A TOTALLY B[... ...]US
NINETIES CHRISTMAS

Thomas A. Christie

Other Books by
Thomas A. Christie

Liv Tyler: Star in Ascendance

The Cinema of Richard Linklater

John Hughes and Eighties Cinema

Ferris Bueller's Day Off: The Pocket Movie Guide

The Christmas Movie Book

Notional Identities

The Shadow in the Gallery

The James Bond Movies of the 1980s

Mel Brooks: Genius and Loving It!

The Spectrum of Adventure

A Righteously Awesome Eighties Christmas

Contested Mindscapes

John Hughes FAQ

The Golden Age of Christmas Movies

The Heart 200 Book [with Julie Christie]

A Very Spectrum Christmas

Mysteries and Secrets of the Heart 200 Route
[with Julie Christie]

A TOTALLY BODACIOUS NINETIES CHRISTMAS

Festive Cinema of the 1990s

Thomas A. Christie

A Totally Bodacious Nineties Christmas: Festive Cinema of the 1990s by Thomas A. Christie.

First published in Great Britain in 2022 by Extremis Publishing Ltd.,
Suite 218, Castle House, 1 Baker Street, Stirling, FK8 1AL, United Kingdom.
www.extremispublishing.com

Extremis Publishing is a Private Limited Company registered in Scotland (SC509983) whose Registered Office is Suite 218, Castle House, 1 Baker Street, Stirling, FK8 1AL, United Kingdom.

A CIP catalogue record for this book is available from the British Library.

ISBN: 978-1-7398543-5-5

Typeset in Goudy Bookletter 1911, designed by The League of Moveable Type.

Printed and bound in Great Britain by IngramSpark, Chapter House, Pitfield, Kiln Farm, Milton Keynes, MK11 3LW, United Kingdom.

This book is dedicated to
my dear friends

Mrs Ivy D. Lannon
&
Mr Ian G. Cranston

It was a true privilege to know them both,
and they will forever be greatly missed.

Contents

Also in This Series:

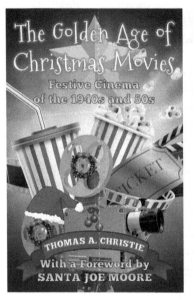

'I heard the bells on Christmas Day,
Their old, familiar carols play,
And wild and sweet
The words repeat
Of peace on earth, good-will to men!'

Henry Wadsworth Longfellow,
Christmas Bells **(1863)**

A TOTALLY BODACIOUS NINETIES CHRISTMAS

CHRISTMAS

Festive Cinema of the 1990s

Introduction

IF the 1940s had been witness to the creation of the Christmas movie genre as we recognise it today, it was the 1980s which became its second (or modern) golden age. During the eighties, Christmas cinema underwent a rapid evolution where it swiftly became more relevant to popular culture than it had been for decades. Suddenly new subgenres of festive film began to spring up – some proving to be more successful with audiences and critics than others – while experimentation with the key conventions of the Christmas movie moved more quickly than ever before.

Prominent features such as *Santa Claus: The Movie* (Jeannot Szwarc, 1985) enjoyed a considerable cultural profile on account of aggressive marketing campaigns and merchandising, which brought Christmas cinema right back into the public eye after the long wilderness years of the 1960s and 70s. But the period was also noteworthy for the way in which it interrogated the conventions of the genre before, in most cases, reinforcing their relevance to a rapidly changing world. Richard Donner's darkly comic *Scrooged* (1988) not only updated Charles Dickens's *A Christmas Carol* from the streets of Victorian London to the skyscrapers of New York City, but it also re-examined the novella's much-referenced moral concerns through the lens of corporate politics, exploring in-

terpersonal dynamics in a avaricious and increasingly solipsis-
tic age. Other films of the decade, including John Landis's
Trading Places (1983), more directly examined the complex
conflict between the ruthlessness of late monopoly capitalism
and the altruism of the festive season. Even some of the most
successful action movies of the period, such as *Lethal Weapon*
(Richard Donner, 1987) and *Die Hard* (John McTiernan,
1988), employed Christmas settings as an unlikely backdrop
for their high-octane thrills. Suddenly, the Christmas movie
wasn't just popular at the box-office again – it had fully re-
gained cultural and critical relevance, the likes of which it
hadn't enjoyed since its post-war heyday.

If the eighties had been witness to a reinvention of the
Christmas movie, it would be the nineties which saw the reaffirmation of the genre's key themes. While the central tropes
of festive movie-making remained as perennially steadfast as
always, Western society itself was in a state of rapid cultural
flux. The world was changing in many ways, from the geopo-
litical ramifications stemming from the end of the Cold War
through to domestic challenges to the traditional nuclear family, and these subjects all had an impact on the cinema of the
time. Throughout the nineties, film-makers found themselves
having to strike a delicate balance between confirming the
ongoing relevance of Christmas cinema as a discrete genre and
acknowledging the way in which features were being forced
to adapt and develop in a fast-moving world where there was
greater demand for diversity, inclusion, and creative heteroge-
neity. If movies such as *Home Alone* celebrated the comfort
and succour of the nuclear family, others such as *The Santa
Clause* were to instead acknowledge that sometimes family
can extend far beyond blood ties, suggesting that our domicili-
ary relationships can sometimes consist of relatives and extra-

domestic connections alike. These themes were revisited and re-examined regularly throughout the decade.

The Christmas movies of the nineties would be about far more than the rise of the constellation family, however – even if the topic was addressed frequently by features such as *All I Want for Christmas* and the high-profile Les Mayfield remake of *Miracle on 34th Street* (with wildly differing results). The decade was noteworthy for the way in which tradition and modernity were to clash – and often in unexpected ways. Some films, such as *The Preacher's Wife*, were to directly refashion classics of the genre's 1940s golden age while emphasising the relevance of their central stories to the modern day. Others, including *Trapped in Paradise*, were to riff on the sensibilities and themes of Christmas films of an earlier vintage (in that instance, Michael Curtiz's inspired 1955 comedy *We're No Angels*) while transplanting their action to different settings.

While a preoccupation with tradition and modernity permeates the festive cinema of the 1990s, the decade was just as noteworthy for its more experimental features. *The Nightmare Before Christmas* brought such a highly distinctive visual approach to its stop motion animation, it became one of the most instantly-recognisable features of the period. Brian Henson's *The Muppet Christmas Carol* breathed new life into the oft-related Dickens tale thanks to the presence of the late Jim Henson's unforgettable character creations, creating a fresh and truly virtuoso cinematic adaptation. *A Midnight Clear*, an atmospheric adaptation of William Wharton's war novel of the same name, was perhaps the most effective film of its type until the production of *Joyeux Noël* (Christian Carion, 2005) over a decade later. And of course, the nineties also presented a diverse array of festively-situated comedies, some meeting a degree of critical success – including *The Ref* and *29th Street* – whereas other films such as *Mixed Nuts* and *I'll Be Home for Christmas* proved to be considerably more of an acquired taste.

Although the nineties saw the production of many made-for-TV Christmas movies, this book concerns itself only with the discussion of full-length motion pictures intended for theatrical exhibition. Such was the prolificity of festive TV movies throughout the decade, to give them the credit they are due would necessitate at least another volume of a similar size to this one, and as such they – along with the period's many short Christmas features – are generally referred to only in passing. By that same token, the selection of films under discussion have been carefully chosen to provide a cross-section of the Christmas cinema of the decade – the features which were most prominent in pop culture, which enjoyed particular critical acclaim, or which performed well at the box-office. In fact, the nineties were witness to well over a hundred film releases which either contained Christmas themes or featured a festive setting, some of which enjoyed a higher profile than others, and a more complete list is included in an appendix at the end of the book.

If the 1980s had blended the genre's core conventions with uncompromising modernity to striking effect, the 1990s were instead to herald a subtle return to renewed traditionalism which would revisit, reinterpret and ultimately reinforce the established themes of the festive movie-making as never before. This melange of contemporaneousness and time-honoured convention not only came to characterise the festive movie-making of the nineties – it would also set the stage for the major production boom in the genre which was to follow in the new millennium. The way in which Christmas cinema was to evolve in the era of brand-new DVD home entertainment technology, increasingly discerning (and sometimes cynical) audiences, and a febrile political scene on both the international and domestic stages, is every bit as fascinating as the narratives of the films themselves. The nineties were to be the perfect coda for the century that had brought about the holiday movie. By the end of the decade, the Christmas film would not only have been firmly established as a genre which was here to stay – proving that its critical and commercial revival in the 1980s was not simply a temporary development – but would also lay the groundwork for a whole new century of festive movie-making.

1

Home Alone (1990)

Hughes Entertainment / Twentieth Century Fox Film Corporation

Director: Chris Columbus
Producer: John Hughes
Screenwriter: John Hughes

B Y the time of the early 1990s, the world was in a state of precipitous change. The Berlin Wall had fallen, the Soviet Union was on the verge of collapse, and then-U.S. President George H.W. Bush was speaking of the emergence of a unipolar geopolitics with the United States as the sole superpower at its epicentre. So too were cultural attitudes beginning to shift, with the 'greed is good' ethos of the eighties giving way to new common concerns beyond the economic factors which had dominated much of the social commentary during the past decade.

Just as these far-reaching changes would affect the world of cinema in general, so too would the Christmas film adapt to reflect this newly-developing domestic and international outlook. The energetic defence of the Christmas spirit in the face of corporate excess – which had been so regularly referenced throughout the nineties – was steadily to fade in relevance, gradually being replaced by a move towards a greater celebration of the family and the community as well as the re-emergence of another traditional theme: the need for a sense of belonging in a world that seemed to be progressing more abruptly into an age of uncertainty than ever before.

Home Alone marked the return of legendary writer-producer John Hughes to the Christmas film genre after the previous year's well-received *National Lampoon's Christmas Vacation* (Jeremiah Chechik, 1989), and the movie would further develop the themes of the importance of dysfunctional familial bonds and sincere affection towards the festive season that he had established throughout his earlier feature. While he has been widely lauded for his pioneering teen movies and eighties comedies, Hughes was also to have a significant impact upon Christmas cinema – a contribution which has often been obscured on account of the scale of success enjoyed by his directorial output throughout the mid-eighties thanks to the huge cultural profile of features such as *The Breakfast Club* (1985), *Ferris Bueller's Day Off* (1986) and *Planes, Trains and Automobiles* (1987). The festively-themed features produced by Hughes Entertainment may not have reached quite the same level of lasting admiration that has accompanied many of his other movies, but they have nonetheless earned their place within a well-populated and commercially popular genre, ensuring that they are still regularly screened and appreciated by audiences even today.

While *National Lampoon's Christmas Vacation* and *Home Alone* shared some common factors – an inviting home in the Chicago suburbs, and Christmas plans that go drastically awry – the approach that Hughes would adopt for his screenplay on this occasion would to prove to be drastically different. *Home Alone* was a heartfelt tribute to the nuclear family by Hughes, and one which appears unerringly traditional in comparison to later nineties films with similar themes of domestic relationships and reconciliation at Christmas. In the same manner as movies such as Robert Lieberman's *All I Want for Christmas* (q.v.), *Home Alone* promotes the traditional benefits of marriage and the stable, nuclear family unit, whereas the decade's later offerings became significantly more inclusive, emphasising that the term 'family' can – and should – encompass a very diverse range of relationships extending beyond blood ties. But as was the case with his other Christmas features, Hughes seemed much more intent upon ensuring that his audience was being entertained than attempting to overtly influence their worldview with excessively profound socio-political points, meaning that he and director Chris Columbus would work in tandem to maintain a warm-hearted, festive atmosphere throughout the film.

Home Alone was to feature as its star the popular child actor Macaulay Culkin, with whom Hughes had worked during his earlier family comedy *Uncle Buck* (1989). Culkin's wryly mature performance in that film had been favourably received by the critics of the time, making it almost certainly his most instantly-recognisable performance at that point in his career, but few could possibly have predicted the meteoric box-office success that was soon to come. However, as Kirk Honeycutt observes, Hughes's unwillingness to compromise his creative vision – a film with a character portrayed by talented child actor at the very centre of its narrative – almost meant that *Home Alone* didn't see the light of day at all:

> Few in Hollywood thought it was wise to build an entire comedy around a small child. But John [Hughes] felt otherwise, so Warner Bros. agreed to make *Home Alone*. Then the studio ran the numbers. This is what every studio does: compare a project to similar movies and the box office

achieved. The highest total Warners came up with for *Home Alone* was $40 million domestically and overseas. Since the budget for John's screenplay was $19 million, Warner Bros. insisted John cut his budget by $1 million. John refused. So Warner Bros. promptly put the film into 'turnaround,' essentially making the film an orphaned project. Twentieth Century Fox chairman Joe Roth picked the film up quickly enough, and at $19 million. But the decision by Warners to put *Home Alone* into turnaround would have lasting repercussions at that lot. *Home Alone* became the highest grossing comedy of all time, at $285.8 million domestic. It is also among the few Hughes films to score with an international audience and, of course, it launched a franchise.[1]

Home Alone came relatively early in the filmography of director Chris Columbus. Prior to the film's release, he was best-known for helming the cult comedy *Adventures in Babysitting* (1987) (also known as *A Night on the Town* in some international territories), and nostalgic comedy-drama *Heartbreak Hotel* (1988). Later a producer of note, he is also a well-regarded screenwriter, having composed scripts throughout the eighties for films such as Joe Dante's *Gremlins* (1984), James Foley's *Reckless* (1984) and Barry Levinson's *Young Sherlock Holmes* (1985). Later to direct features including *Mrs Doubtfire* (1993), *Stepmom* (1998) and *Bicentennial Man* (1999), his profile was raised even further due to the success of fantasy adaptation *Harry Potter and the Philosopher's Stone* (2001) and its sequel *Harry Potter and the Chamber of Secrets* (2002). His later films have included action fantasy *Percy Jackson and the Lightning Thief* (2010) and the video arcade-themed sci-fi comedy *Pixels* (2015). But in the view of many commentators, *Home Alone* seems likely to remain one of the most immediately identifiable of all his films.

Chaos reigns in a cosy, upmarket home near Chicago; decorated for Christmas, its peaceful exterior gives little hint of the pandemonium that is taking place inside. Members of the McCallister family are frantically busying themselves with last-minute holiday packing before they head off on a vacation to Paris the next day. The extended group of family members have gathered together at the house to share the flight over to France. Nobody seems to notice seemingly-affable policeman Harry Lyme (Joe Pesci), who is fruitlessly trying to catch the attention of a member of the family. His unexpected presence in the front hall has escaped the attention of the house's owners, Peter (John Heard) and Kate McCallister (Catherine O'Hara), who are busy getting packed upstairs. Their son, eight-year-old Kevin (Macaulay Culkin), is puzzling over what to put in his own suitcase, though he receives neither help nor sympathy from the plethora of siblings and cousins who are weaving their way through the house. Frustrated at being virtually ignored in his own home, Kevin exasperatedly cries out that as soon as he's old enough to move out, he plans to live alone. But his self-pity is interrupted when he glances out of the window and spots his ageing neighbour, old man Marley (Roberts Blossom), clearing snow from his driveway. Kevin's brother Buzz (Devin Ratray) spins him a yarn that Marley had been a notorious serial killer in the late fifties, having murdered his victims with a snow-shovel very similar to the one that he is currently using. Kevin looks on with a new sense of awe as the seemingly-innocuous elderly gent continues to grit the road outside.

Aided by the opportune arrival of a pizza delivery man, Harry eventually manages to get hold of Peter and explains that he is doing a spot-check of houses in the area to ensure that everyone is aware of the dangers posed by burglars in the run up to Christmas. Peter gives him a rough outline of his home's defences, but is drawn away before Harry can finish pumping him for information. The cop continues to wander the ground floor until he encounters Kate, who tells him that the family will be departing early the next morning for France. Seeming unusually satisfied by this news, Harry departs with a promise that the McCallisters should rest assured that their house will be watched carefully while they are out of the country. Meanwhile, Kevin starts a fight with Buzz in the kitchen and accidentally drenches everyone's passport when he spills milk over them. As his tantrum is the last thing that the already-frenetic family needs to deal with, Kate orders him to go up into the house's converted loft and stay out of trou- ble. Aggrieved at this perceived injustice (he only attacked Buzz because his older brother had deliberately eaten his share of takeaway pizza), Kevin fires back that he would be much happier if he had no family at all.

During the night, a storm knocks out power to the house, resetting all of the alarm clocks. Thus the McCallisters are awakened by the arrival of airport courier minibuses at eight o'clock, which is when they were expected to be pre- pared to leave. A frantic dash takes place as they desperately try to get ready on time. As the luggage is loaded onto the minibuses parked outside, a head-count accidentally includes Mitch Murphy (Jeffrey Wiseman), a nosey kid from across the street who is rummaging through the McCallisters' bags. Thus when the family depart, even more flustered than be- fore, they are completely unaware that they are one person short – particularly as their attention is diverted by a last minute warning from an electrical company lineman (Peter Siragusa) that although power has been restored to the house, the phone lines will be out of operation for the foreseeable future. Racing through the airport, the family are relieved when they manage to check in for their flight with mere moments to spare.

Back at the house, Kevin is bewildered when he wakes up and emerges from the attic to discover that his home is empty. He drifts from room to room, not quite believing the house to be vacant and completely oblivious to the fact that his family are now heading over the Atlantic towards their Parisian holiday destination. Growing increasingly concerned, he heads over to the garage and discovers that his parents' cars are still parked there. As Kevin had never seen the long-departed airport minibuses, having been asleep when they had arrived, he begins to wonder whether his continual desire to see the back of his bickering family has finally paid off: from his point of view, they seem to have simply disappeared into thin air. At first, he seems mildly troubled by this prospect, but after remembering their harsh words to him the night before he soon decides that the solitary life may not be so bad at all.

Deciding to make the most of his new situation, Kevin is soon eating popcorn while jumping on his parents' bed and taking potshots at the laundry chute with Buzz's prized air rifle. He settles down in front of the TV with a massive bowl of ice-cream and marshmallows to watch an old forties gangster movie, blissfully unaware that his parents are only now realising – to their horror – that he is absent from their flight. But as the rest of the McCallister clan continue to head to Paris, full of guilt and unable to contact the house by phone, a carefree Kevin is having the time of his life careening down the stairs on a wooden sledge.

That night, two burglars are parked in a plumbers' van at the end of Kevin's street. One of them is none other than Harry, now revealed to be no policeman at all – he has been impersonating a cop prior to the holiday season, using his scam home security checks to trick householders into revealing if they will be away from their homes over Christmas. He is even able to tell when electric timers are set to activate, meaning that lit-up windows and doors are no deterrent: Harry is fully aware of which houses are fair game for a raid. This impresses his enthusiastic but slow-witted partner in crime, Marv Merchants (Daniel Stern), who is more than ready to put his crowbar to good use.

Knowing that the McCallisters' home contains particularly rich pickings, they decide to make it their first stop on the street. But Kevin sees their shadows passing the lounge window as they head for the entry to the basement, giving him enough time to switch on as many lights as possible before they are able to force entry. Startled by the sudden activity – Harry had expected the house to be empty after his earlier discussion with Peter and Kate – the felonious pair waste no time in departing. Petrified by the prospect of the house being broken into, Kevin cowers under his parents' bed until he can hear that the burglars' van has gone. Once they have left the street, he chastises himself for having been scared and heads out of the house proudly proclaiming that he will no longer be made to feel afraid. A few moments later, however, he runs into Marley and – not dissuaded by the elderly man's kind smile – promptly takes to his heels, screaming in terror until he is safe in his parents' bedroom once again.

At an airport in Paris, Kate and Peter are becoming increasingly frustrated at their inability to contact Kevin. With the phone lines still not restored to their street, they are unable to contact any of their neighbours, and the rest of their acquaintances are either away for the holidays or otherwise out of reach. Eventually they manage to persuade the local police force to send an officer to the house in order to check that Kevin is safe. But as Kevin refuses to answer the door to a stranger, the police assume that the call has been a hoax. The earliest flight back to Chicago is still two days away, so Kate elects to stay at the airport in the hope that a cancellation will become available beforehand. Peter and the rest of the family head for the home of his brother, who has moved to Paris for work some years beforehand, in the hope of getting in contact with Kevin by telephone one way or another.

The next morning, Kevin discovers that he can't find his toothbrush and decides to head out to buy a new one. In search of money, he resolves to raid Buzz's savings box... but as it is placed on the topmost point of a set of wall-mounted shelves, he inadvertently brings the whole lot crashing down when he tries to climb them to retrieve the cash. As Kevin gathers together the purloined dollar bills, he is oblivious to the fact that the collapsing shelves have shattered Buzz's tarantula tank, setting loose his brother's cherished pet spider. Heading out onto the snowy street, he is confused to discover a van parked in the Murphys' driveway across the street. Little does Kevin realise that it belongs to Harry and Marv, who are currently clearing out the Murphys' home. While the pair are gathering valuables into swag bags, the answering machine kicks in – Peter is leaving a message, stating that he is still in Paris and asking if the Murphys will ring him back. Realising that the McCallisters' house is vacant after all, the burglars are ecstatic; they resolve to target it again as soon as night falls.

Kevin goes into a pharmacy to buy a toothbrush, but is shocked when Marley enters the shop and – gripped with fear – races away without paying. Believing him to be a shoplifter, the store's clerks (Jim Ortlieb and Ann Whitney) send the stock boy (Jim Ryan) to catch him. But Kevin is too hysterical with panic to see sense, and makes a break for it across a crowded park, losing his pursuers by skidding across a frozen pond filled with ice-skaters. When he eventually calms down, he becomes ashamed at having stolen property from the drugstore and wanders along the street in a daze. Meanwhile, Harry and Marv are leaving the Murphys' house, their efforts at breaking and entering quite superbly unsubtle. Determined to leave a calling card, Marv blocks the Murphys' drains and sets the taps running, thus fostering their criminal reputation as 'the Wet Bandits'. As they draw their van out of the driveway, they narrowly avoid hitting Kevin, who is still a little stupefied at the earlier events. Kevin immediately recognises Harry from the older man's earlier visit to his home while dressed as a policeman, now realising with shock what has been going on. Harry does not reciprocate Kevin's recollection, but notices his shocked expression nonetheless. Suspicious, he and Marv decide to follow Kevin in their van to see which house he enters, but Kevin diverts the burglars by ducking into a nearby church, causing them to lose his trail.

True to form, the Wet Bandits return to the street that night, and are stunned to discover that a party appears to be in full swing at the McCallisters' house. Puzzled at this latest unexpected development, and yet knowing that the family couldn't have returned from France so quickly, neither of them can fathom what is going on. But inside the house, Kevin has rigged up some mannequins with a series of ropes and pulleys, along with employing a variety of other improvised gadgets including cardboard cut-outs and an electric train set, to help throw the burglars off the scent. Now totally baffled, Harry determines that they should return the following night in the hope that the 'guests' will have departed by then. Marv fires up the van's engine and heads off before they can be recognised; Kevin watches with immense satisfaction as they recede from view.

Over in Paris, a frustrated Peter continues without success to reach someone in Chicago who can get in contact with Kevin. While he continues to worry, the kids are resolutely unimpressed by their status quo – especially Buzz, who believes that Kevin richly deserves his current predicament. But he has no idea that back home, Kevin is currently ordering up his favourite pizza via home delivery, appearing to revel in the fact that he is using his irascible older brother's money to pay for it. At the airport, Kate has had some success of her own; with a mixture of smooth-talking and blatant bribery, she has managed to trade her two first-class seats on a later flight in order to board a plane back to the United States that same evening.

Kevin is starting to miss his family, but keeps himself busy with housework to distract himself from his unusual situation. Harry and Marv are once again casing the house, and are surprised that it should look so quiet in the daylight after having been so busy during the 'party'. Marv decides to head to the back of the house for a closer look, but Kevin pre-empts him by playing his favourite gangster movie on the kitchen TV set; the obtuse burglar believes the dialogue to be a violent conversation that is going on inside the house, and makes a run for it when he hears gunfire (actually Kevin setting off some firecrackers). Racing back to the van, he advises Harry that they should leave quickly, but his partner is not so sure. Keen to see exactly who else is in the house, and thus giving them valuable evidence if the police should make enquiries into any crimes in the area (thus providing convenient cover for their own criminal activities), Harry decides that they should stay put for the time being.

Kate is back in the United States at last, though she has been forced to take a number of domestic flights in the hope of returning to Chicago by any means necessary. She is now trapped in Scranton with no available flights and, as it is now Christmas Eve, the airline ticket agent (Alan Wilder) is not hopeful that she will have any luck finding a way home any time soon. Physically exhausted and emotionally drained, Kate seems to be on the cusp of psychological meltdown when help comes in the most unlikely of forms. Gus Polinski (John Candy), a musical performer and self-proclaimed 'Polka King of the Midwest', has been forced to hire a truck to take his band to Milwaukee after their flight has been cancelled. As their route will take them through Chicago, Gus offers to bring Kate along and return her to Kevin as soon as is possible.

The Wet Bandits are shaken out of their stakeout slumber when an oblivious Kevin emerges from the house, intent on chopping down a fir tree in his garden so that he can decorate it in time for Christmas. Recognising him, Harry realises that he and Marv have been tricked – Kevin has been the house's only occupant all along. Marv is reluctant to break into a house with a lone child living in it, but Harry is determined: the McCallisters' house is a burglar's paradise, and he is hell-bent on stripping it bare. Neither of them realise that Kevin can overhear their exchange, including their plan to return and force entry at nine o'clock that night.

Knowing now what his timetable for the rest of the day must be, Kevin is able to squeeze in a visit to a local Santa Claus (Ken Hudson Campbell), who is en-route to a party now that his grotto has been locked up for the season. Kevin asks Santa if he will consider giving him no presents the following day, on the condition that he return his family to their home instead. Baffled at the boy's deadly earnestness, 'Santa' tells him that he will do what he can to help. Making his way home, Kevin finds it difficult to watch other families gathering together in warm, cosy homes when he knows that he will have to return to an empty house once again. He stops by at his local church, where a choir are practicing for a Christmas Eve service later that night. Kevin takes a seat on a pew, only to be joined soon afterwards by Marley. Much to his amazement, the old man is friendly and conversational; he assures Kevin that although many tall tales are told about him, there is no need to be afraid. Slowly, the boy comes to realise that his mortal fear of the kindly gent has been based entirely upon fabrication and urban myths. Marley explains that his granddaughter is singing in the choir that night, and that he is attending the rehearsal to hear her sing as he is keen to avoid his son, who will be attending the later service. In response to Kevin's further questioning, Marley reveals that he and his son have been estranged following a raging argument many years beforehand, and although he has become keen for rapprochement he is wary of extending an olive branch for fear that it may be rejected. Kevin advises him to make the attempt anyway; if his hand of friendship is rebuffed, Marley will have lost nothing. In return, Marley emphasises the importance of family, telling Kevin that no matter what comes between him and his parents or siblings, the bonds of love will still remain.

Realising that time grows short, Kevin runs home and gets ready to defend his home from Harry and Marv's intended burglary. Devising a highly elaborate series of booby-traps, Kevin moves at breakneck speed to get all of his snares into position before the Wet Bandits can arrive. Sure enough, the van pulls up right on time, and Kevin knows that the game is on. After their attempt to gain entry through the back door leads to a painful encounter with Buzz's air rifle, the Bandits elect to divide their efforts – Marv heads for the basement, while Harry goes to the front door. Only just managing to gain entry to the house (though accruing many bumps and bruises along the way), the burglars soon find themselves victim to an overabundance of jury-rigged, damage-inducing devices which include irons, tar, nails, a blowtorch, glue, feathers, model cars, red-hot metal, paint pots, tripwires and Christmas tree ornaments. Even Buzz's escaped tarantula manages to save Kevin from potential disaster when it makes an opportune appearance. After a prolonged game of cat and mouse, Kevin leads the Bandits away from his home and across the street to the Murphys' house – now flooded, due to Marv's earlier calling-card intervention. Once there, Kevin seems to have been outwitted at the last minute by his adversaries, but he is saved by the surprise appearance of Marley who knocks the two burglars unconscious with his snow shovel. Concerned for Kevin's wellbeing, he returns the boy to his home, where Kevin watches in comfort as the police (responding to his own tip-off) arrive at the Murphy's home and take Harry and Marv into custody. Thanks to Marv's watery trademark, the officers know each and every property that the Bandits have broken into, and they are determined that the pair will face appropriate justice.

Now safe, Kevin quickly returns his home to normality, anticipating the arrival of Christmas. But all the festive embellishment and comfortable warmth of the house can do nothing to assuage his loneliness. The next morning, he awakes to a white Christmas and races downstairs in the hope that his family will have returned to him. He is deeply disappointed when he discovers that everything is exactly as he had left it the previous night, but his regret soon turns to delight when his mother arrives at the front door almost immediately afterwards (courtesy of Polinski and his rental truck). Kate and Kevin enjoy a tearful reunion, but neither is prepared for the sight of Peter and the rest of the McCallister kids, who pile in after having got home on the scheduled early-morning flight from Paris. (Because of all the hitches with her domestic journeys, Kate has – in real terms – only beaten them home by a matter of minutes.) The family are overjoyed to be back together again; even Buzz is grudgingly pleased to see that Kevin is safe and well. While Peter puzzles over the discovery of Harry's gold tooth, which is lying dislodged on the living room floor, Kevin looks out of the window and sees a jubilant Marley warmly embracing his son, their long-standing differences now settled. Satisfied that all has turned out well in the end, Kevin takes a moment to marvel at the unifying power of the Christmas spirit... that is, until Buzz discovers what remains of his room.

While *Home Alone* is often held up as a gold standard example of a successful family comedy, the film's achievement extends far beyond its commercial triumph at the box-office. Even now, several decades after *Home Alone*'s initial release, the film's events and iconography continue to dominate popular culture. The building used as the McCallister home, which is located on Lincoln Avenue in Winnetka, a well-known suburb of Chicago, has become a well-known tourist attraction, and the film's famous promotional artwork – prominently featuring Culkin – remains one of the most instantly-recognisable movie posters of the 1990s. One of the most conspicuous of all allusions to visual art in any movie produced by Hughes, the famous scene where Kevin McCallister silently shrieks with his hands clapped to either side of his face was immediately immortalised; the gesture closely (and deliberately) imitated Edvard Munch's famous 1893 painting *The Scream* to great effect. While that work has become forever associated with existential dread and internal angst, and has been endlessly referenced and parodied in popular culture, its influence on *Home Alone* was instead to be one which presented a rather more innocent depiction of childhood panic and youthful exuberance. Hughes had a famously keen interest in artwork, which often surfaced in films he produced such as *Ferris Bueller's Day Off* and Howard Deutch's *Some Kind of Wonderful* (1987), but the homage to *The Scream* was almost certainly the most well-known example of it. 'Divorced from the landscape context that is an intrinsic part of the [Munch] painting's meaning, the screamer pops up in the strangest places',[2] art expert Monica Bohm-Duchen once memorably noted, using Kevin's unwitting pastiche as an example, and indeed this distinctive tableau – which is now synonymous with the *Home Alone* franchise – has been recreated by Culkin on various occasions in the years since.

The McCallisters' luxurious home in an affluent Illinois suburb offers Kevin the widest possible range of opportunities to defend his property against the Wet Bandits, and indeed his inspired range of improvised security countermeasures are a joy to behold. Hughes dreamt up the inspired concept behind *Home Alone* after asking himself how one of his children might fare if they were accidentally left behind while the rest of the family flew off on holiday, and reasoned that the idea of intruders breaking into their home while they were alone would almost certainly be their worst fear. While the film has, of course, become most affectionately regarded for its climactic sequence where Kevin repels the burglars from his house – visually inventive scenes which owed at least some inspiration to the gleefully deranged contraptions of illustrators William Heath Robinson and Rube Goldberg, and would ultimately lead to the production of many similar home defence comedies in subsequent years – it is also notable for the poignancy of its emotional heart, which emphasises the need to belong and feel wanted (especially at Christmas) without ever inadvertently drifting into the realms of over-sentimentality. As Hal Hinson of *The Washington Post* noted, this juxtaposition led to a surprisingly effective fusion of contrasting styles: 'Basically, the film has two influences: Frank Capra and the Warner Bros. animator Chuck Jones. The first part of the movie belongs to Capra, and Columbus lets it dawdle along without much distinction or comic zip. But when the burglars arrive, the Jones spirit kicks in and the movie becomes a sort of live-action cartoon, with Kevin playing Road Runner to the crooks' Wile E. Coyote'.[3]

Certainly, Hughes is careful to take a decisively light-hearted approach to the film's events as they unfold, providing a kind of near-ironclad internal logic which belies the relative implausibility of much of the narrative. Although the conceit of the disconnected telephone line works well in the days immediately prior to the omnipresence of cellphones, it would otherwise seem overly convenient that absolutely no family acquaintances are left in the Chicago area to check on Kevin, or that – terrified by the prospect of being completely alone for so long – even the most independent of adolescents would be able to resist the temptation to call on one of the few remaining non-vacationing neighbours for help (or even to find a nearby public call-box – still common during the early nineties – and phone the police for help). Hughes somehow manages to keep the tone so blithe and upbeat, largely due to Culkin's captivating lead performance, that the audience is never allowed time to consider the grave implications that so easily could have befallen a child who had really been left in Kevin's situation.

In order to keep up the pretence of Kevin's inability to communicate with the outside world, Hughes's screenplay is unable to completely avoid the odd narrative goof here and there. Early in the movie, it is established that the telephone lines are all inoperative throughout the neighbourhood where Kevin and his family live, heightening the drama as of course this development means that his parents are unable to call him and check on his safety when they reach France. Yet in spite of the fact that the lack of telecommunications is a key plot point that is continually emphasised throughout the movie, there are a number of occasions where internal logic is somehow circumvented altogether. Kevin manages to order a pizza to be delivered to the door of the McCallister house without any explanation of how he managed to do this without the aid of a functioning phone line, and yet there is no indication of the telecoms company having reconnected the house as Kevin's father Peter is seen attempting and failing to call him from Paris directly beforehand. Similarly, during the Wet Bandits' climactic invasion of the house, Kevin somehow manages to call the police from an extension line in the master bedroom where his parents usually sleep. Again, there has been no suggestion that the functionality of the telephone line has been restored.

While audiences followed the misadventures of the adolescent Kevin as he revelled in his new-found independence and then gradually began to struggle as bungling adversaries closed in on his home, it was easy to forget the joyless experiences of his family as their long-distance holidays were unexpectedly cut short. Almost as a kind of karmic punishment for their inadvertent parental neglect in accidentally leaving Kevin at home in the first place, the McCallister clan faces a rather grim experience on their intercontinental excursion. Realising rather too late that their son is missing, parents Peter and Kate are forced to immediately spring into action as soon as they arrive at Paris Orly Airport (actually filmed at Chicago's O'Hare International Airport, the same location where the family depart at the start of the movie though slightly redressed). Crammed into a soulless Parisian hotel room, where a traditional festive broadcast of Frank Capra's festive classic *It's a Wonderful Life* (1946) can be seen on a television set – albeit broadcast in the French language (another reminder of annual Christmas customs seeming familiar and yet turned slightly askew) – Kate manages to head back to the United States ahead of her family to reunite with Kevin. But unable to book a flight to Chicago, she is forced to take the most circuitous route imaginable (including, most memorably, being forced to accept a ride from Polinski's travelling polka band) before she eventually manages to return home on Christmas Day. It is made clear that for Hughes, vacationing is a family endeavour which is at its best when the experience is uniting people and allowing everyone to feel its benefits equally (a theme which he expounded upon at length throughout *National Lampoon's Christmas Vacation* the year beforehand). Because the McCallisters violate this premise, albeit accidentally, their time away from home becomes a logistical and bureaucratic nightmare: all hope of a restful break is abandoned as every effort is subsequently focused on returning to Kevin as quickly as possible and ensuring his safety. This may not have been new ground for Hughes, whose championship of family stability was one of the key themes of his work throughout the eighties and nineties, but in its incisiveness the motif of the vacation as a uniting and universal activity was to extend from his adult-oriented comedy through to his more family-focused features.

Also typical of a John Hughes production, *Home Alone* contains many witty references to classic films, and to popular culture in general. Joe Pesci's hapless burglar Harry Lyme, of course, shares his name with Orson Welles's famous character in Carol Reed's seminal Graham Greene adaptation *The Third Man* (1949). The much-loved gangster movie that Kevin watches, *Angels with Filthy Souls*, is an obvious pastiche of Michael Curtiz's influential crime movie *Angels with Dirty Faces* (1938), which had starred James Cagney and Humphrey Bogart. That tale of gangland violence and armed robbery was every bit as grim and uncompromising as Harry and Marv's supposed reign of terror transpired to be plagued with blunders and missteps. However, Kevin's familiarity with the (fictional) classic *film noir* is just one factor which foreshadows his eventual ability to run rings around the interlopers later in the movie.

Other cinematic allusions in *Home Alone* include a clever homage to the advertising poster for Fritz Lang's crime thriller *M* (1931), which featured the palm of Peter Lorre's character Hans Beckert bearing a branded letter 'M', signifying his wanted status. In *Home Alone*, Joe Pesci's burglar

Harry unsuspectingly grabs an electrically-heated doorknob which is engraved with the initial letter of the McCallister family. Once the burn has cooled, Harry discovers that the flesh of his hand has become imprinted with the aforementioned letter, in a manner identical to that of the Lang movie's poster motif.

Similarly, Macaulay Culkin's Kevin McCallister brandishes a Daisy Red Ryder air rifle which is an low-key tribute to the prized BB gun so greatly desired by Peter Billingsley's Ralphie Parker in eighties Christmas classic *A Christmas Story* (Bob Clark, 1983). Amusingly, though Hughes makes clear the fact that Roberts Blossom's seemingly-terrifying Old Man Marley is not a mass-murderer but actually a kind and caring elderly gentleman, Blossom had received some degree of notoriety some years beforehand due to his starring role in *Deranged: The Confessions of a Necrophile* (Alan Ormsby and Jeff Gillen, 1974), in which he had portrayed a serial killer named Ezra Cobb.

Sometimes the villains in a Hughes screenplay were more than simply counterproductive or spiteful; on occasion, they may even tip into the domain of outright criminality. Yet felonious intent did not necessarily call for a dark portrayal of such characters; *Home Alone* owed part of its appeal to the ineptitude of its two ham-fisted housebreakers, the hopelessly inept Harry Lyme and Marv Merchants. While the prospect of a burglar team intent on robbing a home which is being defended by a single adolescent may have seemed like a nightmarish scenario in other hands, Hughes presents these massively incompetent criminals in such a humorous light that it eventually becomes almost impossible to take the duo seriously – even if their unlawful objectives proved to be anything but casual in nature.

Part of the reason why Harry and Marv make for such an effective pairing, quite aside from the perfectly-pitched performances from Joe Pesci and Daniel Stern, lies in the surprisingly delicate balance with which their characters are presented. The home defence scenario which plays out at the film's climax, where Kevin relies on an inspired variety of jury-rigged traps to repel the intruders from his family's house, may well be considered the movie's defining sequence, but there was more to this pair of amateurish burglars than was immediately obvious from their relentless injuries at Kevin's hands. At times they employ unpredictably clever techniques, such as Harry infiltrating the McCallister home disguised as police officer in order to gain the family's trust under false pretences, thus discovering more about their travel plans (and, by extension, determining when the house will supposedly be empty for a prolonged period). Marv similarly has delusions of grandeur which extend beyond the pair's abilities, conferring upon themselves the flamboyant title of 'The Wet Bandits' as their criminal calling card to enhance their notoriety – a moniker which he fastidiously puts into practice by flooding the homes of their victims following a successful burglary. (This conceit later backfires on them spectacularly, of course, as the criminal damage directly links them to the sites of all their previous crimes.) At the conclusion of the movie, when the bruised and beaten Harry and Marv angrily advance on Kevin (whose abundant reserve of defensive strategies has finally run dry), we see a suggestion of genuine danger hitherto only hinted at – an indication that they might just consider more serious retribution for the indignities they have suffered, if their threatened reprisals were not so swiftly curtailed by the timely appearance of unexpectedly protective neighbour Mr Marley.

Kevin's constant aptitude in outmanoeuvring the ham-handed adults is part of the feature's ongoing charm; Harry explicitly mentions that he never reached sixth grade at school, suggesting that in intellectual terms the pair has met their match in the guilefully inventive youngster. Yet on every occasion that Kevin manages to thwart the plans of the Wet Bandits, the more determined Harry and Marv become to successfully rob the McCallister home, until it eventually becomes a matter of professional pride (and personal obsession) to them. Here, as in his screenplays for the first two *Home Alone* sequels, Hughes is able to blunt the potential edge of a scenario which places a minor in peril by frequently emphasising the immaturity and sheer idiocy of the antagonists.

Core to the movie is a focus on Kevin's resourceful craftiness over the burglars' greed and disregard for the common good, ensuring that the innocent and virtuous prevail over those with nefarious ends. However, even the clockwork precision of *Home Alone*'s much-admired criminal repulsion sequence was not without its occasional foibles. Harry is tarred and feathered at an early stage in his burglary of the McCallisters' home, and yet as the housebreaking continues he appears to be noticeably less feather-laden as time goes by. Similarly, when Kevin is soaking the steps leading up to the house's front door they quickly freeze, making it perilous for the burglars to enter and suggesting that the exterior temperature is sub-zero. Yet nearer the conclusion, when Kevin is racing away from the house, the ground is clearly free from ice and he is able to break into a sprint without any danger of skidding or falling – even though there has been no suggestion of a thaw.

Columbus's direction is efficient and capable throughout, nicely contrasting the frantic, accelerated mayhem of the bustling McCallister house in the early scenes with Kevin's later escapades alone in his deserted home. His deft understanding of visual comedy is also evident in the many pleasing sight gags which occur (and recur) throughout the film, such as the McCallisters' constantly-capsized garden statue which appears to be in the line of every car or van that approaches it, and also wry humour such as Ken Hudson Campbell's affable neighbourhood Santa and his gift of lime-favoured Tic-Tacs (being the night of Christmas Eve, he had given all of the remaining candy-canes to his elf assistant before closing up for the evening). The screenplay's sly cultural observations are never less than a treat, such as when Kevin orders takeaway pizza from a business named 'Little Nero's' – the imperial Roman name being an obvious spoof of the famous Little Caesar's Pizza company. (Founded in Michigan in 1959, Little Caesars rapidly grew to become the third-largest pizza chain in the entire USA, after Pizza Hut and Domino's Pizza.) The film also gains by the exceptional set decoration from Eve Cauley and Dan Clancy; the McCallister house could never have seemed quite as festive if its interior had not been so visibly decorated in Christmas-themed colors of green and red throughout – something that is reflected in many of the characters' clothing and several of the props within numerous scenes of the movie, which helped greatly in underscoring its late December setting.

Home Alone features a number of nicely understated supporting performances such as Gerry Bamman's memorably crass Uncle Frank, moaning snidely one minute and then shamelessly pilfering complimentary airline goodies the next, and John Candy's warm-hearted cameo appearance which is heavily reflective of his earlier role as travelling shower curtain ring salesman Del Griffith in Hughes's celebrated *Planes,*

Trains and Automobiles. *Home Alone* also had a considerable advantage in its sweeping score, written by legendary film composer John Williams. Moving effortlessly between tender contemplation and frenetic action, the soundtrack is uniformly impressive, though the atmospheric title theme, up-tempo 'Holiday Flight' and intense 'Setting the Trap' are standout pieces. The film also features the song 'Somewhere in My Memory', with music by Williams and lyrics by Leslie Bricusse, which is performed while a melancholic Kevin watches other families in the neighbourhood getting ready for Christmas as he dejectedly faces returning to the loneliness of an empty house.

Though still only ten years old at the time of *Home Alone*'s release, Macaulay Culkin was already a well-established screen actor, having made his debut in Jack Bender's made-for-TV horror movie *The Midnight Hour* (1985). Following this was an episode of television series *The Equalizer* in 1988, and appearances in moving family drama *Rocket Gibraltar* (Daniel Petrie, 1988) and romance *See You in the Morning* (Alan J. Pakula, 1989). His profile was considerably enhanced with his much-praised performance in John Hughes's late eighties comedy hit *Uncle Buck*, in which he was to appear with his later *Home Alone* co-star John Candy. Culkin has remained active in theatre, television and cinema over the past three decades; prominent amongst his film work has been appearances in *Only the Lonely* (Chris Columbus, 1991), *My Girl* (Howard Zieff, 1991), *The Nutcracker* (Emile Ardolino, 1993), *Richie Rich* (Donald Petrie, 1994), and – more recently – in four episodes of Seth Green's avidly-followed cult TV series *Robot Chicken* (broadcast between 2005 and 2006), as well as six episodes of anthology series *American Horror Story* in 2021. However, the precocious skill of his portrayal of Kevin has meant that Culkin has remained forever connected with *Home Alone* and its meteoric success; as Peter Bradshaw has observed, 'Perhaps it is impossible to see this film without thinking of Culkin's melancholy adult career, but [here] he is a vivid screen presence, almost incandescent with confidence'.[4]

Almost as central to the film's success as Culkin's winning performance were the two ill-fated antagonists – an appealing portrayal of quite possibly the least-competent burglars ever to terrorise a suburban street. Joe Pesci had appeared occasionally on film and television since the early 1960s before making an indelible impression on audiences with his performance in Ralph De Vito's *The Death Collector* (1976). He achieved considerable critical acclaim throughout the early 1980s due to his high-profile appearances in films including *Raging Bull* (Martin Scorsese, 1980), *Easy Money* (James Signorelli, 1983), and *Once Upon a Time in America* (Sergio Leone, 1984), as well as the short-lived but well-received TV series *Half Nelson* (1985). Later in the eighties he continued to diversify, with performances in movies such as action thriller *Man on Fire* (Elie Chouraqui, 1987), lavish musical fantasy *Moonwalker* (Jerry Kramer and Jim Blashfield, 1988) and crime comedy sequel *Lethal Weapon 2* (Richard Donner, 1989). Pesci was nominated for an Academy Award in the Best Actor in a Supporting Role category for his performance in *Raging Bull*, and would later go on to win an Oscar in the same category for his role as Tommy DeVito in Martin Scorsese's *GoodFellas* (1990). Years later, he would be nominated for an Academy Award and a BAFTA Award in recognition of his supporting role in *The Irishman* (Martin Scorsese, 2019). Among his many other awards and nominations were a BAFTA win in 1982 for

Most Outstanding Newcomer to Leading Film Roles (for his appearance in *Raging Bull*), and Golden Globe Award nominations in 1981 and 1991 (for *Raging Bull* and *GoodFellas*). Casting a heavyweight actor like Pesci – often noted for playing sinister and intimidating characters – as the stooge in a family comedy may have seemed like a recipe for disaster, given that he had become so widely known for playing emotionally complex figures and even borderline-sociopathic organised crime operatives, but it was ultimately to prove a masterstroke: his Harry Lyme was to prove the most bafflingly congenial of rogues, happy to illegally clear out someone's house one minute and then thoughtfully advise wandering kids about road safety the next.

It is much to Pesci's credit that we feel every little indignity and burst of pain that his character is exposed to during the film's climax (his one-man battle with a flight of icy steps is singularly unforgettable), and he shares this skill with his co-star Daniel Stern: the two actors' performances complement each other perfectly. Similarly known for serious dramatic roles throughout the eighties, often as eccentrics or intellectuals, Stern transformed himself for the part into a wide-eyed, zealous but ultimately rather dense character. Marv seems more concerned with the adrenaline rush of burglary than the monetary value of his ill-gotten gains, and his doomed desire to establish the criminality of Harry and himself as a kind of urban legend ultimately proves to be the duo's downfall. Stern had made his cinematic debut in the late seventies with his performance as Cyril in Peter Yates's sporting comedy drama *Breaking Away* (1979). In the eighties he combined roles in prominent films such as John Schlesinger's *Honky Tonk Freeway* (1981) and Barry Levinson's *Diner* (1982) with quirkier cult movies such as *C.H.U.D.* (Douglas

Cheek, 1984) and *Frankenweenie* (Tim Burton, 1984). Following a stint as Joey Nathan in TV series *Hometown* (1985), Stern's success continued in many diverse features which included *Hannah and Her Sisters* (Woody Allen, 1986), *D.O.A.* (Annabel Jankel and Rocky Morton, 1988), *Leviathan* (George P. Cosmatos, 1989) and *My Blue Heaven* (Herbert Ross, 1990). He would later go on to further prominence in Ron Underwood's high-profile western comedy *City Slickers* (1991) and its sequel, *City Slickers II: The Legend of Curly's Gold* (Paul Weiland, 1994).

Although John Hughes's stellar reputation as a producer and film-maker had already been well established during the eighties, no-one could have predicted just how well *Home Alone* would go on to perform at the box-office when it was released in November 1990. With an estimated budget of just over $18,000,000, it eventually reached a total of $285,761,243 in domestic takings.[5] It enjoyed a long run in cinemas, eventually grossing $190,922,300 at the international box-office – an extraordinary total of $476,683,543 in combined commercial performance.[6] This meant that *Home Alone* not only became the top-grossing film of 1990, but would also earn a place as one of the most profitable movies in film history. As Rowana Agajanian explains: 'Costing a mere $18.2 million to produce, *Home Alone* grossed $17.1 million in its first three days. Its early success can partly be attributed to timing, clever promotional publicity and "saturation" screening. *Home Alone* opened on Thanksgiving weekend and was shown on 1,202 screens in its first week. Earning nearly $280 million in domestic gross and a further $200 million abroad, the film not only became the top-grossing film of 1990 but joined the ranks of the 20 top-grossing films of all time'.[7]

The film's meteoric commercial success has meant that its decidedly uneven critical reception at its time of release is often forgotten today. Some reviewers, such as Jeanne Cooper, applauded *Home Alone*'s dry sense of humour and its refreshing avoidance of sentimentalism: 'The film's best gags are repeated, and the comedy stops altogether for an obligatory heartwarming scene in which the child is father to the man. Unlike the similarly cynical *Scrooged*, though, *Home Alone* skips the treacle ending to let anti-sentiment have the last laugh. It's one you'll have anticipated – but you may want to laugh anyway. You won't be too busy wiping away tears'.[8] Others, including Dave Kehr, felt that Hughes's occasional tendency towards moral pondering had a tendency to bog down the expression of its characterisation:

> Hughes creates characters that are immediately recognizable and immediately likable, though there always comes a point in his films when he breaks faith with them – when he goes behind their backs to impose a heavy moral lesson or a blunt ideological point. He doesn't seem to trust his characters to carry his film – a former advertising man, he's always got something to sell. [...] With its quotes from *Miracle on 34th Street* and *It's a Wonderful Life*, *Home Alone* seems to be nominating itself as a Christmas classic, and although it's much too self-conscious in its sentimentality (Kevin, who has earlier wished his family away, discovers that he loves and needs them), the film does go some way toward getting the job done. If only Hughes would learn to relax, to stop selling for a minute and allow his characters a little breathing room.[9]

Numerous critics of the time took issue with the implausibility of the film's plot dynamics; Jonathan Rosenbaum, for instance, believed that the sheer improbability demonstrated by the situations which unfold ultimately taxed the viewer's patience to some degree: 'The movie is quite enjoyable as long as it explores the fantasy of a neglected little boy having an entire house of his own to explore and play in, and it still manages to be fun when he exhibits superhuman ingenuity and resourcefulness in holding down the fort – with Culkin doing a fair job of mugging. But the physical cruelty that dominates the last act leaves a sour taste, and the multiple continuity errors that make the last scene possible strain one's suspension of disbelief to near the breaking point'.[10] This criticism was further explored by Roger Ebert, who praised Culkin's lead performance just as he echoed the scepticism aimed at the unlikelihood of *Home Alone*'s events and their outcomes: 'The plot is so implausible that it makes it hard for us to really care about the plight of the kid. What works in the other direction, however, and almost carries the day, is the gifted performance by young Macaulay Culkin, as Kevin. Culkin is the little boy who co-starred with John Candy in *Uncle Buck*, and here he has to carry almost the whole movie. He has lots of challenging acting scenes, and he's up to them. I'm sure he got lots of help from director Chris Columbus, but he's got the stuff to begin with'.[11]

Marc Savlov expressed the somewhat radical view that *Home Alone* was one of the worst films that Hughes had ever been involved in producing – an opinion that was shared by few at the time: '*Home Alone* is the apex, the pinnacle, the culmination of every bad bit Hughes has ever written or directed. It overflows with primitive, disastrously unfunny sight gags and neo-hateful familial humor'.[12] Other commentators, including Caryn James, found that any danger of the film lapsing into schmaltziness was carefully balanced out by the dexterous skill of Hughes's screenplay, which artfully advanced comedy over mawkishness: 'Even so carefree and wry a comedy needs its redeeming lesson, though. For Kevin, it comes when he runs from the robbers and hides in a church, where carolers sing and where he encounters the gruff-looking old man next door – the man seen earlier shoveling his walk and called by Kevin's older brother "The South Bend Shovel Slayer." Of course he turns out to be kinder than Santa. He and Kevin teach each other the true importance of family. Yet even this scene, the most sentimental, is not overplayed. Neither is the ending, when Kevin gets his new fondest wish – his family reappears. *Home Alone* does, after all, have its sweet side. But it's a side best appreciated by the kind of ultramodern kids who might wonder about Santa's passport'.[13]

Interestingly, while later appraisals of *Home Alone* have been considerably more overarchingly receptive, reviewers have been much more inclined to view the film through the lens of Christmas cinema given that the passing years had more firmly associated it within the genre. Owen Gleiberman, for instance, discerns that 'the movie, written and produced by Hughes and directed by Chris Columbus (*Adventures in Babysitting*), succeeds – at least for a few scenes – at tapping into the universal terror and exhilaration of being left alone in an upper-middle-class home stuffed with leisure-time goodies. Hughes, though, can't resist turning *Home Alone* into a sadistic festival of adult-bashing. [...] Then, since this is the holiday season, we get incongruous scenes of Christmas-spirit, family-reunion toastiness, and also a bit in which the lonely old man next door (Roberts Blossom) is reunited with his family, who are wheeled in from out of nowhere for a teary climax. By then, Hughes is pulling our strings as though he'd never learned to do anything else'.[14]

This qualified approval is mirrored by Edison Smith, who indicates the movie's adroit recognition of the connection between the wistful nostalgia of the festive season and the communication of emotional observations about the importance of friends and family:

> John Hughes will never win any awards for pure artistry, but with *Home Alone* he achieves something much rarer. There are films we can discuss on a more cerebral level, films that possess the kind of depth we can derive greater insight and emotional analysis from. It isn't profound or poetic or imbued with clever subtext, but it possesses its own special magic, the kind almost exclusive to juvenile sensibilities. For all the beauty that comes with maturity, nothing comes close to the innocence and imagination of an unaffected mind, and *Home Alone* communicates with kids like an enchanted dog whistle bearing the sound of sleigh bells. It's pure magic. For the rest of us, that's where nostalgia comes in. Nothing stokes the sentimental fires like the festive season; in a world of adult constraint, it reminds us of an innocence we are rarely able to rekindle.[15]

At the opposing end of the critical spectrum, later reviewers of the film have continued to disparage the implausibility of numerous plot twists. Chris Hicks typifies this line of analysis, noting that, 'It's easy to pick apart a movie like this: Would it really take the family that many hours to notice that Kevin isn't with them? Even if they neglected to

notice he was not aboard one of their two airport transporta-
tion vans, when they boarded the airplane they'd have to find
themselves with an extra ticket. Or the other kids would surely notice he wasn't with them. And even the most
independent 8-year-old in the world is likely to be more upset
than Kevin when he realizes he's in his house all alone and his
family has left the country. And even the dumbest would
probably go to a neighbor's house for help. But this is the
world of John Hughes, and it's best not to ask questions. The
script is inventive and the payoff is worth the wait'.[16] Others,
such as Noel Murray, have praised *Home Alone* for the way
in which it slotted so seamlessly into Hughes's wider canon of
movies: 'What's most fascinating now is how *Home Alone* fits
into Hughes' scattershot filmography. Hughes was nearing the
end of his prolific period when he knocked out the *Home
Alone* screenplay – reportedly in a single weekend – and
while the story feels cobbled together from leftover pieces of
Sixteen Candles and *Planes, Trains and Automobiles*, and is
directed by Columbus with an eye toward keeping the budget
down and the energy manic, a lot of Hughes' hooray-for-
suburban-misfits sensibility survives the milling process. The
chain of mishaps and misunderstandings that lead to Culkin
being left behind is of a piece with other Hughes films about
how the world is unfairly stacked against the little guy. Even
at his hackiest, Hughes expressed a worldview that would've
been fun to watch evolve. Why did he abandon us?'[17]

Curiously enough, the depth of characterisation for
which Hughes had become so well known actually inclined
some critics to consider *Home Alone* lacking in the dimension
of the film's own range of characters by comparison. Representative of this kind of disapproval, Leonard Norwitz
considered that 'between writer John Hughes, who usually

has better insight into his young characters, and director Chris Columbus, who wasn't much older than Culkin from the look of him, they neglected to make Kevin's transition into self-confident kid believable – or even interesting. In fact, there is no transition. It's as if Kevin had been keeping his talent a secret all these years – which is quite possible, given what I know about large families. But the realization of his inner strength surprises no one but the criminals'.[18]

The immense commercial success of *Home Alone* in cinemas heralded a new boom-time for Christmas-themed films. However, it has been noted that the film contained a faint whiff of criticism towards upper-middle class lifestyles, calling attention to the fact that the value placed on material-istic pursuits and pursuing a comfortable quality of life was simultaneously underscoring the need for parents to ensure that they adequately prioritised their offspring before the work that made accumulating these trappings possible. As Chris Jordan remarks, *Home Alone* 'offers an extension of the yuppies-with-children cycle by playing upon the idea that par-ents too caught up in their own pursuit of material gratification can easily overlook their responsibilities to their kids. [...] Beneath this comically inflected premise is a deep-seated anxiety about the safety of latchkey children left unat-tended by two working parents'.[19] While this aspect of the film is never unduly laboured, proving that *Home Alone* sig-nified a move away from the manifest (and often rather heavy-handed) cultural commentary that had sometimes proven conspicuous in the Christmas movies of the eighties, it did signal a preoccupation with the family that would contin-ue throughout later festive cinema of the 1990s. Jordan explains that only by shifting emphasis from the individual self to the family unit can order be restored and deeper emotional realisation achieved:

> Parental negligence results in [Kevin's] lapse into sloven laziness and bad eating habits as he gorges himself on pizza and allows the house to lapse into disrepair. However, the movie also constructs the unattended child as a remarkably self-sufficient loner who ably protects the family home from bumbling criminals who repeatedly attempt to break into it on Christmas Eve. Slapstick comedy diffuses the potentially horrific implications of the situation as the boy arranges a series of booby-traps to foil the intruders. [...] While the entire family is suddenly reunited in their home on Christmas morning, incumbent in this aspect of the story is an extension of the yuppie movie's contention that a consumer society's emphasis on lifestyle has compromised parents' focus on their children and their kids' ability to establish meaningful and lasting emotional bonds with others.[20]

Home Alone performed well at a number of award ceremonies following its release. It received two Academy Award nominations in 1991: one for John Williams's original score, and the other for Williams and Leslie Bricusse in the Best Original Song category for 'Somewhere in My Memory'. Williams's music was also successful at other ceremonies: his score won a BMI Film Music Award in 1991, and 'Somewhere in My Memory' was also nominated for a Grammy Award in the category of Best Song Written Specifically for a Motion Picture or for Television in 1992. *Home Alone* was nominated for a Golden Globe Award for Best Motion Picture: Comedy/Musical, with Macaulay Culkin also nominated for Best Performance by an Actor in a Motion Picture: Comedy/Musical at the same ceremony. Culkin was to win a Young Artist Award for Best Young Actor Starring in a Motion Picture in 1991 with the film winning in the Most Entertaining Family Youth Motion Picture: Comedy/Action category, while Angela Goethals was nominated for the Best Young Actress Supporting Role in a Motion Picture Award. The Casting Society of America was also to present Jane Jenkins and Janet Hirshenson with an Artios Award for Best Casting for Feature Film: Comedy.

Given the film's massive box-office success, a sequel seemed inevitable, and sure enough the main cast and production team were to reunite soon after to create *Home Alone 2: Lost in New York* (1992). Once again directed by Chris Columbus and featuring a John Hughes screenplay, the similarly Christmas-situated *Home Alone 2* centres upon a mishap which sees Kevin separated from his family on the way to a family holiday to Miami and eventually winding up (as the title suggests) in New York City instead. Once there, he manages to trick his way into renting a well-appointed room at an upmarket hotel, and is then faced with the twin difficulties of reuniting with his family while simultaneously thwarting an attempt by the recently-escaped Wet Bandits (now rechristened the 'Sticky Bandits') to burgle a vast toy store in the city over the holidays. As well as Macaulay Culkin, all of the central characters were portrayed by the original actors, including John Heard and Catherine O'Hara as Kevin's beleaguered parents and Joe Pesci and Daniel Stern as the increasingly browbeaten two-man burglary team. The film also featured excellent supporting performances by the ever-charismatic Tim Curry as a snooty hotel concierge and Irish actress Brenda Fricker, who portrays the unhoused 'Bird La-dy' – a character with a very similar function to Roberts Blossom's Marley in the original film. Although the film was a huge financial success, it was unable to replicate the monu-mental box-office achievement of the first *Home Alone*, and the many similarities between the sequel's narrative and inci-dents which had taken place in the original were not lost on critics, who gave *Lost in New York* a decidedly mixed re-sponse at the time of its release.

Following this was another sequel, *Home Alone 3* (1997), which retained Hughes as screenwriter but was to see the directorial duties taken up by Raja Gosnell (who had been the editor of the first two films). Starring Alex D. Linz as eight-year-old Alex Pruitt, the film features an entirely differ-ent cast of characters, with none of the original performers returning this time around. Presenting a convoluted plot which centres on a smuggled computer chip that has acci-dentally fallen into the hands of a young boy (who must subsequently defend his home from a team of terrorists that are determined to retrieve it at any cost), the film featured a similarly wintry atmosphere to the first two *Home Alone* movies but otherwise had little in common with its considera-bly more profitable predecessors.

In spite of general critical hostility to *Home Alone 3*, a further sequel – this time a made-for-TV movie – was broad-cast on ABC in 2002. Returning to the story of young Kevin McCallister, now portrayed by actor Mike Weinberg, Rod Daniel's *Home Alone 4: Taking Back the House* featured a rematch between Kevin and burglar Marv Merchants (French Stewart), now joined by his wife and partner-in-crime Vera (Missi Pyle). The first *Home Alone* film not to feature a John Hughes screenplay (the script was penned by Debra

Frank and Steve L. Hayes), the narrative focuses in part on Kevin coming to terms with his parents' recent divorce, but by now the novelty of the cycle's madcap home-defence slap-stick had worn decidedly thin.

In more recent years, a further two *Home Alone* films have been released to general critical disparagement. *Home Alone: The Holiday Heist* was a made-for-TV film which premiered on the ABC Family channel in 2012, directed by Peter Hewitt with a screenplay by Aaron Ginsburg and Wade McIntyre. This film featured a new family named the Baxters, who move from California to a house in Maine... blissfully unaware that a group of burglars led by veteran criminal Sinclair (Malcolm McDowell) are attempting to break into the building to steal a lost Edvard Munch painting from a secret room in the basement. Adolescents Finn (Christian Martyn) and Alexis (Jodelle Ferland) are the only ones standing in the way of the intruders, leading to a fiesta of mostly Christmas-themed booby-traps. At time of writing, the latest entry in the series has been *Home Sweet Home Alone*, produced by 20th Century Studios for the Disney+ subscription video-on-demand service in 2021. Directed by Dan Mazer and with a screenplay by Mikey Day and Streeter Seidell, the story involved a series of misunderstandings between the McKenzie and Mercer families regarding a doll with a rare manufacturing defect. *Home Sweet Home Alone* retained a Christmas setting and the now-expected home defence sequences, but met with generally scathing reviews from critics.

Although Chris Columbus has made further contributions to festive film-making thanks to the well-received *The Christmas Chronicles* (2018) and its 2020 sequel, both starring Kurt Russell as Santa Claus, it seems likely that *Home Alone* will be his best-remembered involvement with the genre.

While the film could conceivably have taken place at numerous other times of the year, the Christmas holiday setting is
what makes it really memorable, and is certainly what ce-
ments it as one of the early highlights of 1990s festive cinema.
By emphasising traditional values in a manner that was relevant to – and popular with – contemporary audiences, the
influence of Columbus's film was to be far-reaching enough to
set the pace for later family-oriented features in the Christmas
film genre not just throughout the decade, but also the new
century ahead. As Michael Mackenzie declares, 'This, for me,
is *the* quintessential festive film, and in my house the year just
wouldn't be complete if the *Home Alone* DVD (and previously VHS) didn't get played at least a dozen times. This
remains by far my most oft-rewatched movie, and despite
knowing every line by heart it never seems to get old. [...]
Home Alone is, when all said and done, damn good fun, and
despite the criticism it often receives, it remains one of the
most enjoyable Christmas movies ever made'.[21]

     While many critics could never have realised the film's
ultimate impact upon Christmas cinema at the time of its release, *Home Alone* has aged well (even in spite of modern
communications technology rendering its central conceit even
less likely than before), and even today it continues to amass
new fans with very passing holiday season. As Smith explains,
it is the combination of Hughes's warm wit and droll dialogue,
Columbus's directorial confidence with both frenetic action
and emotional character moments, and winning performances
led by Culkin's winning central appearance as Kevin which
creates such an unforgettable work of festive cinema:

> Today [*Home Alone*] inhabits a lofty position near
> the top of a magical niche sub-genre, is part of a
> time-honoured tradition that very few films of

note qualify for. There are countless Christmas movies out there. Some cashed in on the silly season before disappearing into the recesses of bad movies past. Others went straight to video, TV, or in today's climate, one of a plethora of streaming platforms. Fewer still made a good first impression but failed to stay the course, giving us a good ol' ride on Santa's sleigh before vanishing in a slither on the snowy horizon. A select few proved much more resilient, touching us deeply and living on in not only our hearts, but in the hearts of future generations, capturing those qualities that most resonate during the festive season. Not only are they movies that we watch during yuletide, they're as fundamental as turkey dinners, Christmas crackers and family games by the tree. Heck, they're as essential as Santa Claus himself, because they bring us together at a time when everything is that more special, a time when we stop to appreciate those who are most important to us. Living somewhere in our memories, ready to be unwrapped at just the right moment, *Home Alone* is certainly one of those movies.[22]

REFERENCES

1. Kirk Honeycutt, *John Hughes: A Life in Film* (New York: Race Point Publishing, 2015), pp.159-60.

2. Monica Bohm-Duchen, *The Private Life of a Masterpiece* (Berkeley: University of California Press, 2001), p.151.

3. Hal Hinson, '*Home Alone*', in *The Washington Post*, 16 November 1990.
    <https://www.washingtonpost.com/wp-srv/style/ longterm/movies/videos/homealonepghinson_a0a9b9.htm>

4. Peter Bradshaw, '*Home Alone* review: 1990 Christmas cracker resurfaces', in *The Guardian*, 30 November 2018.
    <https://www.theguardian.com/film/2018/nov/30/home-alone-review-yuletide-rerelease>

5. Budgetary and box-office data from *BoxOfficeMojo.com*.
    <https://www.boxofficemojo.com/release/rl3629745665/>

6. Box-office data from *The-Numbers.com*.
    <http://www.the-numbers.com/movie/Home-Alone>

7. Rowana Agajanian, '"Peace on Earth, Goodwill to All Men": The Depiction of Christmas in Modern Hollywood Films', in *Christmas at the Movies: Images of Christmas in American, British and European Cinema*, ed. by Mark Connelly (London: I.B. Tauris, 2000), 143-164, p.149.

8. Jeanne Cooper, '*Home Alone*', in *The Washington Post*, 16 November 1990.
    <https://www.washingtonpost.com/wp-srv/style/ longterm/movies/videos/homealonepgcooper_a09ecc.htm>

9.   Dave Kehr, '*Home Alone*', in *The Chicago Tribune*, 16 November 1990.
        <*https://www.chicagotribune.com/ct-home-alone-review-1990-20150929-story.html*>

10.   Jonathan Rosenbaum, '*Home Alone*', in *The Chicago Reader*, 26 October 1990.
        <*https://chicagoreader.com/film/home-alone-2/*>

11.   Roger Ebert, '*Home Alone*', in *The Chicago Sun-Times*, 16 November 1990.
        <*https://www.rogerebert.com/reviews/home-alone-1990*>

12.   Marc Savlov, '*Home Alone*', in *The Austin Chronicle*, 11 January 1991.
        <*https://www.austinchronicle.com/events/film/1991-01-11/home-alone/*>

13.   Caryn James, 'Review/Film: Holiday Black Comedy for Modern Children', in *The New York Times*, 16 November 1990.
        <*https://www.nytimes.com/1990/11/16/movies/review-film-holiday-black-comedy-for-modern-children.html*>

14.   Owen Gleiberman, '*Home Alone*', in *Entertainment Weekly*, 25 July 2007.
        <*https://ew.com/article/2007/07/25/home-alone-2/*>

15.   Edison Smith, 'Keep the Change, You Filthy Animal: How *Home Alone* Became a Festive Record Breaker', in *VHS Revival*, 17 December 2020.
        <*https://vhsrevival.com/2020/12/17/keep-the-change-you-filthy-animal-how-home-alone-became-a-festive-record-breaker/*>

16. Chris Hicks, 'Film review: *Home Alone*', in *Deseret News*, 21 November 2000.
    <*https://www.deseret.com/2000/11/21/20087760/film-review-home-alone*>

17. Noel Murray, '*Home Alone*', in *AV Club*, 13 December 2006.
    <*https://www.avclub.com/home-alone-1798202206*>

18. Leonard Norwitz, '*Home Alone* (Blu-ray)', in *Lens Views*, 8 December 2008.
    <*http://www.dvdbeaver.com/film2/DVDReviews43/home_alone_blu-ray.htm*>

19. Chris Jordan, *Movies and the Reagan Presidency: Success and Ethics* (Westport: Praeger, 2003), p.156.

20. ibid., pp.156-57.

21. Michael Mackenzie, '*Home Alone: Family Fun Edition* Review', in *DVD Times*, 1 December 2006.
    <*https://www.thedigitalfix.com/film/dvd_review/home-alone-family-fun-edition/*>

22. Smith.

2

All I Want for Christmas (1991)

Paramount Pictures

Director: Robert Lieberman
Producer: Marykay Powell
Screenwriters: Thom Eberhardt and Richard Kramer

HOME *Alone* (q.v.) had expertly established one of the most prominent motifs of 1990s Christmas film-making: namely that of reconciliation. In its fondly-remembered reunion between Kevin McCallister and his long-suffering parents, the family unit is restored, order re-established, and the comforts of domestic stability reaffirmed. Yet that movie's meteoric success signalled another trait that would become recognisable throughout the decade: that of the need to balance the traditionalism of conventional festive tropes with the progressiveness of a rapidly-changing socio-cultural milieu.

All I Want for Christmas (incidentally, not to be con-fused with Mariah Carey's smash hit uptempo festive ballad 'All I Want for Christmas is You', which was released three years later in 1994 and has since become the definitive musical starting pistol for many a festive party in the lead up to De-cember) was a high-profile but morally problematic movie which paid lip-service to changing social mores at the same time as idealising established cultural traditions. This contra-dictory approach led to a headlong clash of tropes which would ultimately result in considerable critical hostility, but – quite in spite of that – it was a project that launched amid general enthusiasm on the part of Paramount Pictures. Torene Svitil notes that 'this is the film that new Paramount studio head Brandon Tartikoff rushed through production so fast that snow had to be manufactured in the midst of a Los Angeles summer for the appropriate seasonal look'.[1]

Just as some critics had raised eyebrows at *Home Alone*'s romanticised defence of the nuclear family, so too was there suspicion on the part of commentators regarding *All I Want for Christmas*'s willingness to confront the difficulties of divorce only so far as to reaffirm and venerate the tradi-tional value of the nuclear family. This scepticism has continued into the present day, with reviewers such as Ryan Cracknell offering the opinion that, 'For whatever reason, family films don't often show how life is for many. Mom and Dad often sleep in separate homes today, yet Hollywood seems slow to reflect it. And when they are apart, the chil-dren seem to be scheming on ways of getting them back together. *All I Want for Christmas* is one such film. Generic at its core, the idea behind the movie is valiant enough but happy themes aren't enough to carry an otherwise boring film. [...] *All I Want for Christmas* has the look and feel of a gener-ic family sitcom. At a half-hour, I could have handled it and its generic characters. But stretched out to more than 90 minutes, it's a lot harder to handle, no matter how interested in the subject matter I might have been'.[2] What part, then, does the film play in the wider pantheon of 1990s Christmas movies – and how would its creative approach correspond with the themes that were being established throughout the decade?

The director of *All I Want for Christmas* was Robert Lieberman, a highly prolific industry professional who founded the Harmony Pictures production company and has been responsible for the direction of around two thousand TV commercials. His work for television included helming episodes of series as diverse as *ABC Afterschool Specials* (1978), *Dream Street* (1989) and *The Young Riders* (1989), though he would later move on to even greater success on many iconic TV shows which included *The X-Files* (1993 and 1999), *Dexter* (2006) and *The Expanse* (2016). While he had been the director of TV movies including *Fighting Back: The Rocker Bleier Story* (1980) and *Will: G. Gordon Liddy* (1982), he was especially well-known at the time for directing 'I'll Be Home for Christmas', the 1987 Christmas special of ABC's popular, multiple award-winning drama series *thirtysomething* (1987-91), which had been scripted by Richard Kramer from a story by Susan Monsky. The creative team of Lieberman and Kramer would reunite for *All I Want for Christmas*, with the widely-publicised intent of recreating the earlier festive magic they had conjured for the small screen. In the eyes of many critics, including Desson Howe, their artistic objective was to prove something of a qualified success: '*Miracle on 34th Street* this ain't. Children will fidget. Parents will cross their legs, then uncross them again. Oh, the restless sea of discontent in neighborhood theaters. The story's just too dull and pre-rigged. [[...]] According to the film's press notes, director Robert Lieberman and co-screenwriter Richard Kramer had a blast working on a Christmas episode for *thirtysomething*. They thought they'd repeat the success. Dick, Bob? It didn't happen'.[3]

In an upmarket school in New York, young Ethan O'Fallon (Ethan Randall) has little enthusiasm for the establishment's pre-festive offerings. It is the first Christmas his family will be celebrating since his parents divorced and his father departed, so he has some trepidation about what the festivities will feel like this year. He and his precocious younger sister Hallie (Thora Birch) head home after school, where they meet up with their glamorous former actress grandmother Lillian Brooks (Lauren Bacall) and their doting mother, publisher Catherine O'Fallon (Harley Jane Kozak). Catherine is less than impressed, as the kids' estranged father Michael (Jamey Sheridan) is hours late to pick up his offspring for an arranged trip to a museum. This leads to an argument, where it becomes clear that the couple's recent divorce has been the result of a lack of communication between them as well as Michael's decision to abandon his upscale corporate lifestyle to run a diner on 12th Street – a sweeping professional choice with a major impact on their lives, which Catherine feels was made without her having been properly consulted.

As the O'Fallons bicker, Catherine's new boyfriend Tony Boer (Kevin Nealon) arrives to take her on a date at the theatre. Lillian and the kids seem less than impressed by the smarmy financier, and Catherine makes a speedy departure before further disagreements can break out. Ethan and Hallie are untroubled by the prospect of seeing dinosaur skeletons on exhibition at the museum, and ask their dad if they can join him at the diner instead. The kids clearly love the hustle and bustle of the busy inner-city café, with its good-natured patrons and warm-hearted waiter Sonya (Camille Saviola), and they waste no time in getting involved with preparing and serving food to customers. It is clear that both siblings have retained a strong emotional bond with their caring father, in spite of his recent departure from the family home.

Later on, Hallie covertly reveals her big wish for Christmas – she intends to ask Santa Claus to reunite her quarrelling parents and reverse their divorce. Ethan is aghast, sensing that this ambition will only lead to disappointment, but his sister is adamant and manages to sweet-talk him into taking her to a city department store so that she can speak to Santa (Leslie Nielsen) herself. In spite of Ethan's protestations that she should ask for a more realistic gift, Hallie won't be dissuaded that Santa can succeed at overcoming the impossible when no-one else can. As her brother is forced to rapidly re-treat in order to avoid being seen by his classmates queuing to meet Santa (a major social *faux-pas* at his age), Hallie sees her chance and unveils her wish to the jolly old elf. Even Santa is slightly taken aback by her request, considering it rather out of the ordinary... but the young girl is determined that thanks to the magic of Christmas, everything will work out for the best.

Back at the family home, Catherine is hosting a pre-Christmas party for several high-class guests. The kids are unimpressed by the glamorous socialites making small-talk, and their waspish grandmother – who has seen it all before – is similarly underwhelmed by the preening display. However, Ethan's interest becomes piqued when Susan (Felicity LaFor-tune), one of Catherine's colleagues at the publishing house where she works, introduces her daughter Stephanie (Amy Oberer). The pair appear to share a mutual appreciation as Lillian conducts the lighting ceremony of the family's opulent Christmas tree, though the smitten Ethan's attempts to ap-pear suave soon hit the skids when his chair gives way during a musical recital, and an amused Stephanie watches as he tries to retain his composure while hitting the ground in the least dignified of ways.

Having overheard Susan telling Catherine that Stephanie can't wait to visit the New York Museum of Modern Art, Ethan ensures that he's there the next day in order to get to know her. In spite of initial awkwardness, they soon strike up an easy conversational rapport, and the shared attraction becomes apparent to both of them. Ethan discovers that Stephanie has also had to deal with parental divorce, but attends school in Boston as she had already been enrolled there before her mother and father had split up.

While Ethan takes Stephanie for the cheapest meal in New York – collecting free samples from food appliance salespeople at a department store – Hallie is back home taking a piano lesson. She overhears Catherine and Lillian, where the latter is voicing concern over the unsuitability of the former's unctuous new beau. Lillian clearly has no time for the oily Tony, but Catherine insists that she plans to marry him – a decision which devastates Hallie, as it throws her secret Christmas wish into disarray.

Ethan walks Stephanie to a railway station so that she can catch her train, and tries to arrange a date with her only to discover that they have constantly clashing schedules. Feeling rather deflated as he watches her go, Ethan seemingly resigns himself to the possibility that his romantic ambitions have been thwarted by distance. Returning home, he is met with an confounded Hallie, who tells him of their mother's marital plans. However, Ethan has little time to process the enormity of this development before Tony arrives to drop Ethan off at the diner. Catherine and her boyfriend, along with Hallie, are heading for an evening at the ballet, but Ethan manages to persuade his mother to come into the diner to see the now-finished interior – and meet Michael. In-trigued, as the diner was still in the process of being developed before the divorce, Catherine agrees. Ethan is relieved to see that his parents still have obvious chemistry between them, and Catherine is quietly impressed by Michael's love for the business he has built from the ground up. However, Michael is distraught when Catherine breaks the news that she in-tends to remarry.

At a performance of Tchaikovsky's ballet *The Nut-cracker*, Hallie attempts (with very little subtlety) to derail the evening by feigning illness. Tony sees through her ruse, and with growing resentment. Meanwhile, at the diner Ethan and Michael are sharing their misgivings over Catherine's marriage plans. Ethan implores his father to stop the wedding, but Michael admits that there's little he can do to intervene – Catherine has every right to do what she feels will make her happy. But Ethan doubts Tony's suitability as a partner, and entreats Michael to tell Catherine he still has feelings for her while he still can. However, his father is nonplussed, explain-ing that there is never time to properly discuss anything with her as they are always so busy. This desire for romantic isola-tion seems to give Ethan an idea.

After the ballet has ended, Catherine pleads with Hal-lie to give Tony a chance, feeling that her boyfriend's attempts to connect with the kids are being rebuffed at every turn. Hallie turns the conversation around and asks her moth-er if she is really sure that Tony is the kind of person she wants to form a relationship with in the long term. Catherine seems taken aback at her daughter's frankness, but their dis-cussion is interrupted by Tony's return. Hallie again pretends she has some ill-defined malady – successfully this time – much to the visible frustration of the sleazy Tony.

Back home, Ethan is watching old home movies and be-comes upset as he reflects on the breakdown in his parents' marriage and the regrets he has about the impact on his family unit. This causes him to oversleep the following morning, and as such he is unaware that Hallie has decided to make her way alone back to the department store where she met Santa Claus. Alarmed at the thought of his wilful seven-year-old sister walking the streets of New York City unaccompanied, Ethan goes racing after her and eventually catches up. It turns out that she wanted to reinforce to Santa the nature of her request – not just that she wanted her mother to remarry, but that she specifically wants the marriage between her parents restored. Santa assures her that he will do his best, but Ethan arrives and whisks Hallie away, upset that she would wander the busy city alone. However, even he is taken aback at how emotional Hallie has become, and he realises just how much stock she has put into Santa being able to somehow save the day.

Later, at a Christmas Eve social dance, Ethan finds himself bored rigid by the sombre etiquette of the event. He soon perks up when Stephanie arrives unexpectedly, and the two briefly share a dance before Ethan sees a chance to ditch the tedious occasion and infiltrate a wedding reception being held at the same hotel. The event is so well-attended, every-one assumes that the two youngsters must be invited guests, and thus they tuck in to delicious food while Ethan outlines his plan to trick his parents into spending time together in the hope that they will reconcile. Stephanie finds his optimism somewhat misguided, but he assures her that it stands more chance of success than Hallie's faith in Santa's magical powers.

Hallie and Ethan visit a local pet store and stock up on mice, hatching a plan for when Catherine and Lillian are meeting with a wedding planner later that day. Once back home, they release the mice in the hope of disrupting the consultation, but the wayward rodents make a beeline for the front door instead. While the two go racing after the lost mice, they are oblivious to the fact that one of them has made its way onto the wedding planner's saucer, causing her to recoil in shock. Lillian seems quietly pleased; the upscale planner (who has been hired by Tony) was recommending that hundreds of guests be invited to the wedding at a substantial cost.

A pest control team are called in, and Lillian makes arrangements to stay overnight at a hotel while the search for wayward vermin is underway. Catherine calls Susan, who agrees that she can stay with Stephanie while she's in town. Stephanie, who knows of Ethan's schemes, is overjoyed to know that his outlandish strategy is going to plan. Meanwhile, Ethan phones the police and reports a mysterious 'abandoned car' parked in a loading bay in front of the diner, supposedly left there for several days. He also cooks up a ruse with his friend Marshall (Patrick LaBrecque) to make Catherine think he has arranged to stay at his home. His mother is confused, wondering why Ethan would prefer to stay overnight on Christmas Eve with a school friend rather than his father, but he convinces her that he wants to avoid sad reminiscences of when the family was still together. Tony, who has arrived to take Catherine on a date, is delighted at the thought of the kids staying elsewhere. He offers to drop Ethan off at Marshall's house, and to take Hallie to the diner.

Tony's car arrives on 12th Street, and he is forced to park in a loading bay due to an ice cream delivery van unloading at the front of the diner (which Ethan knew in advance was scheduled to be there). Hallie then releases the one remaining white mouse, which she has named Snowball, onto the sidewalk and starts to behave hysterically. Concerned, Tony rushes out of his car in pursuit of the runaway rodent, and Ethan tricks him into believing the mouse has entered the refrigerated van. Tony tries to catch it, only for Ethan to slam and lock the van doors behind him. Tony is livid at having fallen foul of the ruse, but before he can escape the van's driver, Frankie (Michael Alaimo), returns and heads off for his next delivery. As Frankie is profoundly hard of hearing, Ethan knows that he will be in New Jersey before he realises that Tony is locked in the van's refrigerated storage.

Just as Hallie heads into the diner to see Michael, a local authority pickup truck arrives outside to impound Tony's illegally-parked BMW – a response to Ethan's phone call, and all part of his prearranged plan. As a rather dejected Michael puts up his doleful-looking Christmas decorations, Hallie talks him into dressing up for the evening, suggesting that a smart suit is called for in order to make the most of the season. Over at the hotel, Catherine is confused at Tony's non-appearance, but her thoughts are interrupted when Michael calls to say that Hallie has taken ill. In reality, their daughter simply wants to lure Catherine over to Michael's apartment above the diner. Stephanie knows that this is all part of the plan, and sure enough Catherine aborts her intended dinner date (with the absent Tony) to head back to Hallie.

Sure enough, Catherine arrives at Michael's apartment and is puzzled to discover that both of them are dressed for a formal night out. Hallie is now sleeping, her illness feint once again a success. Stephanie phones Catherine and pretends that Tony has been in touch to say that an emergency has come up, meaning that he will have to pull out of their dinner date. Catherine feels insulted at having been stood up, little realising that Tony is still trapped in the back of an ice cream delivery van.

Ethan, who his parents believe is staying with Marshall, is waiting around outside the diner. A yellow cab arrives to pick up Catherine, but Stephanie arrives in the nick of time, pretends to be Catherine and pays the driver to take off without Mrs O'Fallon. Puzzled at the apparent non-appearance of the taxi, Michael and Catherine watch snow fall outside and reminisce about happier times. Catherine decides to go out hunting for a cab, but Michael dissuades her – with the snowfall turning into a blizzard and visibility worsening, it's unlikely that she would find a taxi that late on Christmas Eve. Reluctantly, she decides to stay.

Little do either of them realise that Ethan and Stephanie are below them in the now-deserted diner, enjoying a romantic meal of their own. Stephanie reveals how excited she is to be taking part in an unexpected adventure over Christmas, having anticipated a rather dull festive season otherwise. The couple reflect on their shared affection; even though they seem slightly melancholic at the realisation that with the geographical distance between their respective home cities, they need to make the most of the moment as their budding romance seems fated to be a short-lived one.

Hallie creeps out of Michael's bedroom, where she has been pretending to sleep, and discovers her parents slumbering comfortably on the same couch together. She sneaks downstairs to break the news to Ethan and Stephanie, and the trio celebrates their scheme apparently having come to fruition. As they clown around in the snow outside the diner, a strange multicoloured light shoots past them in the sky above – presumably Santa, out on his annual deliveries. Hallie is elated, believing her festive wish has come true.

The next morning, Michael and Catherine awaken on the couch, somewhat self-conscious at being in each other's arms again – though far from uncomfortable with the notion. However, shock soon takes hold when they realise that Hallie appears to be missing. (In actual fact, she is fast asleep in the diner with Ethan and Stephanie.) Catherine begins to smell a rat, and phones Marshall to speak to Ethan... little fathoming that he has never been staying with his friend as claimed. Not expecting the call, Marshall panics and confesses that he has no idea where Ethan is. No sooner does he end the conversation, a hypothermic Tony rings from a police station in New Jersey, less than impressed by the trick that Ethan has played on him.

As the kids exchange presents at the diner, Ethan is perturbed when he sees a flustered Michael and Catherine jumping into a yellow cab. He knows that his scheme has finally been rumbled. The O'Fallons arrive back at Catherine's home just as Lillian returns from the hotel, and they discover not only that the kids had never stayed in their rooms the previous night, but also – just to complicate things further – that the family's genial nanny Olivia (Andrea Martin) has just gone into labour.

Stephanie, Ethan and Hallie race back to the house on foot, frantically brainstorming credible-sounding excuses for the previous night's events, but they are stopped in their tracks by the arrival of a speeding ambulance which parks in front of the house... right next to a police car. Ethan fears the worst, and vows to take the blame for everything that has happened. They enter the house, reconcile with Michael and Catherine, and are relieved to discover that the emergency services are there for Olivia and not to take them into custody.

A livid and dishevelled Tony arrives by taxi and angrily rants that the O'Fallon kids will soon learn respect for their elders once he and Catherine are married. But Catherine calmly informs him that Christmas is for families, and she and Tony are not family... nor are they going to be. Delighted to finally see the back of the superficial financier, Lillian shows him out just as Susan arrives, relieved to discover that the apparently-missing Stephanie is safe and well. Ethan tries to explain his plan, but quickly realises that it would be pointless to summarise and instead tells the assembled family that he had come to realise how much he missed them all being together. Michael admits to Catherine that he now realises how difficult his unilateral decisions had made things for the family, and that he owes them greater responsibility. The couple seal their reconciliation with a kiss.

As the family celebrate, Hallie discovers someone at the door – the department store Santa. He admits that fulfilling her wish was a tough task, but wanted to drop off a little something to make the festive season complete: her pet mouse Snowball, thought missing outside the diner the previous night. Hallie is overjoyed to be reunited with her little friend. Ethan is stunned into silence, realising that this Santa is no random store employee but the real deal.

Later, Stephanie and Ethan share a tender moment as they realise they will soon be parted. Ethan regrets the fact that it may well be Christmas the following year before they will see each other again. However, Stephanie interjects that like Hallie, she has had a dream of her own – that the two of them will find true love together. As she and Susan are driven off in a taxi, Ethan is elated, realising that it isn't just Michael and Catherine who have kindled a wonderful romance that fateful Christmas Day.

All I Want for Christmas is a film that is so saccharine, it could make your fillings squeak. The wintry New York City that it depicts (actually filmed during a midsummer heatwave) seems to be entirely populated by upper-middle-class professionals on the verge of ennui – along with their equally jaded offspring – and the convoluted action of the plot seems motivated by endless happy coincidences and unlikely occurrences. This sometimes leads to strange plot inconsistencies, such as Ethan telling the authorities over the phone that Tony's car has been abandoned for several days, but yet – when the tow-truck eventually pulls up at the diner – nobody ever questions why the headlights of the BMW are on and the engine is still running. Similarly, the always-busy streets of New York sometimes seem strangely deserted, even on the usually-social evening of Christmas Eve, and – like *Home Alone* before it – much of Ethan's plan would have been promptly derailed if any of the characters had access to cell-phones. There are also various ethical questions raised, simply on account of the time of the film's production; for instance, the purchase of eight mice from a pet shop simply to act as a diversion – and with no thought to the creatures' long-term safety or wellbeing – would obviously attract objections from animal rights groups in the present day.

The film does riff knowingly on the Christmas movie genre, not least in Hallie's assertion that it's important not to consult just any costumed Santa for advice, but rather 'the real Santa'... who is, of course, to be found only at Macy's Department Store. The cultural references reach beyond *Miracle on 34th Street* (George Seaton, 1947), of course; the jovial owner of the pet store insists that an unusually prone caged rabbit is 'not dead, just resting', recalling the famous 'Dead Parrot Sketch' immortalised on the BBC's *Monty Python's*

Flying Circus in 1969, while Lauren Bacall as Lillian effortlessly parodies her own soaring reputation as a silver screen icon of decades past (a fourth-wall-breaking approach which is typified by Catherine having a framed, real-life publicity photo of Lauren Bacall in her heyday placed prominently in her home). Bacall was, of course, the star of innumerable major features which included *To Have and Have Not* (Howard Hawks, 1944), *The Big Sleep* (Howard Hawks, 1946), *Dark Passage* (Delmer Daves, 1947) and *How to Marry a Millionaire* (Jean Negulesco, 1953), amongst countless others.

It is, however, in its treatment of divorce that the film came to be most controversial. In some sense, its largely-innocuous action was really little more than a contemporary updating of films such as *The Parent Trap* (David Swift, 1961), while its theme of an insouciant father gradually waking up to his familial responsibilities would be echoed by later Christmas films of the decade such as *Jack Frost* (Troy Miller, 1998). However, in introducing the idea that Santa Claus had the power to reverse a parental divorce, the film offered a hint of false hope to young children which seemed almost as irresponsible as the idea of Santa bringing a parent back from the dead in the previous decade's *One Magic Christmas* (Phillip Borsos, 1985). By that same token, as Marjorie Baumgarten notes, the serious issue of divorce and the major impact it has on the lives of children made for an awkward fit in a film that was otherwise upbeat and inviting: 'Call this one *Miracle on 12th Street*. No it's not precisely the same story as the 34th Street model (or even one-third the story), but it borrows much of the same whimsy, grit and Christmas sentiment from the original. [...] This New York they inhabit is a fantasy land, all serendipity and good cheer. Really, just about the only dark cloud in this Manhattan Island paradise is the nasty fact of divorce. And for the few lucky youngsters out there whose lives so far have not been touched by divorce, this movie may stir up illegitimate (or, at least, unnecessary) worries. Such realism in an otherwise fantasy-based tale makes for an awkward combination'.[4]

The gradually changing domestic circumstances of family life in the United States would, of course, lead to re-examinations of the concept of family later in the 1990s, with films such as *The Santa Clause* (q.v.) acknowledging the shift in attitudes regarding blended families while others, including Les Mayfield's remake of *Miracle on 34th Street* (q.v.) would instead reaffirm a continued relevance of the nuclear model of family structure. In *All I Want for Christmas*, however, the estranged O'Fallon parents clearly retain so much emotional connection and shared affection for each other that it seems like a genuine mystery as to why they ever divorced, whereas Kevin Nealon is given a thankless task in portraying the snobbish Tony, a Wall Street financier with all the charisma of a rainy weekend. It seems quite clear that any effort Tony makes to ingratiate himself with Catherine's family is entirely driven by expediency, making the character seem shallow and insincere, and yet the kids' dismissive treatment of him still manages to seem manipulative and offhand. In combination, as Svitil notes, all of these factors lower the stakes of the action and make the outcome seem more of an inevitability than the hard-won fruits of a struggle for true love that the audience may have been led to expect: 'Clearly meant to be adorable, the kids crack jokes like screenwriters rather than children, and the plot is just as contrived as the self-conscious dialogue. Judging by his loft, Dad is making a darn good living at the diner and since Mom and Dad still seem to be in love with each other and the boyfriend is such a jerk, where's the conflict?'[5]

The film benefits from the mature performances delivered by its youthful leads, Ethan Randall and Thora Birch. Randall, who would later be credited as 'Ethan Embry' (the name by which he has subsequently become better known in the film industry), also starred in the Thanksgiving-themed road comedy *Dutch* (Peter Faiman, 1991) the same year, and would go on to later success in movies including *Empire Records* (Allan Moyle, 1995), *That Thing You Do!* (Tom Hanks, 1996), and *Can't Hardly Wait* (Deborah Kaplan and Harry Elfont, 1998). In the role of Ethan O'Fallon, Randall creates a likeable, wisecracking and yet subtly self-conscious lead who is all too aware of the rapid changes taking place in his own life during his early teens – further underscoring the effect of his parents' divorce on his personal development. His projected confidence does much to mask his sense of insecurity, and his desire to reassemble his family unit to provide the stability he knew in the past. It says much for Randall and his co-star, Amy Oberer, that the chemistry of the blossoming romance between Ethan and Stephanie generally appears more believable than that of Michael and Catherine. In spite of her young age at the time, Thora Birch had already appeared in numerous commercials and episodes of TV series, as well as making her acting debut in the science fiction comedy *Purple People Eater* (Linda Shayne, 1988). She would go on to greater acclaim throughout the nineties thanks to performances in films such as *Hocus Pocus* (Kenny Ortega, 1993), *Alaska* (Fraser Clarke Heston, 1996) and *American Beauty* (Sam Mendes, 1999). Birch gives a confident and frequently droll performance as Hallie, never allowing the character to drift too far into the territory of cutesy mawkishness, and her likeability (though arguably the character is something of an acquired taste overall, often proving to be manipulative and calculating) helps to brighten the scenes she appears in. Both Randall and Birch would be nominated for Best Young Actor Starring in a Motion Picture Awards at the Young Artist Awards for their on-screen accomplishments in *All I Want for Christmas*.

While the film's child stars bring both appeal and amiability to their roles, many of their adult counterparts seem to be largely going through the motions – though in their defence, the script often gives them little to work with. Lauren Bacall seems to enjoy gently sending up the cliché of the fading acting legend in her twilight years, but Harley Jane Kozak and Jamey Sheridan struggle to bring any real emotional believability to the relationship between Michael and Catherine. Both bring a sense of intelligence and professional aptitude to their respective characters, but while the screenplay makes clear that the O'Fallons' shared sense of attraction has been neglected rather than truly severed, the actual rekindling of their romance seems awkward and strangely artificial. Kozak was a well-known figure in the acting world at the time thanks to her roles in films such as *When Harry Met Sally...* (Rob Reiner, 1989), *Parenthood* (Ron Howard, 1989) and *Arachnophobia* (Frank Marshall, 1990), whereas Jamey Sheridan had been nominated for a Tony Award for his appearance in the 1986 revival of Arthur Miller's stage drama *All My Sons* and had made regular appearances on TV and in film throughout the 1980s in a wide variety of roles.

Often cited as one of the best aspects of *All I Want for Christmas* was Leslie Nielsen's 'special appearance' as Santa Claus. While his scant screen time essentially amounted to little more than an extended cameo, the always-watchable Nielsen has a definite twinkle in his eye as the white-bearded

North Pole-dweller, and in addition to his famously poker-faced wit he brings substantial charm to the man in the red suit. While Nielsen's long and prolific career had seen him appearing in everything from influential science fiction drama *Forbidden Planet* (Nicholas Nayfack, 1956) to cult disaster movie *The Poseidon Adventure* (Ronald Neame, 1972), his brilliantly deadpan comic delivery won him a new generation of fans in later years thanks to being cast in parodies *Airplane!* (David Zucker, Jerry Zucker and Jim Abrahams, 1980) and *The Naked Gun* (David Zucker, 1988). He would reprise the role of Santa Claus some years later in William Dear's fantasy TV movie *Santa Who?* (2000), and again on CBC's animated series *Chilly Beach* (2003).

Bruce Broughton brings a characteristic touch of class to the original musical score of *All I Want for Christmas*, while the title song by Stephen Bishop also does a decent job of bringing to life the film's themes of domestic warmth and reconciliation. The movie also benefits from some choice cinematography by Robbie Greenberg, which beautifully captures snowy New York at its best, and superb set decoration by John M. Dwyer, which excels at evoking aspects of the various characters in their respective habitats – from the early *Star Trek: The Next Generation* poster in Ethan's room through to the top-notch pinball machine flashing away in Michael's apartment.

All I Want for Christmas received a decidedly frosty reception from critics at the time of its release – and not in the festive sense of the word. Many railed at the inauthenticity of its sentiment and the convolutions of the storyline, with reviewers such as Roger Ebert reflecting that, 'All I want for Christmas is to never see *All I Want for Christmas* again. Here is a calculating holiday fable that is phony to its very bones – artificial, contrived, illogical, manipulative and stupid. It's one of those movies that insults your intelligence by assuming you have no memory, no common sense, and no knowledge of how people behave when they are not in the grip of an idiotic screenplay. [...] There was not a moment of the movie I could believe, not a motivation I thought was plausible, not a plot development that wasn't imposed on us by the requirements of the plot'.[6] Others, such as Rita Kempley, instead complained about the treacly sentimentality which the film served in excessive abundance: 'When it comes to yuletide cheer, *All I Want for Christmas* ranks just under dead reindeer on the roof. [...] The script, originally submitted by Thom Eberhardt, is as peaked as Tiny Tim, a coy wisp that was no doubt doctored into its present pablum-like state by cowriter Richard Kramer'.[7]

Not all appraisals were entirely negative, however, with some critics acknowledging that the film was inoffensive enough if audiences happened to be in the right mood for its melange of schmaltziness and artfulness. Jonathan Rosenbaum, for instance, observed that 'this 1991 feature is not for diabetics or connoisseurs of real people, but everyone else should have a ball. [...] Leslie Nielsen (as Santa Claus) [...] and multiple plugs for Ben & Jerry's ice cream are enlisted to bring some much-needed class to the proceedings, and Robert Lieberman directs it all with a straight face'.[8] There were even a few reviewers, such as Leonard Pitts Jr., who gave positive appraisals of the film's merits, opining: 'What a charming, sweet-natured little fable this is – warm and funny but smart, too. *All I Want for Christmas* is that rare bit of family fare that tickles the tykes but entertains the older set at the same time. [...] Yes, the film is at times manipulative and, especially toward the end, far-fetched. But it is such a beguiling piece of entertainment that you willingly forgive its faults and happily go along for the ride'.[9]

In spite of a general lack of appreciation from the commentators of the time, *All I Want for Christmas* gradually established a modest cult following thanks to screenings on television and home entertainment formats, and as such the film has come to be viewed slightly more favourably in more recent times. This has led to some thoughtful retrospective appraisals by critics such as Neil Baker, who sagely notes that it is Ethan's crafty artifice rather than Santa's ability to grant wishes which really saves the day: 'A movie about family separation and divorce, with the kids stuck in the middle, doesn't exactly sound like a festive fair, and as a result, critics were not impressed in 1991. Many critics would argue that the subject of divorce was too depressing for a kid's Christmas movie, while others pointed to the film's occasionally fall into sickly sweet territory. However, while not perfect, many critics missed the point of *All I Want for Christmas*; after all, this is a film about childhood dreams disrupted by family conflict. Here *All I Want for Christmas* reflects the growing teenage realisation that wishes only come true if you work to make them real'.[10] By that same token, others such as Caroline Ames have echoed the initial criticism that the issue of divorce reversal fits uncomfortably within the framework of the Chirstmas movie: 'This film is by no means a Christmas classic but you can easily see the messages which are linked to the film. But probably giving children false hope when there parents have split up. Surely there was a reason so it shouldn't be messed with? But Hallie did of course ask Santa, played by Leslie Nielsen in the lead to up Christmas for her parents to get back together'.[11]

More prominent in recent reviews than those of the film's original run is an appreciation of Birch and Randall's performances, with critics including Troy Rutter acknowledging the talent of both young actors: 'The film owes itself to the duo of Embry and Birch. Coming off a rather successful Thanksgiving movie, *Dutch*, Embry's performance as Ethan is endearing even though he could easily have turned into a snotty, rich, entitled brat. His relationship with his sister is enviable and almost too sweet. Birch was just coming off the release of *Paradise* with Elijah Wood, Melanie Griffith and Don Johnson prior to the film's release. All the performances in the film are great, and the music and cinematography complement the story. Fun Fact, Leslie Nielsen has played Santa only 3 times. Seems like more'.[12] Cracknell, on the other hand, has reflected the concerns of early nineties' commentators that the movie's outcomes were so heavily signposted in advance, they are essentially robbed of dramatic consequence:

> Because *All I Want for Christmas* is geared towards a family audience, the outcome is largely ever in doubt. But even in taking it outside of the genre, the construction of relationships between the adults makes it far too obvious. The film begins with the children's parents already apart. We don't see any of their fights or differences that drove them away from each other in the first place and when they're shown together they really don't seem all that different. Their mother Catherine (Harley Jane Kozak) is engaged to be remarried, but her fiancé (Kevin Nealon) is set up as a child-hating villain. He's clearly not cut out to be Hallie and Ethan's stepfather. Therefore, getting their parents back together cannot be a far stretch be-

cause we're not given much of a reason as to why they should have been separated in the first place.[13]

With a domestic gross of $14,812,144,[14] *All I Want for Christmas* would ultimately earn less at the box-office in its entire run than *Home Alone* had made in the first weekend of its release. It may have been a disappointing commercial result for a film that had contained performances by so many talented actors, but *All I Want for Christmas* has nonetheless continued to be watched over the decades with a regularity that defies its critical reception. Director Robert Lieberman would helm a number of later films including *D3: The Mighty Ducks* (1996), *The Tortured* (2010) and *Breakaway* (2011), as well as CBS's two-part TV miniseries *Titanic* (1996) and episodes of many TV series, but to date he has never returned to the Christmas movie genre.

Along with *Home Alone*, *All I Want for Christmas* helped to solidify the theme of family relations as being at the core of 1990s festive cinema. As the decade was to progress, the topic would diversify greatly in its scope, as would the related subject of reconciliation – whether between friends or kin. Yet for all its occasional assertion of modernity, especially in its acknowledgement of increasing rates of divorce (not least in Marshall's tongue-in-cheek deal to help Ethan get his parents back together if he will give him a hand to split up his own feuding mother and father), *All I Want for Christmas* was ultimately a film that had greater concern with a bygone past – whether reflected in the sardonic Lillian's feted acting career belonging to Hollywood's golden age, Michael's desire to eschew the corporate rat-race in order to pursue the American Dream and become his own man, the crushingly outmoded format of Caroline's Christmas party and Ethan's formal school dance, or simply the yearning of all the characters for a good old-fashioned happy ending (no matter how implausible this heartwarming resolution may have seemed in the cynical world of the nineties). But as would be the case with so many other festive films of the decade, the irresistible power of the Christmas spirit had the demonstrable capacity to overcome all opposition: neither level-headed pragmatism nor emotional realism would be allowed to stand in its way.

REFERENCES

1. Torene Svitil, '*All I Want for Christmas* Review', in *Empire*, 3 December 2012. <*https://www.empireonline.com/movies/reviews/want-christmas-review/*>

2. Ryan Cracknell, '*All I Want for Christmas*', in *Movie Views*, 10 December 2003. <*http://movieviews.ca/all-i-want-for-christmas*>

3. Desson Howe, '*All I Want for Christmas*', in *The Washington Post*, 8 November 1991. <*https://www.washingtonpost.com/wp-srv/style/longterm/movies/videos/alliwantforchristmasghowe_a0ae7f.htm*>

4. Marjorie Baumgarten, '*All I Want for Christmas*', in *The Austin Chronicle*, 8 November 1991. <*https://www.austinchronicle.com/events/film/1991-11-08/139224/*>

5. Svitil.

6. Roger Ebert, '*All I Want for Christmas*', in *The Chicago Sun-Times*, 8 November 1991. <*https://www.rogerebert.com/reviews/all-i-want-for-christmas-1991*>

7. Rita Kempley, '*All I Want for Christmas*', in *The Washington Post*, 8 November 1991. <*https://www.washingtonpost.com/wp-srv/style/longterm/movies/videos/alliwantforchristmasgkempley_a0a27d.htm*>

8. Jonathan Rosenbaum, '*All I Want for Christmas*', in *The Chicago Reader*, 3 December 2012.
    <*https://chicagoreader.com/film/all-i-want-for-christmas/*>

9. Leonard Pitts Jr., '*Christmas* is Beguiling: A Predictable Plot is Wonderfully Executed', in *The Miami Herald*, 8 November 1991, p.61.

10. Neil Baker, 'Seven Underrated Christmas Movies', in *Cinerama Film*, 12 December 2020.
    <*https://cineramafilm.com/2020/12/12/eight-underrated-christmas-movies/#h-all-i-want-for-christmas-1991*>

11. Caroline Ames, '*All I Want for Christmas* (1991) Review', in *Let's Go to the Movies*, 17 December 2013.
    <*https://letsgotothemovies.co.uk/2013/12/17/all-i-want-for-christmas-1991-review/*>

12. Troy Rutter, 'Film Review: *All I Want For Christmas*', in *Heartland Film Review*, 4 December 2020.
    <*https://heartlandfilmreview.com/2020/12/04/film-review-all-i-want-for-christmas/*>

13. Cracknell.

14. Box-office data from *The-Numbers.com*.
    <*http://www.the-numbers.com/movie/All-I-Want-For-Christmas*>

3

29th Street (1991)

*Twentieth Century Fox / JVC Entertainment Networks /
Largo Entertainment / Permut Presentations*

Director: George Gallo
Producer: David Permut
Screenwriter: George Gallo, from a story by
Frank Pesce and James Franciscus

ONE of the greatest pleasures of assessing nostalgic Christmas cinema is the fact that, alongside the most high-profile entries in the genre over the years, every now and again an often overlooked diamond in the rough is lying in wait to be found. *29th Street* is just such a film. Often overlooked at the time of its release, it has subsequently more or less disappeared into the annals of Christmas Past – and quite unfairly so, as it is actually one of the warmest and most unconventional festive movies of the 1990s.

While the film's publicity poster made explicit its stylistic indebtedness to the spirit of both Martin Scorsese and Frank Capra, with the inclusion of characters with larger-than-life names like Needle Nose Nipton, Dom the Bomb and Nicky Bad Lungs it's quite possible that viewers may also have expected a nod to the distinctive work of writers such as Damon Runyon – not least Bob Hope in his own festively-themed cinematic yarn, *The Lemon Drop Kid* (Sidney Lanfield, 1951), which had been derived from Runyon's work. In reality, however, *29th Street* very much carves its own artistic path, with director George Gallo crafting a highly distinctive tale that – in a manner characteristic of much Christmas movie-making in the 1990s – blended the traditional and the contemporary to striking effect.

Although *29th Street* was directed by George Gallo, a screenwriter and producer (also musician and painter) who at the time was most famous for penning the script for Martin Brest's popular action comedy *Midnight Run* (1988), which had starred Robert De Niro and Charles Grodin, the figure who dominates the movie is that of actor Frank Pesce. A prolific actor on TV and film from the 1970s, Pesce led an interesting life which involved encounters with many prominent industry talents due to supporting appearances in films as diverse as *Rocky* (John G. Avildsen, 1976), *Beverly Hills Cop* (Martin Brest, 1984) and *Top Gun* (Tony Scott, 1986). It was while working on *Midnight Run*, however, that the plan was hatched for him to turn his life experiences into an autobiographical film. As Alonso Duralde has observed, 'The project was born when Pesce played a supporting role in *Midnight Run* (1988), which Gallo wrote. He entertained cast and crew between takes telling the story of his life, and Gallo decided it was a tale worth filming'.[1]

While Pesce's life has become of most interest to film historians due to his many appearances in major movie releases throughout his career, the biographical *29th Street* was to instead focus on his early life, his family and the many colourful friends who came to shape his worldview. With its festive setting and atmospherically snowy New York locale, the stage was set for arguably the most unconventional Big Applesituated Christmas movie since *Bell, Book and Candle* (Rich-ard Quine, 1958). Yet as R.D. Francis has noted, the film's origins were even more interesting than the abovementioned summary may suggest:

Once upon a time in Italy, Antonio Margheriti cast James Franciscus (of the '70s [*Planet of the*] *Apes* franchise) and Frank Pesce as co-stars for his *Jaws* rip, *Killer Fish* (1979). The two became friends and came to write a screenplay on based Pesce's win-ning $6 million dollars in the New York state lottery. But his dad (mob flick mainstay Danny Aiello of the early mob romps *Godfather Part II* and *Once Upon a Time in America*) has some gambling debts to the mob. So, does Frank (Aus-tralian actor Anthony LaPaglia nailing the New York accent) give up the ticket to the mob to save his pop? Sure, there's no blood or bullets and the mob-angle is all played for comedy, but it's still a great directorial debut by George Gallo, the writer behind *Bad Boys* [and] De Niro's *Midnight Run*.[2]

With popular actor Anthony LaPaglia in the role of Frank, and Pesce himself playing his real-life older brother Vito, the part of the Pesce family patriarch fell to well-known star Danny Aiello – an instantly-recognisable face thanks to appearances in films including *The Purple Rose of Cairo* (Woody Allen, 1985), *Moonstruck* (Norman Jewison, 1987), *Harlem Nights* (Eddie Murphy, 1989) and an Academy Award-nominated performance in *Do the Right Thing* (Spike Lee, 1989). As Aiello himself explained in his autobiography *I Only Know Who I Am When I Am Somebody Else*, 'I sat in a restaurant discussing the project. Today a small plaque marks the counter where we ate, with this inscription: "This is where George Gallo wrote *29th Street*." My film agent Jimmy Cota told me that studio backing for the film depended on my signing on. When I read the script, I immediately responded to the father-and-son relationship that was central to the story. David Permut, the producer of *29th Street*, called Jimmy and a deal was struck'.[3] The result would be one of the least orthodox – and most intriguing – of all 1990s Christmas movies.

It's 1976, and the lead-up to the festive season in New York City is underway. In the style of *It's a Wonderful Life* (Frank Capra, 1946), the film begins with an earnest prayer – in this case, from a man named Frank Pesce Jr. (Anthony LaPaglia), curiously pleading with God to help him to avoid winning the New York State Lottery. Sure enough, on Christmas Eve Frank Jr. enters the arena for the lottery draw – 'The Empire Stakes' – but attends alone in spite of six seats being reserved for his family. With the prize total set at $6,200,000, the tension is at fever pitch as the winning numbers are drawn. When the announcer declares that Frank Jr. is the winner, however, he looks on in stunned horror before quickly removing his name badge and exiting the arena.

Making his way through the snowy streets of the city, Frank Jr. stops to throw snowballs at a local church, breaking windows and damaging the Nativity scene. He angrily rails at God for having given him such good fortune and claiming that he had never even wanted ownership of the lottery ticket in the first place. The church's kindly priest, Father Lowery (Richard K. Olsen), emerges to find the source of the disturbance, but an increasingly irate Frank Jr. turns on him too. The middle-aged cleric is puzzled at Frank's bizarre behaviour, but a police patrol car arrives and takes him into custody before any explanation can be offered.

At the police station, Sergeant Tartaglia (Robert Forster) informs Frank Jr. that Father Lowery intends to press charges, but Frank pleads with the priest to let him go, claiming that he has little time left. The policeman, like Lowery, is bewildered – Frank Jr. has no prior criminal record, and his brother is a serving police officer, so why would he be vandalising a church Nativity manger on the night before Christmas? Before Frank can answer, a news report is broadcast on the sergeant's office television, covering Frank's lottery win and explaining that he had left the arena without claiming his prize funds. The police are now thoroughly baffled, and Tartaglia demands that Frank explain his full story right from the beginning.

Frank Jr. takes this request literally, and tells the policeman that he has always been miraculously lucky – even from a young age. This apparently goes right back to his birth, when he was unexpectedly delivered at a hospital in 29th Street while the maternity ward he was supposed to be born in was burned to the ground on the same night. From an early age, Frank Jr. aspires to get his name on a news ticker, but his warm-hearted father Frank Sr. (Danny Aiello) carefully balances his sense of ambition with the realism of life. Frank Sr. is also cautious to guide his son away from the apparent allure of organised crime in the area, though Frank Jr. is bedazzled by the expensive car of local mobster Louie Tucci (Vic Manni). The young Frank Jr. is confused at why his father consorts with Tucci when he clearly can't stand him, little realising that Frank Sr.'s business fortunes have collapsed and he is keen to remain on respectful terms with the local crime families… even if he has no real wish to deal with them.

The adolescent Frank becomes close friends with Jimmy Vitello, whose own father is a prominent mobster in the area. They find a hastily-discarded camera on their urban adventures and pawn it for ten dollars, thus discovering an early talent for entrepreneurship. In spite of the attraction of the organised crime taking place in the area, Frank's older brother Vito (Frank Pesce) graduates from the police academy and becomes a cop – much to the pride of his family. The teenaged Frank, meanwhile, spends his days idly wasting time with an array of colourful friends including the nasally-intoned Needle Nose Nipton (Paul Lazar), out-of-tune singer Dom the Bomb (Richard Cerenzio), hypochondriac Rocky Sav (Philip Ciccone), and of course his now-grown-up childhood friend Jimmy (Rick Aiello) – an enterprising huckster.

While Frank Jr. is enjoying a carefree existence, however, his hard-working father has become a truck driver and spends five days of the week hauling goods through the endlessly busy traffic of the city. Becoming frustrated with his lot, not least as he still resents the closure of his own company, Frank Sr. dreams of moving his family to a better neighbourhood in Queens. However, he is frustrated by his son's constant pie-in-the-sky dreaming rather than Frank Jr. ever being willing to put in any practical hard graft to help improve the family's fortunes.

By the time Frank Jr. reaches his eighteenth birthday, Frank Sr. has achieved his ambition of moving the family out of the city and into the suburbs of Queens. Shortly afterwards, his sister Madeline (Donna Magnani) marries a self-assured Sicilian named Tony (Pete Antico), who soon becomes part of the family. With the Vietnam War now raging, Frank Sr. and his friends are called up before the draft board to sign up for the war effort. However, Frank's nonconformist attitude flummoxes the draft sergeant (Don Blakely), and he is excused from duty after being billed a 'calculated risk'. Frank Sr. and Vito are both less than impressed by the outcome; they feel that Frank Jr.'s apparent dereliction of duty will reflect badly on the family and gravely impact his ability to find employment. Frank himself, however, simply chalks up his expulsion from the armed forces – and the dangers of combat – as another example of his lifelong good fortune.

In spite of his family's misgivings, Frank soon lands himself a job as a customer enquiries operator at Penn Station… and finds himself besotted by his beautiful colleague Maria Rios (Karen Duffy). However, his insouciant attitude towards the rules – and an eyebrow-raising approach to customer care – soon leads to him being fired. Frank Sr. congratulates him for having held the post for eight months – a new record for his son in employment – but Frank Jr. is unrepentant. He feels that with his newly-discovered talent for figures, he might be well-suited to better-paid work like accountancy. His brother Vito, who has just been promoted to detective, is highly sceptical of Frank Jr.'s chances. Frank Sr. is also unhappy that his son has started dating Maria, reasoning that as they are Italian-Americans and she is of Puerto Rican heritage from Spanish Harlem, there will inevitably be a spark of historical conflict in any relationship between them.

Frank, however, brushes off his father's warning as outdated prejudice and heads off to see Maria anyway. While they obviously enjoy a shared attraction, the date ends badly when Frank is stabbed by Maria's brother Jesus (Tony Monte) and is rushed to the local hospital's emergency room. Once again, Frank's legendary luck is in evidence, for when his wound is being treated the surgeon discovers a tumour that is in an early stage of growth which would otherwise have been missed. Thus he not only makes a full recovery from the assault, but avoids a potentially even more serious health scare.

Once he has been discharged from hospital, Frank heads back to his old childhood haunt of 29th Street and soon meets a warm welcome from his friends at the club of narcoleptic Philly the Nap (Ron Karabatsos). Sensing Frank's seemingly inhuman supply of luck during a card game, Philly beseeches him to make the most of his good fortune rather than continually squander it. Frank Jr. takes this advice to heart and decides to make his own luck. Having followed the straight and narrow all his life but feeling that he has nothing to show for it, Frank decides to explore the world of organised criminality instead.

Hearing that a crime family has recently taken over a local bakery, Frank asks Jimmy Vitello to put in a good word for him, and he soon ends up working for the mob. Frank Sr. is less than impressed at his son's induction into the underworld, reasoning that sooner or later Frank Jr. will find himself caught up in serious violence. He urges him to settle down, find a respectable job, get married and make the most of his life. But Frank Jr. is unwilling to believe that this is all there can be to living, and has ambitions for something greater. Frank Sr. suggests trying the new State Lottery, the launch of which has just been announced.

Later on, Mrs Pesce (Lainie Kazan) quietly explains to Frank Jr. that his father has just been laid off from his job. Knowing that this will mean hard times for the family, who had only just been managing to get by, the two Franks react in wildly different ways. Frank Sr. becomes obsessed with winning the new lottery, while Frank Jr. has illegally been collecting unemployment welfare cheques during his time in the employ of the mafia. Keen to avoid any scrunity by the banks, Frank waits until a public holiday and cashes the cheque at a pawn shop. The owner, Irv (Sam Shamshak), reluctantly agrees, but only if Frank will buy something from his shop equalling a minimum of ten dollars in value. Frank decides to buy a pair of binoculars that have seen better days, but realising that they are only worth nine dollars he ends up buying a lottery ticket to make up the difference.

Some time later, in November, Frank Jr. is reading a newspaper on the subway and realises that he is among the named lottery ticket-holders in with a chance of winning the jackpot. He is ecstatic at becoming a finalist and races home, sensing that this may just be the answer to his family's financial woes. But he has little time to celebrate before Frank Sr. thunders through the front door, proudly declaring that *he* is a finalist in the lottery. The family look shocked, not quite knowing how to tell him that the numbers correspond to Frank Jr.'s ticket – the one that is actually in line for the jackpot. Frank Sr., who has spent just about every penny he has on countless lottery tickets, is crestfallen to discover that his son has won through to the final with the one single ticket he has bought.

Word of Frank's good fortune starts to spread, and mobster Zippers Bad Lungs (Vinnie Curto) requests his presence at an underworld gambling den to see if his famous luck extends to other games of chance besides the lottery. Sure enough, he proves to be a success at the dice table – rather too successful, in fact, as he ends up winning big against Louie Tucci, who is so enraged that he has Frank Jr. ejected from the premises. Hearing word of this altercation, Frank Sr. again warns his son against risking the ire of the mob – he doesn't want to risk winding up dead, especially this close to the lottery draw.

With the Pesces' financial worries growing ever deeper, Frank Sr. makes the decision to wreck the family car and claim for the loss from their insurers. But despite leaving it abandoned and unlocked in the Bronx, the authorities find it in perfect condition save for the damage caused by Frank Sr. himself. This not only derails his insurance scam, but also means that he owes hundreds of dollars to get the breakages repaired. Frank's legendary luck has thus proven decidedly unfortunate for his family.

Feeling guilty, Frank Jr. enlists his burly cousin Leo (David Ferraro) to help him dump the car in a lake in New Jersey. After the car has been missing for several weeks, the insurance company eventually agree to pay out, but when Frank Sr. goes to collect the cheque he discovers that the car has been discovered at the bottom of the lake at the last minute. Eventually Frank Sr. sells the car to Leo as a last resort... only for it then to be stolen for real.

With the family's income now at crisis levels, a desperate Frank Sr. borrows money from his son to go gambling. However, he overplays his hand and loses every penny. Distraught by his lack of success, he has a heart attack and collapses on his return home. Frank Sr. is rushed to hospital and eventually recovers, but his brush with death gives Frank Jr. pause for thought about his own happy-go-lucky lifestyle. Frank thus decides to put his fast-talking talents to work and secures a post as a sales rep for a toy company. Thanks to his easy charm and abundant charisma, he soon has retailers eating out of his hand.

A week before Christmas, Frank Jr. is strong-armed into a meeting with Louie Tucci. His earlier indignation now seemingly forgotten, the mobster has a proposition for Frank: given the younger man's fabled run of luck, he is willing to offer $10,000 cash-in-hand for Frank's lottery ticket. He really believes that Frank's ticket can't lose at the final... but even if it does, he suggests, the Pesce family will still be substantially better off. Frank is reluctant to part with the ticket, but fears Tucci's retribution if he refuses the offer. He thus assures the mob boss that he will think about it. Telling no-one of the exchange, Frank returns home and feels humbled when his parents tell him how proud they are of him working in reputable employment. He assures them that he has no intention of squandering his lottery winnings if his ticket is called, but that he is considering going to college to enhance his career prospects.

The night of Christmas Eve arrives, and Frank Jr. decides to visit the club on 29th Street before heading to the lottery draw. As he enjoys a drink with Philly, a group of mobsters storm into the club and demand money from Frank, insisting that his father owes Louie Tucci a sum of $10,000... and payment is several weeks overdue. Frank Jr. is aghast at this news, having had no idea of his father's debt – or its extent. Frank is unable to pay, so the enforcers tell him in no uncertain terms that they will be at his family home later that night to collect the money they are due.

Deeply rattled, Frank speeds home and tells his family that he has decided to go to the lottery draw alone. The others are hurt and confused, as they are already dressed for a night out and ready to go. Both Franks enter into a raging argument, Frank Jr. blaming Frank Sr. for putting the entire family at risk by dealing with the mafia. But as Frank Sr. explains, the situation is not as his son supposes – he didn't end up in debt to Tucci because of a gambling addiction, but because he had to beg for the mobster's help when Frank was born, due to Mrs Pesce suffering a problematic delivery. This led to Tucci taking over Frank Sr.'s business, and starting the Pesces on a downward cycle of debt which has now come to a head. Upset and unnerved by these revelations, Frank Jr. storms out, but is warned by the family not to bother returning – no matter whether he wins the lottery or otherwise.

Frank gets into his car and drives through a blizzard to one of Tucci's clubs. Intercepted by a go-between, Frank offers to exchange the lottery ticket for the cancellation of his father's debts, provided that Tucci will promise no violence towards his family. Seemingly taken aback by the offer, Tucci's henchman agrees on his boss's behalf, and Frank – with supreme reluctance – parts with the ticket. It seems that for once, Frank Jr.'s good fortune has failed him.

Back at the police station, some hours later, Frank finishes his story by telling the sergeant and priest that this is the reason for his frustration – he may technically have won the lottery, but it is the thuggish Tucci who will be the beneficiary of the prize money. Somewhat awestruck by Frank's incredible story, the sergeant reiterates that there is no need for his continued presence at the precinct – Father Lowery has agreed to drop the charges of criminal damage – and he instructs a couple of officers to drive Frank back home to Queens.

Unsure of the reception that awaits him, Frank steps through the door of the house with considerable trepidation... only to be greeted by a party of friends and well-wishers, ready to congratulate him on his lottery success. While everyone is elated to see Frank back, he is unable to share in their excitement, knowing the truth about what has happened. None of them realise that Tucci's car has pulled up outside the house, or that he and his goons are heading straight for the Pesces' home.

The family's celebrations are interrupted when Tucci bursts in and demands the money he is owed. Frank Jr. is shocked, believing that he had held up his end of the bargain, but Frank Sr. calmly produces an envelope containing $10,000 and hands it over to the mobster. Tucci brusquely departs with his entourage and Frank Jr. is distraught, believing that the mobster has left his family destitute. But then Frank Sr. reveals the reality of the situation: having heard about his son's encounter at Philly's club, he realised that Frank Jr. would attempt to exchange the ticket with Tucci to bring about the cancellation of the debt. Thus he made arrangements with an old friend to intercept Frank, pretend to be a go-between for Tucci, and take possession of the lottery ticket... only to then secretly pass it back to Frank Sr. He then borrowed the money from Jimmy Vitello to pay off Tucci and, the crime boss now safely out of the way, the family can really celebrate – the Pesce family really *is* six million dollars richer. Father and son reconcile, and with renewed appreciation for each other's qualities: Frank Sr. now knows his son to be noble and selfless, and Frank Jr. realises that his dad is smarter and more resourceful than he ever knew. And after all that, Frank Jr. finally achieves his lifelong dream of seeing his name in lights at last.

29th Street is a film with real heart and inventiveness, with appealing, larger-than-life characters and quirky situations. From Frank Sr.'s hopeless home-made pizza recipes and his obsession with tending his garden lawn at his house in Queens, through to Frank Jr.'s fast-talking charm and endless selection of colourful friends, the movie oozes emotional warmth and wry observational comedy throughout. The many scenes of affectionate Italian-American family life are brilliantly depicted, with the film very much belonging to

Danny Aiello and Anthony LaPaglia as the seemingly-mismatched father-and-son team who realise that in spite of appearing to be poles apart, they are actually more similar than either of them could initially comprehend.

While most discussions of the film tend to naturally veer towards its autobiographical content, the fantastical elements which start to creep in midway through the film did lead some reviewers to question the veracity of the narrative. Roger Ebert, for instance, noted that 'the ending is so unlikely, indeed, that I suspect it is the literal truth, and that such a thing did happen, exactly like that, to the real Frank Pesce Jr. No screenwriter could have dreamed it up. [...] The ending aside, 29th Street is a movie of considerable energy and good humor, with the expansive Aiello, the uninhibited Kazan and the screwy LaPaglia having a lot of fun with the material'.[4] In the grand tradition of real-life adaptations, however, a certain amount of poetic licence is sometimes in evidence – or, in the case of 29th Street, a very large quantity of it. As Doug Fisher remarks, 'After believing for years that 29th Street was the true story of Frank Pesce, I learned that Frank Pesce did not win the first New York state lottery. He was a finalist, but did not win. Does that taint my opinion of the film? Absolutely not. Many films "based on true stories" take dramatic license with the stories. [...] This is such a common practice that [David O. Russell's] American Hustle (2013) satirically displays in the prologue, "Some of this actually happened"'.[5]

Regardless of how many of the stories Pesce relates are accurate recollections or tall tales, the movie articulates events with considerable charm, even though the period details can sometimes prove inconsistent. For instance, when working as a toy company rep Frank Jr. is seen demonstrating a pedal car based on a 1980s-era Corvette, in spite of the sequence supposedly taking place in 1976. Even throughout the more dramatic scenes, there is always a keen sense of humour in evidence just beneath the surface, reflecting the lively interactions of family life. While the Frank Capra influences are most overtly discernible in the film's opening and closing sequences, blending the support mechanism of a close family with elements of the fantastic and outlandish, others were to comment instead on the inspiration from the films of Martin Scorsese and his finely-honed observations of Italian-American culture – made manifest throughout the film in the interplay between the various members of the Pesce family as well as their many friends. Given the light-hearted nature of the film, the criminal underworld is explored largely in humorous terms, with only the merest suggestions of the organised lawbreaking, institutional corruption and threat of violence that are being implied by the presence of flamboyant mobsters and their sinister, often loud-mouthed entourages. Instead, the film seems more eager to explore the subtle dynamics of a vibrant extended family, where every member is a distinctive individual in their own right – and certainly has plenty to say. However, the stylistic influences were ultimately so palpable in their application, some critics became sceptical of the film's merits in comparison to the renowned material that had inspired its creative approach. As Desson Howe observed:

> *Street* is a dead end. It's also a little thief. When LaPaglia (in voice-over narration) introduces the Little Italy of his childhood, featuring zany pals 'Needle Nose Nipton,' 'Dom the Bomb' and others, the movie's clearly filching from Martin Scorsese's *GoodFellas*. When *Street* isn't going though Scorsese's pockets, it's robbing from Frank Capra. In this dull, derivative fantasy, LaPaglia is born with

91

incredible luck. [...] What happens in the end is a farce-fantasy full of twists, leading to an *It's a Wonderful Life* finale. After the winning ticket is announced, father and son hug each other, secure in the knowledge that money isn't everything. Besides, no one can lose as bad as this movie.[6]

Like so many later Christmas films of the 1990s, *29th Street* was acutely concerned with family, with reconciliation, and with the challenges involved with the main character finding a sense of belonging – a theme which would recur in movies ranging from *The Muppet Christmas Carol* (q.v.) to *The Nightmare Before Christmas* (q.v.). What makes the emotional heart of *29th Street* so convincing is the touching interplay between the main characters – the complex Frank Sr.; the grounded, unerringly practical (and intriguingly unnamed) Mrs Pesce; the independently-minded Madeline; the laconic Vito; and of course, the carefree dreamer that is Frank Jr. himself. The success of the film relies on the audience's depth of emotional investment with these figures, and everything from the family's worsening financial circumstances through to the furious rift between the two Franks only becomes meaningful because viewers have come to care about the fortunes of these attention-grabbing people. Thus when we reach the mutual understanding between father and son which embodies the film's conclusion, the signficance of this moment is magnified not only by the likeability of the two characters but also by the fact that they are surrounded by a plethora of family and long-term friends who can join in the celebrations sincerely – not out of potential self-interest, as in the case of crime boss Louie Tucci, but rather because they sincerely want the best for the Pesce family's future.

Key to the film's success is the touching and believable relationship between Franks Sr. and Jr., with both Danny Aiello and Anthony LaPaglia delivering nuanced and creditable performances throughout. The award-winning Aiello had already become a well-established figure in the acting world, active in film since the early 1970s, but LaPaglia was a much newer face on the big screen, having made his debut in *Cold Steel* (Dorothy Ann Puzo, 1987) and then moving on to features such as *Betsy's Wedding* (Alan Alda, 1990) and *One Good Cop* (Heywood Gould, 1991). His later work would see him win several industry awards, perhaps most notably a Primetime Emmy Award for his guest appearance in NBC's *Frasier* in 2002, and he has been nominated for many further plaudits over the years.

The real Frank Pesce had appeared with Danny Aiello much earlier, in crime drama *Defiance* (John Flynn, 1980), and among his many other performances were roles in films as diverse as *Tilt* (Rudy Durand, 1979), *Flashdance* (Adrian Lyne, 1983) and *Relentless* (William Lustig, 1989). Pesce brings a comparatively low-key, almost contemplative aspect to the portrayal of his own older brother Vito, and this provides an effective contrast to his headstrong, outspoken and warm-hearted Madeline, as played by Donna Magnani – probably best-known at the time for her appearance in *Prime Suspect* (Bruce Kimmel, 1989) which had starred Frank Stallone. Providing stalwart support as the Pesce family's formidable matriarch was Lainie Kazan, a Golden Globe Award-nominated actress and singer who had appeared in a varied range of movies including *My Favorite Year* (Richard Benjamin, 1982), *The Delta Force* (Menahem Golan, 1986) and *Beaches* (Garry Marshall, 1988). She was also nominated for a Primetime Emmy Award, and later would be nominated for a

Tony Award (for her performance in the stage musical adaptation of *My Favorite Year*).

29th Street was a low-key release when it first arrived in cinemas, and reviewers were divided over their evaluation of the film's merits. Many, such as Ebert, were inclined to praise the affection and mutual compassion on display in Gallo's depiction of family life, noting that 'the Pesces in this movie have their origins in real people (indeed, the real Frank Jr. is a character actor who appears as his own older brother, Vito), but in *29th Street* they seem to emerge mostly from the long tradition of Italian-Americans in the movies. They are loosely related to the characters in *GoodFellas, Married to the Mob, True Love* and *Spike of Bensonhurst*, and Aiello, as the head of the family, has all the necessary warmth and passion to lead them'.[7] Others, such as Rita Kempley, were less convinced of the film's merits, being decidedly underwhelmed by Gallo's aspirations to create a heartwarming Christmas tale: 'A trite comedy about a loud, lovable family of Italian Americans, *29th Street* is thinner than the tires on a Domino's delivery truck. Based on events in the life of character actor Frank Pesce, it's less a movie than a scrapbook of Pesce's fond memories of growing up in the neighborhood. [...] George Gallo, who wrote *Midnight Run*, directs his own cliche-riddled screenplay based on a story by the late James Franciscus and Pesce. Gallo and company probably imagine that *29th Street* makes for a magical holiday movie – what with the storms of instant mashed potato flakes. But it would take a miracle, and that was on 34th Street'.[8]

Overall, however, while the film's release went unnoticed by many critics, the merits of the cast's heartfelt performances and Gallo's subtle, human-centred and earnest creative approach were praised by commentators such as

Fisher, who reflected that '29th Street contains big laughs based on the personalities of its people. They are seen loving-ly, with all of their foibles and creative ways of expressing themselves. George Gallo, who writes and directs, handles the material with a light touch. [[...]] Little scenes like that may be throwaway in other comedies, but 29th Street is more about its people than what actually happens to Frank Jr. The film's ending is something that seems dreamed up by a Hollywood screenwriter, but it is so goofy that it may have actually oc-curred. I've rarely seen a film in which the characters surprise me with what they do or say next. Whether it's based on real life or not, 29th Street is full of life and energy you don't see that often. I had a grin throughout the entire film'.[9]

The general critical appreciation for the film has im-proved in more recent years, with its subsequent home entertainment releases bringing it to the attention to a wider audience than during its cinematic release. The analysis of Andy Webb, for instance, spoke of the growing reputation of 29th Street as something of an unfairly hidden gem of 1990s Christmas film-making: 'This isn't just a *GoodFellas* knock-off which also has a certain Christmas element to it as the strength of the story ends up taking over to make it more than just another movie about a family and the mob. And because I don't want to spoil 29th Street for anyone who haven't [[sic]] watched it before let me just say there is a beautiful positive side to this drama almost Capra-esque as the story unfolds. What this all boils down to is that 29th Street is a nice little movie which combines styles reminiscent of various movies with the main one being *GoodFellas*. But whilst some really love this movie it is just for me a good movie, with a good cast and a nice style'.[10]

While reviewers such as Dennis Schwartz have remained sceptical of the film's longevity due to claims of the narrative's sometimes pedestrian reliance on cliché, they still found room for praise: 'Gallo's debut as a director results in a film filled with colorful New York characters and plenty of ethnic love. They are all working-class types with big dreams, and their earthy reactions to life's ups and downs make this unchallenging film easy to take but it is much too trite to be memorable'.[11] Yet some, such as David Nusair, have instead given an appraisal suggesting that in spite of the film's imperfections, it still had potential to be remembered as one of the great curiosities of nineties festive cinema: '29th Street's been written and directed by George Gallo, and it seems obvious that the filmmaker has a real affection for these characters and their respective problems (that the real-life Frank Pesce has a role here as his own brother confirms that notion). But it's also clear that Gallo was far too close to the material to effectively edit the film; 29th Street is peppered with sequences that are either overlong or entirely superfluous. The result is a well-acted film that's pleasant enough, but marred by an egregiously padded-out running time. Still, there's no denying that the movie's conclusion is genuinely uplifting, ensuring that – among certain viewers – 29th Street will likely have a place as a perennial favorite'.[12]

Nobody would claim that 29th Street was among the most instantly recognisable of the decade's Christmas films, but in its unconventional approach – and equally eccentric range of affable characters – it has nonetheless been a movie which has acquired a growing number of fans over the years. It also offered a flipside to the kind of New York Christmas offered by *All I Want for Christmas* (q.v.), being just about as different as any two films could be while sharing the same city as their location. Following this directorial debut, director George Gallo would go on to helm, write and produce many other features, but his artistic ambitions within the Christmas movie genre hadn't yet been satisfied. Some years later, in 1994, he was to be the creative driving force behind *Trapped in Paradise* (q.v.) – a movie which would reunite *29th Street* castmates Frank Pesce, Vic Manni and Paul Lazar with an artistic approach which would prove to be poles apart in comparison to its absorbing predecessor.

REFERENCES

1.   Alonso Duralde, *Have Yourself a Movie Little Christmas* (New York: Limelight Editions, 2010), p.83.

2.   R.D. Francis, 'Exploring: Gangster Films Inspired by *GoodFellas*', in *B&S About Movies*, 20 November 2021. *<https://bandsaboutmovies.com/2021/11/20/exploring-gangster-films-inspired-by-goodfellas/>*

3.   Danny Aiello, with Gil Reavill, *I Only Know Who I Am When I Am Somebody Else: My Life on the Street, on the Stage and in the Movies* (New York: Gallery Books, 2014), p.232.

4.   Roger Ebert, '29th Street', in *The Chicago Sun-Times*, 1 November 1991. *<https://www.rogerebert.com/reviews/29th-street-1991>*

5.   Doug Fisher, '29th Street', in *Bohica*, 14 September 2015. *<https://movieguy1970.blogspot.com/2015/09/29th-street-1991-12.html>*

6.   Desson Howe, '29th Street', in *The Washington Post*, 1 November 1991. *<https://www.washingtonpost.com/wp-srv/style/longterm/movies/videos/29thstreetrhowe_a0b356.htm>*

7.   Ebert.

8.   Rita Kempley, '29th Street', in *The Washington Post*, 1 November 1991.

<https://www.washingtonpost.com/wp-srv/style/longterm/movies/videos/29thstreetrkempley_a0a27b.htm>

9. Fisher.

10. Andy Webb, '29th Street', in *The Movie Scene*, 2005. <https://www.themoviescene.co.uk/reviews/29th-street-1991/29th-street-1991.html>

11. Dennis Schwartz, '29th Street', in *Dennis Schwartz Movie Reviews*, 24 June 2004. <https://dennisschwartzreviews.com/29thstreet/>

12. David Nusair, '29th Street', in *Reel Film Reviews*, 20 April 2005. <https://www.reelfilm.com/anchbay2.htm#29th>

4

The Muppet Christmas Carol (1992)

Jim Henson Productions / The Jim Henson Company /
Walt Disney Pictures

Director: Brian Henson
Producers: Brian Henson and Martin G. Baker
Screenwriter: Jerry Juhl, based on the novella
by Charles Dickens

IF films such as *Home Alone* (q.v.) and *All I Want for Christmas* (q.v.) had determined a new tone for Christmas films in comparison to the previous decade, indicating a sort of back-to-basics approach for the genre as the nineties progressed, then *The Muppet Christmas Carol* was to fit snugly into this new remit of rediscovered traditionalism. A determinedly family-oriented take on Charles Dickens's acutely well-known tale, the warm and charming approach of the Jim Henson Company towards the source material was to seem far removed indeed from the playful contemporary cynicism that had been on display in Richard Donner's *Scrooged* (1988), almost certainly the most high-profile adaptation of the Dickens novella to appear in the 1980s. Yet for all its emphasis on fidelity to the original text, this Muppet-led reworking of *A Christmas Carol* was certainly to prove anything but conventional in execution, and would firmly establish itself as an adaptation that only the Muppets Studio could have achieved.

Devised by celebrated puppet creator and performer Jim Henson, the Muppets are characters which are operated by means of an amalgamation of marionette and puppet technology. Their colourful bodies and expressive features made them immediately popular with audiences when they first appeared on American television on the *Sam and Friends* series (1955-61). After numerous appearances on national TV, Henson's work achieved mass exposure with the debut of acclaimed educational entertainment series *Sesame Street* in 1969. Following this in the seventies was the television phenomenon that, in the minds of many viewers, will always be Henson's crowning achievement: *The Muppet Show* (1976-81). Using its variety stage show premise to full effect over the course of five seasons, the series' massive success with audiences led to the Muppets becoming firmly established in popular culture on both sides of the Atlantic.

By the time that James Frawley's *The Muppet Movie* was released in 1979, the characters had become so well-known amongst the general public that they had largely ceased to be considered as manually operated marionette-puppets, but rather as autonomous celebrities in their own right. Kermit the Frog's long-running (and sometimes reluctant) flirtations with Miss Piggy, Fozzie Bear's doomed ambitions to become a comedy legend and the Great Gonzo's likeably bizarre behaviour had all passed into the cultural consciousness, with different generations finding entertainment in the frenetic hijinks of Henson's characters. Throughout the eighties Jim Henson Productions were to release a further two well-received Muppet movies, Jim Henson's *The Great Muppet Caper* (1981) and Frank Oz's *The Muppets Take*

Manhattan (1984), along with many other TV series and specials which included *Fraggle Rock* (1983-87) and *The Storyteller* (1988). Although Henson died in 1990, his artistic legacy has lived on and continued to flourish in the years since. His creations have remained perennially popular with audiences throughout the world, with the Muppets appearing on television and in film productions regularly up until the present day.

The Muppets have a long and fruitful relationship with the festive season, with TV highlights over the years having included *Emmet Otter's Jug-Band Christmas* (Jerry Juhl, 1977), *Christmas Eve on Sesame Street* (Jon Stone, 1978), *John Denver and the Muppets: A Christmas Together* (Tony Charmoli, 1979), *The Bells of Fraggle Rock* (Doug Williams, 1984), *The Christmas Toy* (Eric Till, 1986), *A Muppet Family Christmas* (Peter Harris and Eric Till, 1987) and, in more recent years, Kirk R. Thatcher's *It's a Very Merry Muppet Christmas Movie* (2002) and *A Muppets Christmas: Letters to Santa* (2008). *The Muppet Christmas Carol*, however, remains their only cinematic outing to date which has featured the festive season as its focus.

Directed by Jim Henson's son and long-time industry expert, Brian Henson, the film was to follow in the tradition of the preceding three Muppet movies in that it would present a variety of musical numbers to punctuate the action. Furthermore, this unique adaptation of Dickens's story would blend together a variety of Muppet characters who would, in turn, be portraying characters from the original text. Thus audiences were, for instance, presented with performer Steve Whitmire operating Kermit the Frog, who in turn is playing Bob Cratchit. As Roger Ebert observed, this led to an interesting cinematic sleight of hand which made the presence of

Henson's colourful, larger-than-life characters seem entirely logical even in the milieu of a period setting: 'Like the earlier three Muppet movies, it manages to incorporate the Muppets convincingly into the action; we may know they're puppets, but usually we're not much reminded of their limited fields of movement. Ever since Kermit rode a bicycle across the screen in *The Muppet Movie* in 1979, the Muppeteers have managed to bypass what you'd think would be the obvious limitations of the form. This time, they even seem to belong in Victorian London, created in atmospheric sets that combine realism and expressionism'.[1]

Brian Henson's association with 'Muppetry' is a long one which stretches back to an appearance in Jim Henson's short film *Wheels That Go* (1967) as well as the first episode of *Sesame Street* back in 1969. His performances throughout the eighties included puppet operation in Jim Henson's *The Great Muppet Caper* (1981) and *Labyrinth* (1986), Frank Oz's *The Muppets Take Manhattan* (1984) and Walter Murch's *Return to Oz* (1985), while he contributed special effects for episodes of TV's *Fraggle Rock* in 1984 as well as on *The Muppets Take Manhattan*. Active as a producer since 1991, his directorial career began with the TV series *Jim Henson Presents Mother Goose Stories* (1987-88). His work as a director, writer and producer has continued since then, and he has since helmed *Muppet Treasure Island* (1996) and episodes of TV's *Muppets Tonight* (1996-98), as well as acclaimed TV science fiction drama *Farscape: The Peacekeeper Wars* (2004) and surreal comic fantasy *The Happytime Murders* (2018), amongst many other features. In 1992 he was to win the Scientific and Engineering Award, along with co-nominees Faz Fazakas, Dave Housman, Peter Miller and John Stephenson, at the Academy Awards. In later years, he has been the recipient of numerous Daytime and Primetime Emmy Awards.

It is the nineteenth-century, and in London on Christmas Eve, novelist Charles Dickens (The Great Gonzo/Dave Goelz) and his close associate Rizzo the Rat (Steve Whitmire) introduce themselves as the narrators of this ghostly festive tale. Just as they have announced themselves, they are interrupted by the arrival of the callous and unfeeling Ebenezer Scrooge (Michael Caine), who is among the city's most prosperous – and detested – moneylenders and private landlords. Arriving at his place of business, it becomes abundantly clear that Scrooge has no time for the festive season – or indeed for his fellow human being (or even Muppet).

His cheerful young nephew Fred (Steven Mackintosh) arrives in the vain hope of kindling some embers of yuletide joy in Scrooge's heart, but the moneylender is singularly unmoved. Fred issues his annual invitation to Scrooge to join him and his wife Clara (Robin Weaver) for Christmas dinner at their home, only to find his offer coldly rebuffed... just as it has been during every previous December. Two charity collectors (Bunsen Honeydew/Dave Goelz and Beaker/Steve Whitmire) pay a visit to solicit donations in support of the poor and destitute at Christmas, but Scrooge has obvious disdain for their benevolent aims. He even throws a decorative Christmas wreath at a passing carol singer (Bean Bunny/Steve Whitmire) in a fit of anti-festive pique.

Scrooge's meek office clerk Bob Cratchit (Kermit the Frog/Steve Whitmire), speaking on behalf of his book-keeper colleagues, asks his employer if he will be honouring the Christmas holiday the following day. Scrooge is initially reluctant, but grudgingly accepts the logic of Cratchit's argument that as no other companies (or indeed individuals) will be doing business on Christmas Day, he will essentially be wasting money by keeping his own premises open. Decidedly miffed at the prospect of being forced to observe Christmas, if only inadvertently, Scrooge grumpily leaves the office – much to the relief of his employees, who are finally free of his watchful eye.

Back home, the solitary Scrooge is startled when his door-knocker suddenly transfigures itself into a spectral apparition. Convincing himself that he has been fooled by a trick of the light, he settles in for the night with a meagre supper only to be interrupted by the shocking materialisation of his long-dead business partners, Jacob Marley (Statler/Jerry Nelson) and Robert Marley (Waldorf/Dave Goelz). The sarcastic pair are chained by heavy spectral manacles, and explain that they have been punished in death for the greedy and uncaring attitudes they demonstrated while still alive. Jacob and Robert sternly warn Scrooge that he must change his own behaviour before it is too late, or he too will be bound for all eternity. They tell him to expect the arrival of further spirits later that night.

Sure enough, in his bedchamber at the stroke of one o'clock, Scrooge finds his slumber interrupted by the arrival of the Ghost of Christmas Past (Karen Prell/Robert Tygner/William Todd Jones/Voice of Jessica Fox) – an angelic being in the form of a child, who has the power to turn back time and force Scrooge to face his past actions. She takes the ill-starred moneylender back to his childhood, and a lonely life at boarding school where his family left him to continue working over the Christmas holidays while his classmates are all away celebrating the festivities. Scrooge watches as his old headmaster (Sam the Eagle/Frank Oz) gives his younger self some austere advice about how to prosper in business.

A short time-jump later, and Scrooge perceives himself as a young man in the employment of Mr Fozziwig (Fozzie Bear/Frank Oz), the kind-hearted owner of a rubber chicken factory. It is Christmas time at the business, and Fozziwig has organised an exuberant party for his hard-working staff. He is perplexed to find Scrooge still grafting away at his book-keeping duties and encourages him to have a little fun instead. Sure enough, he soon encounters a beautiful woman named Belle (Meredith Braun) and the two immediately feel a mutual attraction. However, the Ghost of Christmas Present reveals that only a few years later, the pair are parted when Belle realises that Scrooge loves money more than he does her. The younger Scrooge seems dispassionate about her departure, seemingly indifferent to the demise of their romance, but the present-day miser becomes deeply emotional when looking back at the happy marriage that might have resulted from their shared affection. Deeply regretting his disastrous actions, the emotional Scrooge begs the Ghost of Christmas Past to return him to his home – and correct time.

Scrooge is instantly back in his bedchambers, but barely has a chance to gather his thoughts before the huge, bacchanalian Ghost of Christmas Present (Donald Austen) appears and declares that he wishes to introduce Scrooge to the marvels and pleasures of Christmas Day. This comes as something of a mystery to Scrooge, who has spent most of his life avoiding the festivities. The Ghost first whisks him to the home of Fred and Clara, and to a party which will be taking place the following day. Scrooge is initially intrigued by the parlour games taking place and the good-natured conviviality between his nephew and his guests, but his mood sinks when he becomes the butt of all the jokes: though Fred makes a half-hearted attempt to defend his (unseen) uncle, the others call out the cheerless man's tight-fistedness, short temper and generally unpleasant disposition.

Next is a visit to the rather more modest home of the Cratchits, where Scrooge is amazed at how the large family is so happy to be together even in spite of their humble Christmas celebrations. Matriarch Emily Cratchit (Miss Piggy/Frank Oz) oversees the festivities with a warm eye, and it is obvious that all the family members need to be content is the presence of each other. Shortly after, Bob arrives from a Christmas church service with his son, Tiny Tim (Robin the Frog/Jerry Nelson), who suffers from complex health issues. The Ghost of Christmas Present explains to Scrooge that due to the Cratchit family's financial problems, they lack the funds to seek medical treatment for Tim. Taking the old skinflint to an eerie graveyard, the Ghost explains that the ailing Cratchit child may not last much longer – inferring that he might not even live to see the following Christmas.

After the departure of the Ghost of Christmas Present, Scrooge is somewhat alarmed to meet his successor: the silent and sinister Ghost of Christmas Yet to Come (Robert Tygner/Donald Austen). This spirit appears as a large, ominous individual in a long dark cloak, reminiscent of the Grim Reaper. He wordlessly takes Scrooge into the future, where he overhears a group of wealthy financiers talking about the death of a businessman in the area. They seem unmoved by his demise, and unwilling even to attend the funeral – unless a free lunch is on offer, of course. Scrooge seems disturbed by their lack of concern for their departed colleague.

Later, Scrooge witnesses a group of local people – including arachnid charlady Mrs Dilber (Louise Gold) – attempting to sell off the belongings of the unnamed businessman to Old Joe (David Shaw Parker), a trader in the criminal underworld. Even the cynical Joe himself is taken aback at the singular lack of feeling towards the dead entre-preneur. Scrooge is next transported to the home of the Cratchits, where the dejected family are grieving the death of the beloved Tiny Tim. The money-lender is appalled that such a bright young life has ended so needlessly.

Next, Scrooge is returned to the graveyard, and the Ghost of Christmas Yet to Come reveals the overlooked and disregarded resting place of the dead business owner... who turns out to be Scrooge himself, unlamented and quickly for-gotten. Now realising not only the error of his ways but also his potential to do good in the world, Scrooge pleads with the Ghost to return him to the present while there is still time to make a difference.

Sure enough, he is soon sent back to his bedchamber one final time, and is overjoyed to realise that it is still Christmas morning. Deciding not to waste a second longer, Scrooge hurriedly gets dressed and makes arrangements for an enormous turkey to be delivered to the Cratchits' home. Along the way, he amazes past acquaintances such as the charity collectors and the carol singer by revealing his new, benign and generous character, and stuns Fred and Clara by arriving at their home in time for their Christmas party for once – a transformed figure, full of kindness and munificence.

Finally, he raps the front door of Bob Cratchit's house and momentarily imitates his former demeanour, terrifying his employee who dreads losing his job. However, before the in-dignant Emily can give him a piece of her mind, Scrooge dumbfounds everyone by telling Bob that he will be increasing his salary with immediate effect... and also single-handedly paying off the family's mortgage. The Cratchits are dumb-founded at the utter transformation of the formerly-parsimonious Scrooge, and welcome him into their home to celebrate Christmas together with many of his new-found friends. As the story closes, Charles Dickens/Gonzo explains that thanks to Scrooge's intervention, Tiny Tim did not die during the year ahead, but instead found a second father in the once-cantankerous money-lender – a man who came to love Christmas more than anyone else in old London town.

Given that the overwhelming majority of the characters in Henson's adaptation of *A Christmas Carol* are being portrayed by the madcap Muppets, it is surprising – and commendable – to note how loyal the film remains to the spirit and nature of the original Dickens text. So profoundly integrated are the Muppet characters in the popular cultural psyche that at no point are the audience inclined to think of them as human-operated devices: they appear, quite simply, to be nothing less than individual actors in their own right. And it is precisely because of this notion of the Muppets as autonomous performers that the film works so well: like *The Muppet Show* before it, the film toys with the employment of a kind of teasing postmodernity, creating a film which is wholly a Muppet feature just as much as it is wholly a faithful adaptation of a Dickensian novella. As Thomas M. Leitch has explained, 'The keynote of *The Muppet Christmas Carol* is not so much faith in Dickens or the Muppet franchise as faith in the possibilities of play already implicit in both franchises. By refracting its realistic Scrooge through the unlikely lens of Muppet neighbors, victims, and author figures, it invites its viewers to play with him and through him quite as closely, though in somewhat different terms, as Alastair Sim's playfully malevolent, and finally playful, Scrooge, who constantly looks as though he had just eaten a piece of bad meat'.[2]

Perhaps the most apparent exponent of this strategy is the inspired use of The Great Gonzo (Dave Goelz), among the most eccentric of all Muppet characters, in the role of Charles Dickens. Accompanied by his friend, a laconic rat with a New Jersey accent named Rizzo (Steve Whitmire), Gonzo is acutely aware of the fact that he is playing the part of Dickens largely in order to act as the film's narrator. Rather than approaching the role in a direct way, as a conventional narrator might be inclined to, Gonzo playfully utilises his portrayal of Dickens throughout the film to explore the range and reach of its narrative function. As James Chapman perceptively notes, 'The film even throws in the concept of the deconstruction of the author for good measure when Rizzo wonders how Gonzo can say what Scrooge is doing when they cannot see him on screen. [...] The film also reminds audiences of the education-with-entertainment purpose of the Muppets by asserting its cultural provenance. As Gonzo concludes: "If you liked this, you should read the book."'[3]

The fourth wall is regularly broken throughout the film when Rizzo continually calls into question the plausibility of Gonzo's depiction of the nineteenth century literary genius (considering, for instance, the likelihood of the real Dickens being blue and furry, or having a talking rat as a friend), and also when the pair regularly discover that they have difficulty keeping up with the action – a narrator may be omniscient, after all, but omnipresence is discovered to be another matter entirely. The latter factor leads to numerous scrapes throughout the film, where Gonzo discovers that he has been temporarily (and inadvertently) cut off from the main focus of the film and must employ devices such as grappling hooks to get back into spotlight when necessary. As Hugh H. Davis has remarked, *The Muppet Christmas Carol* 'is at once both an homage to the work it is adapting and a spoof of the genre of literary adaptation in film. With the Great Gonzo playing the part of the author Charles Dickens (yet revealing all along that he is only playing a role), this narrator links the film directly with its literary source, establishing this film's acknowledged indebtedness to the work. Because Gonzo knows he is an actor playing a literary role, he reminds the viewers throughout that they are watching a movie version of a book'.[4]

Gonzo and Rizzo's continual commentary on the film's cultural relevance and faithfulness to the source material is highly entertaining, and is one factor of the film which makes it an unerringly unique and distinctive adaptation of such a familiar tale. Commentators such as Davis have favourably considered the skill of screenwriter Jerry Juhl in employing this technique to engage audiences with the characters – as Muppets, familiar from previous televisual and cinematic outings – while simultaneously offering an accurate depiction of Dickens's characters from the original source text:

> Charles Dickens's *A Christmas Carol* is arguably the most famous fictional Christmas story. The traditions inherent in this story are so well known that they virtually have become a part of the story itself. *The Muppet Christmas Carol* addresses this seeming paradox – that to be faithful to the original novel is to recognize all that has occurred since – by treating the text both self-reflexively and reverentially. This simultaneous recognition of the novel's importance as literature and its importance as culture serves to mark the Muppet version of the story as unique. The many adaptations have attempted to tell straight versions of the story which

follow the book closely, while the various transformations have attempted to tell the story with a
wink and a nod to the conventions that surround
the book. This version successfully does both. Brian Henson's film both recreates Dickens's world,
with language, sets and character designs lifted
from the novella's prose, and playfully toys with
the conventions which surround such adaptations,
with meta-cinema and cinematic intrusions which
remind the audience of the nature of film adaptation.[5]

There is also the fact, as Chapman has discussed, that
the film simultaneously calls upon audience awareness of the
individual Muppet characters and their behaviour as well as
preconceptions about the story and presentation of *A Christmas Carol* in popular media, thus making it a filmic experience
that is acutely concerned with its own textual identity: 'It
might seem pretentious to claim *The Muppet Christmas Carol* as a postmodern text, but that is precisely what it is. In the
first place, like *Mickey's Christmas Carol*, the concept is in-
herently inter-textual, drawing on the audience's knowledge
of both the Dickens story and the Muppets' universe. *The
Muppet Christmas Carol* goes further, however, in that it
frequently disrupts the narrative to engage in a discourse
about its own status as a cultural artefact'.[6]

Certainly, a working knowledge of *The Muppet Show*
and its many characters adds an extra dimension to the film,
though it is certainly not essential to the enjoyment of *The
Muppet Christmas Carol*. Statler and Waldorf, the two senior citizens who were forever sardonically scoffing at the
performance talents of the other Muppets in the TV show,
appear in the twin roles of Jacob and Robert Marley: because

the two characters are inseparable within the Muppet universe, their function with audiences who are familiar with their earlier appearances would seem impaired (or at least unusual) if only one were present, and for this reason the story's *dramatis personae* is amended accordingly. Likewise Scrooge's old employer Fezziwig becomes 'Fozziwig', the owner of a rubber chicken factory, referencing one of the props used by Fozzie Bear in his perpetually ill-fated attempts to become a successful stand-up comedian in earlier Muppet appearances (and some distance from the Nigel Fezziwig of Dickens's original novella, who – though similarly kind-hearted – ran a small owner-controlled trading business). Sam the Eagle, a proud patriot who always espouses the virtues of truth, justice and the American way, needs to be reminded at the last minute that he is supposed to be British – or, at least, playing a character who is British – for the purposes of fulfilling his role as Scrooge's old schoolmaster. (In a nice touch, an elderly version of Sam/the schoolmaster and Fozzie/Fozziwig can be seen at the end of the film when Scrooge momentarily visits their retirement home.)

Other minor roles from the Dickens original, such as that of Bob Cratchit's wife, are expanded and embellished to accommodate the relative prominence of their Muppet actor (in this case, the glamorous but infamously capricious Miss Piggy, cast somewhat against type as the pragmatic and sweet-natured Emily). It almost seems strange, then, that no amount of augmentation to fit Dickens's story into a Muppet-oriented framework ever seems to compromise the film's truthfulness to the textual source, or even threaten the suspense of disbelief – and considering that the production calls for singing fruit and vegetables at one point, this is no mean feat.

There are other minor deviations from the original, such as the elimination of Scrooge's sister Fan from the Christmas Past sequences, and the considerable curtailing of the climactic scenes at the home of his convivial nephew, Fred. But generally, the tale is related with such close consideration to the original novella that even the film's subtle visual in-jokes are in no danger of overstaying their welcome: later scenes reveal a store named 'Statler and Waldorf', whereas another shop bears the name 'Micklewhite's' – famously a reference to Maurice Micklewhite, the real name of the film's human star, Michael Caine.

The necessity for the presence of human actors in the film is summed up perfectly by Ginger Stelle, who observes that as Scrooge is characterised by a capacity for fundamental change in his very nature (leading to the emergence of an entirely different temperament and disposition), the use of a Muppet character/performer for the part would be inappropriate precisely because the audience had become so familiar with each of their particular personalities: 'Why not cast a Muppet as Scrooge? Quite simply, the nature of the Muppets does not allow for the kind of dramatic character shift that Scrooge undergoes. Clearly no-one would ever accept that Kermit could be that mean and heartless. Kermit is not mean and heartless, nor can he pretend to be so. At the same time, neither Statler nor Waldorf could ever be accepted as the nice and loving Scrooge because that would go entirely against their established characters. Even a new Muppet would not do. The filmmakers created some new characters for this film, most notably the Spirits of Christmas, but even they possess static characters. They do not change. In the end, only a human actor could play Scrooge because audiences are used to seeing human actors portray more fluid parts'.[7]

Therefore, any of the more prominent Muppets – known by audiences to behave and react in a certain way – would not be plausible in the role of Scrooge due to the fact that many viewers would have a preconceived notion of their likely actions and conduct, thus potentially damaging the film's dramatic credibility. As Scrooge is human, of course, his earlier selves are also played by humans, as are his one-time fiancée and also his nephew Fred and his wife Clara. Yet it is much to the credit of Brian Henson's direction that the human actors and Muppet performers mix so seamlessly on screen: not even the final scenes around the Christmas dinner table appear jarring, where scores of Muppets prepare themselves for a turkey dinner in immediate proximity to the human cast members, due to the film's innate balance of unconventional internal logic and sheer festive charm. However, not every commentator was convinced by this approach; Peter Rainer, for instance, was quick to compare the Muppet characters' established traits with their effectiveness in their Dickensian roles: 'If Caine is first-rate, the Muppets fare less well. The problem may be that, for the first time in their movie careers, they are playing characters, and the Muppets have always been *sui generis*. Kermit, for example, is irreducibly Kermit; as Bob Cratchit, we can sense him straining to erase his own personality and blend Method-style into the part. But at least he's trying. As Emily Cratchit, Miss Piggy doesn't even bother to pretend she's playing a part. It's a self-indulgent piece of work that completely loses sight of Emily's selfless, poignant love for her husband and Tiny Tim. It's a piggy performance'.[8]

Michael Caine makes for a very restrained Ebenezer Scrooge: judiciously, he chooses to make no attempt to compete with his furry co-stars when it comes to dominating the screen, instead presenting a nuanced performance of great subtlety. His transformation during his three spiritual visitations is carefully underplayed, and even his display of reformed character on Christmas Day is delicately drawn while remaining warmly sincere. There may be no dancing in the street as with Albert Finney's Scrooge in Ronald Neame's 1970 musical of the same name, nor even the barely-contained glee of Alastair Sim in Brian Desmond Hurst's highly influential 1951 version, but Caine's evocation of the penny-pinching Ebenezer is touching precisely because of its suggestion of wistful regret over wasted opportunity rather than the customary display of joy and merriment that had become so common to other big screen versions of Dickens's famous miser.

One of the most successful British actors of the post-war era, Caine began appearing in films and on television in the early 1950s. His breakthrough role came in 1964 as British Army officer Lieutenant Gonville Bromhead in Cy Endfield's *Zulu*, following which Caine went on to make some of his best-known appearances in films such as Sidney J. Furie's *The Ipcress File* (1965), the title role in Lewis Gilbert's *Alfie* (1966), and in Guy Hamilton's *Battle of Britain* (1969), quickly establishing himself as a household name in British cinema. Beginning the seventies with his masterful portrayal of Jack Carter in *Get Carter* (Mike Hodges, 1971), his acclaimed performances included roles in *The Man Who Would Be King* (John Huston, 1975), *The Eagle Has Landed* (John Sturges, 1976), and *A Bridge Too Far* (Richard Attenborough, 1977). He remained highly active throughout the eighties, starring in Lewis Gilbert's *Educating Rita* (1983), Woody Allen's *Hannah and Her Sisters* (1986), John Mackenzie's *The Fourth Protocol* (1987) and Frank Oz's *Dirty Rotten Scoundrels* (1988), amongst many others. His long and distinguished acting career has been recognised many times at awards ceremonies, including his presentation with the prestigious Academy Fellowship Award at the 2000 BAFTA Awards. He has been nominated for BAFTAs on some eight occasions, winning in the Best Actor category for his performance in *Educating Rita*. Additionally nominated for twelve Golden Globe Awards (winning for appearances in *Educating Rita*, David Wickes's TV drama miniseries *Jack the Ripper*, 1988, and Mark Herman's *Little Voice*, 1998), he has also received three Emmy nominations. At the Academy Awards he has been nominated six times, receiving the Best Actor in a Supporting Role Award for *Hannah and Her Sisters* as well as his performance in Lasse Hallström's *The Cider House Rules* (1999). Caine remains a highly-visible actor today, most notably with recent appearances in the films of Christopher Nolan including *Inception* (2010), *Interstellar* (2014), and *Tenet* (2020), as well as in the role of butler Alfred Pennyworth in Nolan's box-office-conquering *Dark Knight* trilogy (2005-12), which won him a whole new generation of fans. Among his many other accolades, he was made a Commander of the Order of the British Empire (CBE) in 1992, received a Knighthood in 2000, and was made a Commander of the *Ordre des Arts et des Lettres* in 2011.

While Caine made clear at the time of *The Muppet Christmas Carol*'s filming that he intended to take a very serious, sober-faced approach to his portrayal of Ebenezer Scrooge – thus not competing with his Muppet co-stars when it came to screen presence – his refined, understated performance met with a mixed critical reception. Some, such as Caroline Westbrook, opined that 'the biggest contributor to the success though is Michael Caine, wisely underplaying it as a mean Scrooge who is later almost embarrassed by his own generosity. In fact, Caine's so right in the part, you can almost forgive his singing. Almost'.[9] Yet conversely, others such as Gary J. Svehla have disparaged this approach, remarking that Caine's methodology was essentially too subtle and nuanced for its own good: 'The reborn Scrooge is almost the same man as the nasty "bah humbug" Scrooge. There is little sense of a former-ly decent man who descends into materialistic hell by loving money more than humanity and who, confronting his mistake, miraculously gets a second lease on life coming through here'.[10] In spite of this divergence in critical opinion, however, Caine – who spoke openly about his desire to play the charac-ter during the time of production – nonetheless has become one of the more memorable actors to portray Scrooge in re-cent decades.

The other human performers are well-employed, even if their appearance often amounts to little more than an extend-ed cameo. Most notable are Steven Mackintosh as Scrooge's sanguine nephew Fred, Robin Weaver as the bubbly, relent-lessly cheerful Clara, and Meredith Braun as a beautiful and suitably melancholic Belle. The sets are flawless throughout, with decorator Michael Ford creating a highly detailed envi-ronment which conveys aspects of Victorian style and warm touches of larger-than-life Muppet character in a combination which is as classy as it is seamless. Special note is also due to the detailed costume design by Ann Hollowood and Polly Smith, particularly in their work on Scrooge's meticulously-crafted attire which helps to make Michael Caine's appear-ance one of the most dapper versions of all cinematic iterations of Dickens's curmudgeonly old skinflint.

Miles Goodman provides the film with a likeable, at-mospheric score and, like almost all of the Muppets' cinematic outings, the film also includes a variety of musical numbers –

in this case featuring music and lyrics composed by Paul Williams. Standout pieces include the opening song 'Scrooge', where the protagonist is introduced as he makes his way briskly through the streets of Victorian London; 'Marley and Marley', the introduction of Scrooge's old partners in their spectral form; and 'Thankful Heart', where the reformed Ebenezer voices gratitude for his change in character.

Perhaps the best-known song from the film, 'When Love is Gone', is performed by Scrooge and Belle at the cusp of their separation, and was controversially excised from the original cinematic release of the film before being reinstated for the 1993 VHS and LaserDisc releases. Director Brian Henson was said to be displeased by the song's removal from the theatrical release, given that its themes are mirrored by the later 'When Love is Found', sung by the assembled cast at the conclusion. (Singer Martina McBride also performs a reprise of 'When Love is Gone' during the film's end credits sequence.) The song appears on some DVD releases of the film while being absent from others, and has also been missing from Blu-ray versions. In 2020, Henson confirmed that the original film negative of the song had been recovered thanks to the researches of Disney archivists, and as such this footage would be included in future 4K releases of the movie.

A somewhat lopsided critical reception awaited *The Muppet Christmas Carol* at the time of its release. Some reviewers, such as Janet Maslin, applauded the way that Henson and his team had evoked a sense of timelessness throughout the film, incorporating the Muppets faultlessly into a particular place and era which were quite different from their usual contemporary adventures: '*The Muppet Christmas Carol* was co-produced and capably directed by Brian Henson, whose supervision of puppetry and special effects keeps the film on a par with earlier Muppet efforts. The screenplay, by Jerry Juhl, is less inventive, but then it must cope with the challenge of retelling Dickens in terms that will register with young children. In this regard the film does work well, bringing home the story's impact and reinforcing its central message. Even if it takes two dancing black-and-white Muppet Marleys, a passel of quill-wielding rats as Scrooge's office clerks and a collection of young frogs and pigs in the Cratchit household, this *Christmas Carol* makes a clear case for kindness and successfully warms the heart'.[11] Conversely, others commentators found that the adaptation was lacking in much of the drive and energy that had been typical of *The Muppet Show*. Desson Howe, for instance, argues that:

> The dullness is surprising, given guest headliner Michael Caine's central presence and the usually bright material we've come to expect from the Muppet corner. Director Brian Henson, son of the late, great Muppet founder Jim Henson, is obviously dedicated to the show's going on. Yet the spark that usually animated that show is missing. [...] *The Muppet Christmas Carol* isn't terrible, by any means. But it's resoundingly moderate, with merely passable songs by Paul Williams, and only occasional real laughter. It's no particular fault of Caine's. He makes a perfectly adequate curmudgeon. When he tells Kermit to prepare the latest round of eviction notices, Kermit respectfully reminds him this is Christmas Eve. 'Very well,' he replies, 'you may gift-wrap them.' But Scrooge's character evolution – from nasty to humanity-hugging – is insufficiently flavored with comic relief.[12]

Although many reviews of *The Muppet Christmas Carol* were decidedly lukewarm, finding that the film was technically competent but (it was argued) had brought little that was new to the telling of Dickens's oft-told moral fable, even the more sceptical reviewers were mindful of the artistry necessary to bring about the metafictional aspect of fictional characters playing other fictional characters with considerable panache. Jonathan Romney's evaluation is characteristic of this line of analysis, noting that 'it's hardly surprising that the Muppets look more comfortable than the humans in this Victorian London heritage ride. It's like a department-store Xmas grotto after lights-out with the toys taking over and sending up the tawdriness of the whole thing simply by indulging their cynicism and sentimentality, while Michael Caine's Scrooge wanders round like a disgusted caretaker. The film's best joke is its ongoing symposium on the problems of narration, between "Dickens" (The Great Gonzo, neither bird nor beast but a misbegotten bendy-nosed thing) and his skeptical stooge Rizzo the Rat. They have to keep climbing walls and hitching lasso rides to get the story told'.[13] Similarly, Philip Kemp acknowledges the movie's ingenious postmodern flourishes, sparing Gonzo's cleverly self-aware narrative abilities from wider censure of the film's merits: 'The film's neatest trick is the Gonzo-Rizzo double act, with Rizzo providing a welcome undertow of scepticism ("A blue furry Charles Dickens who hangs out with a rat?") to counteract excess sentimentality. By clarifying the storyline for the benefit of children who may not know it, while at the same time cracking distancing jokes to amuse the adults, they keep the narrative moving – and even manage to toss in a hint of death-of-the-author deconstruction'.[14] Overall, however, the most prominent critical hostility was aimed at an attempt to revisit the often-adapted Dickens story in the first place, questioning whether Henson's film had brought enough to the tale that was new in order to truly engage audiences. As Pamela Bruce comments, 'Despite cutesy cleverness in the construction of most scenes, the spirit segments are the real imaginative core of this film, where Muppet stylization and special effects merge to create a refreshing look to a familiar face. But in the back of one's mind, the suggestion still creeps: there was no reason for this film to be made – aren't there already better Christmas films out there to satisfy holiday viewing rituals?'[15]

Retrospective reviews of *The Muppet Christmas Carol* in more recent times have become less polarised thanks to the warm glow of nostalgia, and the movie has continued to be discussed regularly on account of its numerous re-releases on formats such as DVD and Blu-ray. Several commentators, including Chris Olson, have praised the film's irresistible charm and the dexterity of Brian Henson's direction which maximises the appeal of Dickens's classic: 'From the outset the movie creates a brash tone which is synonymous with the Muppets, who are able to transcend the usual confines of human narrative. They regularly break the fourth wall with their two narrators, who are also in the shot rather than performing as an overvoice. Their version also massively picks up on the comedy elements of Dickens' beloved literary classic, even poking fun at the great author himself. [...] *The Muppets Christmas Carol* delivers everything you could want from a Christmas film, whilst caring not at all for decorum or grace – such is the way any rendition of a festive film should be'.[16] Others have applauded the way that the movie works not just as a festive Dickens adaptation but also as a treat for aficionados of Henson's inspired character creations. As Mike

Long explains, 'The Muppet Christmas Carol is a departure from the previous films, as it tackles a pre-existing story. Placing Kermit, Miss Piggy, and Fozzie in supporting roles was a risky maneuver which could have easily turned off longtime fans. However, Gonzo and Rizzo do a fine job in the lead, as Gonzo drops his usual "weirdo" act and actually shows some charisma. And, of course, Rizzo makes for a great comic sidekick. So, the movie then becomes almost like a game where we try to spot familiar Muppet characters like Animal, Beaker, Sam the Eagle, and Lew Zealand. While the movie contains some dramatic moments, we also get some classic corny Muppet humor, and the dinner scenes with Kermit, Miss Piggy, and their children is very funny'.[17] Overall, Peter Bradshaw's analysis best sums up the prevailing critical response to the film in the modern day when he emphasises how well the warm and transformative spirit of the movie has held up even in the present day: 'When Dickens was writing A Christmas Carol in 1843, he was said to have taken long night walks through London in a state of passionate euphoria, covering 10 or 15 miles at a time, dreaming his masterpiece into existence. I like to think if in the course of these walks some spirit could have taken him into the future to show him the adaptations to come, this is the one he would have especially favoured. Only an obtuse snob would not see the sweetness and good-nature of The Muppet Christmas Carol'.[18]

While the commercial performance of Henson's movie at the box-office was respectable, it was adversely affected on account of the fact that it was released into cinemas at the same time as a number of other high-profile features, most notably the blockbuster Home Alone 2: Lost in New York (Chris Columbus, 1992) which dominated popular interest at the time. Nonetheless, the film has achieved lasting cult success due to its place in the pantheon of Muppet features, and its profile has been further enhanced by its repeated releases on home entertainment formats over the years. *The Muppet Christmas Carol* was also to win Brian Henson the Best Direction Award at the Fantafestival Awards in 1993, while its soundtrack was nominated for the Grammy Award for Best Musical Album for Children the same year.

Today, *The Muppet Christmas Carol* remains almost certainly the most prominent cinematic adaptation of Dickens' story to have been produced in the 1990s. Although there were other versions released throughout the decade, some of them highly acclaimed by critics, they were generally broadcast on television rather than released into cinemas. Foremost among these was Patrick Stewart's strikingly austere Ebenezer Scrooge in David Hugh Jones's *A Christmas Carol* (1999), shown on TV's Hallmark Entertainment channel. This followed Stewart's hugely successful one-man performance of the Dickens novella in 1991, where he was to play every character from the book on stage to great critical acclaim and was later nominated for the Drama Desk Award for Outstanding One-Person Show for his efforts. Amongst other noteworthy Scrooges of the nineties was Jack Palance in Ken Jubenvill's TV movie *Ebenezer* (1997), an interesting Wild West interpretation of the story where the story of Scrooge is transplanted to nineteenth-century America.

A Christmas Carol is a story which has continued to maintain cultural relevance and mass appeal due to its perennial festive themes of altruism, positive character transformation, and the importance of family and friends. One of the most family-friendly live action versions of the tale, *The Muppet Christmas Carol* had treated the style and content of Dickens's work with great respect while also introducing original new stylistic angles to the story in order to retain contemporary interest. Its blend of traditionalism and modernity was perfectly in tune with much festive cinema of the 1990s. While the film contains plenty to entertain younger viewers, adults (particularly those who grew up with *The Muppet Show*) appreciated the film's loyalty to the distinctive characters of the many different Muppet players, as well as the knowing narrative ingenuity of Charles Dickens in the guise of the wacky Gonzo. But the film also suggested a retreat from the darkness of eighties adaptations of the tale, lacking both the commanding sobriety of Clive Donner's 1984 version starring George C. Scott and the sardonic bite of Richard Donner's *Scrooged* in 1988. There is also, in the closing scenes where Caine's Scrooge acknowledges the importance of his family and new-found friends, a warm appreciation of personal responsibility and the benefits of mutual co-operation: surely amongst the most long-established of all Christmas messages. But as we shall see, Scrooge was far from the least conventional character to seek a sense of belonging in the Christmas films of the nineties.

REFERENCES

1. Roger Ebert, '*The Muppet Christmas Carol*', in *The Chicago Sun-Times*, 11 December 1992. <*https://www.rogerebert.com/reviews/the-muppet-christmas-carol-1992*>

2. Thomas M. Leitch, *Film Adaptation and its Discontents: From* Gone with the Wind *to* The Passion of the Christ (Baltimore: Johns Hopkins University Press, 2007), p.92.

3. James Chapman, 'God Bless Us, Every One: Movie Adaptations of *A Christmas Carol*', in *Christmas at the Movies*, ed. by Mark Connelly (London: I.B. Tauris, 2000), 9-37, pp.31-32.

4. Hugh H. Davis, 'A Weirdo, a Rat and a Humbug: The Literary Qualities of *The Muppet Christmas Carol*', in *Studies in Popular Culture*, Vol. 2, No. 3, April 1999, 95-105, p.96.

5. ibid., pp.101-02.

6. Chapman, p.31.

7. Ginger Stelle, '"Starring Kermit the Frog as Bob Cratchit": Muppets as Actors', in *Kermit Culture: Critical Perspectives on Jim Henson's Muppets*, ed. by Jennifer C. Garlen and Anissa M. Graham (Jefferson: McFarland and Company, 2009), 94-102, p.101.

8. Peter Rainer, 'Movie Review: Muppets Take on Dickens' *Carol*', in *The Los Angeles Times*, 11 December 1992. <*https://www.latimes.com/archives/la-xpm-1992-12-11-ca-1527-story.html*>

9.   Caroline Westbrook, 'The Muppet Christmas Carol', in
        Empire, January 1993.
        <https://www.empireonline.com/movies/reviews/muppet-
        christmas-carol-review/>

10.   Gary J. Svehla, 'The Muppet Christmas Carol', in Gary J.
        Svehla and Susan Svehla, It's Christmas Time at the Movies
        (Baltimore: Midnight Marquee Press, 1998), 197-99, p.199.

11.   Janet Maslin, 'Review/Film: Kermit, Etc. Do Dickens Up
        Green', in The New York Times, 11 December 1992.
        <https://www.nytimes.com/1992/12/11/movies/review-
        film-kermit-etc-do-dickens-up-green.html>

12.   Desson Howe, 'The Muppet Christmas Carol', in The
        Washington Post, 11 December 1992.
        <https://www.washingtonpost.com/wp-srv/style/
        longterm/movies/videos/
        themuppetchristmascarolghowe_a0af54.htm>

13.   Jonathan Romney, 'The Muppet Christmas Carol', in The
        New Statesman, December 1992-January 1993, p.60.

14.   Philip Kemp, 'The Muppet Christmas Carol', in Sight and
        Sound, February 1993.
        <https://www2.bfi.org.uk/news-opinion/sight-sound-
        magazine/reviews-recommendations/muppet-christmas-carol-
        deconstructed-dickins>

15.   Pamela Bruce, 'The Muppet Christmas Carol', in The Aus-
        tin Chronicle, 11 December 1992.
        <https://www.austinchronicle.com/events/film/1992-12-
        11/the-muppet-christmas-carol/>

16.   Chris Olson, 'The Muppet Christmas Carol', in UK Film
        Review, 24 December 2015.

\<*https://www.ukfilmreview.co.uk/post/the-muppet-christmas-carol-1992-film-review*\>

17.   Mike Long, '*The Muppet Christmas Carol*', in *DVD Sleuth*, 8 November 2012. \<*https://www.dvdsleuth.com/MuppetChristmasCarolReview/*\>

18.   Peter Bradshaw, '*The Muppet Christmas Carol* Review: Michael Caine shows spirit in magical extravaganza', in *The Guardian*, 29 November 2017. \<*https://www.theguardian.com/film/2017/nov/29/the-muppet-christmas-carol-review-michael-caine-kermit-miss-piggy*\>

5

A Midnight Clear (1992)

A&M Films / Beacon Pictures

Director: Keith Gordon
Producers: Bill Borden and Dale Pollock
Screenwriter: Keith Gordon, from a novel by
William Wharton

WARTIME may not seem like the most likely backdrop for a Christmas movie, and yet some of the most touching depictions of the festive season are evoked when they are pitched directly in contrast to a backdrop of strife and conflict. Films such as *White Christmas* (Michael Curtiz, 1954) had featured significant scenes set during wartime, whereas the action of others – including *Merry Christmas, Mr Lawrence* (Nagisa Oshima, 1983) – were all the more harrowing for the way in which the traditional yuletide sentiments of peace and goodwill were juxtaposed with harrowing scenes of inhumanity and brutal combat. *A Midnight Clear* was a highly effective exemplar of this subgenre of Christmas film-making, presenting a wartime scenario which featured both ruthlessness and common humanity while encouraging the viewer to consider the ways in which the spirit of Christmas can become a light that illuminates even the darkest of situations.

A Midnight Clear was an adaptation of William Wharton's 1982 novel of the same name, and followed the book's action closely. Wharton was the pen name of author Albert William Du Aime, an American writer who saw action with the United States Army during World War II, eventually being badly injured in combat during the Battle of the Bulge. Those harrowing experiences, together with his later academic experience – he gained a doctorate in psychology from the University of California in Los Angeles following his discharge from the Army – came to inform many of his novels, not least the Pulitzer Prize-nominated *Birdy* (1978) which was adapted into an acclaimed film by Alan Parker in 1984, starring Matthew Modine as the eponymous, Vietnam War-traumatised protagonist. As James Deutsch notes, the novel differed from the film in its choice of the historical setting for its conflict, pointing out that 'Wharton, the pseudonym for an American painter living in Paris since the 1960s, earlier wrote *Birdy* [...], a first novel that dealt with the horrors of World War II and the psychosomatic problems that combat can bring'.[1] *Birdy* was later adapted for the stage by Naomi Wallace in 1997. Wharton's first-hand experiences of conflict – and specifically the World War II Ardennes Offensive of December 1944 to January 1945 – are even more explicit in *A Midnight Clear*, and the haunting story makes clear his views on the futility of international warfare.

The film's director was Keith Gordon, who had made his start in the world of showbusiness as an actor – often playing nerdy intellectuals with a slyly comic angle. He appeared in roles across numerous genres including films such as *All That Jazz* (Bob Fosse, 1979), *Dressed to Kill* (Brian De Palma, 1980), *Christine* (John Carpenter, 1983) and *Back to School* (Alan Metter, 1986). During this period, he developed experience as a screenwriter on Mark Romanek's *Static* (1985), before moving into directing with his cinematic debut, the youth rebellion drama *The Chocolate War* (1988). His preoccupation with interpersonal empathy, common humanity and themes relating to coming of age would continue to be in evidence throughout *A Midnight Clear*, which was to be only his second directorial feature.

While anti-war films were far from a new development, even within a Christmas setting, *A Midnight Clear* was to establish a unambiguous moral sentiment that would have been familiar to audiences of earlier World War II movies such as *Castle Keep* (Sydney Pollack, 1969), based on William Eastlake's 1965 novel of the same name, and *Catch-22* (Mike Nichols, 1970), adapted from Joseph Heller's famous 1961 novel, which both employed surrealistic flourishes which provided highly effective contrast with the tragic realism which delineated the horrors of armed conflict. Gordon produces a melange of non-aggression, contemplation and psychological observation to produce a memorable feature which laid the groundwork for later, more prominent war movies such as the mixture of non-violence, humanity and pragmatism evident in Terrence Malick's *The Thin Red Line* (1998) at the end of the decade. As Michael Wilmington explains, *A Midnight Clear* was a response to other stylistic influences which further delineated Gordon's artistic approach:

> Great war movies never glorify war, even if, sometimes, they praise the courage of the men who fight it. *A Midnight Clear* (at the Hillcrest Cinemas) – not quite a great war movie but certainly a sensitive, bright and supremely moral one – shows how courage itself can be a kind of insanity. [...] Gordon's favorite director is Stanley Kubrick, but

his film doesn't suggest the remorselessly mechanical, ironic perfection of a Kubrick war movie, a *Paths of Glory* or *Full Metal Jacket*. Instead, *A Midnight Clear* [...] is closer to something Fred Zinnemann might have done: It has some of the same precision, lucent craft and unapologetic humanism. At its best, it's a barely muted cry against war's stupidity and injustice. With a clear eye, the movie shows us midnight.[2]

It is December 1944, and the Second World War is entering its final stages in Europe. In the deceptively still, snow-covered Ardennes forest, adjacent to the border between Germany and France, a detachment of American troops has been deployed against Nazi aggressors. In a trench, 26-year-old soldier Vance Wilkins (Gary Sinise), known as 'Mother' by his comrades, is driven to a state of extreme psychological distress when he discovers that his first child has been stillborn back in the United States. His nickname comes from his tendency towards obsessive tidiness, but he is far from fastidious when consumed by intense emotional grief. Mother's aberrant behaviour is of concern to his immediate superior, Sergeant Will Knott (Ethan Hawke), who beseeches him to seek psychological evaluation. But Mother refuses the offer, preferring to work his way through his grief on the battlefield without the aid of care professionals.

The rest of the squad includes Paul 'Father' Mundy (Frank Whaley), who had to give up his ambitions of entering the priesthood when war broke out; Corporal Mel Avakian (Kevin Dillon), who takes his soldiering very seriously; Bud Miller (Peter Berg), a talented mechanical expert; and Stan Shutzer (Arye Gross) who, being Jewish, has particular reason to loathe all that the Nazis stand for. In spite of the fact that an Intelligence & Reconnaissance Squad is intended to have twelve members, Knott's has been reduced to only six. They are under the command of the hard-nosed Major Griffin (John C. McGinley), who – in peacetime – was a mortician by trade. Due to the number of casualties sustained under Griffin's watch, Knott feels that he has been promoted to the rank of sergeant more rapidly than is justified by his actual combat experience.

The squad is made up of members who each scored very highly on the US Army intelligence scale, but due to Griffin's ill-advised operations they have already lost half their number to enemy fire. Knott laments the loss of such talented soldiers to badly-planned manoeuvres, perceiving that the world has lost unique intellects – and young lives – as a result. To Griffin, however, everyone under his command is expendable in times of war. Their orders are to move north into the Ardenne forest to await relief troops and guard against enemy incursions over the border. Their superior, Lieutenant Ware (Larry Joshua), was of the opinion that the performance of Intelligence & Reconnaissance had been sub-par and reasoned that smarter troops would be required to drive up the success rate of operations, hence Knott and his subordinates being requisitioned for their current role. But with half his troops now dead, the sergeant is less than convinced by Ware's reasoning.

Griffin explains to Knott and Ware that a Nazi offensive is expected in the area, and that a taskforce of advance troops sent to investigate the rumours has not returned. To this end, Knott and his five colleagues are to take up residence in an abandoned country house near the area where the Germans are judged most likely to attack, reporting their findings to Ware via radio. Knott has some trepidation about these orders, as there is no intelligence on whether the house in question has already been occupied by enemy troops. In theory, he and his troops could be walking straight into the lion's den without even knowing it.

Knott and the men under his command drive two jeeps to the house in question, with the weather worsening as heavy snow closes in. Mother, whose nerves are still worryingly on edge, starts to fire one of the jeeps' mounted machine guns indiscriminately, believing that enemy soldiers are about to attack. But when Knott investigates, the obstruction on the road turns out to be the frozen corpse of another American soldier, locked in silent combat with the (similarly ice-covered) body of a German trooper. The surreal scene is highly discomfiting to Knott and his men, as the two dead soldiers almost appear as though they are embracing like old friends. Mundy performs a brief blessing as the two cadavers are removed from the road.

The squad arrives at the empty house and immediately checks for the presence of enemy soldiers, as well as landmines and other traps. Thankfully there is nothing to be found other than a young deer, whose presence suggests that the rural property has been unoccupied for some time. A room-by-room search produces no sign of recent habitation, but the troops are elated to discover fine wine and tinned sardines along with mattresses, pillows and warm bedding – it seems that their stay might be more comfortable than they had feared. They retrieve their equipment from the jeeps and set a fire to keep the extreme cold at bay, even at the risk of the chimney smoke alerting the Germans of the house's occupation.

Lookout posts are set up and operated through the night, and Mother calls back to the house to report seeing unexplained movement in the distance – though Father, who is also on sentry duty, can't confirm this due to poor visibility. Soon after, however, Avakian relays a report of unexpected sounds in the vicinity, leading Knott to come racing to the watch position. Sure enough, Germans can be heard laughing and signalling to each other nearby, and one surprisingly jovial voice makes clear that they are all too aware of the 'Amerikaner' presence at the house. Knott feels sure they are being taunted and readies a grenade, planning to scout the area around the house when the German voices suddenly fall silent. Avakian discourages him, sensing that they would be walking into an ambush, but the men are all disconcerted by the encounter – not least as the Germans had parted ways with an ominous instruction to 'sleep well'. This convinces them that the enemy troops are gearing up for an offensive.

Later, Ware calls the house and demands an update. When he hears of the German presence in the area, he orders Knott and his troops to find the enemy command post as quickly as possible. The soldiers thus set out, camouflaged and wading waist-deep through snow in broad daylight, to search the area where the voices had been heard the previous night. Sure enough, they soon find a small guard house nearby – chimney smoke giving away its position. Knott's men spot three German soldiers, but rather than attack he reasons that as the enemy troops had spared them the previous night, he will pay them the same respect.

On the way back to the abandoned house, the American troops are intercepted by three German combatants, their rifles trained on their position. Knott and his men panic, but by the time they have composed themselves it becomes clear that their enemies have already left the scene. This baffles them, and they flee before they can come under hostile fire. In their haste to depart, however, their scope and map are lost.

Returning to the others, the combatants confer and dejectedly point out the fact that while they tracked down the Germans, their enemy seems to have a much better idea of the corresponding American position. Everyone is ill at ease about the fact that the German soldiers had every opporunity to kill the American troops and yet, for some unknown reason, chose not to. Mother, meanwhile, has separated himself from his comrades and taken up residence in the building's attic. He contemplates the house's collection of fine artwork, which has presumably been moved to the top storey for safe-keeping. The intense soldier marvels at the fact that the creative expression behind the creation of these paintings was the product of love and passion – a significant observation in a combat zone during the horrors of war.

Night falls, and once again the sentries hear the sound of German voices approaching. A grenade is thrown at their position and explodes, but no returning fire is forthcoming. Confusingly, the Germans start to chant an anti-Hitler slogan, then start throwing snowballs at the American position. Having expected grenades and gunfire, Knott's troops are baffled and send more snowballs flying back to the Germans. After a while, the enemy troops depart, and the Americans realise that before retreating their adversaries have returned their missing map.

Shutzer notices that a location and time have been marked on the map, and reasons that the Germans must be suggesting a rendezvous. Knott feels certain that this will be a trap, but Shutzer is not so sure – the frozen corpses on the approach to the house had been deliberately arranged in a hug, suggesting a desire for co-operation, and the Germans have now had multiple opportunities to kill the Americans but have refused to do so at every encounter. Knott suspects that their enemies are merely lulling them into a false sense of security while they await reinforcements, and resolves to radio the situation back to Ware. However, Shutzer begs him not to throw away the potential for a peaceful resolution – if the Germans want to surrender, they may do so peacefully, but Ware and Griffin will instead insist on an armed offensive no matter what the circumstances might be.

Thinking on his feet, Shutzer hatches a plan. If the Germans really do intend to give themselves up, the Americans can stage the situation to make it look as though Mother has taken them all prisoner single-handed. As a perceived war hero, the top brass would likely send him home, where he would have more chance of being able to heal his wounded psyche. This solution appeals to Knott, who knows that Wilkins is clearly cracking up as a result of emotional pain and the stress of continuous conflict. Avakian is appalled, believing the plan to be doomed to failure, but Knott has made up his mind and sets off with Shutzer to the rendezvous point. However, knowing how psychologically unstable Mother has become, they all agree not to tell him what they have planned.

Sure enough, the Germans are waiting where they had indicated, and Shutzer enters a conversation with their leader (Curt Lowens). The officer wants to speak with the American soldier in authority, so Knott approaches and Shutzer does his best to translate with what little German he knows. Knott is shocked by the fact that the officer's guard (Kelly Gately) looks even younger than he is. Eventually they come to understand what the Germans want. They have been transferred to the area from the Russian Front, vicious hostilities which they had only just survived, and are desperate not to get involved in the Battle of the Bulge which is currently raging near their position. Realising that Germany now has no way of winning the war, they want to find a way of being taken prisoner by the Americans without appearing to have surrendered. That way, they will avoid having to take part in what they believe to be a suicidal counter-offensive.

Miller is decked out to look like an American officer, in order to give the Germans the impression that he is in charge of the unit and to add legitimacy to the plan. They then arrange to have Mother put on sentry duty that night, given that he is the only soldier who is oblivious to the Germans' desire to be taken into custody. Before this can happen, the enemy soldiers are spotted dragging heavy ordnance towards the house, and there is an immediate fear that they are training a mortar on their position. Any concern about a double-cross is soon allayed, however, when closer inspection reveals that all seven Germans – soldiers and officer – have brought a Christmas tree, which they have decorated. Knott and his troops look on speechless as the Germans burst into song, performing Christmas carols and offering gifts. They warmly exchange food and other presents, hands are shaken, and an American hand grenade is given as a decoration for the Germans' tree. Everyone is stunned at the unexpected display of goodwill from their mortal enemies.

The Americans retreat back to the house with their collection of gifts from the German soldiers. As they discuss the highly unusual encounter, a confused Mother arrives and enquires why nobody has been answering the field telephone. He alone is oblivious to the meeting with the Germans, and is bewildered at having heard singing. His colleagues reluctantly explain that the enemy combatants have offered presents and wishes of goodwill to mark the festive season, but make no mention of the Germans' plans to give themselves up without a fight. Mother is very uncomfortable at the prospect of being on good terms with their wartime opponents, reasoning that things tend to work more smoothly if enemy soldiers stay out of each others' way unless they are actually fighting.

The next morning, there is another meeting between Knott and the German officer, with Shutzer again acting as translator. The Germans are eager to give themselves up as quickly as possible, as they feel certain that their army is about to advance through the area. However, if it appears that they have surrendered without a struggle, they fear that reprisals will take place against their families back home. Thus they suggest that a fake battle take place, where spent bullet cartridges will be found on the scene to give the impression of a real confrontation. Knott is reluctant, believing it may be a Nazi trick, but the German officer desperately blurts out that he and his troops are not members of the Nazi Party – they are simply soldiers in the Wehrmacht, the German armed forces. He clearly wants to distance himself from the genocidal, totalitarian ideology of Nazism. After a heated discussion with Shutzer and Miller, Knott eventually decides to go along with the German plan.

Back at the house, they telephone base camp and tell Ware that they believe there will soon be an opportunity to take an enemy soldier as a prisoner, and that they will escort them back to Major Griffin as soon as they are able. They then tell Mother to stay in the house and to call for reinforcements if they do not return within two hours, thus keeping him occupied while they go to stage the mock battle with the Germans. Knott and the other four troops then go to the German command post, where they find their opponents are more than ready to hand themselves over. As per their earlier plan, both sides discharge their weapons harmlessly into the air, leaving spent bullet cartridges as an indication of a non-existent skirmish. Just as the strategy appears to be working perfectly, however, a fatal shot rings out – Mother has secretly followed his fellow soldiers and, unaware of the scheme, believes that the battle is real. The Germans panic and retaliate, but Knott's men – knowing that they now have no choice – respond with lethal force. Within seconds, all bar one of the German soldiers are dead.

Father is mortally wounded by enemy gunfire, and dies in Knott's arms. Mother is distraught, unable to understand why Father would have tried to stop him when he had the enemy in his sights, but Knott tries to salve his anxieties by saying that their comrade must simply have acted irrationally in the heat of battle. Shutzer has also been hit by a German bullet, but it seems to miss his vital organs and he manages to survive. The remaining troops agree to alter their plan so that when questioned, they will tell their superiors that the enemy had them pinned down until Mother arrived to save the day.

The officious Griffin has arrived at the abandoned house and immediately takes charge of the situation. Far from being impressed by the apparent wipeout of the German post, however, Griffin upbraids Knott for the haphazard condition of their temporary waystation and warns him that he would have the sergeant court-martialled if not for the impending German attack that is expected in the area. He demands that Knott transfer the tyre chains from one of his jeeps to his own vehicle (having left camp in the snow without them), and plans to leave with the wounded before the enemy incursion can begin. Even Lietenant Ware is shocked by his superior's insensitivity – and his cravenness at retreating in the face of a looming enemy attack.

Ware informs Knott that according to Griffin's orders, the sergeant and his remaining troops are to remain at the post and await the commencement of the German incursion. At the first sign of an enemy advance, he is to signal the command base immediately. Knott is dumbfounded, knowing this to be essentially a suicide mission, but also understanding that the orders fit Griffin's underhanded character perfectly. Once the officers have departed, however, the four remaining soldiers feel desolate at how things have unfolded and wonder if the war is worth surviving if amoral sadists like Griffin will be in charge of the world that's left. Seeing no need to occupy sentry posts, reasoning that they will hear a major German advance long before they see it, the soldiers bathe Father's dead body in respect for their fallen comrade.

Shortly after, the house comes under attack from German artillery. The phone line back to base is inoperative, so Knott gives the order for the surviving soldiers to board the jeeps and make a retreat to the American command post. As Griffin has commandeered the tyre chains from one of the vehicles, however, it struggles to get through the dense snow. They spot a German armoured column arriving just as they leave the area, but somehow manage to avoid the relentless bombardment which ensues. In their haste to leave, Knott's jeep skids off the road onto a rock face, meaning that the troops have no choice but to depart the area in the one remaining vehicle.

Knott and his surviving troops reach the American base camp, but discover that Griffin has ordered a retreat – the entire encampment has been uprooted, with no indication of their whereabouts. The sergeant therefore has little choice but to keep following the road for as long as they can. With no map, however, they quickly realise that they have no idea where they are travelling. Eventually their vehicle runs out of fuel, and they are forced to continue on foot – but with no way of knowing even what country they are now in, they watch as a detachment of German armoured vehicles and hardened *SS* troops pass by. The young Americans wonder if their enemies are on the attack or trying to retreat.

Unsure whether they will be taken prisoner or find their own side first, Knott and the other soldiers bury their weapons and equipment, then masquerade as army medics – carrying the body of their dead comrade, Father. They set off through the frozen landscape, bearing the corpse between them, as they pass scenes of carnage. Eventually they encounter a lone American sentry and, keeping to their story, have Father's body delivered to an army mortician. They are then returned to their regiment, where Ware coolly informs Knott that he is to be immediately returned to the field with anti-tank soldiers assigned to replenish the numbers of his squad. He also confidentially admits that Griffin decided not to bother informing Knott of the news of the German advance, hence the radio silence prior to the retreat. Mother is reassigned to the motor pool, but Ware remorsefully explains that Shutzer and the one surviving German prisoner both died on the journey back to the American camp. Coldly handing Knott the paperwork to take responsibility for his missing equipment, Ware tells him that they will soon be advancing on the German lines... before, as an afterthought, wishing him a Merry Christmas. Stunned by the seemingly endless bloodshed of the war, Knott simply stares in silence, shocked into a state of numb devastation by the profound losses he has suffered.

While *A Midnight Clear* could hardly be considered uplifting yuletide entertainment, it is a film which clearly articulates the warmth and unifying power of the festive season – if only to ultimately stress the value of these qualities by subverting them. Gordon's film, like Wharton's novel before it, is ultimately far more concerned with the senselessness and slaughter of warfare than it is with the transformative power of Christmas celebrations. However, the Christmas scenes are nevertheless significantly employed to offer a better answer to conflict resolution than endless butchery; in the plan hatched between the mutinying German soldiers and Knott's troops, a non-aggressive and orderly simulated surrender is offered under the guise of shared Christmas goodwill. Only the tragic misunderstanding of Mother, himself deeply traumatised by personal tragedy and the heightened stress of constant warfare, derails the scheme before it can be brought about. As David Denby explains, 'The movie's tragic denouement seems to emerge less from the nature of war than from ordinary human error. *A Midnight Clear* is too much an absurdist allegory (with religious overtones) and not clear enough on the moment-to-moment physical level. But youth's deep dismay is there – and Hawke's numb disbelief when he's sent back into the field after his adventures is a memorable moment of despair'.[3]

In addition to reflecting Wharton's own wartime recollections of the Battle of the Bulge, it is no coincidence that the film's events unfold against the closing months of the war. The combatants on both sides are tired and worn out, supplies are running low, uniforms are tattered and tempers are frayed. Having witnessed death on an industrial scale for years at this point, everyone we see just wants the conflict to be over. Yet Gordon's screenplay throws a curve-ball to expectation in a variety of ways. The German soldiers, who are *de facto* representatives of a murderous, hateful and genocidal regime, are shown as pragmatic and contemplative – as their commander points out, they personally belong to the regular German army, not the actual Nazi Party, and are following orders because it is their professional duty rather than their ideological impulse to do so. These troops are made up of frightened teenagers and weary old draftees who are long past the age of retirement from the field, and their unusually collegiate behaviour is deliberately contrasted with the psychotic zeal of the *Waffen-SS* killing machine which makes a few chilling appearances near the conclusion of the film. The message here seems clear: that in war, it is always those on the front lines who suffer more than the strategists and top brass, and that nobody in any armed force is necessarily immune from the abuses or injustices of their superiors. The rebelling Germans' sympathetic portrayal is contrasted with the self-serving and glory-seeking Major Griffin (a brilliantly cold-blooded performance from veteran character actor John C. McGinley), whose blustering arrogance can't conceal the fact that the men under his command mean nothing to him and are simply pawns to be sacrificed at his whim. The swaggering Griffin's unfairness towards Knott and his troops, to say nothing of his acute moral cowardice, underscores the fact that he has no interest in the wellbeing of the soldiers serving under his command, and further emphasises the harshness of their situation – even a senior officer on their own side appears wholly disinterested about whether they live or die.

In spite of its Christmas setting (Knott points out that with no way of telling the time and date, it's hard to know with any degree of accuracy exactly when Christmas Day itself takes place), *A Midnight Clear* is depressing and bleak, but its narrative still offers some hope of common humanity. The lack of German subtitles is a powerful artistic choice, ensuring that most English-speaking audiences will be left just as much in the dark regarding the enemy soldiers' intentions as Knott and his men, reliant on Shutzer's rudimentary translation skills to uncover their adversaries' intentions and gauge how far they can be trusted. Here, as James Berardinelli discerns, 'Hitler's war has so depleted the Germany army that they're left with "old men and boys." They're tired and scared and, like many Axis soldiers in Europe, recognize that hope has fled. They don't want to die so they seek an alternative to fighting. Surrendering to the Americans doesn't seem like a bad one, as long as they can make it look like they were taken after a battle. The first challenge is to conquer the language barrier, something they attempt not with bullets but by stoking the Christmas spirit. After a tree, a few carols, and an exchange of gifts, the Germans and Americans are able to regard one another with something closer to trust than hostility. Until, of course, it all goes wrong. In war, it seems, that almost always happens'.[4]

Because Christmas conventions are used as a kind of shorthand for cross-cultural goodwill and mutual understanding, the deadly misapprehension of the surrender plan – where the oblivious Mother opens fire on the stunned and unsuspecting Germans – feels all the more devastating when it comes. By echoing the co-operative sentiment of the famous Christmas Armistice of the First World War, *A Midnight Clear* offers a familiar cultural image of collaboration and mutual aid between representatives of warring nations, but it also concludes in the same way: with the promise of greater understanding eventually drowned out by the inhumanity and psychological detachment of war. Here, as Vincent Canby suggests, the warmth of festive celebrations gives way to a deeper meditation about the brutality of international warfare: '*A Midnight Clear* recalls the often told story about a Christmas Eve in the trenches during World War I. At midnight, so the story goes, Allied and German soldiers met in the middle of no man's land to sing carols and toast each other's health. *A Midnight Clear* expresses something of the same longing, but without the greeting-card sentiment. The film is seriously angry. From time to time it comes close to losing its way, but even a possibly superfluous flashback to the squad's last night before shipping out is redeemed by the discipline of the film making'.[5]

The American soldiers' battlefield numbness is accentuated by many surreal moments – the frozen corpses of combatants arranged in a macabre embrace, the young deer living in the abandoned rural property (which trots nonchalantly past the puzzled American soldiers as though they are the true interlopers), the snowball fight when an exchange of grenades is expected, and of course Shutzer's makeshift snowman which is modelled after Adolf Hitler (complete with stick arms arranged in a Nazi salute). All of these images are striking in their sheer incongruity, and the rarefied situations they allude to are contrasted with brief recollections of the troops' more innocent time spent during training in the United States. This includes the closeness of the group's formative friendships and their enigmatic encounter with a grieving woman named Janice (Rachel Griffin) during a night on the town, but none of their drill exercises can prepare them for the harsh realities of actual conflict on the front lines, where mass death is commonplace rather than simply the subject of newsreels. Yet Susan E. Linville makes the point that even here, not everything is quite as it seems: 'The film reminds us that home, the domestic, and "domestication" are not simply synonymous with the beautiful as rational or readily narratable. Instead, congruent with Freud's view, they emerge as sites of trauma and anxiety-producing epistemological uncertainty – or, for that matter, as a *mise-en-scene* whose beauty defines a fantasy firmly at odds with those conventional visions of "home" and oedipal identity on which the combat film traditionally depends'.[6]

A *Midnight Clear* debatably works best when it is juxtaposing the common humanity of its youthful protagonists with the depressing and merciless insensitivity of the war machine. Griffin, for instance, is completely unconcerned by the trauma suffered by Knott and his men or the losses they have endured, instead castigating them for hair-splitting matters such as the physical condition of their mobile operations post and the state of their uniforms. Likewise, when the young soldiers later manage to escape near-certain death at the hands of the battle-hardened German *Waffen-SS*, they are so geographically disorientated that they can't even tell if their adversaries are advancing or retreating. These are exactly the types of developments which, as Michael Upchurch discerns, help to carve out the film's feeling of young lives blighted and lost by a grindingly uncompromising conflict: 'A *Midnight Clear* is an anti-war movie in the vein of *Slaughterhouse Five* and *Catch-22*. Its fantasy element is less pronounced, but its voice is similarly young, skeptical and bitterly rueful. [...] The anti-war message is driven home by some touches that go beyond the usual blood-and-gore, notably in a brief scene where an Army coroner inserts a dog tag in a dead soldier's mouth for ID purposes and then slaps the dead man's jaw shut with unnerving efficiency. A *Midnight Clear* doesn't do as much as it might with its characters. But as a parable of human folly and fragile hope, it has considerable impact'.[7] The impact of the film's strident depiction of the excesses and weariness of constant warfare feel all the more stark when cast against a wintry backdrop and the heartfelt Christmas conventions used by the German soldiers to communicate their desire to co-operate. It is, as Berardinelli comments, a collocation which highlights the need to value the optimism and mutual understanding of the festive season even in the most rarefied of circumstances: 'The typical movie set in and around Christmas embraces the mood of the season: Peace on Earth and Goodwill to All People. *A Midnight Clear* has a sharper and less idealistic perspective of things. Viewed through the lens of war, the absurdity of human nature is laid bare. We see the good, the bad, and the ugly – all packaged together in events spanning a few days leading up to December 25. It's a reminder, as if any is needed, that, despite the birth being celebrated at Christmas, humankind is still very much in need of salvation'.[8]

Some commentators have criticised the fact that *A Midnight Clear*'s snow-covered surroundings give away its Utah-based location filming; the woodland seems to be mostly composed of white birch trees, native to North America but not to be found in the Ardennes forest. However, Tom Richmond's cinematography does a highly creditable job at recreating the bleakness of the western European landscape in the freezing cold, and certainly adds an element of seasonal authenticity to proceedings. Yugoslavia had initially been considered as a possible location, but weather forecasting could not predict snowfall with any degree of certainty – and generating artificial snow in the quantity required would have been financially unworkable given the film's budget (estimated at a slender $5 million). Instead, White Pine Canyon in Utah's Park City was used... and as luck would have it, the area experienced one of its most extreme winters in almost a century during filming, adding to the authenticity of the action. The expansive woodland areas used for the production later became the site of a development of luxury homes.

The film's central cast are uniformly excellent in portraying the mix of youthful courage and war-weary lethargy. Ethan Hawke had appeared in *Explorers* (Joe Dante, 1985) and then in *Dead Poets Society* (Peter Weir, 1989) followed by *Dad* (Gary David Goldberg, 1989), which had also been adapted from a William Wharton novel. He has since gone on to considerable acclaim not just for his acting performances, but also as a director and novelist. Gary Sinise was at the time perhaps best-known for directing the 1988 film *Miles from Home*, starring Richard Gere and Kevin Anderson, and he would of course achieve considerable fame throughout the 1990s with performances in films including *Forrest Gump* (Robert Zemeckis, 1994), *Apollo 13* (Ron Howard, 1995) and *Ransom* (Ron Howard, 1996). Arye Gross had appeared in numerous films of the 1980s, especially in comedies including *Just One of the Guys* (Lisa Gottlieb, 1985), *Soul Man* (Steve Miner, 1986) and *The Couch Trip* (Michael Ritchie, 1988). Peter Berg had performed in movies including *Miracle Mile* (Steve De Jarnatt, 1988), *Heart of Dixie* (Martin Davidson, 1989) and *Late for Dinner* (W.D. Richter, 1991), and would later enjoy success as a writer, director and producer. Kevin Dillon's prolific acting career had included roles in *Platoon* (Oliver Stone, 1986), *The Rescue* (Ferdinand Fairfax, 1988) and *War Party* (Franc Roddam, 1988), whereas Frank Whaley had appeared in features including *Field of Dreams* (Phil Alden Robinson, 1989), *Born on the Fourth of July* (Oliver Stone, 1989) and *Career Opportunities* (Bryan Gordon, 1991), and would later also attain success as a screenwriter and director.

When *A Midnight Clear* arrived in cinemas in 1992, critics were largely approving of the film's qualities – though their praise was not without qualification. Some, such as Hal

Hinson, commended not only the direction but also the skilled performances of the main cast: 'Aside from ⟦Gordon's⟧ confidence with the camera and his impeccable sense of pace, his real strength is his work with the actors. Though the cast – which includes Frank Whaley, Peter Berg and Kevin Dillon – is young, there is no sign of Brat Pack-style self-indulgence. Instead, the ensemble functions just as a group of combat-tested soldiers would; as if, in fact, their lives depend on an almost telepathic sense of unity. The personalities of the actors are distinct, but it's as an ensemble that they most distinguish themselves. And, as their leader, Gordon shows the kind of filmmaking talent that creates genuine excitement'.[9] On a divergent note, Roger Ebert instead celebrated the indefinable atmosphere and symbolic inscrutability of the movie, taking note of the qualities which differentiated it from other war cinema of the time: '*A Midnight Clear* is a little too much of a parable for my taste – there are times when the characters seem to be acting out of the author's need, rather than their own – but it's a good film, and Gordon is uncanny in the way he suggests the eerie forest mysteries that permeate all of the action'.[10]

Not all reviewers of the time were uniformly in favour of the film, however. Marc Savlov, for instance, felt that the narrative momentum eventually faltered, and that the careful build-up which frames the action was ultimately squandered:

> Based on an actual occurrence, the film places a battle-weary squad of young GIs in the surreal, snowbound French-German border. They're tired and sick to death of all the killing they've seen; as squad leader Hawke puts it, even the beautiful Ardennes remains unnoticed by the men, fatigued as they are. [...] When the worst that can happen

does, it comes as little surprise. Unfortunately, three-quarters of the way through what was shaping up to be one heck of a unique take on The Big One and the nature of war in general, it all falls apart. There are whole segments in *A Midnight Clear* that have little or no use here and scream of padding, which is really too bad. Having made brilliant use of Utah's very Ardennes-like scenery and after positing so many interesting questions regarding the politics of war and the question of 'The Enemy,' it's a shame that this film sputters out as badly as it does.[11]

As the years have passed, the critical reputation of *A Midnight Clear* has gradually been enhanced, with more recent appraisals of the movie extolling not just its stylistic virtues, but also the power of its storytelling. As John Bishop has mentioned, 'The real brilliance of *A Midnight Clear* is in Keith Gordon's preternatural knack for economy as both writer and director. Working within limited means both scenic and sensational (filmed as it was in a vengefully chilling Park City, Utah), Gordon strips the firepower and narrative clutter from the mostly Vietnam-centric war films before him to craft a character piece about intelligent if inexperienced young men demonstrating grace under pressure. [...] Gordon has himself copped to anti-war intentions in his story, but they are more organic than matter-of-fact when you watch his film. Compositionally, Gordon is on-point in the bleak humor, realistic dialogue and tableaux of frostbitten violence which he has sourced from Wharton's tome'.[12] Other critics have been somewhat more moderate in their judgements, with some taking particular note of the budgetary limitations which the creative team were forced to overcome throughout the production. Sam Turner notes that 'you do get the impression with Keith Gordon's *A Midnight Clear* 〚...〛 that it was a film somewhat ahead of its time; a post-modern war film some six years before Terrence Malick blew that sub-genre out of the water with *The Thin Red Line* in 1998. 〚...〛 〚The film's〛 failings, though somewhat minor, can perhaps be traced back to an over-reliance on the prose of William Wharton's source material and to the occasional arrival of ultimate superior, John C. McGinley, who steps on to the wrong side of parody. The budget too, clearly hampers early interactions with the Germans, which could have, and should have, been much more haunting'.[13]

Although a majority of commentators were to focus their analysis on *A Midnight Clear*'s fidelity to the tropes of the war movie genre and its innovative qualities, some have also considered the film more explicitly in terms of Christmas cinema – and have offered it high praise in this regard. Mike D'Angelo was among those who have celebrated the central premise of the movie and its congruence with the traditional Christmas themes of reconciliation and benevolence: 'My own favorite Christmas movie falls into the 〚yuletide marginality〛 category, within the further subcategory of films so obscure that nobody remembers them well enough to think of them as anything at all. 〚...〛 A war movie in which neither side actually wants to fight – except as a kid's game – could hardly be more appealing. What better Christmas gift could one ask for than the discovery that the folks you thought were trying to kill you actually want to play? Kindness is most touching when least expected, and here it rains down from out of nowhere'.[14]

While there have been more effective and considerably angrier anti-war movies over the years, as a Christmas-situated example of the subgenre *A Midnight Clear* would arguably be the most successful exponent of conciliatory yuletide sentiment in times of conflict until the arrival of *Joyeux Noël* (Christian Carion, 2005) in the following decade. For his work on *A Midnight Clear*, Keith Gordon was nominated for a Best Screenplay Award at the Film Independent Spirit Awards in 1993, and while the film has not achieved quite the level of cultural prominence of many other Christmas films of the nineties, it remains a powerful work of contemporary filmmaking which challenges audience expectation in often surprising ways. With its compelling themes of generosity, compassion and bringing adversaries together under a common cause, it was a highly distinctive and emotionally earnest contribution to the festive cinema of the 1990s.

REFERENCES

1. James Deutsch, '*A Midnight Clear*', in *War and American Popular Culture: A Historical Encyclopedia*, ed. by M. Paul Holsinger (Westport: Greenwood, 1999), 284-85, p.285

2. Michael Wilmington, 'Movie Review: *Midnight* a Clear-Eyed Anti-War Film', in *The Los Angeles Times*, 1 May 1992.
    <*https://www.latimes.com/archives/la-xpm-1992-05-01-ca-1382-story.html*>

3. David Denby, 'Getting Serious', in *New York Magazine*, 18 May 1992, p.55.

4. James Berardinelli, '*A Midnight Clear*', in *ReelViews*, 20 December 2018.
    <*https://www.reelviews.net/reelviews/midnight-clear-a*>

5. Vincent Canby, 'Review/Film: *A Midnight Clear*; War Recalled as Surreal Muddle', in *The New York Times*, 24 April 1992.
    <*https://www.nytimes.com/1992/04/24/movies/review-film-a-midnight-clear-war-recalled-as-a-surreal-muddle.html*>

6. Susan E. Linville, *History Films, Women, and Freud's Uncanny* (Austin: University of Texas Press, 2004), p.62.

7. Michael Upchurch, '*Clear* and Present Danger', in *The Seattle Times*, 1 May 1992.
    <*https://archive.seattletimes.com/archive/?date=19920501&slug=1489485*>

8. Berardinelli.

9.   Hal Hinson, '*A Midnight Clear*', in *The Washington Post*, 1 May 1992.
     <*https://www.washingtonpost.com/wp-srv/style/longterm/movies/videos/amidnightclearrhinson_aoa76a.htm*>

10. Roger Ebert, '*A Midnight Clear*', in *The Chicago Sun-Times*, 1 May 1992.
     <*https://www.rogerebert.com/reviews/a-midnight-clear-1992*>

11. Marc Savlov, '*A Midnight Clear*', in *The Austin Chronicle*, 5 June 1992.
     <*https://www.austinchronicle.com/events/film/1992-06-05/a-midnight-clear/*>

12. John Bishop, '*A Midnight Clear + Inside Monkey Zetterland*', in *Mind of Frames*, 25 March 2015.
     <*https://mind-of-frames.blogspot.com/2015/03/a-midnight-clear-inside-monkey.html*>

13. Sam Turner, '*A Midnight Clear*: Blu-ray Review', in *Film Intel*, 10 April 2012.
     <*http://www.film-intel.com/2012/04/midnight-clear-blu-ray-review.html*>

14. Mike D'Angelo, '*A Midnight Clear*', in *AV Club*, 27 December 2010.
     <*https://www.avclub.com/a-midnight-clear-1798223380*>

6

The Nightmare Before Christmas (1993)

Touchstone Pictures / Skellington Productions Inc.

Director: Henry Selick
Producers: Tim Burton and Denise Di Novi
Screenwriter: Caroline Thompson, based on a story
and characters by Tim Burton

L IKE *The Muppet Christmas Carol* (q.v.) before it, the subtly-employed postmodernism of *The Nightmare Before Christmas* was to foreshadow the rather more amorphous, deconstructed approach to the festive season that was to continue developing far beyond the turn of the century. Although the film's deft employment of stop-motion techniques was to lend it a highly distinctive visual aspect which remains instantly recognisable even today, at its heart is an ebulliently vibrant collision of two diametrically opposed worlds: a narrative of playful juxtaposition which, for all its lack of convention, nonetheless remains acutely involved with the traditional concerns which underpin Christmas.

Just as *Home Alone* (q.v.) had introduced one of the predominant themes of 1990s Christmas film-making, namely the issue of the centrality of the family unit within the traditional Christmas narrative, *The Nightmare Before Christmas* was to concern itself more with the other prevalent topic to emerge throughout the decade: the importance of belonging. Although viewers had by now become well accustomed to festive narratives which stressed the significance of community and striving to have a positive effect upon the lives of those around us, the nineties came to lay new emphasis upon this familiar theme by instead examining the way that Christmas's unique seasonal blend of goodwill and altruism could help individuals to consider and redefine themselves, even if this meant challenging long-held perceptions about their lives and their past. *The Nightmare Before Christmas* was to establish itself as the very epitome of this premise, and its appealingly outlandish approach to its subject matter has meant that it has since come to be considered one of the most prominent festive films of the decade.

The film's origins reached all the way back to a poem that had been composed by Tim Burton in 1982, at a time when he was employed by Walt Disney Productions as an animator. This original verse is said to have been inspired by Burton watching an elaborate Halloween display being dismantled in a department store, and gradually being replaced by a brightly-lit display of Christmas merchandise. The visual divergence of supernatural monsters with the rather more comforting imagery of Santa Claus was to set his fertile imagination in motion. Burton had initially envisaged *The Nightmare Before Christmas* being developed into a short film or perhaps a made-for-TV special, though these plans never came to fruition. Given his rapid rise to fame throughout the eighties, Burton's creative options gradually broadened as time went by, and eventually in 1990 he was to return his attention to the story when he struck a development deal with

Disney to bring it to life on the big screen as a stop-motion feature. It was to be the culmination of Burton's lasting dedication to the project; believing strongly in the characters and premise, he had fought over a lengthy period to bring the project to life. As Mimi Avins explains, 'No stranger to alienation, [Burton] felt a kinship to Jack Skellington, tortured by his own soul-sickness. Since the visual imagery, story, and characters of *Nightmare Before Christmas* were close to his heart, Burton had felt particularly frustrated when Disney and all the TV networks to whom he and [production designer/art director Rick] Heinrichs originally brought the project rejected the idea of making it as a half-hour television special. [...] With the contractual promise of creative autonomy, a deal was struck to make *Nightmare Before Christmas* as Disney's first stop-motion animated feature'.[1]

Upon seeing the completed film and weighing up the subject matter, Disney executives eventually decided to distribute the film under the corporation's Touchstone Pictures label as they were concerned that the outlandish fantasy/horror elements of the movie would prove to be too scary to be suitable for younger children. While Burton was to act as the film's producer along with Denise Di Novi, the directorial and screenwriting responsibilities were taken up by others, and yet there was no denying that his characteristic flair for the macabre and the eccentric were instantly recognisable. As John Hartl has put it, 'Tim Burton's name is prominently displayed everywhere in the publicity for this Disney release – he even gets a possessive credit in the official title – even though he didn't write or direct it. This was, of course, true of Walt Disney's own projects, and it's usually true of John Hughes and George Lucas'.[2]

The Nightmare Before Christmas was directed by Henry Selick, a talented animator and stop-motion expert who had worked for Walt Disney Studios and in a freelance capacity before beginning work on this, his debut feature film. Known for his earlier short works which included *Seepage* (1982) and, for television, *Slow Bob in the Lower Dimensions* (1991), *The Nightmare Before Christmas* remains one of the greatest triumphs of his career, winning him critical acclaim as well as recognition at awards ceremonies. The film has, however, always been considered much more closely aligned to the inimitable visual style of its producer, Tim Burton, whose story and characters formed the basis for Caroline Thompson's screenplay. Burton had, by the early nineties, achieved great fame and the approval of many critics due to a well-regarded string of high-profile features which had included *Pee-Wee's Big Adventure* (1985), the monumentally successful superhero blockbuster *Batman* (1989) and its sequel *Batman Returns* (1992), the latter being a film which had demonstrated its own, uniquely dark take on the festive season. *The Nightmare Before Christmas*, however, owed the approach of its design more to the eccentric look of Burton's macabre *Beetle Juice* (1988) and the similarly off-the-wall peculiarities of *Edward Scissorhands* (1990), but few would deny that the finished product was a work of visual art which proved to be entirely original; a filmic experience which was charmingly offbeat and yet breathlessly inventive.

In a strange land where every holiday season has its own dimensional reality, Jack Skellington (voice of Chris Sarandon/singing voice of Danny Elfman), the Pumpkin King, rules over Halloween Town, a moody realm of vampires, witches, werewolves, and monsters under the stairs. The skeletal, good-natured Jack is the very epitome of Halloween, being full of enthusiasm for the morbid and ghoulish. The denizens of the town, including the Mayor (voice of Glenn Shadix), offer their heartfelt gratitude to their leader for another successfully scary season, glad that they have fulfilled their purpose of frightening people and generally being ghastly for another year. Jack has a particular secret admirer in Sally (voice of Catherine O'Hara), the Frankensteinian creation of the grisly scientific genius Dr Finklestein (voice of William Hickey). But unbeknownst to the townsfolk, Jack is secretly becoming disenchanted with conjuring up the same old terrors every year. Saddened at his growing lack of contentment, he sneaks away from the throng to find space for contemplation, little realising that he is silently being followed by Sally, who shares his sense of existential dissatisfaction.

The next morning, the Mayor arrives at Jack's house with the plans which have been drawn up for the following year's Halloween, but is confused when he discovers that the Pumpkin King is not at home. He doesn't realise that Jack has been walking all night in the forests outside the town. But the situation has become confusing to Jack too, for he is starting to discover that he has walked so far, he has left Halloween Town altogether. Arriving at an intersection point between different seasonal worlds, he finds unfamiliar markers on trees in a clearing which indicate a range of holidays that seem new and strange to him, including Easter, Thanksgiving and Valentine's Day. Becoming entranced by a particular symbol which looks like a decorated fir tree, Jack soon finds himself drawn into a curious vortex and whisked away from the familiarity of the dark forest.

Jack is eventually deposited in an ice-covered wonderland, full of snowmen, elves, skating penguins and colourful toys as far as the eye can see. He is stunned by this bizarre sight of comfort and joy, as the ways of Christmas Town are completely foreign concepts to him. Amazed by the strange sense of goodwill that he senses, Jack watches in astonishment as he sees the many different customs of Christmas played out in front of him: elves making toys, trees being decorated, mistletoe being hung, and electric fairy-lights being draped everywhere. Yet he is also puzzled by the complete absence of things that he has taken for granted in his native land, such as abundant creepy-crawlies and night terrors.

Over in Halloween Town, panic is beginning to grip the residents. Everyone has searched high and low for Jack, but to no avail. Then, just as they are beginning to lose hope, the Pumpkin King himself makes a triumphant return on a snowmobile, a large and suspicious-looking sackcloth bag tied up beside him. Jack hurriedly arranges a town meeting, where he explains all the wondrous things that he had seen in the land of Christmas. However, he soon finds that he has difficulty explaining the notion behind festive gifts and Christmas stockings to the assembled gathering of ghosts and monsters, all of whom expect every newly-presented idea to have a more sinister undertone than that which actually exists. Disappointed that they do not share his zeal for the wonders of this new season that he has discovered, Jack enthrals them with an account of the terrifying ruler of Christmas Town: a horrifying, dark-hearted fiend in a red suit who he calls Sandy Claws.

Back in his home, Jack is voraciously reading through every literary exploration of the festive season that he can lay his bony hands on, including Dickens's *A Christmas Carol*. He is growing increasingly exasperated at his inability to rationalise the goodwill and happiness of Christmas with his macabre, horror-centric mindset. Jack eventually decides to pay a visit to Dr Finklestein's laboratory to borrow some scientific equipment, and is soon setting up off-the-wall experiments with sprigs of holly, cuddly toys and candy canes in a last-ditch attempt to unlock the secrets of Christmas. But no amount of research is sufficient to allow Jack to reduce festive cheer into a simple equation, no matter how hard he tries. Even a surprise visit from Sally, who has temporarily slipped from the notice of her over-protective creator Dr Finklestein, can entirely brighten Jack's mood.

The next morning, the townsfolk are beginning to voice concern for Jack's single-minded obsession with fathoming the Christmas spirit when he proudly proclaims that he has had a moment of enlightenment: surely it isn't necessary to fully understand Christmas in order to enjoy it. To this end, he decides that Halloween Town will launch its own, rather unique version of Christmas... with some 'improvements' along the way. Jack enlists Dr Finklestein to create some Halloween-style flying reindeer, while the mischievous trick-or-treaters Lock, Shock and Barrel (voices of Paul Reubens, Catherine O'Hara and Danny Elfman) are given a secret task to which they are all sworn to secrecy: they must kidnap Santa Claus himself and bring him to Jack. But the impish trio are also henchmen of the spectral Oogie Boogie (Ken Page), who has his own rather more malign plans for Santa, to say nothing of Christmas in general.

Jack is holding auditions for Christmas acts (with rather mixed success) when Sally arrives and tells him that she has received a grim premonition of disaster arising from his attempts to construct a new kind of festive season from elements of Halloween. But her warning falls on deaf ears, as Jack is far more concerned with asking her to tailor him a Santa Claus outfit in time for Christmas. Sally's concerns are soon interrupted with the arrival of Lock, Shock and Barrel who, to Jack's manifest disdain, have kidnapped the Easter Bunny by mistake. This is but a temporary setback in Jack's plans, however, as he watches in satisfaction as his fellow towns-people work tirelessly to get ready for the imminent arrival of the festive season, busily constructing gifts which add a little deathly peril to the usual Christmas cheer. Even Dr Finklestein's efforts have come to fulfilment, with a set of levi-tating skeletal reindeer newly-constructed just in time to pull Jack's sleigh.

Back over in Christmas Town, everyone is blissfully aware of Jack's ill-conceived intentions as Christmas Eve ar-rives. Santa Claus (voice of Ed Ivory) is just in the process of checking his 'naughty and nice' list when his doorbell rings unexpectedly. Answering it, he discovers three diminutive trick-or-treaters... who promptly capture him in an oversized bag and take him to Halloween Town. Once there, Santa is shocked at the grim sight that meets him: a bizarre hotchpotch of the grim and the ghastly, all engaged in an effort to bring Christmas to life by the ghoulish power of Halloween. He demands to know why he has been kidnapped, but Jack seems content to simply tell him that he can consider this a well-earned vacation from his usual duties; this year, Christmas will be taken care of by his neighbours in Halloween Town. Pausing only to steal Santa's hat, Jack tells Lock, Shock and Barrel to keep jolly old Saint Nick comfortable until the fes-tive season is over, little realising that they plan to take him to Oogie Boogie's lair. Sally, meanwhile, pleads with Jack to re-consider his ill-intentioned plans, telling him that he is not being true to himself or even to the spirit of Halloween. But once again, Jack is too wrapped up in his plans to take heed of her sage warning.

The night of Christmas Eve comes at last, and Jack rises from what appears to be a coffin (actually his sleigh), resplendent in his somewhat avant-garde Santa Claus suit and ready to spread his own special brand of festive cheer. In an eleventh-hour attempt to force him to come to his senses, Sally creates a chemically-induced fog to impede the skeletal reindeers' take-off. Jack is momentarily devastated, his Christmas plans seemingly ruined, until he discovers that his ghostly pet dog Zero's nose is able to glow brightly enough to lead the way through the mist. Sally watches in dismay as the gruesome sleigh lurches into the night, Jack and the reindeers careening off into the sky.

Jack quickly sets about distributing his gifts in characteristically enthusiastic fashion, but his range of chilling presents – which include deadly snakes and shrunken heads – don't exactly go down well with their recipients, who react with widespread terror. The police are soon inundated with complaints about Jack's actions, which leads to a public service broadcast advising everyone that an impostor has ruined Christmas (an announcement which meets with widespread glee when it is heard in Halloween Town). The broadcaster explains that the U.S. Armed Forces are preparing to take action against this malign impersonator, a statement which spurs Sally to seek out the real Santa Claus in order to release him before Jack's sleigh is shot out of the sky.

While Jack dodges fire from anti-aircraft batteries (mistakenly thinking that the people of the Earth are thanking him with fireworks for his efforts), Sally makes her way to Oogie-Boogie's hideout where Santa is being held against his will. There, she launches an audacious attempt to spring the hapless hostage from the villainous ghost's clutches, but is ultimately defeated when her ruse is uncovered. Meanwhile,

Jack discovers too late that the military are trying to bring an end to his distinctive strain of festive cheer when a surface-to-air missile launcher scores a direct strike on his sleigh. Tumbling to the ground, the flaming wreckage eventually lands in an inner-city graveyard, where a bewildered Jack – his Santa suit now decidedly singed – wonders where it all went wrong. Finally realising the error of his ways, he reverts to his original persona as the Pumpkin King of Halloween and resolves to set things right while there's still time.

Back in Halloween Town, Oogie-Boogie is preparing to drown Santa and Sally in a vat of molten lead. Before he is able to do so, however, Jack returns in the nick of time and confronts his ghostly nemesis. Oogie-Boogie subjects Jack to a variety of mechanical defences, all of which he narrowly manages to overcome, before the malicious spectre eventually falls foul of his own bubbling vat. Jack sets Santa free with an apology, beseeching him to correct the terrible mistake that has been made. Now seriously miffed, Santa tells Jack that he will do his best, but suggests that in future Jack should listen to Sally's advice rather than arbitrarily wresting control of other holidays for no reason other than pure caprice.

As Jack finally begins to realise the true extent of Sally's feelings for him, Santa makes good on his promise and travels around the world faster than ever before, not just delivering 'real' Christmas gifts but efficiently removing all of Jack's horrifying presents into the bargain. He even makes the time for an impromptu visit to the skies above Halloween Town, delivering its first fall of snow (and deeply confusing the residents as a result). While the townsfolk come to terms with the night's tumultuous events, Jack meets Sally in the graveyard where he declares his love for her, all thoughts of his bungled attempts to take over Christmas now far from his mind.

If there is one thing that can be said for *The Nightmare Before Christmas*, it is that Tim Burton's stylistic imprimatur is clearly stamped upon each and every frame of the film. Director Henry Selick performs an incredible technical feat to bring the action to the screen with breathtaking energy, avoiding the jittery motion that had plagued some earlier stop-motion features – though he was no doubt aided by the fact that the movie required a group of around a hundred specialist film-makers and took around three years to complete, with many stop-motion movements making up a single second of the finished feature. Joshua Zyber is among many commentators who have praised the film's blend of artistic talent: 'Although technically directed by animator Henry Selick (later of *James and the Giant Peach*), Burton created the characters, wrote the story treatment, and designed just about everything in the picture. Pretty much the only thing he didn't do was actually manipulate the puppets frame by frame. The visual and thematic sensibilities are all his. The story of a misunderstood loner searching for meaning and acceptance in his life is a familiar concern from many, if not all of Burton's films, from *Pee-Wee* to *Edward Scissorhands* and beyond'.[3]

Burton's inimitable sense of the innovative and the macabre come to the fore in very rewarding ways, not least in the film's wealth of acutely-observed small details, and the celebration of traditional Halloween frights would strongly foreshadow many of Burton's later features, such as *Sleepy Hollow* (1999) and – most especially – *The Corpse Bride* (2005). Yet the keen creative eye of director Henry Selick is very much in evidence too, giving a foretaste of his later critical acclaim with films such as *James and the Giant Peach* (1996) and *Coraline* (2009). The film is positively brimming with entertainingly gruesome facets, from Jack's bizarrely ill-conceived experiments to deduce the meaning of Christmas through to the extensive raft of inventive character designs which include the trick-or-treaters' walking bathtub, the changing expressions of the Mayor's swivelling head, and the often-mystified Dr Finklestein who, when confused, scratches not his head but his exposed brain (thanks to a convenient flip-top scalp). The hapless inventor is the brunt of much of the film's darkest humour, not least during Sally's many innovative attempts to poison her domineering creator (as everyone in Halloween Town is already dead, of course, concotions which would otherwise prove lethal actually have little more than a soporific effect on him). Even the title is wickedly well-judged, the film's style and narrative being as far removed from Clement Clarke Moore's comfortingly traditional vision of the night before Christmas as it is possible to conceive. Yet as Kenneth Turan notes, behind this frenetic artistic dynamism lay a considerable technical challenge which had to be addressed even before the cameras started rolling:

> Bringing this genially demented world to life meant solving two different but interlocking problems. First off, Burton's drawings had to be turned into three-dimensional figures, and that has been done brilliantly. *Nightmare*'s crones, ghouls and grotesques – topped off by the ultimate incarnation of evil, the Oogie Boogie man (wonderfully served by Ken Page's jazzy phrasings) – are completely beyond description. And even if they weren't, it wouldn't be fair to ruin the fun of having them pop up unexpectedly in their own

disturbing way. The other problem was making everybody move. Given that each second of on-screen action involves 24 different frames, and possibly 24 separate character movements, the amount of painstaking planning and grinding work involved in this was daunting. To ensure a variety of expressions for Jack, for instance, 800 different replaceable heads were made. No wonder that at maximum efficiency, the *Nightmare* crew could turn out no more than 70 seconds of finished film per week. What they did turn out, however, is so profligate with exotic images that it overflows with a demented kind of genius, taking stop-motion to places it's never been before.[4]

Aside from the film's gleefully sinister wit and visual flair, screenwriter Caroline Thompson manages to weave engaging emotional observation into the narrative without her efforts ever relying overduly on the traditional sentimentality of conventional Christmas storytelling. Indeed, it has become clear that the film's engagement with the cultural conventions of Halloween are so central to its narrative, it has even sparked debate about whether *The Nightmare Before Christmas* should even be considered solely a Christmas movie at all. Chris Olson, for instance, observes that: 'Only a bespoke group of movies cause mass hubbub when the question of genre classification comes up at Christmas. To make it on to a list of "Festive Films" the criteria can differ greatly from person to person, such is the experience for a film like *Die Hard* (1988) or franchises which viewers typically watch at Christmas time, such as *Star Wars* or *Harry Potter*. But none of these movies compare to the intensely heated debate which arises when one tries to classify Henry Selick's movie, written by the incomparable Tim Burton, *The Nightmare Before Christmas*.[5] This clash of styles and traditions has led to numerous interpretations of the film's narrative amongst critics, some of them more far-reaching than others. In Jack's eagerness to cross-pollinate the conventions of Christmas and Halloween, some – such as Richard Corliss – were quick to pick up on a possible allegory of cross-cultural competition in an increasingly postmodern world: '*Nightmare* can be viewed as a parable of cultural imperialism, of the futility of imposing one's entertainment values on another society. (Euro Disneyland might come to some minds.) The apolitical moral is: cultivate your own garden or graveyard. Don't try to be somebody else. Know your place and your strengths, and make the most of them'.[6] Others have suggested a more vexed reading of cultural mores on Burton's part, reflecting a depth of consideration that surpasses many other entries in the same genre. M. Keith Booker, for instance, conjectures that the film's culture-clash premise may be seen as a critique of society's consumption of traditional conventions more generally: '*The Nightmare Before Christmas* contains potential layers of complexity that are decidedly non-Disney. For one thing, the contrast between Halloween Town and Christmas Town suggests contradictions in American (and Western) religious observances that go beyond simple cultural richness. The values commonly expressed in these two holidays as currently celebrated in our society are incompatible. [...] The film thus presents a potentially carnivalesque challenge that reverses the official priorities of Western society'.[7]

As his festive plans turn awry, Jack's woes stem from the fact that he is trying too hard to be someone that he is not, and in the process is therefore neglecting who he truly is. Jack is so keen to evade the tedium of yet another Halloween, a holiday that he knows so well, that he is willing to do any-thing to usurp Christmas, even if – by his own admission – he has next to no understanding of the indefinable alchemy that actually makes the season tick. In so doing, he not only feels compelled to forcibly remove Santa from his traditional role, but his obsessive focus on his plans to give Christmas a radical make-over allows the genuinely malign Oogie-Boogie the op-portunity to hatch his own, rather less altruistic scheme. Through misfortune Jack eventually learns the importance of being true to himself, and just in time to restore Christmas to normality. The ethereal Oogie-Boogie is vanquished, Santa released back to his annual duties, and – in finally recognising Sally's affections – Jack appears to accept that sometimes common sense and a realistic recognition of one's own limita-tions can be positive, self-enhancing factors rather than the symptom of a humdrum, stagnant mundanity as he had origi-nally believed.

Much of what makes *The Nightmare Before Christmas* so unique amongst festive films lies in the proficiently-articulated chaos which unfolds as the anarchic, ghoulish Hal-loween Town encroaches upon the ordered jollity of Christmas. As Barry J.C. Purves explains, this is expressed perfectly as a result of Selick's stop-motion approach, which allows for the communication of a meticulous dynamism just as much as it conveys the emotional spontaneity of the charac-ters: 'This is a groundbreaking film in so many respects, but what I really love is its energy. Too often with stop motion this energy is due to rather unruly frenetic animation, but here the energy is exquisitely controlled and dance like. The music and the camerawork sweep the audience along, but it's the animation itself that is so lively. [...] I wonder why there is so much stop motion associated with Christmas. Is this a

time when more stories are told, when more myths are circu-
lated and children are excited by all manner of fantasies? Or is
it about toys? There are always more stop motion pro-
grammes on at Christmas and it is fascinating that things
coming to life are seen to be a special treat'.[8] In casting the
comforting traditions of Christmas against the disorderly chaos of Halloween, rather than subverting either in a more
direct manner, Burton and Selick manage to make the fusion
of the two clashing holidays all the more arresting. There is a
great deal of gentle pathos in Jack's near-total inability to understand why the very things that make Halloween so unique
are anathema to the diametrically-different festive season.
Even by the film's conclusion, there is a nagging sense that
Jack probably still can't comprehend why it would be inappropriate to leave a man-eating snake beneath someone's
Christmas tree, but – we seem to be assured – he is now content to leave Santa to get on with the job of delivering
comfort and joy to the children of the world, and will instead
remain satisfied with rallying his kinsmen in the land of talking pumpkins and vampire bats.

In the creation of such distinctive worlds, both familiar
and yet strangely alien, the visual style of *The Nightmare Before Christmas* has made a continuing impression on cultural
commentators. Richard Harrington, for instance, noted that
'Burton has created his own skewed world, one that suggests
a kinship to a number of tricksters, among them Charles Addams, Edward Gorey, Gahan Wilson, Maurice Sendak and
Roald Dahl. This is a modern classic that enriches the
Christmas tradition by turning it on its head and spinning it
like a bob'.[9] In fact, it is the unabashed strangeness of the environment that is presented by Burton and Selick which adds
so much to the viewing experience; the viewer is lulled into a

false sense of security in the sense that even the more time-honoured aspects of Christmas are cast in a new light, allowing considerable subversion of expectation. As Roger Ebert noted at the time of the film's release:

> One of the many pleasures of Tim Burton's *The Nightmare Before Christmas* is that there is not a single recognizable landscape within it. Everything looks strange and haunting. Even Santa Claus would be difficult to recognize without his red-and-white uniform. [...] *The Nightmare Before Christmas* is a Tim Burton film in the sense that the story, its world and its look first took shape in Burton's mind, and he supervised their filming. But the director of the film, a veteran stop-action master named Henry Selick, is the person who has made it all work. And his achievement is enormous. Working with gifted artists and designers, he has made a world here that is as completely new as the worlds we saw for the first time in such films as *Metropolis* (1927), *The Cabinet of Dr. Caligari* or *Star Wars.* What all of these films have in common is a visual richness, so abundant that they deserve more than one viewing. First, go for the story. Then go back just to look in the corners of the screen, and appreciate the little visual surprises and inspirations that are tucked into every nook and cranny.[10]

It is difficult to overstate the skill by which the film's animated figures are able to articulate a full range of emotional expressions; Selick's painstaking work, particularly with the lead character of Jack, is near-faultless in its capacity to express the broadest extent of feelings and sentiments. Yet the ground-breaking character design is only one part of the artistic success of *The Nightmare Before Christmas*. Danny Elfman provides not just a characteristically lively score but also a full range of songs throughout the film, the most memorable of them almost certainly proving to be 'What's This?', performed by Jack upon being confronted with the many bewildering sights of Christmas Town when he first arrives there. Nominated for Academy Awards on four separate occasions (including two in the same year in 1997), Elfman has been a long-term collaborator with Burton on a wide range of cinematic projects, having provided the original score for many of his projects which, at the time, had included *Pee-wee's Big Adventure* (1985), *Beetle Juice* (1988), *Batman* (1989), *Edward Scissorhands* (1990) and *Batman Returns* (1992), as well as for a diverse range of other feature films such as *Scrooged* (Richard Donner, 1988), *Midnight Run* (Martin Brest, 1988), *Dick Tracy* (Warren Beatty, 1990) and *Nightbreed* (Clive Barker, 1990). Additionally, Elfman was to provide Jack Skellington's singing voice throughout the film, while the character's general dialogue was performed by experienced actor Chris Sarandon.

For a film with such distinctive model-work, where every expression is so faithfully reproduced, it only stands to reason that the quality of the voice acting for *The Nightmare Before Christmas* would prove essential to the film's success. It is fortunate, then, that the movie is aided by such a wide range of well-delivered performances, key among them being Sarandon's astonishingly varied portrayal of Jack. Able to bring the spindly figure alive with great aplomb, Sarandon manages to wring every possible emotion from the conflicted skeleton, conjuring up ennui and dissatisfaction just as ably as he evokes the character's sense of wonder and single-mindedness. The result is a performance that is both charming and accessible throughout, no matter how outlandish Jack's surrounding environment may happen to be at any given time. Sarandon was well-known to audiences from the 1970s onwards, when he had been nominated for the Best Actor in a Supporting Role Academy Award for his extraordinary performance as Leon Shermer in Sidney Lumet's *Dog Day Afternoon* (1975). Later to appear in films as varied as *The Sentinel* (Michael Winner, 1977), *The Osterman Weekend* (Sam Peckinpah, 1983) and *The Princess Bride* (Rob Reiner, 1987), he had already ably proven his horror credentials with prominent roles in films such as Tom Holland's *Fright Night* (1985) and *Child's Play* (1988).

Sarandon is proficiently supported in *The Nightmare Before Christmas* by Catherine O'Hara, well established in the public consciousness at the time for having played ill-fated suburban mother Kate McCallister in the first two entries in the *Home Alone* series. In the role of Sally, the kindly, detachable-limbed creation of Dr Finklestein, O'Hara crafts a strangely likeable character who is full of empathy and compassion... but who is not above a little poisoning and deception where necessary (all in the very best traditions of Halloween Town, of course). A veteran of television's *Second City TV* between 1976-79 and 1981-84, O'Hara had made cinematic appearances in films throughout the eighties which had included *After Hours* (Martin Scorsese, 1985), *Heartburn* (Mike Nichols, 1986), and Tim Burton's own *Beetle Juice*, as well as a range of nineties features such as *Betsy's Wedding* (Alan Alda, 1990) and *Dick Tracy*. In 2010, O'Hara was awarded an Emmy Award in the category of Outstanding

Supporting Actress in a Miniseries or Movie for her performance in HBO's *Temple Grandin* (2010).

The film benefits from an impeccable range of supporting voice performances, delivered by an extremely varied range of actors. These included William Hickey, so memorable as Uncle Lewis in *National Lampoon's Christmas Vacation* (Jeremiah Chechik, 1989) but probably best-remembered by many as ageing Mafia Don Corrado Prizzi in John Huston's *Prizzi's Honor* (1985); Paul Reubens, very well-known in the popular culture of the time for his screen guise as the madcap Pee-Wee Herman; and talented improvisational comedian and voice actor Greg Proops, celebrated for his many appearances in the UK on Channel 4's *Whose Line is it Anyway?* (1988-99). Glenn Shadix impresses as the nervy, indecisive Mayor of Halloween Town, as does Ed Ivory as the permanently bewildered Santa Claus. Particular mention, however, must go to Ken Page for a no-holds-barred performance as the playfully malevolent Oogie-Boogie. Able to perfectly meld the frivolous and the genuinely sinister, Page ensures that his character becomes a truly memorable villain for the most unconventional of films.

The Nightmare Before Christmas generally performed well with critics at the time of its release, with an overwhelmingly positive response from most commentators. Many, such as David Ansen, were effusive in their praise of the film's pioneering visual style: 'This giddily imaginative stop-motion animation musical is so stuffed with visual delights you won't want to blink. [...] The list of marvels could go on and on, testament to the teeming imagination of Burton, who dreamed up this treat more than a decade ago as a young animator at Disney. Now, back at Disney, his magic toyshop of a movie has come to sweetly malignant fife. Chances are, it will be around for many Halloweens to come'.[11] Yet proving (as though it were ever in any doubt) that all taste is subjective, others such as Harper Barnes took aim at the film's employ-ment of stop-motion and the consistency of its narrative: 'In the hands of some Eastern European masters, stop-motion animation has created some fine adult animated films, like Jan Svankmajer's spooky version of *Alice in Wonderland*. But *The Nightmare Before Christmas* is basically a charmless and muddled tale that aims at a target somewhere in the vast gulf between Franz Kafka and Walt Disney and hits nothing'.[12]

These sentiments were echoed by Owen Gleiberman, who considered the film to be rather less than the sum of its parts and found its thematic intentions unfocused: 'As we stare at Jack's empty eyes (and listen to his blandly incongru-ous, nice-animated-guy voice), there's nothing to hook into – no personality, no spark. He's a technical achievement in search of a soul. And so is the movie. I'm not sure I've ever seen a fantasy film that's at once so visually amazing and so emotionally dead. [...] *The Nightmare Before Christmas* is a fable in which the spirit of Christmas finally triumphs over that of Halloween. Yet it's clear that Burton's allegiance will always be with the ghouls, not the goody-goodies. Is it any wonder this *Nightmare* never coalesces? He couldn't make up his mind about whether to be naughty or nice'.[13] Overall, however, most reviewers of the time commended the skilful subversion of recognised Christmas tropes into something en-tirely new and original, with many paying tribute to Tim Burton and Henry Selick's care in presenting an inventive world of gothic scares which never alienates its youthful audi-ence. Yet as Marjorie Baumgarten suggests with tempered enthusiasm, it is for the visual feast which the film conjures up that it is likely to be most fondly remembered: 'You will also find yourself reveling in the sheer majesty of these images. And for that experience alone, the movie is a must-see. Unfortunately, there is little else to recommend *Nightmare*. The story is slight and can best be described as *The Grinch Who Stole Christmas* in reverse. [...] With tie-ins to both Halloween and Christmas, this one's likely to linger in the theatres a while. And while I'd like to encourage the continuance of this sort of animation, I'd like to caution about this type of cast-off storytelling'.[14]

The film has remained enduringly popular in the years following its release, quickly accumulating cult credibility and maintaining a lasting high regard amongst other Christmas features of the same vintage. Its profile has only been bolstered by its re-release in cinemas between 2006 and 2010, this time being issued in Disney Digital 3D, and as such *The Nightmare Before Christmas* has continued to uphold and even enhance its critical reputation in recent years. Modern commentators have continued to pay homage to the film's winning performances and its unique, moody sense of the fantastic, with relatively few dissenting voices in the general chorus of approval amongst reviewers. As Chris Olson notes, 'Like several other Christmas movies, *The Nightmare Before Christmas* is a musical – delivering anthemic melodies that have remained in the popular mindset since the film's release. By opting for this dramatic form, the animated film is able to transcend the rigid borderlines between genres like horror, animation, children's movies and the like, and instead focus on literally sculpting its own place in the Christmas narrative. [...] There is simply too much to love about Selick's film, and Burton's creations, for it to be confined to the shackles of animated horror. In fact, this is a film for October, December, and any month you want to see a hugely impressive piece of animated genius'.[15]

Other reviewers, such as Mike Long, have opined that the film's visual appeal sometimes diverts viewers from imperfections in the execution of its narrative: 'The movie is very different and entertaining, but it's not perfect. Although I'm a huge fan of *The Nightmare Before Christmas*, I must point out its foibles. The main problem with the movie is the Oogie Boogie character, who adds nothing to the movie. The Oogie Boogie scene feels very tacked on and the last thing that this movie needed was a villain. The fact that Jack is going up against great odds is story enough'.[16] Contrastingly, Joshua Zyber revels in the film's dizzying deconstruction of expectations and traditional conventions, holding up its gleefully carnivalesque qualities as being key to its charm: 'In its completed form, *Nightmare* plays like a demented Rankin & Bass holiday special, by way of a German Expressionist silent film, a classic Universal horror picture, and a Hollywood musical. The movie is a giddy mix of pop culture influences, and yet clearly, unmistakably Tim Burton through and through. [...] Released under the Touchstone banner because Disney CEO Michael Eisner deemed it "too dark for kids" and didn't want it to bear the Walt Disney Pictures logo, *Nightmare* opened in the Fall of 1993 to tremendous critical acclaim. The movie didn't have the box office power of Disney's *The Lion King* or *Aladdin*, but performed quite well and has gone on to become a holiday classic that just happens to bridge two holidays, making for a great treat to watch at both Halloween and Christmas every year'.[17] And as Keith Phipps was to argue, even in spite of the varying appraisals surrounding the effectiveness of the film's storyline, the film's unrelenting charm and chaotic vitality seem fated to make it amongst the most memorable Christmas movies of the 1990s: 'Even at a mere 75 minutes, *Nightmare* occasionally seems short on story. What it offers instead – morbid whimsy, a winning sweetness, and an abundance of imagination – makes those flaws easy to overlook. Deftly crafted enough to make a skeleton dissecting a teddy bear or the sight of children terrorized by an evil toy duck seem cute, *Nightmare* taps directly into Burton's unique sensibility, bringing it to life with highly memorable results'.[18]

The Nightmare Before Christmas was nominated for the Best Visual Effects Award at the 1994 Academy Awards, the nomination shared between effects team members Pete Kozachik, Eric Leighton, Ariel Velasco-Shaw and Gordon Baker. Danny Elfman's score for the film was nominated for the Best Original Score (Motion Picture) Award at the Golden Globes in the same year, and he was to win the Saturn Award for Best Music, while the film itself picked up the Best Fantasy Film Award at the same ceremony. There were also Saturn nominations for Best Director for Henry Selick, and in the Best Special Effects category. Additionally, the film was nominated for the Best Dramatic Presentation Award at the Hugo Awards, and the Outstanding Family Motion Picture Award at the Young Artist Awards ceremony. There was further success at the Annie Awards, where Henry Selick was honoured with the Best Individual Achievement for Creative Supervision in the Field of Animation Award, and art director Deane Taylor was conferred the Best Individual Achievement for Artistic Excellence in the Field of Animation Award. *The Nightmare Before Christmas* itself was nominated for the Best Animated Film Award at the same year's Annie Awards ceremony.

Even after almost three decades have passed since its initial release, no other animated Christmas film has managed to come anywhere close to recapturing the dark gothic charm of Burton and Selick's unique festive caper. It is perhaps for this reason that it has remained so popular with audiences, reissued again and again on DVD and Blu-Ray as well as, in recent years, making seasonal appearances in cinemas (both in its original 2D and new 3D incarnations). It has also been the basis for a number of spin-off comics, video games and novels, as well as a live concert which debuted at the Hollywood Bowl in October 2015. *The Nightmare Before Christmas* has proven to be the perfect blend of seasonal charm and creative innovation, conjuring up a hugely distinctive world where the cosy and the macabre collide in a way which seems simultaneously energising and eye-catching. Yet its core theme, which speaks so clearly about the importance of recognising the authenticity of our individual character traits and sense of purpose, is counterbalanced by an exploration of Jack's reliance on – and the support provided by – his honorary 'family', the citizens of Halloween Town. These topics of family and belonging, which proved to be so prominent in nineties festive film-making, would also come to the fore later in the decade, where they would emerge in quite strikingly different configurations.

REFERENCES

1.   Mimi Avins, 'Ghoul World', in *Tim Burton: Interviews*, ed. by Kristian Fraga (Jackson: University Press of Mississippi, 2005), 95-101, p.98.

2.   John Hartl, 'An Animation Dream – *Nightmare Before Christmas* is Visual Treat, But it Lacks Vision', in *The Seattle Times*, 22 October 1993.
      <https://archive.seattletimes.com/archive/?date=19931022&slug=1727371>

3.   Joshua Zyber, '*The Nightmare Before Christmas*', in *High-Def Digest*, 25 August 2008.
      <https://bluray.highdefdigest.com/1207/nightmarebeforec hristmas.html>

4.   Kenneth Turan, 'Movie Reviews: Burton Dreams Up a Delightful *Nightmare*', in *The Los Angeles Times*, 15 October 1993.
      <https://www.latimes.com/archives/la-xpm-1993-10-15-ca-45836-story.html>

5.   Chris Olson, '*The Nightmare Before Christmas* Film Review', in *UK Film Review*, 22 December 2015.
      <https://www.ukfilmreview.co.uk/post/the-nightmare-before-christmas-1993-film-review>

6.   Richard Corliss, 'A Sweet and Scary Treat: *The Nightmare Before Christmas* spins a fun-house fantasy for two holidays', in *Time*, 11 October 1993.
      <https://content.time.com/time/subscriber/article/0,33009 ,979351-2,00.html>

7.	M. Keith Booker, *Disney, Pixar, and the Hidden Messages of Children's Films* (Santa Barbara: Praeger, 2010), p.121.

8.	Barry J.C. Purves, *Stop Motion: Passion, Process and Performance* (Oxford: Focal Press, 2008), p.299.

9.	Richard Harrington, '*The Nightmare Before Christmas*', in *The Washington Post*, 22 October 1993.
<https://www.washingtonpost.com/wp-srv/style/longterm/movies/videos/thenightmarebeforechristmaspgharrington_a0ab93.htm>

10.	Roger Ebert, '*The Nightmare Before Christmas*', in *The Chicago Sun-Times*, 22 October 1993.
<https://www.rogerebert.com/reviews/tim-burtons-the-nightmare-before-christmas-1993>

11.	David Ansen, 'Movies: Tim Burton Looks at Holiday Hell', in *Newsweek*, 31 October 1993.
<https://www.newsweek.com/movies-tim-burton-looks-holiday-hell-194070>

12.	Harper Barnes, '*The Nightmare Before Christmas*', in *The St Louis Post-Dispatch*, 22 October 1993, p.3.

13.	Owen Gleiberman, 'Tim Burton's *The Nightmare Before Christmas*', in *Entertainment Weekly*, 7 August 2012.
<https://ew.com/article/2012/08/07/tim-burtons-nightmare-christmas-2/>

14.	Marjorie Baumgarten, '*The Nightmare Before Christmas*', in *The Austin Chronicle*, 29 October 1993.
<https://www.austinchronicle.com/events/film/1993-10-29/140073/>

15.	Olson.

16.   Mike Long, '*The Nightmare Before Christmas*', in *DVD Sleuth*, 26 August 2008.
       <https://www.dvdsleuth.com/NightmareBeforeChristmas Review/>

17.   Zyber.

18.   Keith Phipps, '*The Nightmare Before Christmas*', in *AV Club*, 29 March 2002.
       <https://www.avclub.com/the-nightmare-before-christmas-1798195605>

7

Miracle on 34ᵗʰ Street (1994)

Twentieth Century Fox / Hughes Entertainment

Director: Les Mayfield
Producer: John Hughes
Screenwriter: John Hughes, from the screenplay by
George Seaton and a story by Valentine Davies

MIRACLE *on 34ᵗʰ Street* (George Seaton, 1947) is widely regarded as one of the most beloved Christmas movies of the genre's golden age, and is a film which has genuinely stood the test of time. With its perennial themes of belief, family and friendship, the feature won three Academy Awards and has been preserved in the United States National Film Registry and the Academy Film Archive in 2005 and 2009 respectively. Arguably best-remembered for Edmund Gwenn's spirited, warm-hearted performance as a department store Santa Claus who turns out to be rather more than he seems (a role which won Gwenn the Academy Award for Best Actor in a Supporting Role), this beloved film has been remade several times for television, with features including CBS's *Miracle on 34ᵗʰ Street* (Robert Stevenson, 1955), starring Thomas Mitchell; NBC's *Miracle on 34ᵗʰ Street*, featuring Ed Wynn (William Corrigan, 1959); and CBS's *Miracle on 34ᵗʰ Street* with Sebastian Cabot headlining (Fielder Cook, 1973). It has also been adapted for radio several times as well as appearing in the form of a Macy's Department Store puppet show in 2012, and was even developed into a stage musical – *Here's Love* – on Broadway in 1963, and as a stage drama in 2000.

Being held in such high esteem by critics and audiences, *Miracle on 34th Street* may have seemed an unlikely choice for a big screen remake in the late nineties, and yet that was exactly what John Hughes would choose to create in 1994 – amidst much public interest. The film saw Hughes continue his engagement with festive film-making with what would debatably be the most challenging entry in his loose sequence of festively-themed movies, which started with *National Lampoon's Christmas Vacation* (Jeremiah Chechik, 1989) and continued with *Home Alone* (q.v.) and its sequel, *Home Alone 2: Lost in New York* (Chris Columbus, 1992). With this popular remake of George Seaton's iconic silver screen classic, Hughes not only revisited his earlier themes of celebrating the family unit and honouring the importance of the domestic over the corporate, but also established the foundation for a renaissance of golden age Christmas movie remakes by other directors later in the decade.

With its genesis harking back to a formative period in the history of Christmas cinema, when the conventions which define the genre were still being laid down throughout the 1940s and 50s, the original *Miracle on 34th Street* had been established for decades as a bona fide landmark in the development of the festive film, with none of the subsequent TV updates coming anywhere close to supplanting its towering status. Even today, Seaton's film remains one of the best-loved of all Christmas movies, and there are very few motion pictures in any genre which encapsulate so vividly the excitement of childhood expectation towards the festive season, or which underscore with such panache a willingness to retain a healthy faith in that which remains indefinable – irrespective of what anyone's ideological, philosophical, or religious background may be.

Hughes's choice to direct the film was Les Mayfield, who at the time was best-known for helming the comedy *Encino Man* (1992) and who would collaborate with Hughes again a few years later on the whimsical comedy remake *Flubber* (1997), starring Robin Williams. This new cinematic revision of *Miracle on 34th Street* was to arrive in cinemas during the November of 1994, just in time for the lucrative Christmas market. Hughes's screenplay was forced to perform a difficult balancing act in the sense that his audience would expect a degree of fidelity to the original film while also anticipating heightened relevance to modern day sensibilities. Atttempting to walk this creative tightrope led to decidedly mixed responses from critics; as Thomas S. Hischak observes, 'The script by John Hughes follows the original story but, the movie being twenty minutes longer than the 1947 version, he adds things that are dead weight, such as a quickie wedding, a silly real estate agent, and some religious nonsense that goes nowhere. [...] The movie often wallows in sentimentality not found in earlier versions yet so much of it seems false'.[1]

Deftly reworking Seaton's earlier screenplay (which itself had been based on a story by Valentine Davies and his subsequent, bestselling 1947 novella-length prose adaptation), Hughes was at pains to take account of the social and cultural changes which had occurred in the intervening decades. That being said, many similarities remained between the two versions. As in the original film, a kindly old gentleman named Kriss Kringle (identified as 'Kris' in the Seaton movie) finds

189

himself persuaded to become a department store's Santa Claus over the holiday period, but winds up a victim of his own success – when Kriss's kindly nature brings about enthusiastic publicity and new customers in their droves, a vindictive rival seeks to call his mental stability into question, leading to his incarceration. (The antagonist in the original film is a crank psychologist with a grudge named Granville Sawyer, portrayed by Porter Hall; the shady forces running a rival – and fictional – department store take up a similar adversarial role in the remake.) This causes particular distress to one of the store's executives, Dorey Walker (Elizabeth Perkins, succeeding Maureen O'Hara's Doris from the original), and her daughter Susan (Mara Wilson, in the role initially made famous by Natalie Wood) – a skeptical child whose friendship with Kriss slowly makes her question her incredulity towards Santa Claus and his mythical powers, mirroring the plot developments of the original movie. Dylan McDermott's compassionate city lawyer Bryan Bedford (named Fred Gailey in Seaton's original and played by John Payne) takes up the subsequent court case resulting from Kriss's evaluation, leading to a lengthy legal battle which ultimately proves not only that Santa Claus exists, but that he does so in the form of the humble Mr Kringle.

As Holly Chard has noted, Hughes's soaring reputation at the time secured the film the confidence of the studio, ensuring that it enjoyed a high profile amongst the year's cinematic releases: 'To ensure that the film had production values befitting of a prestigious release, the studio allocated Hughes a substantial budget of $28 million. [...] To downplay any accusations that the remake was cynically motivated, Fox and Hughes were careful to frame their interest in the project in emotional terms, evoking nostalgia for traditional family

Christmases and building on the original movie's status as a "classic". The movie's executive producer, Bill Ryan, reinforced Hughes's suitability for the project and focused on the personal reasons for his involvement in the remake. Shortly before the film's release, Ryan stated, "The film's themes are very dear to John. Faith; believing in people; and the meaning of Christmas, when people go out of their way to help each other"".[2] In so doing, the creative aim was clearly to preserve the charm and affirmatory themes of the original movie whilst also producing a feature that had heightened social and cultural relevance to the present day.

It is the Thanksgiving period in New York City, and Dorey Walker (Elizabeth Perkins) – events director at a major department store named Cole's – is at her wits' end. Mere weeks before Christmas, and shortly before the company's opulent Thanksgiving parade, she spots a neatly-dressed, elderly gent (Richard Attenborough) berating the company's costumed Santa Claus, Tony Falacchi (Jack McGee), for being drunk on the job and setting a terrible example. Dorey has no choice but to fire Falacchi for dereliction of duty, but is then short of a Santa to lead the parade. With some desperation, she asks the kindly old man – who has a trim white beard and a very pleasant, festive demeanour – if he will consider standing in at short notice. The modest gentleman agrees, and introduces himself as none other than Kriss Kringle.

Kriss makes such an immediate impact as Santa Claus that Cole's decide to offer him seasonal employment in the role over the Christmas period. He immediately becomes a hit with the city's children and families, as his benevolent manner is so authentic everyone becomes convinced that he might just be the real thing. However, Dorey's young daughter Susan (Mara Wilson) remains unconvinced. Her mother has raised her to be rational and sceptical, and she is highly resistant to the wonder of Christmas.

Susan's disbelief troubles Dorey's boyfriend, city lawyer Bryan Bedford (Dylan McDermott), who believes that childhood should be full of exciting dreams and reckons that cynicism is best left until adulthood, where it can be found in abundance. Bryan knows that Dorey's own hard-nosed rationalism and disillusionment are rubbing off on Susan, so he tries his best to foster a sense of fun and adventure in the stubbornly disbelieving young girl. His efforts are unknowingly bolstered later when, during a babysitting session with Kriss, Susan conspiratorially tells the old man that she has a secret trio of Christmas wishes: she wants a father figure, a baby brother, and an idyllic suburban house similar to the one that Cole's has used as a location for their sales catalogues due to its picturesque appearance. Smiling, and knowing that this is a tall order, Kriss enquires whether receiving these three wishes would make Susan believe in Santa Claus. Upon reflection, Susan decides that this would indeed provide the proof that she has been searching for.

Much to the delight of Cole's general manager, the dapper Donald Shellhammer (Simon Jones), Kriss's remarkable rapport with the customers is responsible for greatly increasing the store's sales in the approach to the holiday period, and the top brass are impressed by his efforts. However, little do any of them realise that trouble is brewing. Victor Landberg (an uncredited Joss Ackland), the scheming owner of rival department store Shopper's Express, has hatched a plan to remove Kriss from his post – and ideally create some scandal for Cole's into the bargain. Plotting with Tony Falacchi, the recently-dismissed Santa (who now bears a grudge against Kriss), the underhanded competitors conspire to trick

Kriss into attacking Tony, thus framing him for assault. The accusation thus becomes that Kriss is mentally incapable of fulfilling his role as the store's Santa Claus.

Keen to help her new friend, and seeking to limit damage to Cole's reputation, Dorey enlists Bryan's help in having Kriss's case heard in court. Given that he is beloved by all of the shoppers who visit the department store, the public are very much on his side – even if Cole's management are somewhat nervous at the potential damage to their professional reputation depending on the outcome of the trial. The presiding Judge, Henry Harper (Robert Prosky), finds himself in an impossible situation, as he has no desire to rule that Kriss is not Santa Claus and thus lead to the disillusionment of countless children. There is similar awkwardness for prosecutor Ed Collins (J.T. Walsh), who is all too aware that his success in the case will be predicated on the disappointment of the general public – even though the rule of law must be upheld. However, in order for Bryan to win the case, he must somehow formulate a way to prove two separate factors: firstly, that Santa Claus really does exist – and secondly, that Kriss Kringle is that very same Santa Claus.

Bryan begins to lose hope, but at the eleventh hour he hatches one last desperate plan to save Kriss from being institutionalised. Just as the judge is about to pass his verdict, Susan hands him a Christmas card. Inside is a single dollar bill – but in spite of appearances, bribery is not her intention. On the dollar, the phrase 'In God we Trust' has been highlighted. Thinking quickly, Harper realises that Bryan has inadvertently handed him the escape route he has so urgently been looking for. Because the US Treasury Department can print every dollar bill with this statement on it, it is declaring its faith in a higher being as an act of belief, not a matter of material proof. Thus if the government can act on faith, why can't the many people in the city believe – in the same way – that Kriss Kringle is Santa Claus? Therefore, with some relief, Harper is able to dismiss the case by asserting that not only is Santa Claus a real person, but that he and Kriss Kringle are one in the same.

Now that Kriss's liberty has been assured, Dorey and Bryan are ecstatic and decide to formalise their relationship, marrying in a church following the traditional Christmas Eve service there. The next morning, the family awaken to see the arrival of Christmas Day, and Susan is overjoyed by the discovery that Bryan is now her stepfather. However, there is little time to process this information as the three of them are due to meet with Shellhammer at a house in the suburbs. Upon arrival, they realise that this is not the work-related event they had initially supposed – working behind the scenes, Kriss has orchestrated the possibility of the new family being able to buy the property as their new home. Knowing that this is the dream house that she has always dreamed of, Susan is beyond excited. While it would normally be beyond her price range, Dorey has received a generous Christmas bonus from her employers due to her part in signing up Kriss to work at Cole's, and she is now able to make the purchase. Susan races to her new room, knowing that this is has truly become her best Christmas ever, and Dorey asks her if all of her wishes have now been fulfilled. Her daughter replies that as she now has a new stepfather and her ideal home, all that remains is the arrival of her new baby brother. Bryan and Dorey glance at each other with some degree of astonishment, suspecting that Kriss's magic may just deliver that final wish in around nine months' time. Unfortunately they have no way of thanking their avuncular benefactor, as it seems that he is currently taking care of some pressing business overseas.

Mayfield and Hughes's remake of *Miracle on 34th Street* offers a number of key narrative changes from Seaton's earlier movie; much of the explicit psychological analysis content is eliminated from the plot, including the conniving character of Granville Sawyer, meaning that the guileless Kriss's downfall is engineered in a much more premediated way. Just as prominently, the two major New York department stores of the 1947 film are now replaced by fictional counterparts. As William D. Crump explains, 'The names of the two department stores, Macy's and Gimbels, were changed, respectively, to C.F. Cole's and to Shopper's Express, because Macy's denied the use of its name for the film, and Gimbels no longer existed at this time'.[3] This led to inevitable production challenges, in the sense that participation in the annual Macy's Thanksgiving Parade was also not allowed, meaning that an entirely different procession for the opening sequence of the film had to be staged from scratch.

However, at its core the film retains the same message of remembering the vital importance of belief in the individual, substituting the earlier film's conclusion (where mailbags full of letters to Santa are decanted into a New York courtroom) for a rather more low-key climax which contains an understated subtext focusing on the very concept of faith, drawing subtle parallels between belief in the spirit of Christmas and the simple act of trust. This rather more explicitly religious approach to how people perceive the act of faith led to some controversy amongst commentators, given that the America of the 1990s was a considerably more secular nation than it had been during the immediate post-War period of the original film. This inevitably led to some dispute, though for many critics the defining issue was not that of the material rationalism vs spirituality debate, but rather the sense that Hughes's screenplay labours the disparity in a rather heavy-handed way that the 1947 film had not. Leonard Norwitz, for instance, opines that: 'There's a naiveté in Seaton's original that makes the whole thing work which does not exist in the remake. Hughes analyses and explains and is careful about how he goes about it. The judge's wording when he talks about "In God we trust" is a brilliant exercise in diplomacy, but by the time we get there, what innocence there might have been has been pared away. Seaton's "Faith is believing when common sense tells you not to" may be simple-minded and hardly a generous explanation of faith, but it does describe well enough the relationship between faith and reason'.[4] Furthermore, the decision to change the film's conclusion turned out to be contentious in other ways – namely that the means devised by Hughes to affirm the nature and purpose of Kriss inadvertently contradicts the legal conclusion that was revealed in the original George Seaton screenplay. As Richard Scheib explains:

> There is the end where the court case is won when it is shown that the US Government, by placing the phrase 'In God We Trust' on the dollar bill, confirms the existence of a higher authority. This specific piece of preaching is particularly conspicuous in that it specifically changes the way that the court case was won in the original. In the original, the court case was won when the Postal Service delivered all the dead-letter mail addressed to Santa to the court thus confirming that a US Government department believed that Kriss was Santa. There was no reference to a higher authori-

ty or the existence of God. There is no reason why the old ending would not have worked this time around. [...] The Christian message being preached is certainly an odd one. What, after all, is one to make of Dylan McDermott's rhetorical question: "We ask the court to judge what is better – a lie that brings a smile or a truth that brings a tear?" The religion being offered seems to be one that favours feelgood sentiment – believe it because it should be true, not because it is.[5]

If Hughes's exploration of the significance of faith suggested an underlying preoccupation with traditionalism, so too did the film's handling of the issue of divorce. Back in the 1940s, the original film's handling of marital breakdown was something of a novelty for a family film, with the Catholic Legion of Decency billing the feature 'morally objectionable in part' largely on account of Maureen O'Hara's Doris having undergone a divorce prior to the events of the film.[6] By the 1990s, with the dissolution of marriage having become a much more common fact of domestic life, the way that movies handled the issue – particularly in the context of Christmas – was beginning to change. Features such as *All I Want for Christmas* (q.v) had framed divorce as a kind of existential threat to the nuclear family, considering traditional notions of hearth and home as being central to the ideal Christmas. Others, such as *The Santa Clause* (q.v.) – which was released at around the same time as *Miracle on 34th Street* – took a rather more progressive view of the subject, instead considering family to be a more malleable structure than tradition may suggest and thus advancing the view that it is the people close to us which makes Christmas special; it need not necessarily be a matter of blood relations. Hughes's screenplay for *Miracle on*

34th Street generally favours the former approach over the latter, earning it some critical scepticism that its attitudes were somewhat out of step with the social customs of the time. Douglas Hildebrand, for example, makes the point that, 'Mayfield's *Miracle on 34th Street* has a lot of charm and is generally good-natured, if somewhat sentimental. However, a central theme – that of the virtue of the traditional suburban, nuclear family – is dated, and can be read as a manifesto for "family values" conservatives'.[7]

In defence of Hughes's screenplay, it is clear that he is far from oblivious to the profound social changes to have taken place between the era of the original film and the present day of 1994, and indeed Kriss's occasional sense of despondency over the cynical inability of people in modern times to realise the wonder, kindness and altruism of Christmas seems all the more poignant against the backdrop of the derisive, hard-nosed nineties than it had even done in the comparatively unworldly cultural environment of the late 1940s. Crump notes that 'two particular scenes reflect a 1990s sensibility: Bryan does not invoke the name of any specific deity while saying grace before a meal with Dorey and Susan, and the name on the newlyweds' mailbox reads "Walker-Bedford"'[8] (also a sly evocation of Bedford Falls, the idyllic American community of Frank Capra's 1946 classic *It's a Wonderful Life*), but Hughes's strangely paradoxical meditation on modernity reaches further than that. Reflected in Mayfield's direction, there is some interesting sleight of hand being conducted to ensure equilibrium between the wide-eyed wonder of Seaton's original and an acknowledgement of the sceptical, apprehensive and technologically-advanced environment of the present day. Yet as Hal Hinson has argued, the visual

trappings of modernity do little to distract from the traditionalism at the heart of Hughes's production:

> Strange as it may seem, Hughes and his Santa – Sir
> Richard Attenborough – have the gall to suggest
> that Saint Nick lives, right here in the heart of the
> cynical '90s. [...] Considering the age we live in, it's
> a small miracle that the movie works at all. Like
> the original, the film's subject isn't really Santa
> Claus or Christmas; the real subject is faith. And
> Hughes, who adapted George Seaton's original
> screenplay, has done a savvy job of modernizing
> the setting so that the story becomes a sort of ref-
> erendum on 'believing' in the '90s. The result is
> pure family-values agitprop – a Christmas com-
> mercial for Mom, Dad, God, country and all-
> American conspicuous consumption. To their
> credit, Hughes and his director, Les Mayfield, are
> aware that they are peddling a falsehood. But the
> movie asks which is worse: a truth that draws a
> tear or a lie that creates a smile?[9]

The Mayfield version of *Miracle on 34th Street* benefit-
ed greatly from Richard Attenborough's performance as the
jolly and avuncular Kriss Kringle; the veteran actor throws
everything into the creation of a thoroughly appealing character who embodies the very essence of the festive season.
Wisely, Attenborough chooses not to emulate Edmund
Gwenn's original portrayal of old Mr Kringle, instead carving
out a very different individual who retains his intended connection to the traditions of Christmas while remaining
engaging and relevant to modern audiences. The role was to

earn Attenborough a nomination for Best Supporting Actor at the Saturn Awards in 1995.

Richard Attenborough was one of the most prominent names in British film-making at the time of production, having served as the President of the Royal Academy of Dramatic Arts and the British Academy of Film and Television Arts. Though well-remembered for his acting performances in films as diverse as *Brighton Rock* (John Boulting, 1948), *The Great Escape* (John Sturges, 1963), *10 Rillington Place* (Richard Fleischer, 1971) and *Jurassic Park* (Steven Spielberg, 1993), it was as a director that he would meet with even greater success. To great acclaim, he helmed features including *Young Winston* (1972), *A Bridge Too Far* (1977), *Cry Freedom* (1987), *Chaplin* (1992) and *Shadowlands* (1993), and most especially *Gandhi* (1982) which would win both the Best Picture and Best Director Oscars at the 1983 Academy Awards. Amongst his many other accolades, he was to win four Golden Globe Awards, four BAFTA Awards, and the BAFTA Fellowship for lifetime achievement in 1983. He was appointed a Commander of the Order of the British Empire (CBE) in 1967, was Knighted in 1976, and was created a life peer in 1993 when he was elevated to the House of Lords.

Given that he had earned such a towering profile in the entertainment industry, it is intriguing to note that Attenborough's performance as Kriss Kringle sharply divided critics at the time of *Miracle on 34th Street*'s release. Some, such as Leonard Klady, praised both the casting and the warmth of Attenborough's portrayal: 'Writer/producer John Hughes has done minor and subtle tampering with the 1947 vintage holiday yarn, and that proves both an asset and hindrance to the new version. [...] Hughes and director Les Mayfield have wisely shifted focus to the Santa figure and have a superb St

Nick in Attenborough. Not only is he the embodiment of de-cency, he's having a crackling good time bringing the character to Earth. [...] The overall effect is enjoyable and cuddly like a warm fire on a cold night. It also harkens back to a bygone, simpler time. For those die-hard believers, it's a bit disappoint-ing that the filmmakers huddle in the past rather than press on optimistically into the future'.[10] Others, such as Hollis Chacona, were rather more sceptical about Attenborough's charms in such a well-loved role – especially when compared to Edmund Gwenn's perennially well-loved, award-winning portrayal back in 1947: 'Richard Attenborough? Sure, he has good hair and a beard, but the man simply doesn't twinkle. He more bares his English dental plan teeth than smiles and has a slightly sinister air about him. Unlike the cherubic Edmund Gwenn's Kris Kringle (he won an Oscar for his 1947 perfor-mance), Attenborough's Santa is a hard sell. [...] Cap that with a typically aggrandized Hughesian finale where Santa delivers a big, sumptuously decorated house in the suburbs, filled to the rafters with expensive presents, and the spirit of Christmas in the Nineties becomes painfully clear. And I heard a woman exclaim as the scene faded from sight, "Man, I guess *I* need to talk to Santa tonight!"'[11]

While the original *Miracle on 34th Street* had seemed quite comfortable with the commoditisation of Christmas, provided that commercial endeavour was never allowed to undermine the mutual goodwill of the festive season, Hughes was not unaware of the aggressive interrogation of the over-commercialisation of Christmas which had taken place throughout the 1980s in films as wide-ranging as *Santa Claus: The Movie* (Jeannot Szwarc, 1985) and *Scrooged* (Richard Donner, 1988). With the 1947 film first appearing in an Amer-ica that was only just beginning to emerge from the economic austerity of the war years, the subtle note of caution it sounded regarding the commercialisation of Christmas as a factor which potentially jeopardised the season's characteristic altruism would doubtless have seemed timely. Mr Kringle states quite emphatically his concern that the festive season is ceasing to focus on the importance of giving, and is now in danger of becoming more concerned with materialism and self-interest. Hughes preserves Kriss's altruistic scheme of gently conveying parents to stores other than Cole's in order to track down hard-to-find gifts or better-quality presents – a strategy which initially baffles the corporate top brass with its simplicity and ability to generate public support for the company (even though they risk losing some Christmas revenue, many of their seasonal customers subsequently pledge to become loyal shoppers there throughout the year as a result of Kriss's honesty).

Miracle on 34th Street was one of the earliest and best-known exponents in festive cinema of the need to recognise the importance of unselfishness and philanthropy at Christmas, and yet rather than appearing overtly preachy the film actually blurred the boundaries between commercial trade and individual generosity quite profoundly. In Hughes's film, as in the original, Kris seems perfectly happy to enter the employ of Cole's, and – though he is an unconventional staff member (to say the least) – he has few qualms about jumping through any and all corporate hoops that are presented to him. While he is eager to encourage parents to seek out the best bargains when purchasing presents for their children so that their money can go further, he has no difficulty in accepting the fact that mass-production is the most expedient way of ensuring that as many toys as possible are available at affordable prices to satisfy the gift-buying public.

While Bryan and Dorey's blossoming romance answers Susan's secret Christmas wish for the security of a nuclear family with two loving parents (a classic Hughesian motif if ever there was one), by approaching Kriss in the belief that he can make this desire come true, Susan mirrors Kevin McCallister's late-in-the-day visit to the street corner Santa in *Home Alone* as he tries to find new, untried options in his quest to be reunited with his family. Yet Hughes spends more time on preserving the dual purpose evident in Seaton's original screenplay, celebrating the commercial spread of Christmas – the energetic cultural distribution of festive customs made possible through the mass-market – at the same time as it presents underplayed anxieties about the uncompromising encroachment of mercantilism into the season of giving, which saw the inclusiveness of the traditional Christmas challenged with the obstinate demands of unchecked materialism.

At its core, however, the Mayfield version of *Miracle on 34th Street* is really a film about faith – a simple yet robust belief in the Christmas spirit and the positive effects which can derive from it. Kriss repeatedly makes the point that it is a matter of human nature to sometimes put our faith in things which may appear indefinable or intangible, such as love itself, and that we should never give up hope even when the odds are stacked against us. But Hughes also emphasises that it is important to choose carefully what it is that we put our faith in, because those beliefs will ultimately shape and define us. We see this optimistic outlook at work not just in Susan, whose natural youthful exuberance has been stymied by hard-hearted adult pragmatism, but also in the staid matter-of-factness evident in her mother Dorey's melancholic worldview, her glacial temperament eventually thawing as a result of Kriss's wistful encouragement and the idealistic Bryan's gentle but indefatigable romantic advances. No-one, it seems, can stand in the way of Mr Kringle's irrepressible festive spirit; he has no interest in gaining the upper hand over those who oppose his message of goodwill, for his only goal appears to be propagating a universal message of benevolence to all, typified by Christmas but relevant the whole year through.

Elizabeth Perkins and Dylan McDermott both made for appealing leads, while Mara Wilson's youthful Susan appears suitably star-struck by old Mr Kringle's effortless invocation of the wonder of the holiday season as she makes the transition from jaded cynic to a true believer in Santa Claus. Perkins was arguably best-known to the audiences of the time for her roles in comedies such as *About Last Night* (Edward Zwick, 1986) and *The Flintstones* (Brian Levant, 1994), though her later performances on Showtime's comedy-drama TV series *Weeds* (2005-12) would make her the recipient of three nominations for Primetime Emmy Awards and two nominations for Golden Globe Awards. McDermott had likewise achieved fame thanks to appearances in prominent films such as *Hamburger Hill* (John Irvin, 1987), *Twister* (Michael Almereyda and Suzy Amis, 1989) and *Steel Magnolias* (Herbert Ross, 1989), though he too would go on to even greater success in television. He won a Golden Globe Award for Best Actor: Television Series Drama in 1999 for his portrayal of Bobby Donnell in ABC's legal drama *The Practice* (1997-2004), and has been nominated on numerous occasions for Golden Globe Awards, Primetime Emmy Awards, Screen Actors Guild Awards, and many other accolades. Mara Wilson was at the time best-known for playing Natalie Hillard in *Mrs Doubtfire* (Chris Columbus, 1993) alongside Robin Williams, and would later go on to appear in *Matilda* (1996),

Danny DeVito's adaptation of the popular Roald Dahl story. She took a twelve year hiatus from the acting profession in 2000, but in more recent years has achieved fame not only on television and stage but also as a playwright and author.

Although most critical focus on *Miracle on 34th Street* was concentrated on the appeal of its lead performers and the general visual sumptuousness of the production, much praise is due to Bruce Broughton for his inspired original score for the film, which brilliantly encapsulates the festive atmosphere of proceedings with great warmth and panache. Similarly, the movie's set decoration by Leslie E. Rollins is exceptional, most especially in its appreciation for fine detail (from the interior of Dorey's slightly impersonal apartment right through to the yuletide ambiance of the family's dream home at the conclusion) as much as the elegant, broad-strokes proficiency in bringing the fictional Cole's department store to life. It would also be remiss not to mention the film's strong line-up of supporting actors, which include William Windom, Jane Leeves, Joss Ackland, and especially Simon Jones as the dryly sardonic Donald Shellhammer. Jones would have been immediately recognisable to British audiences as interstellar everyman Arthur Dent from the BBC Radio adaptation of Douglas Adams's *The Hitchhiker's Guide to the Galaxy* in 1978, and then starring on BBC TV in the 1981 television adaptation.

Given the challenges involved in updating one of the most beloved features from the golden age of Christmas cinema, it was no surprise that Mayfield's *Miracle on 34th Street* met with a diverse range of responses from critics which ranged from the enthusiastic to the decidedly sceptical. Kenneth Turan's review for *The Los Angeles Times* was typical of the kind of cautious praise which lay in wait for the film: '*Miracle on 34th Street* is one of the genuinely beloved holiday movies, winner of a trio of Oscars in 1947 and a Christmas season fixture ever since. So producer/co-writer John Hughes, the force behind this remake, has understandably tried hard to be faithful to its spirit. Hughes has shared his screenplay credit with initial writer George Seaton, cast Alvin Greenman (who played a teen-age Santa back then) in a cameo role, and even tried to get R.H. Macy's to repeat its role as the story's pivotal department store. [...] When *Miracle on 34th Street* remembers that it's supposed to be a sweet piece of hokum, when it has the wit to leave Attenborough and Wilson on the screen together and forget about its rash of putative improvements, it does offer well-scrubbed family fare. Kriss himself would want us to forgive its flaws, and at this time of the year it gets harder and harder to turn the old gentleman down'.[12] The appraisal of qualified success was echoed by Roger Ebert, who acknowledged Hughes's achievements while also recognising the enduring status of Seaton's classic original film: 'The movie has been remade by producer John Hughes and director Les Mayfield, who follow the original fairly closely, but with a quieter, more elegiac tone. [...] There will never really be a movie to replace the 1947 *Miracle on 34th Street*, nor a performance to replace Edmund Gwenn's, but this modern update is a sweet, gentle, good-hearted film that stays true to the spirit of the original and doesn't try to make everything slick and exploitative. You know it's a good movie when you walk out humming the songs, and this time, it was *Joy to the World*.[13]

Other reviews at the time of the film's release varied dramatically from the warmly appreciative to the thoughtful but ultimately disappointed. Angie Errigo was among the critics who praised Hughes's evocation of a bygone age of festive film-making in the modern age, writing that: 'Writer-producer-kidmeister John Hughes' remake of the heart-warming, Oscar-winning 1947 comic fantasy might seem a trifle weak in the miracle department, but this tale of a department store Santa who goes on trial to prove he is, in fact, the genuine article abounds in the expensive production values and misty-eyed sentiment that all but guarantee a massive Christmas hit. [...] If you're after an entirely pleasant, inoffensive, feel-good movie at Christmas, this is it: the kind of innocent, utterly charming, hanky-ringing [sic] fare that they aren't supposed to be making any more'.[14] At the other end of the critical spectrum, Caryn James berated Hughes's creative *modus operandi*, considering it too contemporary to be an effective tribute and too tepid to be an successful modernisation: 'The new *Miracle on 34th Street*, produced by John Hughes (the mastermind behind shrewd hits like *Home Alone*) and written by him with George Seaton [who had died in 1979], is a dull project that makes only cosmetic changes [to] the original. It loses the warmth and nostalgia of the old movie, but is too timid to give the story the sharp, contemporary spin it needs. [...] The highlight of the new *Miracle*, which was directed by Les Mayfield, is still Kriss's appearance in court, though as Bryan defends him the audience has to suffer through lines like: "What is worse? A lie that draws a smile or a truth that draws a tear?" And one highlight of the old film, a scene in which the post office delivers bags of mail to Kriss in court, is missing now. Instead, Mr. Hughes has added a religious slant. The instinct that led him to this material may have been sound, but the effect is like a deflated balloon from the Cole's Thanksgiving Day Parade'.[15]

In the final analysis, however, Mayfield's film did tend to be judged rather unsympathetically overall in comparison to the 1947 original. Desson Howe was not alone in lamenting the triumph of style over substance, considering Hughes's approach to be well-intentioned but lacking in emotional sincerity when contrasted with Seaton's movie:

> This lethargic modernization, which stars Sir Richard Attenborough, Elizabeth Perkins and Dylan McDermott, may appeal to audiences because of the themes it labors for: the true spirit of Christmas, the mystique of Santa, children's desires for loving parents and so forth. But for the most part, the movie's a slow-moving, overblown, never-better-than-competent rendition of the original. [...] Amid the seasonal innocuousness, Attenborough's performance is about the most stirring thing in the movie. A dead ringer for the North Pole tubster, he's sprightly, warming and self-assured as he chuckles heartily, charms children and cynics alike, and talks quite matter-of-factly to reindeer. But even if he passes Yuletide muster in the courtroom, all the personality and goodwill in the world can't disguise this movie for what it is – or isn't.[16]

This deep-seated division amongst commentators has continued in more recent years, where retrospectives of *Miracle on 34th Street* have continued to sharply disagree over the film's merits and shortcomings. Kevin Matthews was among reviewers who felt that in accommodating the world of the 1990s, Mayfield and Hughes had missed the mark that had been hit so squarely by the original: 'There's still plenty of fun to be had with the central premise here, and the script by John Hughes tries to retain the spirit of the original while updating everything slightly, but there's just some magic missing. Perhaps it's the way in which the script, and direction by Les Mayfield, feels like 100 other movies from the 1990s aimed at family audiences. Perhaps it's the way in which the balance is ever so slightly disturbed in a way that makes the sweet just a bit too sickly and the moral message just a little overcooked'.[17] This view was mirrored by Ryan Cracknell, who was similarly unconvinced of the film's long-term effectiveness in comparison to the evergreen original: 'I guess I struggle with the cliché question that arises from most every remake: what's the point of messing with something that worked well the first time out. The obvious answer other than box office gold, is to update the classic to fit a modern audience. But the original tells a timeless story that is equally relevant now as it was 50 years ago. As time goes on, one version of *Miracle on 34th Street* will continue to enchant. The other will play in reruns on television over and over again, with a few people stopping in after some long and tiring channel surfing, watching it because it's on rather than actively seeking it out. I'll let you guess which version I think is which'.[18]

On the other hand, Chris Olson looks beyond the long shadow of the 1947 film to consider Mayfield's version on its own virtues, and found much to commend the movie in its own right: 'With intensely warm colours and soft-angled framing, Les Mayfield's film is almost a dreamlike story about a picturesque American family at Christmas. There is no small amount of hokeyness to the plot or the script, but it all seems so forgivable when wrapped in such a tender rendition of a Christmas film, and Attenborough is utterly brilliant. Few performers achieve the gravitas and humanity that he does with this endlessly portrayed character. [...] One of the all-time great Christmas films, *Miracle on 34th Street* is a humanely moving piece of drama and light comedy, a touching story that is driven by brilliant performances and an unyielding dedication to warmth and love'.[19]

When all is said and done, however, the general critical reputation of the *Miracle on 34th Street* remake has fared better in recent years than many commentators predicted, and the gradual emergence of 1990s nostalgia has only helped to enhance its standing amongst other features of the era. As critics such as Andy Webb have observed, while the 1947 George Seaton original will likely always have a special place in the hearts of Christmas cineastes, the Mayfield version has subsequently come to evoke its own sense of wistful reminiscence amongst an entire generation of moviegoers:

> Christmas comes but once a year, but good Christmas movies live long on in our hearts for many years afterwards. Such is the case of the modern classic *Miracle on 34th Street*, a remake of the equally classic *Miracle on 34th Street* from 1947. Although never a fan of remakes, especially those which usually butcher a classic, I have to say that with John Hughes producing and Les Mayfield directing this remake of *Miracle on 34th Street* does more than an adequate job of updating a movie to appeal to a new generation. [...] *Miracle on 34th Street* is without a doubt a very good remake, never straying far from an award winning formula but doing a good job of updating the classic without losing either the magic or message of the original. Like the original I am sure that this one will become an annual favourite in the lead up to Christmas and no doubt may see itself being the subject of a remake in another 50 years. If it's just

to see the magic of Richard Attenborough as Kris Kringle putting on the Santa Claus gear it is worth watching.[20]

John Hughes's inventive range of Christmas movies may never have reached the level of instant recognition that has been achieved by many of his other films – most especially his iconic teen movies of the mid-1980s – but their annual appearances on TV and via home entertainment platforms have ensured that they have certainly never been forgotten. Carrying forward several of the central themes established in his earlier work, not least the importance of the traditional family unit, the need for personal and social responsibility, and the emotional significance of the individual, the festive cinema that he produced has not only retained an audience over the years but has also assumed its own worthy position within the broader canon of Christmas movie-making – not least on account of the way in which it chimed in with many other festive features of the same period. Little could Hughes have realised, however, that Les Mayfield's remake of *Miracle on 34th Street* was to lay the creative foundation for further, fascinating re-examinations of classic Christmas cinema later in the decade, setting another characteristic precedent for the genre in the 1990s.

REFERENCES

1.   Thomas S. Hischak, *American Literature on Stage and Screen: 525 Works and Their Adaptations* (Jefferson: McFarland, 2012), 145-46, p.146.

2.   Holly Chard, *Mainstream Maverick: John Hughes and New Hollywood Cinema* (Austin: University of Texas Press, 2020), pp.183-85.

3.   William D. Crump, *The Christmas Encyclopedia*, 3rd edn (Jefferson: McFarland, 2013), 291-92, p.292.

4.   Leonard Norwitz, '*Miracle on 34th Street* (Blu-Ray)', in *Lens Views*, 22 October 2009.
      <http://www.dvdbeaver.com/film2/DVDReviews47/miracle_on_34th_street_1994_blu-ray.htm>

5.   Richard Scheib, '*Miracle on 34th Street*', in *Moria: Science Fiction, Horror and Fantasy Review*, 2009.
      <https://www.moriareviews.com/fantasy/miracle-on-34th-street-1994.htm>

6.   Jessica Catcher, '12 Awesome Facts You Didn't Know About the Original *Miracle on 34th Street*', in *ViralNova*, 12 December 2014.
      <http://www.viralnova.com/miracle-34-trivia/>

7.   Douglas Hildebrand, 'Les Mayfield', in *Contemporary North American Film Directors: A Wallflower Critical Guide*, ed. by Yoram Allon, Del Cullen, and Hannah

Patterson (London: Wallflower Press, 2001) [2000],
p.360.

8. Crump.

9. Hal Hinson, '*Miracle on 34th Street*', in *The Washing-ton Post*, 18 November 1994.
    <*https://www.washingtonpost.com/wp-srv/style/
    longterm/ movies/videos/
    miracleon34thstreetpghinson_a0a86e.htm*>

10. Leonard Klady, '*Miracle on 34th Street*', in *Variety*, 6 November 1994.
    <*https://variety.com/1994/film/reviews/miracle-on-
    34th-street-2-1200439489/*>

11. Hollis Chacona, '*Miracle on Thirty-Fourth Street*', in *The Austin Chronicle*, 18 November 1994.
    <*https://www.austinchronicle.com/events/film/1994-
    11-18/138400/*>

12. Kenneth Turan, 'Movie Review: The *Miracle* of 1947, 47 Years Later', in *The Los Angeles Times*, 18 November 1994.
    <*https://www.latimes.com/archives/la-xpm-1994-11-18-
    ca-64068-story.html*>

13. Roger Ebert, '*Miracle on 34th Street*', in *The Chicago Sun-Times*, 18 November 1994.
    <*https://www.rogerebert.com/reviews/miracle-on-
    34th-street-1994*>

14. Angie Errigo, '*Miracle on 34th Street Review*', in *Empire*, January 1995.
    <*https://www.empireonline.com/movies/reviews/miracle-34th-street-review/*>

15. Caryn James, 'Film Review: What Do You Say, Virginia?', in *The New York Times*, 18 November 1994.
    <*https://www.nytimes.com/1994/11/18/movies/film-review-what-do-you-say-virginia.html*>

16. Desson Howe, '*Miracle on 34th Street*', in *The Washington Post*, 18 November 1994.
    <*https://www.washingtonpost.com/wp-srv/style/longterm/movies/videos/miracleon34thstreetpghowe_a0b090.htm*>

17. Kevin Matthews, '*Miracle on 34th Street* (1994)', in *FlickFeast*, 23 December 2011.
    <*https://www.flickfeast.co.uk/reviews/film-reviews/miracle-34th-street-1994/*>

18. Ryan Cracknell, '*Miracle on 34th Street* (1994)', in *Movie Views*, 13 December 2003.
    <*https://movieviews.ca/miracle-on-34th-street-1994*>

19. Chris Olson, '*Miracle on 34th Street* (1994) film review', in *UK Film Review*, 23 December 2015.
    <*https://www.ukfilmreview.co.uk/post/miracle-on-34th-street-1994-film-review*>

20. Andy Webb, '*Miracle on 34th Street*', in *The Movie Scene*, 2009.

<https://www.themoviescene.co.uk/reviews/miracle-on-34th-street/miracle-on-34th-street.html>

8

The Santa Clause (1994)

Walt Disney Pictures / Hollywood Pictures /
Outlaw Productions

Director: John Pasquin
Producers: Robert Newmyer, Brian Reilly and Jeffrey Silver
Screenwriters: Leo Benvenuti and Steve Rudnick

RECIPIENT of an ingenious and widespread market-ing campaign, even by Hollywood standards, *The Santa Clause* quickly earned itself a reputation as one of the most high-profile of all nineties Christmas films at the time of its release, and even today it remains amongst the most enduring festive movies to have emerged into the dec-ade's pop culture.

While the engaging performance of its popular star, Tim Allen, was to greatly enhance its reputation during the time of its release, its continued esteem amongst audiences in recent years can perhaps be seen to have stemmed more from the lasting charm of its central premise: that of the transposi-tion of a contemporary everyman onto the ever-captivating canvas of Christmas mythology. With its themes of unconven-tional family relations proving more complex than in many previous festive features (especially in contrast to the forth-right celebration of the nuclear family which had been

depicted in films like *Home Alone* (q.v.) and *Miracle on 34th*
Street (q.v.)), and its fish-out-of-water concept perfectly en-
capsulating the prominent topic of fitting in and belonging –
which was to be explored by many other films of the time –
The Santa Clause would ultimately prove to be, in many
ways, one of the defining Christmas movies of the decade. As
Jay Mechling explains, 'In consumption-driven "late capitalism", a primary topic of public discourse about Christmas has
been the felt tension between spirituality and materialism.
These films appearing every year on network television as
"Christmas classics" explore this cultural contradiction, and
the viewing public never seems to tire of these films' rehearsal
of the problem and its solution. [...] Only time will tell
whether *The Santa Clause* (1994, starring television sitcom
comic Tim Allen) becomes another "Christmas classic," but
its theme of the redemption of a divorced man who neglects
his children until he is forced to become Santa Claus's replacement has all the elements of a narrative resolving
tensions around materialism, family, and sentiment (if not
spirituality)'.[1]

Even more than other 1990s Christmas films, *The Santa Clause* is concerned with the tensions between tradition
and modernity. It thoroughly modernises the Santa Claus leg-
endarium whilst simultaneously reinforcing the long-
established conventions of that yuletide mythos. Because Tim
Allen, the film's well-known star, is portraying a contemporary American figure with relatable modern day concerns and
everyday personal and professional stresses, his eventual transformation into the eternally altruistic, benign and instantly-
recognisable figure of Santa Claus becomes all the more striking. As Mark Connelly has observed:

Santa is a truly immortal American. Cinema has done more than any other medium to promote this message and ensure its ascendancy over other interpretations. [...] The vision of Santa as an all-American hero can sometimes pose problems. *Variety* worried that *The Santa Clause* might not be a success outside the USA: 'off-shore prospects aren't as bright because of the uniquely American flavouring'. How exactly do these films create this impression? *The Santa Clause* employs Tim Allen, star of the popular television sit-com *Home Improvements* [sic], to take on the job. In the movie he plays the character Scott Calvin (note the significance of the initials), an executive in a toy company. [...] Scott reinforces this image of Santa as, in fact, a typically American guy, by reading his son that classic of American Christmas/Santa literature, *A Visit from St Nicholas*, also known as *'Twas the Night Before Christmas*. [...] Later, when Scott has finished delivering toys, we see the sleigh cross the skyscape of a typical American city and the dawn of Christmas Day is heralded by him shouting the last line of the poem, 'Happy Christmas to all, and to all a good-night'.[2]

Bringing this slice of modern Christmas folklore to life was John Pasquin, a director and producer (as well as an occasional screenwriter) whose career had begun in television in the early eighties; his work behind the camera spanned the entire decade, helming episodes of high-profile series including *Family Ties* (1983-88), *Newhart* (1985-86) and *Thirtysomething* (1987). *The Santa Clause* was to form his cinematic debut, though he has returned to the world of film numerous times in recent years, developing movies such as *Jungle 2 Jungle* (1997), *Joe Somebody* (2001) and *Miss Congeniality 2: Armed and Fabulous* (2005), as well as continuing to remain very active in the world of television. Pasquin has been nominated for Primetime Emmy Awards on three occasions – once for his directorial work on *L.A. Law* in 1990, and twice as producer of *Home Improvement* in 1992 and 1993. His energetic approach to *The Santa Clause* won him considerable acclaim – not least in his determination to ensure that the film's child-friendly methodology would not hamper him from producing a feature that also had broad appeal for the whole family. As Lisa Liebman noted, 'It's not just teen-agers who shy away from films that are too saccharine. Parents, too, sometimes find that they cannot face another family outing to a G-rated picture. "I think ⟦a⟧ G ⟦rating⟧ is the kiss of death for a lot of grown-ups," says ⟦John⟧ Pasquin, the director of *The Santa Clause*. "Parents look at a G rating and say 'Whoa! Let's have the baby sitter take the kids'".'³

In the American town of Lakeside, toy corporation owner Mr Whittle (Peter Boyle) is hosting a lavish Christmas Eve event in celebration of the company's best ever sales. He singles out marketing executives Scott Calvin (Tim Allen) and Susan Perry (Judith Scott) for special praise due to their efforts in exceptionally promoting the firm's products. Scott takes great delight basking in his boss's congratulations, but gets so carried away with the office festivities that he ends up leaving much later than intended. This causes friction with his ex-wife Laura (Wendy Crewson) and her new husband, psychologist Dr Neil Miller (Judge Reinhold), as Scott had earlier agreed to look after his son Charlie (Eric Lloyd) – who normally lives with Laura and Neil – overnight while they stay with Neil's parents. Scott's home is notably lacking in festive appeal, however, and Charlie is less than keen on the idea of staying with his slick but cynical father. However, Scott proves to have more of a festive spark than anyone expected when he discovers that Neil has been advising Charlie that Santa Claus is more of an allegorical expression of festive cheer than he is an actual being. Infuriated that Laura should have allowed such cold emotional detachment to put their son's faith in Santa at risk, Scott assures Charlie that jolly old Saint Nick is most definitely alive and well – after all, he is an adult and still fervently believes in him. Laura is indignant that Scott should question Neil's judgement and her own parenting skills.

Scott's noble but ultimately doomed attempts to cook his son a traditional turkey dinner do little to make an impression on Charlie, who seems resigned to a joyless Christmas Eve. After a largely fruitless tour of the town's restaurants, they eventually wind up at their local branch of Denny's, which is currently populated by office workers from a multinational corporation and also, more germanely to Scott and Charlie, single fathers and their children (who have also, it seems, had major troubles with their own respective turkey dinners). Charlie is singularly unimpressed at the prospect of eating his Christmas Eve meal in such clinically impersonal surroundings, especially when it becomes obvious that the restaurant staff have already run out of most of the items on their festive menu.

Back home, Scott is reading from Clement Clarke Moore's *A Visit from St. Nicholas* while Charlie lies in bed. Sensing that his son is close to falling asleep (even if his evening has made Charlie unlikely to be entertaining any visions of sugar plums dancing in his head), Scott tries to withdraw from the room quietly... but the suddenly-awake Charlie has other ideas. Soon Scott is being bombarded by awkward questions about the plausibility of Santa's annual gift-bearing visits. How did his reindeer acquire the ability to fly? How does Santa manage to fit down a house's chimney and, in a modern world which has so few open fireplaces, how is he able to deliver presents to homes without them? Scott does his best to answer his son's questions to the best of his ability and, though he is saddened by Charlie's dispassionate doubtfulness, finds himself secretly cheered when he receives a request to leave out some milk and cookies by the tree – just in case.

Later that night, Charlie is amazed when he hears heavy footfalls on the roof above his head. Believing that Santa is in the process of paying his regular Christmas Eve visit, he races through to Scott's bedroom. Scott, however, comes to the immediate conclusion that the house is being burgled, and races outside to confront the apparent intruder. Sure enough, he soon spots a man on his roof, but in calling out he startles the trespasser and causes him to tumble to the ground. Charlie is initially awestruck, until he realises the uncomfortable truth – Scott appears to have killed Santa Claus (John Pasquin). Confident that he is only dealing with an interloper in fancy dress, Scott frisks the body for identification, finding a calling card (marked 'Santa Claus, North Pole') which instructs him to put on Santa's red suit and trust the reindeer to do the rest. Scott is initially contemptuous of these grandiose directions... until he happens to notice a magic sleigh and full compliment of flying reindeer perched on the roof of his house.

Scott tries and fails to come to terms with this strange turn of events, but discovers that he is unable to check the body for any further documents because it has disappeared into thin air – only Santa's empty suit remains on the snowy ground. Before he can make any further attempt to rationalise the situation, however, Scott finds that Charlie has ascended a ladder which has mysteriously appeared at the front of the house, and is now firmly ensconced at the reins of Santa's sleigh. Still believing the whole thing to be an elaborate hoax, Scott orders his son to move, but the reindeer mistakenly be-lieve that he is talking to them and fly off into the starry night, whisking along Scott and Charlie in the sleigh behind them.

It soon becomes apparent that the reindeer expect Scott to assume Santa's duties for the night: they deposit the sleigh on top of a nearby house, where he is persuaded by Charlie to don the red suit and deliver presents to the children inside. Scott only does so only with the utmost reluctance (not least as the suit is several sizes too big for him), but soon discovers that he has developed the unexpected personal ability to fly – and, what's more, to fit down any size of chimney stack. His first effort is less than successful, as he is harassed by a family dog, sets off the house's burglar alarm and then wakes the inhabitants. However, he soon begins to get the knack of the job, which is just as well given that the reindeer have a long night planned.

Finding that Santa's toy-sack magically refills after eve-ry visit, Scott realises that he has his work cut out for him. But apart from a few ill-tempered moments (he eventually tries to rationalise his situation by deducing that he is halluci-nating, or at the very least having a very strange dream), by dawn all of the gifts have been delivered. Scott orders the reindeer to take him home, but Lakeside isn't where they have in mind. They whisk the sleigh off to the North Pole and then detach themselves and wander into the distance, leaving a rather confused Scott and Charlie in the icy wilderness. A few moments later, however, an elf arrives (apparently from nowhere) and causes a literal North Pole to rise from the snow-covered ground. Keying in a code sequence, the elf watches as the sleigh descends into a vast underground workshop.

Scott is stunned by the seemingly miraculous sight that awaits him. The workshop is staffed entirely by elves; although the beings are impossibly ancient, in physical terms they appear just like small children. Charlie is amazed by the astonishing marvels that are on display, but Scott is still more concerned about the fact that he can make neither head nor tail of their peculiar situation. In his search for answers he stumbles across Bernard (David Krumholtz), a senior elf, who finally explains what is going on. When the previous incumbent of the role fell from the roof of Scott's house, the role of Santa Claus became vacant, and Scott has now formally assumed Santa's identity by wearing his suit. (This, stated in impossibly small print on the calling card that Scott discovered, is the eponymous Santa Clause.) Scott now has eleven months to tie up any outstanding affairs from his existing life before he must return to the North Pole and take over Santa's duties the following December. Still finding the whole state of affairs rather difficult to swallow, Scott asks Bernard what would happen if he simply refused to accept that he was Santa Claus. This horrifies the elves, and a deeply sombre Bernard explains that if there is no Santa, there would – in turn – be no Christmas.

Bernard gives Charlie a special gift – a very old, magical snowglobe – while he charges Judy the elf (Paige Tamada) to sort out Scott's ill-fitting red suit. Charlie is overjoyed to be visiting the legendary workshop at the North Pole, but Scott is troubled at the prospect that, rather than being a visitor, he may soon be a permanent resident there. The kind-hearted Judy explains that it is not surprising that he finds it difficult to believe what is happening to him. After all, she tells Scott, children have no difficulty having faith in Santa because they instinctively know that he is there for them, even though there is no empirical proof of his existence. For adults, no amount of evidence would ever be sufficient, and so they quickly grow out of their youthful trust in the magic of Christmas. This simple statement gives Scott pause for thought.

The next morning, Scott awakens at home in bed and tries to rationalise the previous evening's events as nothing more than a strange dream. However, this notion is immediately challenged by the fact that he is wearing a pair of red silk pyjamas, embroidered with S.C. on the breast pocket, which had been given to him by Judy at the North Pole. Frantically, he races outside to see if he can find any evidence of the fallen Santa or the sleigh which had been on the roof, but ultimately comes up with nothing. Charlie, on the other hand, is still entranced by his Christmas experiences – a fact which doesn't go down well with Neil and Laura when they arrive to collect him later. Laura is indignant that Scott appears to have filled Charlie's head with fanciful notions when she and Neil have been trying to instil him with a sense of rationality and common sense. Scott, for his part, is no longer sure what to think.

Some time later, Charlie's class are giving presentations about the work of their parents. Charlie, who has brought along both Scott and Neil, decides that he wants Scott to give the first presentation. Scott begins to explain about his work in toy production, but Charlie immediately butts in and tells the class that his father is, in fact, Santa Claus. No amount of counter-explanation from Scott will satisfy Charlie to the contrary, which alarms Neil and Laura as much as it does the class's teacher, Miss Daniels (Mary Gross). This leads to a meeting with the school's headteacher, irritable Principal Compton (Joyce Guy), where Scott tries desperately to convince everyone that Charlie is merely explaining the events of a vivid dream that he'd had on Christmas Eve. Nobody is convinced by this account of events, however.

Scott takes Charlie to the zoo and, as they watch polar bears swimming, tries to convince him that the events of Christmas Eve were nothing more than the product of his youthful imagination. But Charlie, who still carries Bernard's snowglobe around with him wherever he goes, is having nothing to do with Scott's attempts to rationalise what happened at the North Pole. He tells his father that he is simply in denial about the revelations at Santa's workshop, but that the truth will eventually establish itself. Scott assures him that this is not the case, but is blissfully unaware that a procession of reindeer has begun to follow him as he heads out of the zoo.

Neil and Laura become increasingly concerned with Charlie's fixation on Christmas, especially as he seems to be spending most of his time role-playing as Santa. When Scott comes to visit his son, Neil explains that he is worried about the effect that he is having on Charlie; he questions whether Scott's continued presence in Charlie's life is now becoming counter-productive to his personal development. Laura also begins to wonder if Scott is trying to assume the larger-than-life role of Santa in an attempt to compensate for the time that he has so far failed to spend with his son. Fearing for the future of his access to Charlie, Scott implores him to keep his

North Pole experiences a secret from Neil, his mother and everyone at the school. Charlie can't understand why this should be, but is eventually persuaded to remain quiet about the strange incident at Christmas.

As it should happen, Charlie's behaviour is not the only problem that Scott encounters. He awakens one morning to discover that he has grown a full beard and, more worryingly, has put on a large amount of weight. This is greeted by bewilderment at his office, where the other executives are stunned at his greatly-altered appearance. Scott tries to explain away his rapid increase in body mass by telling them that he has suffered a massive allergic reaction to a bee sting, but it is clear that nobody believes him even remotely. His colleagues are further concerned when, during an office meal, he orders a large number of different items from the dessert menu and unashamedly gobbles them down, one after the other. Later, during a presentation based on advertising strategies for a toy armoured tank, Scott becomes indignant that the company's proposed promotion exploits the image of Santa Claus, portraying the figure in a bad light by neglecting the true spirit and traditions of Christmas. Eventually the CEO, Mr Whittle, loses his patience and orders Scott out of the conference room. Privately, Whittle tells Scott that he is concerned about his appearance, his behaviour, and his general state of mind. Scott tries to excuse his actions, but Whittle demands that he gets himself sorted out at the earliest possible opportunity – implying that his job is at risk if he refuses.

Increasingly worried about his health, Scott books an appointment with medical doctor Pete Novos (Steve Vinovich) who gives him a full checkup. After a vigorous physical, Dr Novos is baffled to discover that Scott's health is perfect... even although he is continuing to gain weight. His hair is also greying, his beard now having turned almost completely white. The doctor suggests that the unexpectedly rapid growth in Scott's facial hair (although he shaves regularly, his beard grows back completely within hours) can probably be explained away by a hormonal imbalance, and that his greying hair is a natural part of the approach to middle age. However, even he is unable to clarify the reason why Scott's heart, though strong, is beating to the tune of Christmas carols.

Scott goes along to spectate at one of Charlie's school soccer games. While there, he is vexed to discover that many of the children instinctively know that he is Santa Claus. They line up so that they can each, in turn, tell him what they want for Christmas. This does not play at all well with Neil and Laura, who arrive to watch Charlie's game but are so stunned at Scott's appearance that they decide to leave instead, taking Charlie with them. Laura is appalled that Scott should have chosen to change his appearance to win the favour of his son, which she sees as a desperate attempt to capitalise on Charlie's affection. As neither of them realise that Scott has little choice in the state of his current appearance, Neil also recommends that Scott should attend a therapy session at his practice in order to get to the root of his apparent identity crisis. Scott becomes dismayed, as it becomes increasingly apparent that he is now in real danger of losing access rights to his son.

Things continue to grow ever stranger for Scott. First a fleet of delivery vans deposit a vast array of neatly-packaged red boxes at his home, inside which he finds the gargantuan 'naughty and nice' list (which he is under strict instructions to check twice). Then he discovers that no matter how regularly he should decide to shave or apply hair dye, he immediately reverts to having a full white beard and completely white hair. Neil urges Laura to consider a court injunction to suspend Scott's visitation rights to meet with Charlie. Although initially reluctant, Laura goes along with the plan, and when Charlie is interviewed by the examining judge (Ron Hartmann) he explains about Scott's secret life as Santa in great detail. Considering Neil and Laura's concerns about Charlie's wellbeing and Scott's mental fitness, the judge decides to revoke Scott's right to maintain access to his son.

Along with his other woes, Scott is devastated to be apart from his son just as their relationship was starting to improve. He decides to pay a visit to Neil and Laura's home in order to say one last goodbye to Charlie now that his visitation rights have been suspended. Neil is highly resistant to the notion, particularly as they are currently sharing a Thanksgiving turkey dinner, but eventually Laura concedes and allows them a moment in private together. Charlie is desperately unhappy at the prospect of being apart from Scott, and tells his father that he wants to be with him – even in spite of Scott's attempts to tell him that it's far better that he stay with Laura and Neil for the time being. Before Scott can try to reason any further with Charlie, Bernard appears out of nowhere: the time has come for Scott to return to the North Pole. What Scott doesn't realise, however, is that Charlie is coming with them.

When Neil and Laura discover that Charlie is missing, they immediately assume that Scott has abducted him as part of his delusionary behaviour. This triggers a large-scale police manhunt to apprehend Scott, led by Detective Nunzio (Larry Brandenburg). The police are, to put it mildly, bemused at an assignment to find Santa Claus and take him into custody. Charlie telephones Laura from the North Pole and explains that he is safe and well, but hangs up before the call can be traced. Desperate to track Scott down, the police form a ring of steel around the Miller family home, while every passer-by who happens to be wearing a Santa suit is stopped for interrogation – not an easy task, given that Christmas is fast approaching.

At the North Pole, meanwhile, Scott is busily getting ready for his annual Christmas Eve delivery. Now finally reconciled to his new role in life, he looks on with enthusiasm as Quintin (Nic Knight), the elf in charge of research and development, unveils a new Santa suit which is heat resistant and entirely impervious to even the most scorching of fireplaces. Charlie is equally excited about the impending delivery of gifts, unveiling with great gusto the range of new technical innovations that have been built into Santa's (now suddenly rather high-tech) sleigh.

At first, Scott's Christmas sleigh-ride goes perfectly, with presents delivered right on schedule and with great consumption of milk and cookies. However, things take a more problematic turn when Charlie suggests that they visit Neil and Laura's house to deliver their gifts. A squad of police officers are lying in wait in the Millers' living room, ready to arrest Scott for child abduction. The children of the area are upset to see Santa handcuffed and taken into custody in the back of a police patrol car. But in spite of Scott's protestations that Charlie is safe and well in his sleigh, his son goes unnoticed up on the roof of the Millers' home.

Realising that something has happened to Scott, Bernard and Quintin deploy the Effective Liberating Flight Squad (ELFS), who immediately engage in a rescue mission. This jet-packed cadre of elite elves set off for the Miller residence, baffling the inhabitants of a nearby police car as they rescue Charlie from the roof and speed off into the night to save Scott. After circumventing a hapless desk sergeant (Gordon Masten), the ELFS break into the cells of the local police station and rescue Santa. Scott then wastes no time in returning Charlie to Neil and Laura, finally putting an end to their agonising vigil. The Millers are so relieved to see Charlie again that, rather than immediately calling for Scott's re-arrest, they are willing to hear him out. At first, he tells Charlie that it is for the best that he remain with his mother and Neil, though he does ask Laura if she will allow him to spend time with Charlie every Christmas Eve. Finally realising that Scott is not delusional, but really has actually become Santa Claus, Laura burns the injunction papers and tells Scott that he is free to visit his son whenever he pleases. Furthermore, Bernard arrives (once again, out of thin air) and informs Charlie that he can also visit his father at any time of his choosing – all he needs to do is give the magic snowglobe a shake, and Scott will join him.

Neil, who still believes that Scott is unhinged, is becoming concerned that he and Laura are allowing themselves to be caught up in Scott's complex web of illusion and hallucination. But this time, Laura won't be swayed: she is convinced that Santa Claus is real, and has taken the form of her ex-husband. A police SWAT team storm into the house in an attempt to apprehend Scott for a second time, but they are too late – he has returned up the chimney to his sleigh before they can reach him. Faced with the sight of Santa hovering above the ground with a sleigh pulled by flying reindeer, even Neil is forced to face the fact that even the most sophisticated of delusions could not be fooling everyone simultaneously, including the growing crowd of bystanders outside. As he leaves, Scott parachutes gifts to Laura and Neil – a board game and toy whistle respectively, which they had wanted for Christmas as children but had never received. It was that experience which had convinced them both that Santa Claus didn't exist; now that Scott has rectified this omission, they are both left in no doubt of his true identity. Satisfied with Scott's efforts, a group of elves (who have been watching unseen from the crowd) depart at the same time as Santa's sleigh leaves to return on its Christmas Eve journey. Keen to test the effectiveness of his snowglobe, Charlie calls Scott shortly afterwards and joins his father as he begins his new job in earnest, spreading joy and goodwill across the world.

The Santa Clause continued the preoccupation of nineties festive cinema with the family unit, in the sense that – in a similar vein to *All I Want for Christmas* (q.v.) and the 1994 remake of *Miracle on 34ᵗʰ Street* – it was a prominent family drama which was to feature parental divorcees rather than the traditional nuclear family setting that had previously been so typical of the genre. The theme of divorce – and how parental bonds could survive its trauma and aftermath – had established itself in a number of family films throughout the early nineties, most notably in Chris Columbus's popular *Mrs Doubtfire* (1993), while the theme of a cynic rediscovering the wonder of the festive season was also a recognisable trope, having surfaced prominently in films of the eighties including *One Magic Christmas* (Phillip Borsos, 1985) and *Prancer* (John D. Hancock, 1989).

What is especially striking is the way in which the film's drama, centring on the threat of Scott becoming legally estranged from his son Charlie, often seems largely subordinate to the main theme: the transfigurative influence of Christmas. The result is that Laura and Neil are often allowed to come across as rather stolid and mean-spirited (as

Scott himself had been, prior to his transformation), which can make it difficult to warm to their characters even given the validity of their concerns over Scott's apparent identity crisis. Fortunately, Judge Reinhold and Wendy Crewson both give appealing enough performances to soften the harder edges of their characters' apparent lack of sympathy, but there is no arguing that the legal and emotional drama of the film does tend to bog down the narrative momentum just at the exact moment that it should ideally be picking up pace. Yet as Carlos deVillalvilla remarked, even the court subplot has an important function to play within the film: 'There are no villains in this movie – Neil and Laura act out of genuine concern for Charlie and that's kind of refreshing. Some Scrooge-like critics grumbled about the custody issues bogging down the plot but quite frankly I disagree. The movie is about the difficulties created by Scott becoming Santa and in that sense the reaction of other adults to Scott's transformation seems logical and believable to me. Even though there is a certain magic in the North Pole scenes, Scott's coping with his physical transformation are for me the best scenes in the movie'.[4]

The film does, however, give a scrupulously modern take on the Santa mythology, in stark contrast to many other high-profile evocations that had come before it. Whereas *Santa Claus: The Movie* (Jeannot Szwarc, 1985) had taken care to craft an ancient, pagan mythology for the Jolly Old Elf – albeit one which was at odds with established traditions surrounding the character (such as his origins as St Nicholas) – *The Santa Clause* takes great relish in forging another direction entirely, bringing some progressive zest to an overly-familiar concept. Here, too, the film complements several other, then-recent festive features while simultaneously carving

233

its own niche, as Frank Thompson suggests: '*The Santa Clause* shares a conceit with the earlier Disney film *Ernest Saves Christmas* – namely, that there is no one Santa Claus but an ongoing series of them. In *Ernest Saves Christmas*, Santa realizes that he has gotten too old for the job and has chosen his successor. In *The Santa Clause*, the old Santa has to retire due to illness – or maybe death. After he falls to the ground from Scott's roof, he simply disappears, leaving an empty suit for Scott to put on'.[5]

The film's director, John Pasquin, appears to be having no small amount of fun in his small cameo, where he plays Scott's ill-fated predecessor in the role of Santa. This is but one of the film's many mischievous flourishes, for there are also a number of playful nods to the Christmas movies of years past. George Seaton's original *Miracle on 34th Street* (1947) is about to be screened on Scott's TV on the night of Christmas Eve, while a little girl – upset at seeing a hand-cuffed Scott led away by the police – delivers the famous 'Let Santa go!' line of dialogue from Seaton's classic movie. Scott's eventual decision to share Christmas dinner with Charlie at a chain restaurant has distinct echoes of the concluding scenes from Bob Clark's *A Christmas Story* (1983). Similarly, the elves of the North Pole are neatly realised as children and young teenagers with an upbeat, seen-it-all attitude, rather than the diminutive bearded men of tradition, shaking up the conventional formula as it had been portrayed in earlier films such as *Santa Claus: The Movie*. The reindeer also boast dynamic, expressive features, easily proving to be the equal of their counterparts in Jeannot Szwarc's influential movie. As Jeff Shannon has put it, 'There's a giddy logic to *The Santa Clause* that turns the aged yet childlike elves of the North Pole into equal-opportunity employers. [...] The movie's mix

of fantasy is also finely tuned, from the lavish expanse of Santa's underground workshop (a marvelous set designed by
Carol Spier) to the bossy pragmatism of the reindeer (especially Comet), which don't seem to mind a newly designed sleigh
capable of vertical takeoff. It's little touches like this that
make all the difference. When so many other comedies are
falling flat, *The Santa Clause* has enough cumulative laughs to
make it a likely holiday hit'.[6]

It is difficult to describe any festive film which kicks off
with the apparent death of Santa Claus as being anything
other than daring, no matter how tastefully the aforementioned incident is handled by the script. It is therefore quite
fascinating, in this sense, to consider the way in which so
many of the more problematic aspects of Scott's gradually
changing identity are played down by Pasquin and screenwriters Leo Benvenuti and Steve Rudnick. We gain a
tantalising glimpse of Scott, the archetypal corporate go-
getter, losing the respect of his colleagues due to his irrational
behaviour and radical physical changes, but the long-term effects of this transformation on his personal lifestyle are never
fully explored. Nor, indeed, do we visit with any degree of
clarity the issue of Scott becoming increasingly aware of the
fact that his drastically altered appearance has made him cease
to be as attractive to the opposite sex, and the profound effect
that this presumably would have on his self-esteem. Yet as
Thompson explains, this literal transformation has symbolic
significance too: 'Scott's transformation is physical first, and
mental and emotional later. To his dismay, he finds that he is
gaining weight rapidly – possibly due to his new diet of milk
and cookies. His hair has turned white, and no matter how
often he shaves, he still ends each day with a luxurious beard.
[...] For Scott Calvin's ultimate transformation into Santa

235

Claus, the makeup artists studied earlier images of Saint Nick from the twenties and thirties, including some Norman Rockwell paintings. 〚...〛 It's also a pretty perceptive statement about how a father can – must – literally and figuratively transform himself into the kind, gentle, loving – and attentive – dad that he needs to be'.[7]

It would be all too simple to explain these issues away with the fact that *The Santa Clause* is, essentially, a lighthearted family film which would do well to avoid such issues of self-awareness and individual psychological integrity. But the repeated significance attached to Neil and Laura's questioning of Scott's sanity, culminating in the legal separation of father and son, does rather leave the issue open to further and deeper interpretation. It is of note, therefore, that the film was originally intended to be much darker in tone, and interesting to consider exactly what the final product may have looked like with only a few deviations from the established narrative. Framing this difference in tone is the surprising fact that Tim Allen was not the first choice for the starring role; as J.P. Roscoe elucidates, '*The Santa Clause* became a huge holiday hit 〚but〛 the movie had been in production hell for a while, and Tim Allen wasn't the original plan for Santa Claus. Bill Murray was the first candidate and who the film was originally written for and Chevy Chase was also planned for Scott Calvin'.[8] While Murray turned the role down and Chase reportedly had scheduling conflicts at the time which would have made his participation impossible, it is certainly intriguing to imagine what a profound impact such an acute shift in casting would have had on the tone of the film.

As might be expected in a movie which focuses on its central character to the extent that it does, much of the success of *The Santa Clause* hinges on Tim Allen's captivating lead performance as Scott Calvin, the man who would be Santa. It is fortunate, for that reason, that Allen gives a virtuoso performance throughout, from the shallow, cynical marketing yuppie of the film's opening scenes all the way through to the jolly, dedicated symbol of the festive season that he eventually becomes. His well-judged mixture of incredulity and stroppiness is often highly entertaining. Allen seems to enjoy the more fantastical elements of the film as much as he does the dramatic, emotional scenes which occur nearer the climax, appearing to take great delight in Scott's newly-found sweet tooth (especially his growing addiction to milk and cookies) as well as discovering the answer to a question which has no doubt troubled many a parent: exactly how Santa is able to visit homes which have no fireplace. (The solution may well be a great relief for the children who live in such homes, but in practical terms – as the audience discovers – it does not prove to be such good news for Scott.) Allen had achieved huge fame thanks to his starring role as affable TV host Tim Taylor in ABC's *Home Improvement* (1991-99), which won him a Golden Globe Award (and four further Golden Globe nominations during the show's run), though he had made his cinematic debut some years earlier during a small part in Ciro Durán's dark thriller *Tropical Snow* (1988). The success of *The Santa Clause* was only to enhance his already prominent profile, as did his performance the following year as the voice of Buzz Lightyear in John Lasseter's animated smash hit *Toy Story* (1995). His prolific acting career has continued to the present day, and he has also worked as a producer, director and screenwriter – including as Mike Baxter in sitcom *Last Man Standing* (2011-21) – and he was to make a return to festive movies in more recent years as the cynical character

237

Larry Roth in the critically divisive *El Camino Christmas* (David E. Talbert, 2017).

While it is the strength of Allen's likeable performance which ensures the core appeal of *The Santa Clause*, to say nothing of his lightness of touch in his interpretation of the offbeat lead character, the film's supporting cast also do well with the material that they are given. Judge Reinhold was handed the somewhat awkward task of taking Neil, a mildly neurotic psychiatrist with a line in tasteless sweaters, and turning him into an engaging and sympathetic character. Though Neil inevitably comes off worst in his near-constant verbal sparring with Scott, Reinhold's naturally genial screen persona shines through in order to make the prissy shrink as likeable as possible. Reinhold's acting career had enjoyed many successes throughout the eighties, with appearances in films such as *Stripes* (Ivan Reitman, 1981), *Fast Times at Ridgemont High* (Amy Heckerling, 1982), *Gremlins* (Joe Dante, 1984), and most especially as Detective Billy Rosewood in *Beverly Hills Cop* (Martin Brest, 1984) and its two sequels. He continued to appear in diverse films throughout the early nineties, with roles in features including Sam Pillsbury's romantic thriller *Zandalee* (1991) and Nick Mead's crime caper *Bank Robber* (1993), before his performance in *The Santa Clause*. He has also, in more recent years, been active as a director and producer.

Wendy Crewson also manages against the odds to make Laura a reasonably benevolent and concerned individual, bringing the character to life in ways that elevates her beyond the multi-purpose killjoy that she appears to be on paper. Crewson has, if anything, an even more difficult job than Reinhold, for Laura's protectiveness of Charlie seems to be more skewed towards resentment of Scott's desire to curry favour with his son rather than being borne entirely from an attempt to shield Charlie from Scott's seemingly-irrational behaviour. It is fortunate, therefore, that Crewson manages to inject the character with just enough poignancy to make Laura's concerns seem valid and justifiable, in order to avoid her ever seeming entirely unsympathetic. Crewson had, in addition to prolific appearances on television, been working in the film industry since the early 1980s, her roles including parts in *Skullduggery* (Ota Richter, 1983), *Mark of Cain* (Bruce Pittman, 1985) and short film *The Sight* (Francis Mankiewicz, 1985). Later to appear in a number of nineties features, such as *The Doctor* (Randa Haines, 1991), *The Good Son* (Joseph Ruben, 1993) and *Corrina, Corrina* (Jessie Nelson, 1994), she has also more recently assumed production roles in both television and cinema.

Other performers worth looking out for throughout the film include industry veteran Peter Boyle as Mr Whittle – forever fondly remembered as The Monster in Mel Brooks's *Young Frankenstein* (1974), amongst the many other roles that he portrayed in his lifetime – as well as a spiky but sociable turn from the charismatic David Krumholtz as Bernard, the streetwise and sardonic elf. Krumholtz is a well-regarded stage actor whose earlier film work had included appearances in *Life with Mikey* (James Lapine, 1993) and *Addams Family Values* (Barry Sonnenfeld, 1993), and who would go on to many later appearances in TV and film. As Charlie, Eric Lloyd manages to tread a fine line between childhood wonder and obstreperous petulance, thankfully falling on the right side of the boundary almost all of the time. Given his significance to the central ensemble, this is vitally important, for it ensures that the film never spirals into a headlong nose-dive towards sentimentality even at the point of its emotional conclusion.

The Santa Clause generally performed well with the critics as well as in cinemas, even in spite of the fact that it faced stiff competition at the box-office in the form of Les Mayfield's *Miracle on 34ᵗʰ Street* (q.v.), the popular and high-profile John Hughes-produced remake of the perennial forties classic which was released during the holiday season in the same year, and – in its examination of divorce, scepticism, and public perception of the legendary figure of Santa Claus – addressed many of the same themes. Nonetheless, commentators broadly approved of *The Santa Clause*'s mix of contemporary invention and traditional charm, with Roger Ebert offering the qualified praise that '*The Santa Clause* (so named after the clause on Santa's calling card that requires Scott to take over the job) is often a clever and amusing movie, and there's a lot of fresh invention in it. If I found my attention flagging, maybe it's because I am not a member of its intended audience. For kids and many teenagers and their families, this is probably going to be a popular film. I personally found I just didn't care much: That, despite its charms, the movie didn't push over the top into true inspiration. I would have traded a lot of *The Santa Clause* for just one shot of Groucho Marx explaining how there ain't no sanity clause'.[9] Others instead drew attention to the fact that Pasquin never allows the film's technical wizardry to detract from the underlying appeal and breezy goodwill of its core narrative, permitting a sense of wonder to emerge from the interpersonal dynamics of the characters rather than special effects; as Leonard Klady remarks, 'This is a hip, likable spin on the seasonal icon told with a deft mixture of comedy and sentimentality. The mixture should mint some fast Xmas coin and play into the New

Year with upbeat returns. [...] *The Santa Clause* also offers one of those rare instances where the gadgetry and effects don't overwhelm the story. They remain functional and organic, handsomely complemented by Carol Spier's production design'.[10]

While Tim Allen's lead performance garnered appreciation from many reviewers, the film's smartly-pitched humour was often singled out as what really drove its sense of charm. Desson Howe, for instance, observes that: 'Kids of most ages will be able to follow – and enjoy – this comic fantasy. Thanks to unobtrusive (or is that low-budget?) special effects, they'll also enjoy the movie's answers to such cynical questions as: How does Santa fit through the chimneys or get into homes that don't have them? Allen makes things equally pleasant for older audiences, especially when he's trying to deal with his new calling. "Merry Christmas to all," he intones good-naturedly to one and all, before muttering: "When I wake up, I'm going to get a CAT scan"'.[11] For some, however, the movie's allure was significantly less convincing; Michael Wilmington, for instance, was especially biting in his appraisal of its perceived limitations:

A feeble attempt to revive the tradition of heart-warming family seasonal comedies that gave us *Miracle on 34th Street*, *It's a Wonderful Life*, *The Bells of St. Mary's* and many others, this staggeringly inane movie suggests that all the old cinema magic may have expired with the immediate post-World War II era that fostered it. [...] Dull lighting and drab settings abound – and the North Pole workshop resembles the depleted toy section in a department store about to go out of business. What exactly is the audience for this movie? Guilt-ridden divorced toy company executives? Sweater or Santa fetishists? Obsessed *Home Improvement* fans? (They're the ones who should stay away.) It may not be strictly accurate to say the actors, especially Reinhold, look embarrassed throughout *The Santa Clause*. But doing these jokes about unruly reindeer, hard-guy New York elves and Santa on the run from the cops, they should be embarrassed. This is the kind of material that's usually handed to high school freshmen for their initiation skits.[12]

While the above review was somewhat harsher than the general consensus, Wilmington was not alone in voicing scepticism about the film's merits. While some reviewers considered the storyline to have an occasional tendency to stray into the realm of saccharine, others believed that mawkishness ultimately rendered the narrative bland. James Berardinelli, for instance, opined that 'this is what happens when someone takes what might have been a moderately-entertaining television Christmas special and tries to adapt it for the big screen. *The Santa Clause* isn't an unmitigated disaster, but it's also a whole lot less impressive than it could be. [[...]] There's nothing offensive or mean-spirited about *The Santa Clause*, but that's expected from a Disney release. However, there should be more to family entertainment than these "wholesome" qualities, and this film isn't able to deliver them. Tim Allen's movie is in need of something his TV show is very familiar with: improvement'.[13] Overall, however, the reception of the film was positive if sometimes qualified. The criticism of Hollis Chacona praises the film's virtues while emphasising its overall place within the wider pantheon of festive cinema: "Part Oz, part Willy Wonka chocolate factory, this delicious concoction of a Santa's workshop set is fantastic and too much for our wondering eyes to absorb in the short amount of time we're allowed there. But, even in the "real" world of *The Santa Clause*, the jokes are mostly funny, the divorced parents stay happily divorced, and we're treated to yet another earnestly dopey performance by the endearing Judge Reinhold. [...] Okay, so it can't hold a comedic candle to *A Christmas Story*, but I can guarantee that if you take your kids to *The Santa Clause*, you'll never again have to dodge those disconcerting questions about how Santa gets into your fireplace-less house. And that alone could be worth the price of admission'.[14]

This generally receptive critical response has continued into the present day, with some recent appraisals of *The Santa Clause* citing it as being, in retrospect, a modern triumph of its genre. Carlos deVillalvilla observed that: 'This is certainly not the best Christmas movie ever made but it has become a minor holiday classic. It is clever, good fun and essentially harmless. It could have used a little more edge and Santa breaking his neck early on might scar the more sensitive kids for life but other than that this is charming holiday viewing and definitely a movie I don't mind seeing again and again'.[15] In the opinion of Zachary Cruz-Tan, however, the success of *The Santa Clause* was not simply a result of its compelling lead, its dry wit or its technical accomplishments, but rather its emotional heart and willingness to follow through on its thematic intentions, noting that the film 'develops into a sweet parable, more about faith, and the rekindling of faith, than about recovering fathers. [...] What I cherished most about this movie is not the effects, which are dated, nor the performances, which are held rigid by the dialogue, but the path it takes. Scott is pampered by his duties into submission and ultimately earns compassion from his son and wife (Wendy Crewson), which I suppose is expected'.[16] But in general, analysis today remains much as it was at the time of *The Santa Clause*'s release – affirmative but usually with reservations. As Mike Long has put it:

> *The Santa Clause* plays like two movies in one. The basic premise and the play on words with Santa Clause is quite clever and delightful. The idea that anyone can become Santa Claus, and undergo a physical transformation, simply by putting on the suit is a neat one and Tim Allen really milks his natural comedic talents when he puts on the fat suit or reacts to the beard. (If you want to look for deeper meaning in the movie, one could say that it's telling us that the Christmas spirit lives in all of us.) I also like the idea that a man who sells toys for a living had to go through this to fully appreciate Christmas. But, then we have the dark side of the movie. As Scott begins to change, those around him begin to worry. When he starts to believe and tell others that he's Santa, they really begin to worry. Of course, having been to the North Pole with Scott, Charlie tells everyone that his Dad is telling the truth. This makes Laura and Neil accuse Scott of dragging Charlie into his delusion. Scott's sanity is questioned, as is his ability to parent. The bottom line is that this portion of the movie is quite depressing and, while it's trying to make a point, gets too far away from holiday spirit. Yes, the movie has a happy ending, but that rough patch is hard to get over.[17]

The Santa Clause was to put in a strong performance at a number of industry awards ceremonies following its release, including nominations for Best Fantasy Film and Best Make-Up at the Saturn Awards, Best Breakthrough Performance and Best Comedic Performance for Tim Allen at the MTV Movie Awards, and Best Family Motion Picture (Comedy or Musical) and Best Performance by a Young Actor Co-Starring in a Motion Picture for Eric Lloyd at the Young Artist Awards. In addition to the above nominations, Michael Convertino was to win a BMI Film Music Award in 1995 for his original score for the film.

The considerable commercial success of The Santa Clause ultimately gave rise to two sequels in later years. Michael Lembeck's The Santa Clause 2: The Mrs Clause (2002) was to see the overwhelming majority of the original film's main and supporting cast return for a light-hearted caper centring around Scott's discovery that he must observe another, hitherto-unrevealed North Pole clause. This mystical caveat states that he has to find himself a wife (the Mrs Clause of the title) no later than Christmas Eve, or else put the entire festive season at risk. Although the film's critical reception was significantly more mixed than that of the original, it performed very well at the box-office, paving the way for a second sequel in 2006. The Santa Clause 3: The Escape Clause, also directed by Michael Lembeck, mainly concerns the chaos which engulfs the North Pole due to the mischievous shenanigans of Jack Frost (a characteristically high-octane performance from Martin Short), who almost manages to derail the festivities of the holiday season if not for some quick thinking from Scott and his allies. Reviews were more hostile towards this third outing, with many commentators beginning to voice the opinion that the series was now running out of steam, but *The Santa Clause 3* nonetheless retained a healthy showing in cinemas over the festive period of its release.

At time of writing, a new *Santa Clause* spin-off limited series has been announced for the Disney+ streaming video platform, entitled *The Santa Clauses*, with a release expected late in 2022. With star Tim Allen signed to return, along with David Krumholtz as Bernard the Elf, the premise of the miniseries will revolve around the late-middle-aged Scott Calvin's realisation that he cannot continue indefinitely in the role as Santa Claus, and follows his efforts to find and appoint a suitable successor in the role before he can retire.

There has rarely been a more literal interpretation of the transformative power of Christmas than that which was provided by *The Santa Clause*, and while the journey of its protagonist (from materialistic, corporate banality to altruistic kindness and geniality) is in line with other narratives expressed in festive cinema, it is in the deliberate broadening of the central familial sphere of influence that the film seems to be of particular interest. Scott takes care, during the concluding scenes, to emphasise to Charlie that rather than his family being fractured, it has instead been enlarged – he will always have access to both of his parents, but will also have a stable home thanks to the bond between Neil and Laura. Thus while its contemporary – the Les Mayfield remake of *Miracle on 34th Street* – celebrated the traditional nuclear family just as intently as *Home Alone* (q.v.) had done, *The Santa Clause* was to acknowledge that times were changing, and with them attitudes towards social mores. We see that the blended family can be a supportive structure which offers comfort and wellbeing, and that what really matters is how its constituent members respect and treat each other.

The film therefore exhibits a redemptive theme too, in the sense that Scott not only discovers a new and more fulfilling role for himself – becoming a more responsible father and rejecting the soullessly acquisitive nature of his corporate lifestyle – but that he is also able to come to terms with the new and challenging family circumstances surrounding his son's relationship with his former wife and her new partner. In so doing, *The Santa Clause* manages to confidently fulfil a shrewd duality of purpose, typifying many characteristic themes of established festive cinema whilst simultaneously broadening its appeal to encapsulate the changing social conventions of the contemporary world. This collision of the traditional and modern would, of course, be addressed again as the decade continued, but rarely did the characteristic 1990s fusion of established convention and recognised cultural change seem quite so striking as it did throughout the course of *The Santa Clause*.

REFERENCES

1. Jay Mechling, 'Rethinking (and Reteaching) the Civil Religion in Post-Nationalist American Studies', in *Post-Nationalist American Studies*, ed. by John Carlos Rowe (Berkeley: University of California Press, 2000), 63-80, p.76.

2. Mark Connelly, 'Santa Claus: The Movie', in *Christmas at the Movies*, ed. by Mark Connelly (London: I.B. Tauris, 2000), 115-134, pp.116-17.

3. Lisa Liebman, 'Film: The Gentle Art of Creating a Family Film', *The New York Times*, 27 November 1994. <*https://www.nytimes.com/1994/11/27/movies/film-the-gentle-art-of-creating-a-family-film.html*>

4. Carlos deVillalvilla, '*The Santa Clause*', in *Cinema365*, 24 December 2011. <*https://carlosdev.wordpress.com/2011/12/24/the-santa-clause/*>

5. Frank Thompson, *American Movie Classics' Great Christmas Movies* (Dallas: Taylor Publishing Company, 1998), p.209.

6. Jeff Shannon, 'Allen Delivers Belly Laughs In Amusing *Santa Clause*', in *The Seattle Times*, 11 November 1994. <*https://archive.seattletimes.com/archive/?date=19941111&slug=1941324*>

7. Thompson, pp.211-12.

8.   J.P. Roscoe, 'The Santa Clause (1994)', in Basement Rejects, 13 December 2011.
      <http://basementrejects.com/review/the-santa-clause-1994/>

9.   Roger Ebert, 'The Santa Clause', in The Chicago Sun-Times, 11 November 1994.
      <https://www.rogerebert.com/reviews/the-santa-clause-1994>

10.   Leonard Klady, 'The Santa Clause', in Variety, 10 November 1994.
      <https://variety.com/1994/film/reviews/the-santa-clause-1200439443/>

11.   Desson Howe, 'The Santa Clause', in The Washington Post, 11 November 1994.
      <https://www.washingtonpost.com/wp-srv/style/longterm/movies/videos/thesantaclausepghowe_a0b08e.htm>

12.   Michael Wilmington, 'The Santa Clause', in The Chicago Tribune, 11 November 1994.
      <https://www.chicagotribune.com/news/ct-xpm-1994-11-11-9411110127-story.html>

13.   James Berardinelli, 'The Santa Clause', in ReelViews, 11 November 1994.
      <https://www.reelviews.net/reelviews/santa-clause-the>

14.   Hollis Chacona, 'The Santa Clause', in The Austin Chronicle, 18 November 1994.
      <https://www.austinchronicle.com/events/film/1994-11-18/the-santa-clause/>

15.   de Villalvilla.

16.   Zachary Cruz-Tan, '*The Santa Clause* (1994)', in *The Critical Reel*, 26 November 2014.
       <*http://thecriticalreel.com/the-santa-clause-1994/*>

17.   Mike Long, '*The Santa Clause Trilogy* (1994-2006)', in *DVD Sleuth*, 16 October 2012.
       <*https://www.dvdsleuth.com/TheSantaClauseTrilogyReview/*>

9

Trapped in Paradise (1994)

Twentieth Century Fox / Permut Presentations

Director: George Gallo
Producers: Jon Davison and George Gallo
Screenwriter: George Gallo

S OME Christmas movies have become lost gems of the genre; features which, unfairly, have dropped off the radar of popular culture and are rarely watched or discussed in the years following their production. On the other hand, there are films which enjoyed a reasonable profile at the time they were released in cinemas, but – due to the critical reaction from reviewers and audiences which was to meet them – were promptly to disappear into the mists of yuletide obscurity. Director George Gallo has the distinction of having helmed both types of Christmas film. His *29th Street* (q.v.) was an underappreciated slice of modern urban fantasy which has gradually built a cult following amongst fans of Christmas cinema, but remains one of the more obscure festive features of the 1990s. *Trapped in Paradise*, on the other hand, enjoyed greater star power and a considerably more generous budget, but was so pilloried by the critics when it first hit movie theatres that it quickly acquired a reputation as one of the decade's most conspicuous Christmas turkeys.

Arguably the single greatest nail in the film's coffin is not that it is a bad movie, but rather that it has so much un-realised potential for greatness. Gallo, who had earlier achieved so much success as the screenwriter of *Midnight Run* (Martin Brest, 1988), was in place to write and direct the film as well as acting as one of its producers. The cast con-tained a number of popular and well-known performers in the main roles, as well as many talented character actors in sup-porting parts. These included several who had made appearances in *29th Street* – not least Frank Pesce, whose au-tobiographical story had formed the basis of that earlier movie. Thus with so much talent assigned to the movie, what was it about *Trapped in Paradise* which attracted so much critical ire? And did it ever really deserve the level of vitriol that has been aimed at it over the years?

The film's premise owed a great deal, at least in spirit, to *We're No Angels* (Michael Curtiz, 1955) – itself an often unfairly overlooked triumph from the golden age of the Christmas movie, where three convicts on the run from the Devil's Island penal colony end up hiding out in the premises of an unsuspecting family as they try to devise a way to escape to the mainland. All goes to plan until they discover that the family is made up of such kind and thoroughly decent people, they can't quite bring themselves to rob and swindle them, and thus the felons end up helping them out of grave difficul-ty before eventually deciding to give themselves up just as the festive season gets underway. Boasting headline performances from Humphrey Bogart, Aldo Ray and Peter Ustinov – play-ing a fraudster, a hoodlum and a safe-cracker respectively – *We're No Angels* presented the least conventional 'Three Wise Men' imaginable, and the basic principle of three eccen-tric characters trying and failing to flee during Christmas after committing a crime is a very clear influence on Gallo's film, albeit updated to a much more contemporary setting.

With such a solid thematic and narrative foundation for *Trapped in Paradise*, numerous theories have been advanced with regard to its catastrophically bad reputation amongst film commentators. In large part, the purportedly troubled production of the movie has been cited as the most likely factor in the unevenness of the final product that was presented to audiences. Chris Coffel points out that according to anecdotal accounts, it is alleged that 'the cast absolutely hated making the film. [Jon] Lovitz was the most vocally outspoken of the bunch, allegedly referring to the movie as *Trapped in Bullshit*. It sounds like these onset problems stemmed from writer/director George Gallo having little interest in actually directing the movie. Again Lovitz spoke out claiming that [Nicolas] Cage actually directed portions of the film because Gallo simply refused to give direction. I guess this is why Gallo has had a much better career as a writer than as a director'.[1]

Other censure has been focused on the irregularity of the film's setting, which is portrayed as a strange collision of urban modernity and the idealised rural community settings of Christmas movies past – most specifically, of the genre's storied 1940s post-War origins. Here, as Todd McCarthy has observed, there is a lack of consistency in evidence which means that *Trapped in Paradise* never quite succeeds in being either comedically edgy or wistfully nostalgic: 'The film harks back to a time in life and movies when small-town America represented the ultimate in cozy togetherness, warmth and security. In such a context, selfishness assumes the dimensions of a mortal sin, and what could be more selfish than crime for personal gain? This is where the Brothers Firpo come in. [...]

They may as well have traveled by time machine as by stolen car, as the locals seem to be living in a Frank Capra or Leo McCarey film from the 1930s or 1940s'.[2]

It is the lead-up to Christmas in New York, and traffic has ground to a virtual standstill in the populous city as people race around on last-minute business before the holidays. Someone in the crowd drops their wallet, which is kicked around by pedestrians until it falls into the hands of the well-dressed Bill Firpo (Nicolas Cage). Bill discovers that it is stuffed with hundred dollar bills, but – as photos in the wallet show that its owner is a doting family man – his conscience compels him to turn it in rather than steal the cash. He later goes to seek confession at his local chapel, but the priest – Father Ritter (Richard B. Shull) – is confused by his parishioner's troubled conscience. If Bill mailed the wallet back to its rightful owner, why is he feeling guilty? The answer, Bill explains, is that by even momentarily considering keeping the lost money, he felt almost as drawn to wrongdoing as his two felonious brothers, Dave (Jon Lovitz) and Alvin (Dana Carvey), who are currently in prison doing time for their past misdemeanours. He is shocked when the priest then reveals that he may be able to compare misdeeds with his wayward siblings in person sooner than he thinks – due to major overcrowding, the parole board is currently considering prisoners for early release.

Sure enough, Bill is waiting outside the prison soon after as the confabulating compulsive liar Dave and childlike kleptomaniac Alvin are discharged by the authorities. Bill knows that his brothers are incapable of changing their ways, and warns them that he will tolerate none of their usual criminality. As they are both technically on parole, they are under Bill's supervision and unable to leave the State. However, they are unable to resist getting up to their old tricks – within minutes of stopping to buy a snack from a convenience store, Alvin is helping himself to the contents of the cash register. Bill storms in and demands that his brother return it, but the store owner witnesses the theft and calls the police. A chase ensues, but Bill manages to convince the pursuing cop that he is an off-duty detective, ensuring their escape.

Back in the safety of their home, the brothers' mother Edna 'Ma' Firpo (Florence Stanley) is delighted that the family are once again reunited. She refuses to believe that Alvin and Dave have ever been guilty of any criminality – much to Bill's frustration. As far as she is concerned, they just happen to be in the wrong place at the wrong time... a lot. Ma stumbles across a letter held by Alvin which is allegedly from a fellow jail inmate, asking him to connect with his daughter who lives in a small town in Pennsylvania. Bill perceives this as an obvious forgery on Dave's part, possibly as part of a ruse to cross State lines and escape the parole board. However, he is more immediately concerned about the fact that his own wallet now appears to be missing.

At his job as the manager of an upmarket restaurant, Bill is ingratiating himself with high-class clients when Dave comes racing in with some urgent news. Bill's missing wallet has been found at the scene of a crime in the Bronx, and the police are now actively looking for him as a suspect. Alvin is waiting outside in a stolen getaway vehicle, and the baffled Bill sneaks out the back of the restaurant with Dave to make their clandestine getaway. They make it over the State boundary to New Jersey, but Bill immediately smells a rat when Dave claims to call home from a public call-box and tells his brothers that Ma is being interrogated by the police. She has apparently recommended that they get further away to evade capture, and Dave suggests heading for Paradise, Pennsylvania in order to fulfil their promise to their former prisoner acquaintance. Bill knows full well that this must all be part of an elaborate ruse, but is reluctant to take the risk of returning home just in case there is even a remote risk that the police really are in pursuit.

The Firpo brothers arrive in the beautiful, snowy small town of Paradise on Christmas Eve, and immediately bring about chaos by causing one of the sheriff's deputies to be thrown from his horse. The jovial Chief Burnell (Sean McCann) apologises for the inconvenience, blaming it on the poor horsemanship of the deputy – his son, Timmy (Paul Lazar). Bill is less than enthused at being under the close scrutiny of the law yet again, but asks the chief if he knows the whereabouts of a Sarah Mazzucci – the name of the contact given by the prison inmate. Burnell has no knowledge of anyone with that name living in the town, but tells them that the only Sarah he's aware of in the vicinity works at the local bank.

Seeing this as their only lead, the brothers head into the grand building in the hope that Mazzucci might be the maiden name of the Sarah they are looking for. They soon discover the security in the bank to be staggeringly lax, with only one elderly napping guard on duty and closed-circuit security cameras unplugged. They soon encounter Sarah Collins (Madchen Amick), one of the bank clerks, who admonishes Alvin for helping himself to every complimentary pen and candy cane in the foyer. Bill starts gently enquiring whether she is the Sarah they are looking for, but is swiftly interrupted by the constantly-waffling Dave. Deciding that they have reached a dead end, the brothers are just leaving when a private security firm arrive with tens of thousands of dollars for

256

the bank's vault. The kindly manager, Clifford Anderson (Donald Moffat), signs the cash in as Bill looks on in incredulity at the building's near-total lack of defences against criminality.

As the brothers drive away, Bill offhandedly points out that if they had a gun, they could hold up the local bank without even a hint of resistance. Dave gleefully tells him that the car they are driving has been 'borrowed' from a gun store owner, and – sure enough – the trunk is laden with a collection of pristine firearms. Suddenly Bill's morally-upright approach to life dissipates in front of their eyes. Thinking on their feet, the brothers stock up on disguises at a local convenience store and then hotwire a car. They pull up outside the bank and storm in wearing face-masks and brandishing shotguns. The bank manager's talkative wife, Hattie (Angela Paton), admonishes them for holding a robbery just before the town winter-fest... much to Bill's astonishment, as he had expected no resistance. When they demand the key to the bank vault, Hattie informs them that only her husband Clifford has access to it, and he has just gone out for his lunch hour.

Refusing to be deterred, Bill marches Hattie over the street to the crowded coffee shop where Clifford is eating and demands that he bring the vault key back to the bank. However, on account of his bulky disguise, he is forced to withdraw his shotgun, causing the customers to believe he intends to rob the coffee shop. Thus he has no choice but to march every patron and staff member from the busy shop over to the bank, to avoid them having any opportunity to call the police – much to the mystification of the other townsfolk as they watch the bizarre procession. Once everyone has congregated in the one place, Clifford unlocks the bank vault at gunpoint, and Bill wastes no time in grabbing bags stuffed with cash. In his haste to leave, however, he accidentally sets off a security tripwire, raising the alarm.

Outside the bank building, Bill and Dave run towards the getaway car, but Alvin accidentally sets off without them and then inadvertently causes a five-car pile-up. Eventually the three brothers reunite and head off to the outskirts of town to pick up their original vehicle. Bill discovers that he still has Clifford's keys to the bank vault, and Dave jokes that they can hit the building again the following year. They are all unaware that, back in prison in New York, tough convict Vic Mazzucci (Vic Manni) is regaling his fellow inmates with his dream of robbing the lightly-defended bank in Paradise – even though his daughter, Sarah, works there. His tale is interrupted when he is informed that the TV news is reporting that the exact same bank has just been ransacked. Immediately suspecting the Firpo brothers, who knew of his plans, Vic is enraged.

A media circus is descending on Paradise, closely followed by the arrival of FBI Agents Peyser (Richard Jenkins), Boyle (Jonathan Allore), Cooper (Mark Melymick) and Giardello (Scott Wickware). The investigators are keen to know if any unexpected faces had been seen in the vicinity, but the chief of the sheriff's department feels that with the town winter-fest underway and many visitors in town, it would be next to impossible to tell. The FBI have scrambled to intercept traffic out of the town, and sure enough, the Firpo brothers – who have become hopelessly lost – are soon being pursued by a patrol car. In his haste to get away, Alvin puts their vehicle into a spin on the snow-covered road, and it ends up plunging off a road bridge to the ground below.

Although their car is wrecked and overturned, all three brothers are miraculously unharmed by the crash. With an extreme winter weather system setting in, they would be liable to freeze but for the arrival of the benevolent Dick Anderson (Sean O'Bryan), who informs them that the major roads are now blocked by snow but offers to bring them home to avoid the elements. They are soon horrified, however, when he returns them to Paradise, and to the home of their aunt and uncle... who happen to be Clifford and Hattie from the bank. They are unable to believe their bad luck, until it becomes clear that the bank manager and his wife have no idea that they were the felons responsible for the robbery.

The Andersons arrange fresh clothing for the brothers and invite them to join the family for dinner. Bill is surprised to discover that Sarah, the clerk from the bank, lodges with Clifford and Hattie at their home. Just as they are about to sit down to dinner, a TV newsflash reveals that Vic Mazzucci and an accomplice, Caesar Spinoza (Frank Pesce), have escaped from prison and are heading for an unknown location. This greatly alarms Dave, who immediately asks to call their mother back in New York. As he feared, Mazzucci answers the phone and tells the hapless Firpo in no uncertain terms that he expects to receive all the proceeds from the bank robbery – which he claims was all his own scheme – or else Ma's safety will be in danger.

None of them realise that the permanently gruff Ed Dawson (John Ashton) and his sidekick Clovis Minor (John Bergantine), sheriff's deputies who work at the town convenience store, are waiting impatiently outside. Having deduced that the Firpo brothers were responsible for the robbery, based on their earlier purchase of the clothing which later formed their robbery disguises, Ed resolves to hatch a plan in order to steal the cash back from the criminals – not to return it to the authorities, but to keep it themselves.

Over dinner, Clifford conversationally reveals that a total of $275,000 was stolen from the bank. Bill off-handedly suggests that banks always submit inflated claims when they are robbed so that they actually end up better off as a result of a heist, but Clifford is aghast at the dishonesty of the very notion. The sincerity of his moral decency gives a shamed Bill momentary pause for thought. The brothers are further chastened when they realise that such profound monetary losses are likely to put the bank in near-certain danger of a buyout from larger concerns, and that everyone in town had contributed throughout the year to a Christmas club... meaning that the Firpos have unknowingly managed to rob every person with a bank account in Paradise.

Sarah discovers that there is a bus route still open to Philadelphia where, if the brothers are able to catch a train to New York, they could be back in New York by midnight. Bill gladly accepts the offer of a car ride there, but feels appallingly guilty when the Andersons give them some cash for the journey and invite them back any time they are in the area. As Sarah and the Firpos depart, Ed spots Bill's duffel bag and concludes that it must contain the stolen cash from the bank. Just as they all head out of Paradise, however, Vic and Caesar are driving towards the town with Ma Firpo as their hostage. Not trusting Dave and Alvin to return home with the money, Vic has decided to intercept them in Pennsylvania instead.

The Firpo brothers are dropped off at a bus station heading for Philadelphia, but Sarah speeds off without even wishing them goodbye – much to Bill's confusion. Bill heads for the ticket office but is frustrated to discover that the money he was given by Clifford is just short of the required ticket fee. Unable to access the stolen loot from his bag due to near-by police officers, he is chastened yet again as a compassionate bus station clerk (Marcia Bennett) makes up the difference from her own purse. As Bill emerges from the station, Ed and Clovis see their opportunity and try to steal the duffel bag. Bill grabs Ed's gun and fires it into the air, causing a panic and leading the police to focus their attention on the two store attendants rather than the Firpos. The brothers make good their escape, and are long gone before the FBI arrive on the scene.

Chief Burnell vouches for Ed and Clovis, identifying them both as volunteer deputies at the sheriff's department, but the two men feign ignorance of the incident at the bus station. Taken back to the FBI's temporary base of operations for questioning, the pair continue to disavow any knowledge of the bank robbery culprits, but are interrupted when a trio of local kids turn up with a claim that they saw three strange men pushing a car into a local river. As the investigators head off to find the evidence, the Firpos are in the process of trying to steal a rowing boat from a garden while its owners enjoy a Christmas party indoors. Knowing that they now have no chance of leaving by bus, Bill and his brothers have decided that an alternative method of departure will be necessary. They have barely started to make a getaway, however, before a police helicopter with a searchlight necessitates the aban-donment of their escape plans. While Bill and Dave get to shore, Alvin capsizes into the freezing water. Again, the altru-ism of the townspeople comes to the rescue when some elderly onlookers see Alvin clinging to a rock and form a human chain to save him from the strong tide. They bring him indoors and, after a last-minute attempt at reviving him, get the hapless crook back on his feet again.

Acting on the earlier tip-off, the FBI and the town sheriff's department have managed to locate and recover the stolen car from the river nearby. Inside, the ski-masks used in the bank robbery are quickly found. As the investigators ponder their findings, the Firpos have been brought along to a midnight Christmas Eve church service by Alvin's most recent rescuers. They awkwardly meet the Andersons and explain that they had missed their bus, but Sarah – not believing any of it – asks Bill for a quick word. When they are on their own, Sarah reveals that she is all too aware of the brothers' involvement in the robbery, and urges Bill to get out of town while he still can in order to avoid the consequences of his criminality. But Bill is starting to have a crisis of conscience over his earlier actions, knowing that the Firpos have unknowingly threatened the Andersons' livelihoods and the future of the town. He tells her that he wants to make amends, also signalling that he is aware that she is not all that she seems.

Alvin and Dave, meanwhile, have stolen the town's horse-drawn Christmas carriage and suggest that they use it as a getaway vehicle. Alvin sets off on a chaotic path through the churchyard and down main street, the police and FBI soon in hot pursuit. After a lengthy chase, and more by luck than design, the brothers end up causing the chasing vehicles to collide and manage to escape into the countryside. Reaching the interstate, the Firpos abandon the carriage and try to flag down a passing car to hitch-hike their way to safety. However, the horse drawing the carriage strays onto thin ice and is in danger of drowning in the freezing water, causing the brothers to race back to his rescue.

With considerable effort, they are able to free the distressed steed and take him to a nearby diner. As they dry out in the warmth, Bill explains that he has seen the error of his ways and intends to return the money to the bank vault – he still has the keys, and wants to do the right thing. Dave is appalled at the suggestion, given the amount of effort they've already expended in an attempt to escape Paradise, but Alvin agrees that it would be the right moral action to take. When Dave warns Bill that he is still a wanted man in New York, Alvin explains that this is simply not true – the whole episode had been an elaborate set-up to trick Bill into fleeing to Pennsylvania. He returns Bill's wallet, which was never found at a crime scene, and Dave grudgingly admits that the police converging at the restaurant where Bill works had only happened because he had called in advance to falsely report the suspected presence of a sniper in the building. Disgusted at his brothers' duplicity, Bill storms off.

Now bereft of transport, Bill tries to hitch a ride back to Paradise and unwittingly encounters Vic and Caesar. As neither party recognises the other, they offer to drive him into town – though Bill has no idea his increasingly irate mother is being held captive in the car's trunk. On the journey, Vic and Caesar spot a photo of Ma Firpo in Bill's wallet and immediately grasp the family connection. Vic pulls a gun on Bill, who jumps from the car in a panic and races for cover as the escaped convict fires indiscriminately at his fast-receding form.

Fortunately for Bill, Dave and Alvin are in pursuit in the stolen horse-drawn carriage and soon pick him up. The trio head back to the bank and break in, but Bill accidentally sets off the alarm when he uses the wrong key to access the vault. Forced to scramble when the authorities converge on the scene, the brothers instead decide to leave all of their stolen loot at the door of the local church minister with an explanatory note. Father Gorenzel (Gerard Parkes) is stupefied at the sight of all the missing cash when he answers the door, but by then the Firpos are long gone.

Ed and Clovis intercept the brothers and force them at gunpoint into their jeep. The FBI and the sheriff's department notice the vehicle as it speeds past the bank, just as they declare the latest break-in to be a false alarm. Ed explains that they're taking the Firpos to Clifford Anderson, reasoning that the brothers and the bank manager had plotted the robbery between themselves in order to falsely claim back an inflated amount of money from the insurers. They are unaware that Agent Peyser, who suspects foul play, is tailing them in his own car. When the car pulls up at the Andersons' home, Peyser notices a suspicious-looking vehicle with a New York licence plate parked nearby and immediately smells a rat.

As Ed and Clovis manhandle the brothers into the Andersons' house at gunpoint, they are amazed to discover that the family are being held hostage – by Vic and Caesar. The brothers are shocked to discover that their mother, who they believed was still in New York, is amongst the captives. Vic demands the full proceeds of the bank robbery, or he will start killing hostages. Bill explains that while he and his brothers were responsible for the crime, they have realised the error of their ways and have handed every dollar over to the church for safekeeping. This revelation seems to impress Sarah, who is revealed as having been Vic's daughter (under an assumed name) all along. Ma Firpo blasts Vic for the sob story letter that started the caper in the first place, but the criminal is bewildered by her claim... until Dave sheepishly admits that it was he who had concocted the whole scenario just to trick Bill into going to Paradise so he could be hoodwinked into robbing the bank.

Alarmed when the FBI announce that they have the building surrounded, Vic and Caesar try to make a getaway, but the sheriff's son Timmy – who is among the hostages – unexpectedly overpowers Caesar and uses his gun to shoot Vic in the shoulder, allowing the FBI agents to storm the building. The escaped crooks are dispatched back to prison in New York, and Ed and Clovis are taken into custody along with the Firpos. As the suspects are all transported to the FBI's mobile base of operations, Sarah visits Father Gorenzel and is astonished to discover that Bill had been telling the truth – every dollar of the stolen cash is accounted for, along with a note explaining that it belongs to the people of Paradise. She is startled to learn that the brothers really have mended their felonious ways.

Agent Peyser interrogates the suspects in an attempt to piece together what has really happened. Firstly, he asks Hattie Anderson to identify the brothers as the bank robbers, but she is unable to give positive verification because they had been wearing ski-masks at the time of the heist. Ed blurts out that he had sold the brothers masks at his convenience store half an hour before the crime took place, but in doing so he unwittingly admits that he had knowingly withheld information from the investigators. Alvin, being a habitual kleptomaniac, empties his pockets and reveals three ski-masks... along with a multitude of other sundry items. Peyser frustratedly asks the Firpos for their location at the time of the robbery, but Sarah and Clifford arrive and swear that the brothers had been Christmas shopping when the break-in was happening. Then Father Gorenzel appears with a box stuffed full of money and explains that all of the stolen cash has been accounted for – but that he has no idea who left it at his door, as the accompanying note was simply signed 'Three Wise Men'.

Finally admitting defeat, Peyser confidentially informs the brothers that while he is more than aware that something strange has happened in Paradise that cannot be accounted for, he has little choice but to let them go free – with the stern warning that such a miraculous chain of events is unlikely to ever come around again, so they should make the most of it and keep out of trouble. The assembled townsfolk are elated that their new friends have been let off the hook at the last minute.

Christmas Day has dawned in Paradise, and the Firpos are unexpectedly free men. As Ma Firpo voices her pride in her sons' change of heart, Sarah arrives to wish Bill goodbye. She too has been changed by the events of the past few days, and feels humbled that the townsfolk treat her no differently even now she has been revealed as the daughter of a notorious criminal. Bill reveals that he believes his experience in Paradise has been revelatory, and he would like to exchange his life in the big city for the charms of this small town... and the love of Sarah. As Ma, Alvin and Dave head back to New York together, Bill decides to stay with Sarah and start a new life together – a truly reformed character.

On the subject of *Trapped in Paradise*, veteran critic Roger Ebert opined that the film 'should be preserved by the Library of Congress, as an example of creative desperation. It plays like a documentary about a group of actors forced to perform in a screenplay that contains not one single laugh, or moment of wit, or flash of intelligence, or reason for being'.[3] Ebert's disparagement was shared by many reviewers of the time, and yet – while the movie was never to be in any danger of being confused with a masterpiece – it is scarcely as bad as its reputation suggests. Admittedly, as the synopsis indicates, the film is overlong, the plot is needlessly convoluted, and some of the attempts at humour fall flat on their face. Yet as a parody of the kind of relentlessly upbeat, wholesome yuletide venues which have acted as the backdrop of countless Christmas movies past, *Trapped in Paradise* works best when it is turning expectation on its head.

The fictional town of Paradise, Pennsylvania, is exactly the kind of idyllic, small-town American festive utopia that has since been popularised by countless Hallmark Christmas TV movies. The rural location is, as Janet Maslin observes, a very deliberate creative choice – particularly when juxtaposed with the streetwise urban realism of New York (actually filmed in Toronto), where the movie begins: 'Setting his cumbersome story among small-town folks at Christmastime, the writer and director George Gallo (*29th Street*) succeeds all too well in capturing his characters' ordinariness without allowing them any particular spark. Quaint little Paradise, Pa., isn't plastered with neon signs, but if it were, they would tout this as Capra country. This wholesome burg is meant to be a humorously incongruous place to find the Firpo brothers'.[4] As a result of the film's premise that the town is being so besieged by winter weather that the roads are impassable, Gallo's production team shipped in approximately 34,000 kilograms (75,000 pounds) of biodegradable potato flakes to create the illusion that Paradise was essentially submerged in fresh snow. Certainly the near-constant blizzards taking place on the night of Christmas Eve aids greatly in evoking a freezing ambience – as does the excellent location filming in and around Ontario, Canada. Yet even here, something so innocuous as creating the illusion of extreme weather conditions could show up logical inconsistencies in the film, with Jonathan Rosenbaum commenting that, 'If Frank Capra had directed the Three Stooges in a Disney Christmas release, the results would have been considerably better than this godawful Fox comedy. [...] Even the weather seems tailored to the script's shifting needs (one river is iceless, the others completely frozen over) as the bumbling brothers struggle to make their escape'.[5]

The conceit of three cynical criminals landing in a community where everyone is thoroughly decent and kind towards one another has great comedic potential, but the stratagem is ultimately overplayed. Many of the amusing situations which are portrayed become so tortuously drawn out and signposted that they are robbed of their comic capacity, which is especially regrettable given the range of excellent supporting character actors in evidence including Donald Moffat, Angela Paton, Vic Manni, Florence Stanley, Richard Jenkins and Sean McCann. While it is amusing that the aged, slumbering bank security guard manages to sleep all the way through an unapologetically noisy bank heist, for instance, the camera cuts back to him so often that the joke is excessively overdone. Similarly, there is a sense that we never truly come to know most of the townsfolk in anything other than the most rudimentary terms, often giving the impression that their presence is often only arranged to expediently serve the needs of the plot. Thus whether the audience considers the denizens of Paradise to be charmingly decent or self-consciously contrived is very much a matter of subjective opinion. McCarthy makes the point that, 'The politics of the piece, which can hardly be ignored, can be read either as a charmingly idealized portrait of an America that probably existed more in people's imaginations than in real life or as an unrealistic impulse to turn back the clock. One area where the picture gets the short end in the inevitable comparison with the old Hollywood is in supporting performances. Studio-era films were rife with great contract players who only had to show up onscreen to conjure up an array of aspects of, and attitudes toward, society. The community here pales in comparison to those on view in nearly any film produced during the period *Trapped in Paradise* is meant to evoke'.[6]

Gallo's screenplay touches on various themes common to Christmas cinema, not least in its celebration of the community during the festive season and – perhaps most notably – spotlighting the importance of family ties, even when the family in question is as unconventional a group as the Firpos. In actuality, however, attention towards Christmas conventions is often largely underemphasised in favour of the immediacy of the film's comic situations. While the intention seems very clearly to upend several public expectations of festive filmmaking in order to bolster the movie's comedic content – especially when pitching hard-nosed FBI agents and violent escaped convicts against the unerringly decent and upstanding citizens of Paradise – Gallo seems unsure of exactly how far to push the tactic, meaning that the film ultimately doesn't seem to be either one thing or the other. Like its colourful protagonists, it lacks the necessary degree of *legerdemain* to be all things to all people.

With so many supporting characters battling for screen time, very few of them prove to be particularly well-developed, and it says a great deal for the talent of the actors involved that they are able to create watchable performances given the lack of opportunity to expand on the quirks and eccentricities of their fictional personas. Particularly given the film's running length, this can't be seen as anything other than an egregiously wasted opportunity, and – as Charles T. Tatum, Jr. has remarked – is certainly among the reasons why the film has been repeatedly criticised for lack of production polish and editorial discipline: 'Nicolas Cage, Jon Lovitz, and Dana Carvey play three of the most unconvincing brothers ever cast, in a comedy that should never have been made. [...] The script is overly hokey and sentimental. I like a good Christmas movie now and then, but this is so chock full of good tidings and cheer, it turns completely unbelievable. Throw in the loud, bombastic music that drowns out some performers' lines, the fakest snow you have ever seen, and some characters suddenly acting in the complete opposite direction from how they were introduced, and you have an unmitigated disaster. *Trapped in Paradise* clocks in at nearly two hours long and is in desperate need of an editor. I would lose the first half of the film, and then the second half'.[7]

Even in stylistic terms, *Trapped in Paradise* would prove difficult to classify: part crime comedy, part romance and part Christmas fantasy, it never quite seems to be entirely the sum of its constituent fragments, and the jarring clash of creative approaches often works against the film rather than in support of it. The whirlwind romance between Bill and Sarah, for instance, seems all the more implausible given the near-total lack of opportunity given to Cage and Madchen Amick to develop it, while the townspeople's affection for the three bungling bank robbers seems particularly implausible given that they never seem to spend any significant amount of time with any of them throughout the film. With so many competing creative influences, therefore, Gallo's movie struggles to distinguish its own approach, which – as critics such as George Rother have suggested – makes it more of a patchwork of influences rather than a truly inventive work: 'It's something like *Groundhog Day* combined with *Quick Change* with a dash of *It's a Wonderful Life* thrown in for good measure. It's not the most original movie in the world, but it does have its good points that makes it worth watching at least once'.[8]

Carrying the bulk of the film's narrative is the intriguing on-screen trio of Nicolas Cage, Dana Carvey and Jon Lovitz as the mismatched Firpo brothers. Cage has long since earned a reputation as one of the most consistently interesting actors in Hollywood, and he doesn't disappoint here with an energetic and somewhat idiosyncratic performance as the elder sibling Bill which suits the sentiment of *Trapped in Paradise* perfectly. Carvey brings a fascinatingly childlike quality to the ingenuous Alvin, whose constant, compulsive stealing is often the source of amusement in many scenes (not least when trying – and singularly failing – to look surreptitous when purloining a plastic toy from the bottom of a box of cereal in the middle of a busy convenience store). Carvey was said to have based Alvin's curious speaking style on two different people, namely the film producer Brad Grey and the actor Mickey Rourke, complete with a comically exaggerated approximation of Rourke's facial expressions. The loquacious Lovitz also brings an animated approach to the constantly-talkative Dave, playing up the character's uncontrollable lack of truthfulness to amusing effect as well as emphasising his more gregarious traits – perhaps most evident when the character arranges an impromptu singalong and yoga breathing lessons when the bank hostages are forced to wait while Bill desperately tries to find a key to the vault.

Nicolas Cage was already a very recognisable face to audiences by the mid-nineties, having appeared in numerous well-received films throughout the previous decade including *Raising Arizona* (Joel Coen and Ethan Coen, 1987), *Moonstruck* (John Patrick Shanley, 1987) and *Wild at Heart* (David

Lynch, 1990). Cage won the Academy Award for Best Actor for his performance in *Leaving Las Vegas* (Mike Figgis, 1995), and was later nominated for his role in *Adaptation* (Spike Jonze, 2002). He has also earned a Golden Globe Award, and been nominated for many other accolades including BAFTA Awards, Independent Spirit Awards and Screen Actors Guild Awards. His on-screen romantic interest in *Trapped in Paradise*, Sarah Mazzucci/Collins, was portrayed by Madchen Amick, who at the time was almost certainly best-known for her performance as Shelly Johnson in ABC's *Twin Peaks* (1990-91) and its cinematic prequel, *Twin Peaks: Fire Walk with Me* (David Lynch, 1992). Though she continued to make appearances on the big screen in films including *Sleepwalkers* (Mick Garris, 1992) and *Dream Lover* (Nicholas Kazan, 1993), she has been considerably more prolific on television in addition to being the director of several music videos.

Dana Carvey and Jon Lovitz both worked on NBC's *Saturday Night Live* to great acclaim before embarking on film careers. Carvey had made frequent appearances on the big screen throughout the 1980s, mostly in comedies such as *This is Spinal Tap* (Rob Reiner, 1984), *Tough Guys* (Jeff Kanew, 1986) and *Moving* (Alan Metter, 1988) before achieving greater pop culture prominence as Garth Algar in *Wayne's World* (Penelope Spheeris, 1992) and *Wayne's World 2* (Stephen Surjik, 1993). Lovitz had similarly been active in the cinema of the eighties, with roles in films as diverse as *Three Amigos* (John Landis, 1986), *Jumpin' Jack Flash* (Penny Marshall, 1986) and *My Stepmother is an Alien* (Richard Benjamin, 1988), and would go on to further fame throughout the 1990s in movies including *A League of Their Own* (Penny Marshall, 1992) and *City Slickers II: The Legend of Curly's Gold* (Paul Weiland, 1994). He has also achieved considerable success as a voice actor, Broadway performer and stand-up comedian.

The original score of *Trapped in Paradise*, by Robert Folk (almost certainly best-known for creating the instantly-recognisable theme to Hugh Wilson's *Police Academy* in 1984), is suitably lively and hits all the right beats for an uplifting Christmas movie. Gordon Sim's set design is similarly worthy of praise, as the film is packed with wonderfully meticulous fine details – from the knick-knacks in Ma Firpo's kitchen through to all of the welcoming, homespun decorations scattered through the foyer of the Bank of Paradise. Jack N. Green's cinematography also has flashes of inspired virtuosity, making the most of the chilly Canadian scenery to suggest a scenic slice of the Pennsylvanian countryside.

At the time of the film's release, *Trapped in Paradise* faced a wall of near-unanimous critical hostility. Steve Davis was representative of a majority of reviewers when he stated that, 'Interminably unfunny, this holiday offering about how the three Firpo brothers learn the true meaning of Christmas from the inhabitants of the quaint small town whose bank they've robbed is something of a crime itself. Taking bits and pieces from *How the Grinch Stole Christmas* and *It's a Wonderful Life*, but forsaking the heart and soul of both, *Trapped in Paradise* flouts the laws of logic, common sense, humor, and narrative coherency. If it isn't the worst movie of the year, it's definitely in the running. [...] By the time the finale of *Trapped in Paradise* ties itself into a sloppy Christmas bow, you're deadened to any feeling of peace on earth or goodwill toward men. Undoubtedly, this is a movie only a Scrooge could love'.[9] Even the film's central performances, which are perhaps its most consistently attention-grabbing quality, came in for censure due to their unconventional nature. Hal Hinson, for instance, noted that even when the film was playing to the strength of its lead actors, things could still go awry: 'Considering that there isn't a single laugh in the whole picture, the term "comedy" must be used loosely. [[...]] As the actor most likely to combust, Cage is always watchable. By now, his trademark tirades have become breathtaking improvisations, filigreed with rococo brilliance. Unfortunately, he is the only bright spot. And there is the question of what Carvey is actually doing with his voice, which he somehow makes sound like a congested combination of Mickey Rourke and Woody Woodpecker. Now that's something you don't come across every day'.[10]

While it may have seemed that *Trapped in Paradise* faced a barrage of unyielding censure when it arrived in cinemas, not every appraisal was entirely disapproving. Desson Howe was among commentators who remarked that while the film had its inconsistencies, such is the subjective nature of humour it still had potential to appeal if viewed in the right spirit: '*Trapped in Paradise*, a heist caper starring Nicolas Cage, Jon Lovitz and Dana Carvey, gets lost in a snow flurry of subplots and formulaic run-and-chase – right around the time you've settled in for a good comedy. But these three noodleheads are so endearing, it seems wrong to dismiss the whole thing. [[...]] *Trapped in Paradise* is the kind of movie you want to watch, fast-forward button at the ready. Although the second half is cluttered with skidding squad cars (in eternal pursuit of the bank robbers) and smiling faces (constantly killing the fugitives with kindness), you never know when something funny is coming along'.[11]

Quite remarkably, given the sheer level of critical enmity aimed at the film back in 1994, *Trapped in Paradise* has undergone a near-miraculous revival of fortune in the appraisals of more recent years. A number of critics, perhaps inquisitive about the movie's general reputation, not only came to the conclusion that it was not nearly as substandard a production as they were led to believe, but that it actually contained far more entertaining qualities than they had anticipated. Jerry Seravia, for example, comments that '*Trapped in Paradise* is far better than ⟦its reputation suggests⟧ though it is hardly a Yuletide classic. For my money, it has more laughs and charm than I expected from almost any Christmas-themed movie since 1994. ⟦...⟧ *Trapped in Paradise* is a jovial, sweet and warm-hearted comedy, never straining for too much sentiment and never too overplayed or overdone. I laughed a lot more than the critics did at the time, thus I never felt I was trapped in a so-called turkey'.[12] This cautious approbation was echoed by Coffel, who – while similarly qualified in his approval – nonetheless also demonstrated that the film's critical status was being gradually rehabilitated: 'I'm not saying this is a perfect movie. It's certainly flawed and nobody would call it a Christmas classic. But it is goofy, good-hearted fun with Cage and two of my favorite ⟦*Saturday Night Live*⟧ alumni all in a wonderful Christmas setting. The bones for a great movie are there. Put this idea in the hands of the Coen Brothers and you could have a good *Raising Arizona* follow up. Instead what we have is three bumbling idiots robbing Stars Hollow but that's good enough for me'.[13]

The reappraisal of *Trapped in Paradise*'s merits has continued into the present day, with reviewers such as Morgan R. Lewis pointing out that if viewers happen to be in the right mood, the film offers a lot to enjoy: 'While it's not quite as madcap as the premise would allow for, most of the scenes are fairly funny. A few stand out as creative twists such as the way the hostage situation at the bank develops, or the inevitable car chase – which in this instance is short one get-away car. *Trapped in Paradise* may not be a Christmas classic or a comedy classic, but for a change of pace during December, it's a reasonably good choice'.[14] Indeed, a few critics have even been willing to go further still and suggest, as Ezra Stead has, that the movie deserves a more prominent place in the wider pantheon of 1990s Christmas cinema:

> *Trapped in Paradise* remains one of my favorite Christmas movies, and one that I've revisited roughly every other year since seeing it in the theater in 1994. More than anything, what saves it is the cast. [Jon] Lovitz and co-star Dana Carvey had worked together for years on [*Saturday Night Live*] and have great chemistry as the goofy but heist-minded Firpo brothers. [...] Bill's story does follow the familiar beats of your average Lifetime or Hallmark-style Christmas romance, as he has his cold big-city heart melted by a small-town girl [...] as well as the small town itself, a place where everyone is so nice they'll treat you like family even after you rob them at gunpoint. Sure, it's corny, and maybe it's more than a little nostalgia on my part clouding my judgment, but I think this is a damn funny movie in the proper spirit of the season. You could certainly do a lot worse, and every year's crop of new Christmas movies has at least a few that will prove that.[15]

With *Trapped in Paradise*, George Gallo was to draw on many recognised tropes of Christmas cinema – namely re-demption and personal transformation, the triumph of hope in the face of adversity, and the ability of a mutually-supportive community to overcome misfortune. Bill even manages to find a sense of belonging in rural Pennsylvania that he has always lacked amongst the densely-packed urban landscape of New York – a goal that was surely sympatico with so many other Christmas features of the decade. While the film's standing amongst critics was far from stellar back in the nineties, its absolvitory reassessment by commentators in more recent years has led to a significant rehabilitation in the eyes of many audiences who have found it to be considerably more enjoyable than its initial repute may have suggested. The movie may not be the overlooked gem of the genre that 29th *Street* had been, but with its pleasingly eccentric performances and warmly festive creative intentions there is still much to recommend a visit to the town of Paradise. It has become, quite possibly, one of the greatest guilty pleasures to emerge from 1990s festive cinema.

REFERENCES

1.   Chris Coffel, 'The Tao of Nicolas Cage: *Trapped in Paradise*', in *Film School Rejects*, 23 December 2016. <*https://filmschoolrejects.com/the-tao-of-nicolas-cage-trapped-in-paradise-206546a5c8oc/*>

2.   Todd McCarthy, '*Trapped in Paradise*', in *Variety*, 4 December 1994. <*https://variety.com/1994/film/reviews/trapped-in-paradise-1200439821/*>

3.   Roger Ebert, '*Trapped in Paradise*', in *The Chicago Sun-Times*, 2 December 1994. <*https://www.rogerebert.com/reviews/trapped-in-paradise-1994*>

4.   Janet Maslin, 'Film Review: 3 Mismatched Brothers in a Small-Town Caper', in *The New York Times*, 2 December 1994. <*https://www.nytimes.com/1994/12/02/movies/film-review-3-mismatched-brothers-in-a-small-town-caper.html*>

5.   Jonathan Rosenbaum, '*Trapped in Paradise*', in *The Chicago Reader*, 29 November 1994. <*https://chicagoreader.com/film/trapped-in-paradise/*>

6.   McCarthy.

7.   Charles T. Tatum, Jr., '*Trapped in Paradise*', in *500 Terrible Films*, 2 September 2022. <*https://500filmstowatch.blogspot.com/2022/09/82-trapped-in-paradise-1994.html*>

8.   George Rother, '*Trapped in Paradise*', in *MovieGuy 24/7*, 9 December 2012.
      <https://movieguy247.com/iMovies/index.php/blog/holiday-movies/672-trapped-in-paradise>

9.   Steve Davis, '*Trapped in Paradise*', in *The Austin Chronicle*, 9 December 1994.
      <https://www.austinchronicle.com/events/film/1994-12-09/trapped-in-paradise/>

10.   Hal Hinson, '*Trapped in Paradise*', in *The Washington Post*, 2 December 1994.
      <https://www.washingtonpost.com/wp-srv/style/longterm/movies/videos/trappedinparadisepg13hinson_c01357.htm>

11.   Desson Howe, '*Trapped in Paradise*', in *The Washington Post*, 2 December 1994.
      <https://www.washingtonpost.com/wp-srv/style/longterm/movies/videos/trappedinparadisepg13howe_a0b093.htm>

12.   Jerry Seravia, 'The Thieving Magpies of *Paradise*', in *Jerry Saravia on Cinema*, 28 November 2011.
      <https://jerrysaravia.blogspot.com/2011/11/thieving-magpies-of-paradise.html>

13.   Coffel.

14.   Morgan R. Lewis, '*Trapped in Paradise*', in *Morgan on Media*, 8 December 2013.
      <https://morganrlewis.wordpress.com/2013/12/08/trapped-in-paradise/>

15.   Ezra Stead, '*Trapped in Paradise*', in *Ruthless Reviews*, 7 December 2020.

<https://www.ruthlessreviews.com/47463/trapped-in-paradise-1994/>

Mixed Nuts (1994)

TriStar Pictures

Director: Nora Ephron
Producers: Joseph Hartwick, Paul Junger Witt and
Tony Thomas
Screenwriters: Nora Ephron and Delia Ephron

SOME films seem destined from their inception to be box-office flops, and some are the exact opposite: motion pictures which appear to have everything in their favour, yet still – by some means – wind up with underwhelming critical and commercial results when they hit cinemas. Never was the latter description to be truer than in the case of *Mixed Nuts*, which had all the hallmarks of a comedy classic when it first appeared in December 1994. It was written and directed by the hugely talented Nora Ephron, starred popular comedy actor Steve Martin alongside a plethora of other highly-skilled performing talents, and boasted a genius premise which had so much potential for dark humour, it really should have been the basis of a farce to end all farces. Yet somehow, in spite of all these qualities being in its favour, *Mixed Nuts* would nevertheless go on to become one of the biggest critical and commercial disappointments in 1990s festive cinema.

Nora Ephron was widely hailed as a major creative talent by the mid-nineties, and the arrival of *Mixed Nuts* was highly anticipated after her directorial debut *This is My Life* (1992) and the major worldwide success of her second film as director, *Sleepless in Seattle* (1993). Ephron had long established herself as a successful producer and screenwriter, creating the screenplays for movies including *Silkwood* (Mike Nichols, 1983) and *When Harry Met Sally...* (Rob Reiner, 1989) – both of which had won her nominations for Best Original Screenplay at the Academy Awards (an accolade that she would repeat with the screenplay for *Sleepless in Seattle*). Also occasionally active as an actor, and later in her career as a highly successful playwright (receiving a posthumous Tony Award for her 2013 play *Lucky Guy*), Ephron was especially well-known for her achievements as a journalist, while her many accolades included a BAFTA Award in 1989 for Best Original Screenplay and the Ian McLellan Hunter Award bestowed by the Writers Guild of America in 2003.

Mixed Nuts was a very loose remake of French comedy film *Le Père Noël est une Ordure,* otherwise known as *Santa Claus is a Stinker* (Jean-Marie Poiré, 1982), and shared its central premise of mismatched volunteers working a Christmas Eve shift at a telephone helpline for people suffering personal difficulties. The Poiré film was generally darker in tone than the American feature that would follow it, and – aside from a few key aspects such as the building's malfunctioning elevator and a handful of character archetypes – the main concept and venue were the principal factors that would ultimately be carried over to the nineties movie. The screenplay for *Mixed Nuts* was written by Nora Ephron in collaboration with her sister, the bestselling author, playwright and screenwriter Delia Ephron. It was, however, to prove a very rare mis-step in the otherwise-celebrated careers of both Ephrons, leading to critical disparagement and a disappointing commercial performance. As Kristin Marguerite Doidge has noted, 'Fans and critics alike had eagerly awaited ⟦Nora Ephron's⟧ follow-up to the beloved – and Oscar-nominated – *Sleepless in Seattle*. That film had struck box office gold. *Mixed Nuts*, not so much. It earned only $6.8 million at the domestic box office. "I may satirize things to a great degree as I go along, but in the end, I say, 'We believe in love. We believe in the Christmas spirit.' That's what it says at the end of all of my movies. That's true. I think," Nora said'.[1]

Carrying over the unconventional holiday season setting of the French original (itself based upon an earlier 1979 stage play by the Le Splendid troupe), the movie relocates its action from Paris to the sunny coast of California. Much of the film was shot in the Venice area of Los Angeles, with the exterior location of the Life Savers office being filmed at the Venice 'V' Hotel at Venice Beach, while interior scenes were filmed at the Kaufman Astoria Studios in Queens, New York City. This may have seemed like a jarring environment for a genre that is usually much more readily associated with warm fireplaces, icy conditions and blizzards, but the incongruous climate also served to advance the notion of disconnected individuals and disjointed situations which – for one reason or another – had found themselves strangely isolated from traditional festivities. Liz Dance explains that '*Mixed Nuts*, the story of a quirky collection of people is also, as the opening suggests, an exposition of the absurdity of the notion of The Christmas Story – the birth of Jesus – imagined by most Western cultures as being wrapped in the snow and glitter of a Northern climate but which, in fact, has a closer alliance with Southern California, where the climate is more in line with that of the Middle East. But more than a confusion of climatic conditions, Western culture's Christmas celebration is an amalgam of stories'.[2] The Ephrons' screenplay recalls the kind of quirky ensemble comedies more commonly linked with film-makers such as Robert Altman and Woody Allen, but consciously adding an off-kilter, festively-themed backdrop that was deliberately designed to challenge expectation. This strategy was to meet with limited success in the eyes of many commentators, however, with Hollis Chacona remarking that, 'The story is supposed to be one of a Christmas miracle, and the salvation of unhappy, lonely lives. But the characters are so annoying and so lacking in any admirable or affecting qualities that we simply don't care what happens to them'.[3]

Christmas Eve is dawning in sunny Los Angeles, and philanthropic volunteer leader Philip (Steve Martin) is cycling to Lifesavers, a phone hotline which provides help and support to people who are suffering personal difficulties. On the way there, he encounters a pair of rollerblading yuppies (Parker Posey and Jon Stewart) who are carrying a Christmas tree between them. They are accidentally intercepted by Felix (Anthony LaPaglia) who, running away from an argument with his angry and heavily pregnant partner Gracie (Juliette Lewis), accidentally collides with them. The rollerbladers are livid, as their tree was apparently 'perfectly symmetrical' and had taken hours to find, but has now been damaged by the impact. Ever the conciliator, Philip steps in and attempts to defuse the resulting argument, but his efforts are angrily rebuffed. Gracie, who runs an avant-garde fashion shop, returns to her place of work and phones Lifesavers for advice, but finds that all the lines are currently busy.

Meanwhile, at the Lifesavers office, kind-hearted volunteer Catherine O'Shaughnessy (Rita Wilson) is taking a call from someone who is increasingly concerned about the 'Seaside Strangler' – a serial killer who has been terrorising the area. The decidedly less sympathetic office manager, the widowed Mrs Blanche Munchnik (Madeline Kahn), disparages Philip for his lateness – little realising that he is already on his way up to the office, carrying the tree that was casually abandoned by the yuppies. Upon entering the building, he meets the landlord – Stanley Tannenbaum (Garry Shandling) – who gleefully presents him with an eviction notice. Stanley points out that Lifesavers is three months in arrears with their rental payments. Philip begs him for more time; the State has decreased their funding, and they simply can't afford to pay. However, Stanley is insistent – if Lifesavers is unable to make good on their outstanding rent, the organisation will be evicted from the building on the 2nd of January.

Philip finally arrives at the office, just in time for the formidable Mrs Munchnik to take her leave now that her shift is over. She and Catherine are confused as to the reason why everyone in the building has received an eviction notice except Lifesavers, not realising that Philip is hiding the reality from them in the hope that he can find a solution at the eleventh hour. Before she goes, Philip proudly offers a gift-wrapped fruitcake to the formidable Mrs Munchnik, but she recognises it as exactly the same present she had given him the year beforehand and is decidedly unimpressed. Catherine cheerfully waves her colleague goodbye with a heartfelt Christmas greeting, little realising that moments later Mrs Munchnik ends up trapped between floors in the building's ageing elevator.

Felix returns to Gracie's store, and she scorns him for wearing a jolly Santa Claus suit when they are both so miserable – though as he points out, he had little choice in the matter as she had destroyed his clothes earlier as the result of a raging argument. Gracie, like so many others, is living in fear of the Seaside Strangler, but has more immediate issues to consider – such as the imminent arrival of her baby. Felix cheerfully informs her that he has managed to arrange a way of ensuring free hospital care for the delivery, provided that they complete welfare forms asserting that they can't support themselves. Gracie is on the verge of ending their relationship, as she wants a partner who is financially responsible; Felix is a good-natured dreamer whose ambition is to make a life for himself as an artist. She storms off with a warning that Felix shouldn't attempt to follow her.

Back at Lifesavers, an increasingly desperate Philip calls his girlfriend Susan (Joely Fisher), who is a loan officer, and begs her to extend a small line of credit to keep the organisation afloat. However, Susan suggests that he seek better-paid work instead, and awkwardly admits that her psychiatrist has told her that she and Philip should break up. Philip is confused, not realising that she had been seeking psychiatric help, but she confesses that she has actually been having an affair with the aforementioned health professional for the past four months. Philip is devastated by the unexpectedness of this revelation, but she coldly hangs up on him without further explanation. Catherine, who is oblivous to his break-up, observes that the phone lines seem unusually quiet for Christmas Eve, when she imagined that people will be at the end of their emotional tether – little realising that Philip is there already.

Another of the building's eccentric occupants, T-shirt slogan writer Louie Capshaw (Adam Sandler), arrives in the foyer with a potted plant. Seeing her chance of finding assistance, Mrs Munchnik – still trapped in the elevator – calls for help. However, Louie is wearing headphones and singing to himself with a curiously childlike delivery, meaning that her cries go unheeded. As he enters his apartment, Mrs Munchnik desperately sounds a note on a toy trumpet in the vain hope of catching his attention, but she is thoroughly drowned out by a recording of Alvin and the Chipmunks singing 'The Chipmunk Song (Christmas Don't be Late)' from 1958 – apparently Louie's festive music of choice.

While Catherine puts up the office Christmas decorations, Philip frantically tries to plan various fundraising events to keep Lifesavers operating. He is interrupted by a phone call from a lonely person seeking company over the holidays, who asks for the office address so that they can spend time with the volunteers. Philip tells the caller that no private details can be shared, but being soft-hearted he is eventually so moved by the obvious distress of the person on the line that he tells them where Lifesavers is located. It transpires that the caller is a transgender woman named Chris (Liev Schreiber), who feels isolated and misunderstood by their family. Leaving the somewhat overly traditional Christmas celebrations taking place at home, their family indifferent to their feelings of seclusion, Chris heads for the address given to them by Philip.

Philip frets that, as he has no idea who he has been talking to on the phone, he may inadvertently have given away their whereabouts to the Seaside Strangler. But his worries are interrupted when another passing resident of the building finally tips them off to Mrs Munchnik being trapped in the elevator. Philip checks the adjacent circuit breaker but can find no fault, so Mrs Munchnik – now frantic to be released – suggests that he takes a screwdriver from the office's earthquake emergency kit and she will guide him through the repair process to rectify the short in the system. Meanwhile,

Gracie calls her old friend Catherine and asks if she can stay with her over the holidays in order to avoid the increasingly irrational Felix. Her call is interrupted when Felix arrives and gives chase, promising to mend his indolent ways. Their latest row comes to an abrupt end when they again encounter the rollerblading yuppies and, perhaps inevitably, manage to wreck their replacement Christmas tree into the bargain.

Searching for a screwdriver, Philip discovers a Christ-mas gift from Catherine – a drastically oversized pair of pyjamas that she has knitted for him herself. Philip tries to explain that his relationship with Susan is over, but before he can do so she becomes emotional and races off. The jollity of the festive season has driven home to Catherine the fact that she is tired of being single and unappreciated, but she can't seem to find a way of reversing her fortunes – even in spite of her unrelenting personal sense of positivity. She returns to the office just as Philip is ending a call, and he reminds her of his personal philosophy that every bad situation contains within it the possibility of hope – a lesson his father shared with him shortly before being run over by a truck full of mixed nuts.

Much to her surprise, Catherine is presented with a Christmas gift from Philip – a subscription to a 'fruit of the month' club, where she receives a different type of produce every month throughout the year. To his horror, however, the office's eviction notice has become stuck to the gift's wrapping paper, meaning that the secret is now out in the open. This leads Catherine to have a panic attack, but she remains certain that Philip can somehow find a way to reverse their fortunes. He calls the *Los Angeles Times* in the hope of stimulating support for their situation in the press, but is met only by an automated helpline which makes it all but impossi-ble to speak with a human being.

Faced with the increasingly impatient Mrs Munchnik's demands to be extricated from the elevator, Philip tries to pull her through the emergency hatch at the top of the carriage. However, Gracie arrives in the foyer and – oblivious to the elevator problems – hits the call button, freeing the carriage and leaving Mrs Munchnik clinging to Philip for dear life. Before he can pull her clear of the elevator shaft, Gracie heads up towards the top floor of the building – Felix now in close pursuit. Thankfully for them, the carriage stops just a few feet from the building's ceiling, thus avoiding them being crushed.

Gracie and Felix continue their neverending argument, which spills over into the Lifesavers office and causes the usual expected chaos. Mrs Munchnik, ascerbic as ever, asks Felix if he is sure he is the father of Gracie's soon-to-be-delivered child, given that he was only released from prison seven months previously. This leads to an even more heated squabble between the pair, which only concludes when Gracie concusses Felix with Mrs Munchnik's Christmas fruitcake. Meanwhile, a throwaway remark by Philip makes Catherine realise that he has broken up with Susan – much to her elation, as she has obviously been nursing an attraction to him for some time.

Given that Felix is now bleeding from a head wound, it is obvious that he needs medical attention. However, as neither he nor Gracie can afford access to healthcare, Philip suggests taking him to see nearby veterinarian Dr Marshall Kinsky (Rob Reiner) while Mrs Munchnik grudgingly covers the phones. As soon as they have gone, however, Mrs Munchnik discovers the office's eviction notice and is indignant that Philip has kept the truth from her. Gracie decides to make practical use of the legal warning by cutting it up into a paper Christmas decoration.

Kinsky is heading off on a date when Philip and Catherine arrive at his surgery with Felix, but reluctantly agrees to help (mistakenly thinking that Felix is a pet cat). This causes his girlfriend Vanessa (Michele Singer) to leave in a fit of pique, believing he is putting his work before their relationship. Kinsky is therefore less than impressed to discover that Felix is actually a human rather than an animal companion, but he treats the head wound as a favour to his friend Philip. While Kinsky and Philip lament their respective romantic problems, Felix deliberately takes an overdose of strong dog tranquillisers in an attempt to end his life. Kinsky battles to keep him awake while Philip calls for an ambulance. When a baffled Philip asks Catherine how she can have a friendship with anarchic characters like Felix and Gracie, she rounds on him and claims that he is only ever good with people on the phone – in real life, all he ever seems to do is find others to blame for his problems.

Back at the office, Mrs Munchnik is surprised when someone calls at the door; given that Lifesavers is an unlisted address, and she is unaware of Philip's earlier call, she isn't expecting any visitors. Gracie is concerned that it may be the Seaside Strangler, but in actuality the caller is the lonely Chris. As the pair squabble over whether to open the door, Mrs Munchnik is accidentally knocked out. Gracie decides that she is leaving, and asks Chris to make the unconscious manager comfortable in her absence. Not having expected to be left in charge of the office, Chris ends up managing the phone lines, but is disconcerted by intermittent disruptions to the electricity supply.

Philip returns to the office, which is temporarily in darkness, and when light returns he is surprised to find Chris there – and shocked to discover the comatose Mrs Munchnik.

Unable to place Chris, their earlier phone conversation now long forgotten, Philip makes polite but awkward small-talk as he wracks his brains trying to work out who they are. He tries courteously to persuade Chris to leave, given the sheer number of other ongoing issues that are facing him, but they are reluctant to do so. Instead, when Philip launches into one of his long-winded homilies about entering a dancing competition in 1968, Chris suggests that they share a Christmas Eve dance of their own.

As Felix is loaded into an ambulance for transport to the hospital, Gracie arrives on the scene and invites Catherine back to her apartment at the clothing store. Night has fallen as they make their way there. Gracie gives Catherine a fashion and cosmetic makeover, and the usually conservatively-dressed phone operator is astonished to find herself transformed with stylish appeal. The two friends share a Christmas wish; for Catherine, that she can find a partner who loves her as much as she loves them, and for Gracie, that her child will have a better life than she has had.

Chris compliments Philip on his graceful movements as they share a dance in the Lifesavers office. Mrs Munchnik awakens from her dazed state of unconsciousness and rounds on Philip, threatening to sue him for (amongst other things) withholding information about the eviction, being the cause of professional stress, and inappropriate conduct in the workplace. She promises that while she may be about to face the loss of her (admittedly only nominally-paid) job through no fault of her own, she intends to ensure that he becomes unemployable for life. Philip objects when she verbally attacks Catherine, but Mrs Munchnik insists that their colleague isn't as innocent as she seems, noting that she has long had romantic ambitions towards Philip. This revelation comes as a total surprise to him.

Mrs Munchnik heads for her car in high dudgeon, several hours after she intended to leave the office, but finds that the vehicle's engine won't start. Philip, meanwhile, is frustrated by Mrs Munchnik's warnings of legal action and snaps at Chris, causing them emotional hurt and thus making them feel compelled to leave. Appalled at his lack of sensitivity, Philip realises that Catherine was right about him – he really does struggle to be socially empathetic when he doesn't have the emotional distance offered by the safety of operating a phone line.

Much to her irritation, Mrs Munchnik finds that she must wait some time for a repair service to fix her car. She meets Catherine and upsets her again, this time by regaling her with a deliberately exaggerated account of Philip dancing in the office with someone else – which Catherine immediately assumes to be Susan. Gracie, Catherine and Louie from the downstairs apartment all converge on the Lifesavers office, and Philip is stunned by Catherine's drastic transformation. Catherine finds Chris's discarded cape, but disbelieves Philip's explanation that it was left by one of the callers who had come to visit the office. As Gracie tries to give Philip a fashion makeover of his own, Louie breaks into a strange falsetto performance of a song.

Chris, meanwhile, is waking up from the effects of the dog tranquillisers in hospital. Managing to evade medical supervision, he runs home to the fashion store but – discovering that Gracie is nowhere to be found – he withdraws a hidden revolver from a cookie jar. Back at the office, Philip, Catherine and Gracie eat a candlelit takeaway meal while being serenaded by Louie, now dressed as a troubadour. His nonsensical lyrics and idiosyncratic delivery test Philip's patience to break-ing point, particularly as Louie is quite unabashedly flirting with Catherine as he performs the 'song'. After it is over, Philip discovers Mrs Munchnik's abandoned Christmas fruit-cake and is angry that she has so offhandedly disregarded his gift. He throws it out of the window in a fit of pique... little realising that it then immediately smashes through the wind-screen of Mrs Munchnik's only-just-repaired car, sending her into a state of shock.

Mr Lobel (Robert Klein), a dog-loving mechanic who lives in the building and has a long-running antagonism with Mrs Munchnik, sees her obvious distress and offers to help. In an unexpected moment of self-realisation, Mrs Munchnik comprehends that in spite of having terrorised Mr Lobel for months and reporting his dogs to the authorities on flimsy pretences out of spite, she is actually deeply attracted to him – but has never allowed herself to admit it even to herself until now. She kisses him passionately, and the two head for a life-guard's hut on the beach for a romantic tryst.

Just as Philip and the others are finishing their meal, Chris returns to the office as they realise they have forgotten their cape. Catherine then realises that Philip was telling the truth, and that Susan really hasn't reconciled with him. As Chris is leaving again, however, Felix arrives in a manic state and holds everyone in the office at gunpoint. He starts firing indiscriminately, and Chris tries to disarm him only to have their foot accidentally grazed by a stray bullet. Gracie takes the revolver from Felix, but rather than safely ejecting the bullets she decides to fire them around the room in an attempt to unload the gun. However, two shots go through the front door and kill Stanley the landlord, who was attempting to gain access to the office when the gun was fired.

Realising that Stanley had arrived in the building to service the elevator, Philip drags his body into the office. He calls the police to report the incident, but ends up with yet another automated answering service on the end of the line. Catherine becomes traumatised by the events unfolding around her and turns freezing cold, which leads Philip to run her a hot bath in an attempt to calm her down. The pair finally confess their shared feelings for each other, and embrace in mutual affection at last.

Louie tends to Chris's flesh wound, which turns out to be minor, and provides them with pain relief. They soon strike up a rapport, and in no time Louie is serenading them with one of his original songs. Meanwhile, Felix and Gracie try to come up with a way of obfuscating Stanley's manslaughter while avoiding either of them going to prison. They are temporarily interrupted when Susan arrives, having changed her mind about her relationship with Philip, but Gracie quickly gets rid of her. By the time Catherine and Philip emerge from the bathroom, Felix and Gracie have wrapped Stanley's body in burlap sacks and camouflaged it by hiding it within the branches of the office's Christmas tree. Philip despairs, believing this to be absolute rock bottom for Lifesavers – six years of helping countless people over the phone, only to be left with the corpse of their landlord unconvincingly disguised as an unkempt Christmas tree.

Unperturbed, Felix suggests that they dump the 'tree' on the sidewalk near (but not too near) to the building. Being Christmas, nobody will consider its presence to be unusual, and when it is cleared away after the holidays there will be no reason to suspect the party responsible for Stanley's death. As they walk the streets trying to avoid unnecessary attention, they encounter Mr Lobel and Mrs Munchnik... and are rather confused by the latter's greatly-improved mood. When Mr Lobel's dogs take an interest in the unconventional tree (or, rather, what is within it), the group continue on their way in an attempt to avoid being found out. All goes to plan until they encounter the antagonistic yuppie rollerbladers from earlier, who are now out for revenge. Aiming for a collision with the Lifesavers' volunteers' tree, Felix and Philip let it go, causing Stanley's body to lurch through the air. When it falls to the ground, the ruse is most definitely revealed.

A substantial crowd begins to congregate around the corpse, and the police are soon called to investigate. Mrs Munchnik tries to spin a yarn that Stanley had committed suicide, and that Philip and Catherine – wracked with guilt that they couldn't prevent him from taking his own life – had tried to cover up the death. But when the police refuse to believe this, Felix eventually confesses – only for Gracie to start brandishing the (now empty) murder weapon. Keen to avoid a panic, as well as Gracie implicating herself even indirectly, Felix grabs the revolver and races off into the night.

A chase ensues, at the end of which Felix has climbed to the roof of a nearby tattoo parlour. Distraught at the thought of returning to prison – or, worse, Gracie going there in his place – he threatens to end his life there and then. Desperate to avoid a tragedy, Philip steps in and pleads with Felix to abandon his suicide attempt and return to them. Christmas always has a tendency to amplify the worst aspects of life as well as the good, he reasons, and Felix wouldn't want to miss the birth of his child simply because of a tragic chain of accidents and misunderstandings. Seeing the logic behind his reasoning, Felix relinquishes his gun and surrenders, much to the celebration of the assembled gathering on the ground.

As the Lifesavers volunteers – and their assorted friends – await police questioning, Catherine hands over Stanley's carpet bag to a detective (Steven Randazzo). After inspection, the astonished officers discover that it contains the murder weapons used by the Seaside Strangler. Not only has Gracie killed a notorious serial killer, thus exonerating herself from a manslaughter charge, but she is also in line for a $250,000 reward. Gracie promises to pay the outstanding rental fees, ensuring that Lifesavers will not be evicted from the building where it is based. In thanks, she gives the detective Mrs Munchnik's Christmas fruitcake, ensuring that it has finally found a good home.

Overwhelmed with emotion, Gracie finds that she is going into labour. Thankfully Dr Kinsky is on hand to deliver the baby, and the birth takes place beneath a huge public Christmas tree at midnight. Philip, realising that love is the real Christmas miracle, decides to make up for lost time and proposes to Catherine. Felix, whose Santa Claus suit for once seems less out of place than usual, rings a bell as he wishes everyone present a very Merry Christmas.

Eschewing the predominant theme of family and reconciliation that permeated much of 1990s festive cinema, *Mixed Nuts* instead focuses on the issue of community and expounds upon the ability of the holiday season to bring together supposedly disparate people into a coherent and reciprocally supportive group. It could be argued, however, that the film's tonal clash ultimately works against its thematic aims. The first two acts are often rather dark and cynical, with humour being derived from the various people calling Lifesavers. These range from a suicidal man (who, through a tragic misunderstanding, ends up carrying out his threat of shooting himself because the support staff are unable to help him due to a fault on the line) through to random crank callers. Yet alongside this we have individuals such as Chris who, like so many people, feels a genuine sense of loneliness and isolation at the festive season, along with other callers who similarly have immediate anxieties that they are trying to cope with – many of them focusing on the Seaside Strangler being at large over the holidays and the sense of threat this represents to the safety and togetherness normally represented by Christmas. However, any hope of realism is soon jettisoned with the arrival of the third act, where bizarre coincidences and unlikely occurrences combine to wipe clean the slate of sceptical negativism and tart acerbity gradually built up by the opening two-thirds of the film. The caustic Mrs Munchnik is thawed by the romantic attentions of her old nemesis Mr Lobel; Philip realises that the disintegration of his relationship with Sarah has surprisingly paved the way to a more successful and mutually-supportive romance with Catherine; and the tempestuous marriage between Gracie and Felix is mollified by the sudden Christmas arrival of their new child. As in so many festive narratives of years past, true love conquers all and proves transformative in the least expected of ways.

Perhaps the greatest mystery of *Mixed Nuts* is how it could contain so much expert performance talent and still manage to feel so patchy and unrealised. Alonso Duralde was not alone in his analysis that 'if this isn't the single worst Christmas movie of all time, it's at least an astonishing waste of comic talent – how can a movie starring Steve Martin, Madeline Kahn, Rita Wilson, Anthony LaPaglia, Juliette Lewis, and Liev Schrieber, with supporting bits by Parker Posey, Jon Stewart, Garry Shandling, and Adam Sandler be this utterly miserable?'[4] Certainly the film begins confidently enough, making the most of the incongruity of the sun-drenched Venice Beach and its unconventional denizens to frame the narrative as a decidedly less-than-traditional Christmas fable. Yet for all that, it often struggles to overcome the story's stage-based origins, with much of the action confined to the Lifesavers office and the surrounding building. The central mystery of the Seaside Strangler seems largely superfluous to events until the last-minute revelation of the serial killer's identity, and the police's decision to immediately release Gracie – to say nothing of granting her the reward money for bringing Stanley's reign of terror to an end – stretches credulity to breaking point. While a note of fantasy was hardly unexpected in a Christmas film, after an hour of building up a pessimistic and at times borderline misanthropic interplay between the characters the resulting transformations in attitude and reversals of fortune seem rushed and unconvincing.

Mixed Nuts did contain a number of inspired touches, some more successfully employed than others. Director Nora Ephron was to put in a brief but pleasing performance as the (uncredited) voice of *The Los Angeles Times*' automated phone recording, an inclusion which was agreeable for the many fans of her work, while the humorous interplay as Philip tries to re-gift Mrs Munchnik a Christmas fruitcake from the previous year (hoping that she will have forgotten that she gave it to him in the first place) will bring a smile to anyone who has had to take part in office gifting. The fruitcake's early appearance almost functions as a tongue-in-cheek example of the Chekhov's Gun principle, given its later role in Mrs Munchnik's Scrooge-like transfiguration. Steve Martin's gift for physical comedy shines through, especially when Philip frenetically flails around trying to extricate the office's eviction notice from Catherine's Christmas gift before she becomes aware of it. Similarly, Catherine's strange, ongoing knitting habit also amuses thanks to Rita Wilson's extensive comic talents, especially when the character produces (at least at the start of the film) an increasingly unrecognisable woollen garment with an unspecified function.

That being said, other such creative flourishes work less well. Mrs Munchnik's ear-splitting protestations are perfectly executed by Madeline Kahn and her mastery of comedic embellishment, which in lesser hands may simply have been an annoying affectation, but still manages to grate through sheer repetition. However, Louie's peculiar falsetto singing voice and self-indulgently juvenile vocal delivery – as rendered by Adam Sandler – would test the patience of a saint, being deliberately weird simply for the sake of it. Some of the other comic aspects are likewise hammered home with a singular lack of subtlety. For instance, the landlord's name is Stanley Tannenbaum – which, famously, is the German term for a Christmas tree. In a rather obviously signposted development, later in the film – after he is shot and killed – Mr Tannenbaum's body is subsequently disguised by the other characters as… a Christmas tree. The dearth of finesse demonstrated by this conceit was detected by numerous reviewers, who were less than receptive to its transparency. As Janet Maslin observed, 'The dead man wears tennis shoes and stands on his head, covered with branches and disguised as a Christmas tree. *Mixed Nuts*, Nora Ephron's frenetic comedy about a suicide hot line in Venice, Calif., is about as funny as that corpse, and about as natural. Adapted from the French film *Le Père Noël est une Ordure*, it has a farcical tone that loses everything in translation, with only hand-waving, door-slamming and zany costumes left behind'.[5]

Given the amount of time the camera spends exploring the confines of the Lifesavers office (clearly an upmarket residential property that has been repurposed for volunteering purposes, hence the classy domestic kitchen, well-appointed bathroom, etc. on the premises), it is a credit to set decorator George DeTitta Jr. that this workspace is so full of stimulating fine details – not least the building's antiquated elevator which hearkens back to the *film noir* locales of years past. Other locations, such as Gracie's fashion store, are also adroitly fleshed out, especially in the contrast between the eclectic public area greeting customers and the rather more mundane, domestic living space behind the scenes. Director of photography Sven Nykvist shows great skill in the cinematography of the scenes that play out beyond the restrictive boundaries of the office, making the most of the beautiful Venice Beach locality. Matching the eccentric yuletide setting was not just George Fenton's energetic original score, but also a collection of quirky reworkings of well-known Christmas songs including 'Jingle Bells' by Eastern Bloc, 'Silent Night' by Baby Washington and 'White Christmas' by The Drifters.

All of the film's main players enjoyed widespread familiarity amongst the public at its time of release. The multiple award-winning Steve Martin had been active as a comedy writer since the 1960s, then later as a host on NBC's *Saturday Night Live*, before making many highly successful film appearances throughout the eighties including *Dead Men Don't Wear Plaid* (Carl Reiner, 1982), *The Man with Two Brains* (Carl Reiner, 1982), *Planes, Trains and Automobiles* (John Hughes, 1987), and *Parenthood* (Ron Howard, 1989). Madeline Kahn had performed in numerous critcially-acclaimed films including *What's Up, Doc?* (Peter Bogdanovich, 1972) and *Young Frankenstein* (Mel Brooks, 1974), with Academy

Award-nominated supporting roles in *Paper Moon* (Peter Bogdanovich, 1973) and *Blazing Saddles* (Mel Brooks, 1974). Rita Wilson had been active in cinema since the 1970s, with a growing profile at the time thanks to appearances in *Volunteers* (Nicholas Meyer, 1985), *The Bonfire of the Vanities* (Brian De Palma, 1990) and Ephron's own *Sleepless in Seattle* (1993). Of the rest of the ensemble cast, many – such as Liev Schreiber and Adam Sandler – were at the beginning of their success in acting, while others including Juliette Lewis and Anthony LaPaglia were building on early, existing achievements to reach greater prominence later in the decade. Garry Shandling had been a multiple award-winning comedian, actor and writer, nominated for Emmy Awards on no less than nineteen separate occasions, while Rob Reiner had a fruitful career as an actor before achieving far greater recognition as the director of films such as *Stand by Me* (1986), *The Princess Bride* (1987), *Misery* (1990) and the Academy Award-nominated *A Few Good Men* (1992). Watch out also for a blink-and-you'll-miss-it appearance by a very young Haley Joel Osment, several years prior to his breakthrough performance in *The Sixth Sense* (M. Night Shyamalan, 1999).

Mixed Nuts met with more or less undivided antipathy from critics when it was first released in 1994. However, there was considerable variance over exactly where the film had gone wrong, with some reviewers singling out shortcomings which were quite different from others detected by their colleagues in the critical community. Hal Hinson discerned that the movie was an atypical misstep for its director, commenting that, 'Usually, Ephron (who wrote the script with her sister, Delia) is one of the most reliable comic voices in the movies, but here her gifts seem to have deserted her. Though she shows her customary talent for smart one-liners, the spirit of the film is forced and desperate, as if she lacked faith in her gags and were trying to shove them down our throats. The story line itself is as shallow as it is pointless – a flood of weak laughs surrounding little islands of pathos'.[6] Roger Ebert, on the other hand, concentrated on the film's strangely diffuse lack of focus, pointing out that in throwing too many elements into the mix, *Mixed Nuts* eventually becomes rambling, exaggerated and increasingly confused: 'As a general rule, normal people are funnier than zany people, a possibility that *Mixed Nuts* would have done well to explore. ⟦...⟧ The film takes place just before Christmas along the beach in Venice, Calif. – an area where, arguably, a normal person would stand out as a curiosity. ⟦...⟧ Maybe there's too much talent. Every character shines with such dazzling intensity and such inexhaustible comic invention that the movie becomes tiresome, like too many clowns'.[7]

Not every critic of the time was entirely hostile towards the movie, with some considering its merits as well as its pitfalls – while still acknowledging that the overall creative equilibrium suggested more of an artistic deficit than not. Chacona, for instance, explained that, 'Though there's half a cashew of Steve Martin's amazing physical comedy, a couple of pecans of Sven Nyqvist's beautiful cinematography and a few eye-catching filberts of very Venice-y set decoration, it's not nearly enough to satisfy. Be forewarned: Open this can of *Mixed Nuts* and you'll find nothing but a bunch of goobers'.[8] Generally, however, the film was subjected to such a torrent of unrelenting disdain from commentators that it rapidly acquired a reputation as one of the most derided Christmas movies of the decade, largely due to withering appraisals such as that of James Berardinelli, who seemed to speak for a large proportion of the critical community at the time:

Mixed Nuts [is] as unwatchable a motion picture as you're likely to find this Christmas season. [...] It boggles the mind that someone actually allowed this choppy, unpolished script to reach the production stage. There's nothing even remotely funny here. Lines like 'I didn't want to tell you this over the phone – I really wanted to fax you' are representative of the quality – or lack thereof – of the so-called humor. And there's a version of *Deck the Halls* that may make you wish you never hear the song again. *Mixed Nuts* makes a point of stating that there's magic at Christmas. After seeing this movie, I'm a believer. After all, it's virtually impossible to come up with an alternate explanation of how something this awful could make it to theaters across the nation.[9]

Curiously, just as *Trapped in Paradise* (q.v.) – the other critically-slammed festive movie release of 1994 – has experienced a phoenix-like resurrection from its initial drubbing by commentators, undergoing a widespread rehabilitation thanks to significantly more well-disposed analysis by recent reviewers, so too has *Mixed Nuts* started to become better-regarded by critics in the past few years as its perceived failings have been increasingly obscured by the glow of nostalgia. Paul Schrodt, for example, has noted that the film was in many ways to presage the edgier, self-aware comedy which was to become more widely accepted in popular culture a few years later: 'What one has to conclude from watching *Mixed Nuts* again, 20 years after it was largely panned, is that it was ahead of its time. The no-hugs-no-lessons attitude, selfish characters, and observational dialogue about human inanity have a lot in common with the concurrently airing TV shows

Seinfeld and *The Larry Sanders Show*, and with Larry David's derided 1998 comedy, *Sour Grapes*. [...] To paraphrase the film's final message, Christmas is three horrible things and then something wonderful. There's always hope'.[10] Others, such as Andy Webb, instead opined that the success (or otherwise) of the film largely depends upon the spirit in which it is viewed, reasoning that it works more successfully as a festively-themed farce rather than as a cohesive comedy narrative: 'It's not one of Martin's popular comedies, yet watching it now it strangely works. [...] *Mixed Nuts* is strange, disjointed and really doesn't have much of a storyline but curiously the curious collection of characters and circumstances at Christmas end up being amusing. [...] The curious craziness of the characters and the comical circumstances is fun if watched as a collection of comical characters rather than as a movie with a story'.[11]

Not every contemporary critic has exhibited a softened stance towards *Mixed Nuts*. Some, such as Matt Brunson, have echoed the antagonistic sentiment of reviewers from the film's initial release and mirrored their assertion that the movie marked a low point in the Ephron's filmography: 'Even with such high-caliber comedians as Martin, Madeline Kahn, Garry Shandling and Jon Stewart at its beck and call, *Mixed Nuts* is a shockingly laughless affair. The film represents the nadir of the late Nora Ephron's career as a writer and director, and fans of her work on *Sleepless in Seattle* and *When Harry Met Sally...* knew well enough to stay home and roast chestnuts on an open fire instead'.[12] In the main, however, the film's gradual reversal of fortune in the eyes of critics has been remarkable, with reviewers such as George Rother being typical in their more sympathetic evaluation of its qualities: 'It's one of those crazy farces that feature a large cast running around in different directions trying to avert various disasters and only making things worse. It's pretty funny stuff and the movie works, even though it probably shouldn't have. When a comedy movie features an all-star cast, there's always the risk that it's going to be a complete disaster that has the actors tripping over each other as they mug for the camera. While *Mixed Nuts* isn't perfect, it hits the mark more than it misses, the performers have some pretty good chemistry and each actor gets a chance to shine'.[13]

Mixed Nuts was to win Madeline Kahn a nomination for Funniest Actress in a Motion Picture (Leading Role) at the American Comedy Awards in 1995. Though the film's reputation has never entirely recovered from its frosty reception at the hands of critics back in the nineties, it remains a shamelessly unconventional and throughly contemporary take on the festive season which was as original as it was divisive. But even decades after its initial release, there is still heated debate over the cause of its hammering by reviewers and subsequent failure at the box-office, which saw meagre returns of $6.7 million[14] from a production budget estimated at $15 million.[15] Perhaps audience expectation was unrealistically high, given the soaring success of Ephron's much-lauded work both before and after *Mixed Nuts*. Maybe assembling so much distinctive performance talent led to too many gifted actors competing for the limelight. Or possibly the film's chaotic cluster of scattershot comic situations simply failed to hit their mark more often than not. We may never have a definitive answer as to why *Mixed Nuts* has never captured the public imagination to the extent that many other Christmas movies of the 1990s have achieved, but one thing remains certain – whether you love it or hate it, as motion pictures go it proves very difficult not to form a strong opinion about it one way or the other.

REFERENCES

1.   Kristin Marguerite Doidge, *Nora Ephron: A Biography* (Chicago: Chicago Review Press, 2022), p.142.

2.   Liz Dance, *Nora Ephron: Everything is Copy* (Jefferson: McFarland, 2015), p.112.

3.   Hollis Chacona, '*Mixed Nuts*', in *The Austin Chronicle*, 6 January 1995.
   <https://www.austinchronicle.com/events/film/1995-01-06/mixed-nuts/>

4.   Alonso Duralde, *Have Yourself a Movie Little Christmas* (New York: Limelight Editions, 2010), p.226.

5.   Janet Maslin, 'Film Review; Hysterics All Dressed Up for the Holidays', in *The New York Times*, 21 December 1994.
   <https://www.nytimes.com/1994/12/21/movies/film-review-hysterics-all-dressed-up-for-the-holidays.html>

6.   Hal Hinson, '*Mixed Nuts*', in *The Washington Post*, 21 December 1994.
   <https://www.washingtonpost.com/wp-srv/style/longterm/movies/videos/mixednutspg13hinson_a0a884.htm>

7.   Roger Ebert, '*Mixed Nuts*', in *The Chicago Sun-Times*, 21 December 1994.
   <https://www.rogerebert.com/reviews/mixed-nuts-1994>

8.   Chacona.

9.   James Berardinelli, '*Mixed Nuts*', in *ReelViews*, 21 December 1994.

<https://www.reelviews.net/reelviews/mixed-nuts>

10.   Paul Schrodt, 'Why *Mixed Nuts* is the Best Holiday Movie You've Never Seen', in *Esquire*, 24 December 2014. <https://www.esquire.com/entertainment/movies/reviews/a31592/mixed-nuts-holiday-movie/>

11.   Andy Webb, '*Mixed Nuts*', in *The Movie Scene*, 2008. <https://www.themoviescene.co.uk/reviews/mixed-nuts/mixed-nuts.html>

12.   Matt Brunson, 'Ho-Ho-No: The Worst Christmas Movies of All Time', in *Film Frenzy*, 22 December 2018. <https://thefilmfrenzy.com/2018/12/22/ho-ho-no-the-worst-christmas-movies-of-all-time/>

13.   George Rother, '*Mixed Nuts*', in *MovieGuy 24/7*, 1 December 2011. <https://movieguy247.com/iMovies/index.php/blog/holiday-movies/772-mixed-nuts>

14.   Box-office data from *The-Numbers.com*. <http://www.the-numbers.com/movie/Mixed-Nuts>

15.   Budgetary data from *TheMovieDB.org*. <http://www.themoviedb.org/movie/24070-mixed-nuts>

11

The Ref (1994)

Touchstone Pictures / Don Simpson/Jerry Bruckheimer Films

Director: Ted Demme
Producers: Ron Bozman, Richard LaGravenese and Jeff Weiss
Screenwriters: Richard LaGravenese and Marie Weiss,
from a story by Marie Weiss

THE year of 1994 was to yield a bumper crop of festive cinema, revealing a stark contrast between the traditional family fare of *Miracle on 34ᵗʰ Street* (q.v.) and *The Santa Clause* (q.v.), and the decidely less conventional scenarios of *Trapped in Paradise* (q.v.) and *Mixed Nuts* (q.v.). In its artistic approach, *The Ref* would ultimately lie somewhere between these two extremes. While no-one was likely to consider the film to be brimming with seasonal good cheer, with its reconciliatory denouement and focus on the rehabilitation of the nuclear family, it was to prove more congruent with the central themes of 1990s festive film-making than its initial wave of marketing may have suggested.

The Ref was an unusual Christmas movie in the sense that it was released in March 1994 – around nine months prior to the traditional festive release schedule in cinemas – and its poster and publicity gave away no hint of its yuletide setting. Indeed, its core influences were judged by many critics to lie not within the Christmas genre at all, but rather to derive from more diverse source material. Given that the film's action surrounds a kidnapping and home invasion that promptly goes very wrong, some commentators were to draw comparisons to Roman Polanski's 1966 psychological thriller *Cul-de-Sac*, which contained many touches of very dark humour and centred around two gangsters who hold a married couple hostage in their own home after an attempted robbery turns awry. In truth, the similarity between the two movies largely ends there, but – as Jordan R. Young notes – this didn't stop the comparison being made: 'More than one reviewer felt Ted Demme's black comedy *The Ref* (1994) was inspired by *Cul-de-Sac*. Critic Andy Klein described the Demme movie, in which a mismatched couple is taken hostage by a cat burglar (Denis Leary), as a "Disneyfied version" of the Polanski film, despite many similarities. It comes closest when the squabbling couple makes Leary pose as their marriage counselor in front of dinner guests'.[1] Other critics, such as Roger Ebert, instead detected a more literary inspiration behind the film, observing that '*The Ref* is a flip-flopped, updated version of O. Henry's ⟦1907 short story⟧ *The Ransom of Red Chief*, in which a kidnapper naps more than he was counting on. ⟦...⟧ Material like this is only as good as the acting and writing. *The Ref* is skillful in both areas'.[2] In Henry's famous tale, two criminals kidnap the son of an affluent man only to discover that the boy's spoiled behaviour is insufferable; after their ransom demand is rejected, the desperate captors eventually end up paying the boy's family – rather than vice-versa – so that they can return him as quickly as possible. It is, in this sense, much closer to the humorously chaotic spirit of *The Ref* than Polanski's emotionally uncomfortable suspense film ever was.

The director of *The Ref* was Ted Demme, who had been active as an actor and producer before moving on to helming short movies, TV features and, later, motion pictures such as *Who's the Man?* (1993). He established a long-running collaboration with comedian and actor Denis Leary, directing his stand-up comedy TV special *No Cure for Cancer* (1992) and *Denis Leary: Lock 'n' Load* (1997). Demme was nominated for a number of industry awards during his lifetime, winning an Emmy Award in 1999 for his work on the production of the TV movie *A Lesson Before Dying* (1999).

The Ref was to feature a variety of diverse creative talent. Leading man Denis Leary was at the time best-known for his stand-up routines, especially thanks to many high-profile appearances on MTV, and was beginning to make the transition into acting with appearances in films including crime thriller *Action Night* (Stephen Hopkins, 1993) and action comedy *Gunmen* (Deran Sarafian, 1994). Richard LaGravenese had established a career as a screenwriter through his work on features such as *Rude Awakening* (David Greenwalt and Aaron Russo, 1989) and *The Fisher King* (Terry Gilliam, 1991), and would later go on to success as a director and producer. His co-writer, Marie Weiss, who created the story for *The Ref,* would also develop the screenplay for Charles Jarrott's TV movie *The Christmas List* (1997) later in the decade, where the festive flavour of the former film would be maintained – albeit with a slightly less bitingly mordant approach.

In a beautifully picturesque rural Connecticut town, Christmas is coming and spirits are high amongst members of the friendly community there. However, in the office of marriage guidance counselor Dr Wong (an uncredited B.D. Wong), it is animosity rather than festive goodwill that is in abundance. The doctor struggles to keep things civil between warring couple Lloyd Chasseur (Kevin Spacey) and his wife Caroline (Judy Davis), who constantly bicker about their mutual loathing and long-running lack of intimacy. Lloyd is angry that Caroline has had an extramarital affair, whereas Caroline berates Lloyd for their marriage's stale sense of repetitive monotony. Rather wisely, the counselor refuses to take sides and merely tries (without much success) to guide their quarrel rather than try to control it.

Meanwhile, at a large upscale home elsewhere in the town, burglar Gus (Denis Leary) is using a combination of state-of-the-art equipment and criminal expertise to gain access to a heavily-guarded safe. He finds it curious when a hidden nozzle above the safe sprays him with cat urine... but the reason soon becomes clear when, clearing out the safe's contents, he accidentally sets off a complex home defence system and plummets through a trapdoor into the house's basement – and the den of a snarling guard dog. Using all his wits to evade the fearsome canine, Gus is unaware that his driver, Murray (Richard Bright), has fled the scene before the police can arrive.

Dr Wong rapidly realises that the marriage guidance session is going nowhere constructive. Lloyd insists that he is content in his life, though Caroline senses that he is constantly unhappy. By contrast, she feels unfulfilled and unable to find a satisfactory outlet for her personal frustrations. Caroline blames Lloyd's domineering mother for their woes, pointing out that she owns their home, has control over Lloyd's job, and that they are paying her back for a personal loan with a high rate of interest. There is also variance over the upbringing of their son, Jesse, who Lloyd considers to be a antisocial delinquent but who Caroline fears is creatively repressed.

The session having achieved absolutely nothing, the Chasseurs drive home. Caroline feels that they should start divorce proceedings, but Lloyd disagrees – largely, it seems, out of sheer stubbornness as well as a spiteful unwillingness to let his wife move on after her affair. On the way back, they stop at a convenience store for some groceries, little realising that the fugitive Gus is also heading there. Spotting Caroline and considering her a potential hostage, he forces her back to the car at gunpoint. Getting into the back seat, he demands that the shocked Lloyd start the car's engine again.

A group of concerned, well-to-do inhabitants of the community converge on the local police chief's office to demand that he take action against the criminality affecting the sleepy town. Lieutenant Huff (Raymond J. Barry) is contemptuous of their concerns; his force is inexperienced and underbudgeted, and as the affluent townsfolk generally go over his head to call on favours from their influential friends, he pointedly suggests that they all get out of his office. When the chief is threatened with being replaced (one of the group is an old school friend of the mayor), and told that they will use volunteers to enforce their own brand of justice, Huff is singularly unimpressed by their bluster.

Gus becomes alarmed when a radio news bulletin reports that road blocks are being set up on roads out of the town in an effort to track down the fugitive burglar. Seemingly out of options, he demands that Lloyd and Caroline take him back to their home so that he can hide there until the police scrutiny dies down. The couple are so venomous towards each other, they continue to squabble even at gunpoint, and Lloyd becomes so engrossed in the argument he goes straight through a stop sign, only narrowly avoiding a collision at a road junction. Gus despairs at their incessant, pathological backbiting, but knows that he has no choice other than to stick to his plan.

Lieutenant Huff's officers find Gus's cat urine-soaked mask and a few blonde hairs at the crime scene, but they have barely started their investigation before they are informed that the State police will be taking over the case. Huff is livid, knowing that his force has jurisdiction in the local area, but the persuasive locals have pulled strings and gone over his head. In the meantime, over at a prestigious military academy, the Chasseurs' teenaged son – the amoral Jesse (Robert J. Steinmiller, Jr.) – shows similar prowess at underhand dealings, as he is blackmailing one of the staff, Mr Siskel (J.K. Simmons), with incriminating photographs in exchange for money.

The Chasseurs arrive back home, and Gus marches them into their house at gunpoint. He seems impressed by the selection of antique furniture and ornaments on display, obviously sensing criminal opportunities, but Caroline assures him that they are from the antique dealership in town that Lloyd runs on his mother's behalf. Jesse calls the family answering machine and leaves a message to say there is no need to pick him up from the train station; he will make his own way back home for the holidays. Gus realises to his frustration that the Chasseurs are planning to host a family get-together later that night. Little do they realise that Lloyd's sister-in-law Connie (Christine Baranski), brother Gary (Adam LeFevre) and mother Rose (Glynis Johns) are already on the way, having stopped briefly for a meal at a diner because Caroline's cooking is so legendarily bad.

Gus ties up Lloyd and Caroline in their kitchen, then calls the local bar in search of Murray. Sure enough, his criminal conspirator is lying low there in the hope of evading police interest. Gus lambastes him for running at the first sign of trouble, but instructs him to make his way to a nearby harbour and commandeer a boat so that they can make good their escape later that evening. In spite of his gun-toting intimidation, the Chasseurs still can't resist aiming relentless sideswipes at each other, so Gus ends up forcing them to admit that they are lying to each other and are too proud to give the fact away. In essence, they are both as bad as each other.

Just as he tries to dress the flesh wound that resulted from a dog bite while escaping the site of the burglary, Gus is startled when the doorbell rings. He unties Caroline to answer the door. Fortunately for Gus, the interruption is merely the Chasseurs' neighbour, George (Bill Raymond), dropping off a gift of fruitcake for the holidays. Concealed behind the door with his gun to ensure that Caroline doesn't give away his presence, Gus is intrigued to discover that a $100,000 private bounty has now been placed on his head by one of the town's affluent citizens. George also obliquely blames Jesse for having stolen the town's Baby Jesus statue from the community Nativity scene the previous year, but Caroline is appalled that anyone would think her son capable of such a petty act of theft.

On the way upstairs in search of a bandage, Gus is stunned to notice an original painting by the early modernist artist Marc Chagall hanging on the stairway and angrily remarks that such a beautiful work of art is being unappreciated – simply being used as a hallway decoration – because the prosperous Chasseurs want for nothing and have no idea of true value. Caroline angrily responds that the painting belongs to Lloyd's mother Rose, along with everything else in the house. Caroline explains that she and Lloyd had once tried to make a success of an upmarket Italian restaurant, but when it failed they were essentially forced to manage Rose's antiques shop instead to make ends meet. This is obviously a huge bone of contention between Rose and Lloyd, but Gus is uninterested in the domestic tensions between mother and son.

Outside, Jesse has arrived in an expensive private car, but dreads the endless bickering that awaits him at home. Somewhat pleadingly, he asks the driver to take the car around the block again to eke out the maximum amount of time before he must reunite with his warring parents. This is in stark contrast to the joyful Christmas party being held nearby for the community's small kids, with a suitably boisterous George in the role of Santa.

With Lloyd and Caroline now tied up again, and still incessantly quarrelling, Gus thoughtfully looks around the house and seems appalled that the Chasseurs should throw away the potential for a happy and harmonious life together when they live such a materially comfortable existence. With some amusement, he also discovers the stolen statue of the Christ Child from the town's Nativity display, hidden away in a wooden chest in Jesse's bedroom. Caroline frets that Jesse hasn't yet arrived home. Knowing that he must quickly improvise in order to keep all three Chasseurs hostage, he ties Lloyd and Caroline to the opposing posts of an antique bed while freeing bungee cords to tie up Jesse on his arrival. Lloyd urges Gus to give himself up, to which the burglar angrily responds that at least he has to work for a living – even if his activities happen to illegal. He pours scorn on Lloyd for his well-heeled ennui, but the put-upon Chasseur rages that in spite of superficial appearances, his life has never turned out the way he wanted it to.

Lloyd's tirade is interrupted when Jesse finally returns home. However, he unknowingly bypasses the intruder and his captive parents in order to make a beeline straight for his room, where he stashes away a suitcase's worth of ill-gotten blackmail money in a hidden cavity beneath the floorboards. When he does finally check in on his parents, almost as an afterthought, Gus quickly binds him at gunpoint. The singularly unimpressed Jesse realises who Gus is from the police reports, and tells him that a hostage situation never works out for criminals. The increasingly exasperated Gus explains that he can't leave until Murray calls for him, signalling a safe escape route, but Jesse points out that they will soon be expecting Christmas dinner guests – and that these family members will already be *en route* to the town from Boston. They also observe that if Gus isn't caught quickly, the police will almost certainly conduct door-to-door searches until he is brought to justice.

In reality, the local police are watching a screening of *It's a Wonderful Life* at the precinct office while State officers take over the case. Lt. Huff presents the videotape evidence recorded from inside the safe during Gus's burglary, clearly showing the felon's face. He tells his officers to watch this footage intently, as it will hold the key to recognising and tracking down the fugitive criminal. However, when Huff is called away to speak with a county prosecutor on the phone, his bungling subordinates try to rewatch the video but end up recording the broadcast of Jimmy Stewart and Donna Reed over the only copy of the evidence. This inevitably lands Huff in hot water with the country prosecutor, who believes they have the exclusive right to access the footage.

Murray has arrived at the local dock and immediately starts looking for opportunities to steal a means of escape, but is almost immediately intercepted by a suspicious boat-owner. Back at the Chasseurs' house, Gus has become exasperated by the fact that with Jesse's arrival, the non-stop arguing has now become three-way. Jesse clearly resents being sent to board at a military academy, but Lloyd angrily fires back that the family had little choice other than to enrol him there as the young man had managed to get himself expelled from every other school in the area. Finally, Gus finds that he can take no more of the dysfunctional squabbling and demands to know the quickest route to the docks, but the family can't even agree on an answer to that simple question – and Jesse interjects that with only twenty minutes until a curfew is due to be imposed, Gus will never get there in time. As though proving the point, a news bulletin reports that the award for Gus's capture has now been increased to $200,000 – much to his obvious aggravation.

Gus lights a cigarette, inadvertently setting off a smoke alarm. When he is distracted, Jesse breaks free of his bonds and grabs the burglar's gun, training it on him. However, Gus is able to successfully intimidate the inexperienced teenager, grabbing his firearm back just as the house's phone rings. At the other end of the line is Connie, explaining that the family expects to be arriving for dinner within the next twenty minutes. This forces Gus to think on his feet – and fast. To avoid any further interjections from Jesse, he ties him to a chair before locking him in a closet. Before he can be gagged, Jesse offers Gus his blackmail money, explaining that he needed serious cash in an attempt to make a permanent getaway from his unhappy domestic environment. Gus is contemptuous, remarking that Jesse has every opportunity he could ever want but is too spoiled to realise that life rarely goes the way we expect. In response, Jesse fires back that it is easy for Gus to judge him when he seems to have his own life all figured out. But in reality, Gus had expected that evening's burglary to be the last of his criminal career, and had planned to use the proceeds to retire from law-breaking permanently.

With no choice but to release Lloyd and Caroline before their guests arrive, Gus lays down his directives. There is to be no access to television in case news reports identify him, nobody on the same floor as Jesse in case he is discovered, and no use of the phone except the one in the kitchen so that he can oversee all communications. Most importantly of all, they are to remain in Gus's sight at all times, and must refrain from arguing lest they give the game away in the heat of their temper.

Back at the police station, one of the town's leading lights – Bob Burley (Robert Ridgely) – jubilantly marches into Huff's office and tells him that due to the gaffe with the videotape, he is to be replaced as the local police chief the day after Christmas. Until that point, he is to report directly to the county prosecutor (who is an old personal friend of Burley). Having seen this development coming, Huff coldly tells Burley that he had an affair with his wife the previous year which, judging by the resulting reaction, has the expected effect on the pompous socialite.

A couple of police officers stop by at the Chasseurs' home to wish them the compliments of the season prior to the curfew taking effect. Startled, and knowing them to be old friends of the family, Lloyd invites them both in for a cup of coffee – to the great vexation of Gus. Further complicating matters, Murray makes his planned phone call to the house but panics when he hears a police officer answer the phone, promptly hanging up. When he calls back later, he can hear the two officers conversing in the background and believes the line to be tapped, making him abandon the call a second time and infuriating his criminal partner in the process.

The Chasseurs' relatives arrive, and the tension is immediately palpable. Rose is snootily dismissive of Caroline and immediately tries to go to her guest room to change into more comfortable footwear. Lloyd panics, fearing that she will discover Jesse, and manages to deflect her by asking if she will aid Caroline in cooking Christmas dinner – a request he knows she can't resist, as it will give her the perfect opportunity to undermine his wife. Rose is suspicious of Gus's presence as she doesn't recognise him, but Lloyd seamlessly explains that he is their marriage guidance counsellor, there to support them emotionally over the holidays.

Murray calls back yet again, and this time Gus is able to convince him that he is not being monitored. The getaway man explains that he has been able to persuade a boat owner, who is a recently-released convict herself, to give them safe passage away from the town. However, her vessel is in need of emergency repairs before they can depart, delaying their escape by at least another hour. Knowing that the police presence in the town is now overwhelming, Gus tells him to prepare for their retreat as quickly as possible while he puzzles out a way of getting from the Chasseurs' house to the docks while the curfew is still operating.

Caroline serves up a traditional Scandinavian Christmas dinner, which the assembled family considers with great scepticism. Rose and Connie question Gus, who they believe to be a highly unconventional therapist, but they eventually conclude that his methods must nonetheless be effective as the usually-warring Lloyd and Caroline now appear to be a compassionate and loving couple – archetypal model spouses. Rose is also suspicious that Jesse is not present, but Gus explains that he had suggested the Chasseurs' son stay with a friend while he worked on Lloyd and Caroline's relationship. Rose then brings up Caroline's adultery, which immediately rein-troduces sharp discord into the exchange, but Gus tries to pour oil on troubled waters. It becomes clearer than ever that Rose disapproves of the marriage between Caroline and her son, and is determined to continually highlight what she be-lieves are the shortcomings of their union.

Eventually, Caroline has had enough needling and heads to the kitchen. She and Lloyd furiously clash over Rose's high-handed criticism, and even Gus concedes that the matriarch is a heartless and snobbish individual. Caroline con-siders this to be a tipping point in the relationship, and is now determined to seek a divorce. The meal descends into a melan-choly blame game as Caroline becomes increasingly inebriated, so Gus – in an attempt to stop the conflict from getting out of control – suggests that the family abandon the meal and open their Christmas presents early. The strategy proves unsuccess-ful, however, with Rose continuing to provoke Caroline until Lloyd eventually feels forced to announce that they will be separating. This cheers the malicious Rose no end; after fif-teen years, she will finally be able to witness the demise of her son's marriage.

Finally, after everything that has unfolded, the Chas-seurs begin to open up to each other. Lloyd admits that he gave up on their restaurant too easily after a devastating re-view by a prominent critic, but points out that while he has always been afraid of failure, so too has Caroline been afraid of being proved wrong. While she looks back now on the ear-ly years of their relationship with fondness, he remembers being in continual debt trying to live a life in New York nei-ther of them could afford. Last but not least, in spite of her protestations to the contrary, it was Caroline who had initial-ly suggested taking Rose up on her offer of a loan, renting the older woman's house, and running the antiques store – not Lloyd. At last they seem to be on the brink of some kind of resolution, but Rose ruins the moment by trying to bring everyone's attention back around to her again. This causes everybody present to turn on her caustic vindictiveness, knowing that she more than anyone is to blame for the endless conflict between Lloyd and Caroline.

The doorbell rings, and Gus is alarmed when he spots a military officer at the front door – not realising that it is Mr Siskel, Jesse's teacher from the academy. Believing that the search for him has escalated, Gus panics and has the rest of the family tied up and gagged – including the vitriolic Rose. Once Siskel enters the house, however, it seems that he has had a Christmas Eve epiphany and tells the Chasseurs that Jesse has been blackmailing him with photos that prove his marital infidelity. Nobody realises that Jesse has managed to again slip out of his bonds and is hurriedly trying to retrieve the money from his room. Looking for an explanation for their son's actions, his parents – with Gus in close pursuit – confront Jesse, but it quickly becomes apparent that he was only gathering cash (by any means necessary) to escape the constant arguments which have made his life at home untenable. He begs Gus to let him join his escape from the town, but – when the criminal refuses – Jesse instead declares that he will leave of his own volition, being unwilling to spend yet another Christmas surrounded by quarrelling relatives.

The house's doorbell rings yet again, interrupting Caroline as she promises Jesse they will do whatever is necessary to make life better for him. By the time they get to the door, it turns out that their visitor has let himself in already – their neighbour George, dressed as Santa Claus, who has been ejected from a nearby Christmas party for being heavily drunk. Seeing Gus's gun, he immediately identifies him as the absconded burglar and intoxicatedly tries to attack, forcing Gus to knock him out cold. Seconds later, the State police arrive outside the house. The Chasseurs, not realising that they are only there conducting curfew checks, decide that they want to help Gus escape – after everything he has inadvertently done to make the couple realise that they still care for each other, they have no desire to see him sent to prison. Jesse offers to take Gus to the docks via a hidden path through the woods, while Lloyd and Caroline stay behind and convince the police that Gus fled to a small independent airport an hour beforehand.

Now alone at last, the Chasseurs are both relieved that they have finally been open and honest with each other about their feelings – even if it has taken a hostage situation to make these revelations possible. Lloyd reveals that Siskel won't press criminal charges if the incriminating photos are returned to him, meaning that Jesse has the chance of a clean slate as well. The couple embrace, willing to give their fifteen-year relationship another chance... but are happy to leave their squabbling relatives tied up just a bit longer. Meanwhile, dressed in George's Santa suit, Gus makes it to the harbour thanks to Jesse's guidance. There is a near-miss when the police drive by, but – believing Gus to be the Chasseurs' inebriated neighbour – they leave with nothing more than a warning about the curfew. Gus finally gets aboard the boat and makes good his escape as planned, but berates the hapless Murray with a furious tirade so venomous, it is worthy of Lloyd and Caroline.

Known by the inspired title *Hostile Hostages* in some overseas territories, *The Ref* is an excellent antidote for anyone who prefers their Christmas entertainment to be more bitter than saccharine. Demme seems to take considerable glee in presenting the picture-perfect Christmas panorama of the community-oriented rural town of Old Baybrook (filmed not in Connecticut but actually in Ontario) before almost immediately seguing into the vitriolic rowing that incessantly takes place between Lloyd and Caroline. The beautifully snowy vistas, expertly presented by director of photography Adam Kimmel, perfectly encapsulate the festive atmosphere that the screenplay then goes on to cheerfully skewer. As Marc Savlov explains, the incongruence of relentless personal attacks taking place against the backdrop of such a wintry, cosy community setting only aids the effectiveness of the film's subversive qualities: 'What with all the holiday tunage on the soundtrack, and the plethora of Yuletide gags scattered throughout the vitriol, something tells me *The Ref* missed its targeted Christmas release. No matter: an unrepentantly nihilistic 110 minutes of bile like this can play any time of year and still come across as acidic as ever'.[3]

As the film's title suggests, Gus ends up unexpectedly acting as a kind of referee between the warring Chasseurs, and Leary's fast-talking, characteristically serrated wit seems perfectly suited to this function. What works in the movie's favour is the fact that, while the premise itself increasingly stretches credulity, the gradual appeasement between the warring Lloyd and Caroline seems all the more convincing for the fact that it unfolds steadily as their defensive barriers slowly erode in the face of the evening's outlandish events. The Christmas setting is exceptionally effective in this sense, as – while family and reconciliation were perennially important themes in the festive cinema of the 1990s – in this case the appeasement and resolution between the Chasseurs seem particularly hard-fought, and made possible only after painful revelations and long-submerged grievances are brought to light. The prissy, perfectionistic Lloyd and theatrical, waspish Caroline are both so mutually distrustful and argumentative, it seems difficult to imagine finding either of them remotely likeable, and yet when we meet their (even more awful) relatives, it becomes all too clear why they eventually became the disgruntled and dissatisfied people that they are when the audience first encounters them.

Over the course of the evening, each of the main characters come to discover something about themselves – not just the belligerent Chasseurs, who begin to realise what has happened to their happier and more idealistic younger selves (that is, they never truly existed in the first place), but also their son whose apparently-delinquent behaviour can be explained by his emotional repression due to the constant interpersonal hostility that surrounds him – to say nothing of his desire to run away from the simmering resentment of this domestic hell before he can become any more miserable. Even Gus is not immune from self-reflection; eager to get out of the criminal underworld before it has the chance to destroy him, he envies the comfortable lifestyle and nuclear family unit of the Chasseurs as much as he begrudges the fact that they take the potential of these things for granted – and are oblivious to their value because of their ceaseless bickering.

By specifically choosing Christmas Eve as the setting for the evening's explosive relationship disclosures, screenwriters Marie Weiss and Richard LaGravenese are clearly aiming for more than just a Scrooge-like transformation from confrontational adversaries into mutually-supportive partners. Caryn James makes the point that, 'Set on Christmas Eve, *The Ref* evokes a familiar kind of holiday feeling: the high anxiety and claustrophobia of spending a long dinner with feuding relatives. The plot sounds hopeless, but the film is handled with gleeful irreverence, dark wit and cynicism'.[4] Thanks to the emotionally cruel, sharp-tongued Rose and the overbearing Connie, even acts so seemingly innocuous as sharing Christmas dinner and opening gifts become a minefield of spiteful comments and vindictive observations. (Lloyd's brother Gary is, by contrast, shown to be largely ornamental – a nicely-judged comic performance by Adam LeFevre.) Because the family members know only too well how to push each other's buttons in order to cause maximum antipathy, it takes the arrival of Gus – an outsider, who has no prior experience of their familial hostility – to try to shame them into more reasonable behaviour, reminding them of what they constantly undervalue as much as he attempts to persuade them to treat each other more reasonably. As Claire Donner observes, 'Gus carries with him the air of a Dickensian Christmas ghost; he has no explicit history, nowhere in particular to go but out of the life and nothing more special than the ability to compel people into catharsis with his righteous verbal onslaught. [...] It feels like he's symbolically scored one for us all against the enormous, psychological pressure of hosting the holiday spirit'.[5]

Because Gus – a lawless, armed criminal – seems a considerably more sympathetic character than his captives, the audience are encouraged to share his incredulity at the Chasseur family's endless enmity towards one another, and his unexpected presence begins to tease out the various causes of this interpersonal hostility. (There is much amusement to be derived from the tough-talking burglar singularly failing to credibly impersonate an renowned therapist – to say nothing of his inevitable lapse back into his acid-tongued insults as the family test his patience to the limit.) We share his exasperation at the fact that, even when threatening people with potentially lethal violence if they don't comply with his demands, they still can't contain themselves from continuing to persistently wrangle with each other.

The way in which the Chasseurs take their cosseted lives for granted is mirrored in the actions of the rest of the town's citizens. People like George, the Santa suit-clad neighbour, are seen presenting a veneer of polite civility (at least initially) while peppering his discourse with cutting, low-key insinuations. Meanwhile, the local police department are clearly under the thumb of the town's pretentious residents – pompous, well-to-do windbags who are always ready to draw on privilege and connections to get their own way driven. All of this comes to a head at Christmas in a way that seems less possible at any other time of the year, as Michael Wilmington has commented:

> The director (Ted Demme) and writers (Richard LaGravenese and Marie Weiss) probably set the movie at Christmas because they want to point up the emptiness of the usual superficial seasonal sentiment. In this hypocrisy-ridden greed-town, Santa Claus is a drunk. And it takes a desperate crook with a temper to keep everyone from each other's throats. It's not a bad idea, but it's not a good movie, either. It's never clear why Leary's Gus puts up with all this, why he doesn't just turn out the lights, hide the car, hogtie everyone and leave them in the cellar. (Of course, we can sense the reason – that he's sort of a nice guy in a fix – but the scenarists don't play this up).[6]

As Wilmington suggests, the film is far from faultless, and there are numerous intriguing inconsistencies which are barely acknowledged and never resolved. Lieutenant Huff being disregarded and eventually dismissed by the influential occupants of the town seems to build up towards a potential revenge subplot that never actually happens, while Mr Siskel's eventual decision to refuse to be further blackmailed by Jesse – essentially risking his private affairs becoming public knowledge – is never fully expounded. However, where *The Ref* does amply succeed is in its impressively nuanced performances and sharp dialogue, which rewards anyone watching the film more than once. This may, in fact, be one of the explanations for its status as a hidden gem of nineties Christmas cinema; as David Nusair explains, '*The Ref* didn't do much business upon its original release, but has since accumulated a cult following on video. There's a good reason for this; it's the sort of movie that improves on repeated viewings'.[7]

While the eventual appeasement between Lloyd, Caroline and their son is an important reinforcement of a persistent theme in Christmas film-making – namely the ability of the festive season to bring people together and see each other in a new light – it is important to note that the pathos of this morality play is only allowed to reach so far. In the original conclusion of *The Ref*, Gus decided to surrender himself to the authorities in order to provide an example to Jesse that crime does not pay; eager to dissuade the teenager from following his own route into lawbreaking, he seeks to sacrifice his own escape from justice in order to willingly face the consequences of his actions. However, test audiences obviously felt that having had to endure the Chasseurs over the festive period, the curiously sympathetic Gus had more than earned his evasion of the authorities, and they reacted with dissatisfaction to this ending to the movie. As a result, an entirely new conclusion – as it appears in the theatrical release of the film – was recorded a few months prior to its cinematic premiere and incorporated instead.

Because Lloyd and Caroline gradually come to appreciate that their marriage has value that they had not fully understood – and, indeed, learn hitherto-known aspects about each other's lives in the process – they make the eventual decision to reverse their quarrelling ways and start to regard each other with a renewed sense of respect. It takes Gus's interjections to awaken them both to the realisation that they were not only lying to each other, but also to themselves. This arc of emotional redemption sets the film apart from other, considerably less hopeful features which share the theme of relationship breakdown and potential divorce, as Jeff Shannon clarifies: '*The Ref* jumps out of the starting gate as the funniest, most rabidly ruthless comedy of the year so far. Try to imagine what it would be like if you crossed a Don Rickles roast with *Who's Afraid of Virginia Woolf?*, and you'll understand how the Chasseurs and their dysfunctional family can turn Christmas Eve into the holiday from hell. [...] Not even a drunken Santa Claus can dampen the yuletide spirit, however, and even though *The Ref* lacks the uncompromising darkness of *The War of the Roses*, it's only because the Chasseurs see their bickering family as something worth saving. Given what they're willing to put up with, it would be Grinch-like to disagree'.[8]

While personal transformations at Christmas were far from an uncommon motif in festive cinema, rarely were they delineated with quite such gracefully slowly-dawning comprehension as was the case in Demme's movie. The handling of marriage and family is slyly adroit, as these themes are broken down, interrogated and reassessed before any kind of happy ending is made possible. Through the gradual understanding that Rose's emotional manipulation and relentless insults are only tolerated because she holds the purse-strings that bind the family, Lloyd and Caroline begin to understand that there is more to life than the hollow trappings of prosperity. Thus they are able, in the end, to extricate their marriage from the malicious matriarch's hateful grasp. However, as Kenneth Turan has noted, the film remains effective precisely because redemptive sentiment is not allowed to overpower the bite of its comic wit: 'The best part of *The Ref* involves [a] neat reversal of expectations, with the nominal hostage-taker ending up at the mercy of the out-of-control hostages, with Gus having no choice but to attempt to bring order out of the Chasseurs' chaos. [...] *The Ref* gets it into its head to actually solve all of the Chasseur family's multifarious problems – in a typical Touchstone/Disney sort of manner – which is a nice thought except that it forces several of the actors to make regrettably serious speeches. Still, it's not every movie that can create so much comedy out of misery, and it's *The Ref*'s bad intentions that finally carry the day'.[9]

The film's effectiveness can, at least in part, be explained by the fact that its screenwriters understand the thematic apparatus of Christmas movies so well, they are able to expertly subvert audience anticipation of what is to come. The Chasseurs, who initially appear unpleasant and indifferent, eventually start to become concerned with the wellbeing of others and more considerate of each other, while the malicious and manipulative Rose seems singularly incapable of such redemption, proving to be so malevolent that she ends up gagged with Christmas wrapping ribbon in a seemingly-symbolic indication that some people can never change – even in the face of the transformative potential of Christmas. As James notes, '*The Ref* is a film to warm the hearts and touch the nerves of dysfunctional families everywhere. [...] This is a grown-up film that delights in undermining Christmas cliches. Some of us are bound to love a movie in which watching *It's a Wonderful Life* leads to a minor calamity'.[10] While an unwitting mistake by the local police destroys the recorded evidence that identified Gus, catching him in the act of burgling, it is this crucial error which inadvertently guarantees his circumvention of justice and, by extension, his eventual escape from criminality. And the calculating Jesse, who seemed bound for a similar path into wrongdoing and transgression, realises the error of his ways before he can fall into the very trap that Gus has been trying to escape from.

Key to the success of *The Ref* was the skilled performances of its principal cast, from the snide, cutting barbs being ruthlessly exchanged between the warring Chasseurs to the exasperated outbursts of Gus as he endlessly attempts to keep the couple from tearing each other apart. Kevin Spacey had appeared in numerous films from the late eighties, including *Working Girl* (Mike Nichols, 1988) and *Glengarry Glen Ross* (James Foley, 1992), and later in the decade would achieve greater success with performances in films such as dark thriller *Se7en* (David Fincher, 1995) and crime drama *L.A. Confidential* (Curtis Hanson, 1997). He would go on to win an Academy Award for Best Supporting Actor for his performance in *The Usual Suspects* (Bryan Singer, 1995) and then for Best Actor in *American Beauty* (Sam Mendes, 1999). He has won or been nominated for numerous other industry awards, including being conferred a Golden Globe Award, a BAFTA Award and a Tony Award. Judy Davis is currently the most awarded individual in the history of the

Australian Academy of Cinema and Television Arts Awards (the AACTA Awards), having won accolades on a remarkable nine occasions (and being nominated for several further awards beyond that). Her cinematic debut was in the Australian comedy *High Rolling* (Igor Auzins, 1977), and she would appear in many films throughout the eighties and nineties as diverse as *Who Dares Wins* (Ian Sharp, 1982), *High Tide* (Gillian Armstrong, 1987), *Barton Fink* (Joel Coen and Ethan Coen, 1991) and *Naked Lunch* (David Cronenberg, 1991). Davis has twice been nominated for Academy Awards, for her performances in *A Passage to India* (David Lean, 1984) and *Husbands and Wives* (Woody Allen, 1992). She has also won two Golden Globe Awards, two BAFTA Awards and three Primetime Emmy Awards, amongst many other industry honours.

The critical reception of *The Ref* was decidedly mixed when it first appeared in cinemas. Many reviewers, such as Savlov, appreciated the juxtaposition between the cheerfulness of the festive season and the prolonged domestic bickering that the film places beneath its narrative magnifying glass, generating humour from the resulting combination: 'Much of the film's rampant nastiness comes from the genuinely inspired casting of Spacey and Davis: they're a mismatched couple whose domestic problems run the gamut from sexual to financial. [...] Spacey and Davis are great together; their bickering has the painful sense of being all too real, poison that's been flowing a long time. Leary rehashes his Bill Hicks persona for the umpteenth time, but if you can get past the blatant rip-off of his shtick, you'll find an inspired, virulent, often hilarious film that apparently was just too much for old Saint Nick'.[11] Others, including James Berardinelli, lamented the fact that the movie's tightly-disciplined editing may ultimately have worked against it – even in spite of an already healthy running time: 'There's a sense that a lot of *The Ref* was snipped in the cutting room. While this undoubtedly helped the pacing, it also opened a few noticeable plot holes. This is not a seamlessly constructed movie, but as long as you're not expecting great art, it's unlikely to disappoint. The dramatic scenes aren't generally effective, but the comic bits more than make up for most of the deficiencies. [...] *The Ref* is designed more for those willing to empathize with Gus, a man having the kind of day that most of us don't even like to have nightmares about. Merry Christmas'.[12]

The movie's central performances were singled out for praise by many commentators, with Kelly Vance's appraisal echoing that of several within the critical community: 'For anyone who doubts that character counts as much as writing in comedy, *The Ref* is a lesson. The screenplay (evidently a reworking by Richard LaGravenese – he wrote *The Fisher King* – of an idea by Marie Weiss) doubles as a vacuum cleaner. Without trying very hard, we can spot bits and pieces of Edward Albee, Woody Allen, and other bitter hubby-wifey comedies like *The War of the Roses.* [...] Leary, Davis, and Spacey are the show, each trying to top the other like jazz musicians at a cutting contest. They're so good we wouldn't be surprised to hear they were improvising'.[13] While the entertaining bitterness emanating from the film's key cast pairing came in for much admiration, however, some critics – such as Desson Howe – sounded a note of caution that the sense of implied threat at the heart of the hostage situation is quickly blunted by the increasingly droll take on these ostensibly-menacing circumstances: 'That marital enmity transcends fear of death is funny. But it rapidly becomes clear Leary is a Touchstone Pictures, user-friendly kinda villain. The tension –

vital to the comic situation – drops right out of the movie. Leary's tough, profane act becomes tame and, frankly, tedious. [...] Unless you're a junkie for mediocre rejoinders and insults ("I know loan sharks that are more forgiving than you," Leary tells Johns), this is one holiday party you'll want to miss'.[14] Overall, though, more reviewers sounded a note of caution over the film's merits than not, with Hal Hinson being representative of those commentators who appreciated the innovative qualities of the movie's fundamental concept while remaining sceptical about many aspects of its execution:

> *The Ref* is one of those rare movies that seem to have everything going for it – a promising director, terrific actors and an original, unapologetically grown-up script – yet somehow still turns out to be a phenomenal drag. [...] To their credit, the actors do their best to make something out of the material they've been given. But while Spacey and Davis are both talented (and undervalued) actors, they are forced to raise the energy levels of their performances too high too soon, and they can't sustain the effort. Leary is more problematic. A stand-up comic trying to translate his impatient, hipster editorializing to the big screen, he doesn't have the modulation of a trained actor, only one speed (fast) and one mode of attack (loud).[15]

In more recent years, *The Ref* has remained something of an acquired taste amongst critics, with many of the same identified issues continuing to predominate in modern analysis as at the initial time of release. Ryan Cracknell has made the point that, as the movie features a rather low-key festive setting, it has become a somewhat subdued addition to the wider pantheon of Christmas film-making: 'Largely overlooked at the time of its release, *The Ref* is a marvelous vehicle for Leary. [...] I don't know why or how *The Ref* has slipped by relatively unnoticed over the years. Then again, I've only just seen it myself. I guess it's one of those movies that doesn't stand out. It isn't marketed as a Christmas movie, thus limiting the chances of it getting dragged out and put in a prominent spot every December. But just because *The Ref* isn't your typical Christmas movie doesn't mean you should skip it. In fact, it should be just the opposite'.[16] Conversely, critics including George Rother have commented that although the film's unconventional approach to the festive season has marked it out as something of an anomaly amongst many other releases of the mid-nineties, its bleakly humorous methodology has made it a distinctive – if rather subjectively successful – experiment within the yuletide comedy subgenre: '*The Ref* is the kind of movie that will appeal to the grinch in everybody; director Ted Demme (*Blow, Who's the Man?*) has put together what I like to call "the anti-Christmas movie". It's not against the Christmas holiday, it's just unlike a majority of Christmas-themed movies, the most similar title that comes to mind is 2003's *Bad Santa*. The good thing is that this movie really works, it's good adult fun for those with a warped sense of humor. Not everybody is going to find *The Ref* funny, it's likely that quite a few people will be offended by some of what's going on in the movie. [...] This movie will not appeal to those looking for an innocuous feel-good flick. If you like dark comedy, then you'll probably like *The Ref*, all others need not apply'.[17]

Not every commentator has been entirely convinced of *The Ref*'s perceived artistic merits, with some – such as Andy Webb – suggesting that the film's reputation as a neglected

treasure amongst 1990s Christmas movies may not be entirely
deserved: 'Having watched *The Ref* I can't actually see what
all the fuss is; yes it is amusing, yes it has some great lines but
it becomes monotonous as despite the various characters it is
almost a one joke movie. [...] *The Ref* is entertaining but it is
one of those movies which is loved by some people but can
end up underwhelming for those who watch because others
love it so much. As such *The Ref* whilst worth watching may
not make your list of Christmas movies you want to watch
every year'.[18] Ultimately, however, critics including Nusair
have made the observation that part of the film's intriguingly
incongruous creative success was the fact that it has proven to
be fascinatingly problematic to define, leading to its vaguely
enigmatic status amongst the Christmas movies of the time:

> *The Ref* is a really bizarre amalgam of outlandish
> comedy and searing family drama, but it works –
> thanks primarily to the exceedingly enjoyable per-
> formances. [...] *The Ref* is an exceedingly difficult
> movie to categorize, given that it comfortably
> leaps between comedy and drama throughout. But
> that's exactly what makes the film so interesting; it
> hasn't been assembled by focus groups or a board
> of executives. There's a certain amount of unique-
> ness present in the movie, mostly due to the
> surprisingly adult and clever screenplay by Rich-
> ard LaGravenese and Marie Weiss. No doubt a
> good portion of Leary's dialogue was improvised,
> though, as it contains a lot of the snarky one-liners
> we've come to expect from the former comic.[19]

The Ref's casting director, Howard Feuer, was to be
nominated for an Artios Award for Best Casting for a Fea-

ture Film (Comedy) by the Casting Society of America. While the movie has become one of the less well-remembered Christmas features of the 1990s, its reputation has grown in recent years, and it has become especially fondly-regarded amongst fans of Denis Leary's distinctively dark brand of comedy. In its deft challenge to festive truisms and the expected conventions of Christmas film-making, the movie is a master-class in interrogating the principles of yuletide themes while simultaneously reinforcing them with an upbeat conclusion, a sense of tentative hopefulness, and a moral message that the mutual support of the family unit can survive even years of constant deterioration and neglect. It may not have been a film that immediately suggested positivity and optimism, but – perhaps exactly because it refused to offer these facets either readily or easily – its emotional impact is felt all the more keenly.

REFERENCES

1. Jordan R. Young, *Roman Polanski: Behind the Scenes of His Classic Early Films* (Lanham: Applause Books, 2022), p.163.

2. Roger Ebert, '*The Ref*', in *The Chicago Sun-Times*, 11 March 1994.
    <*https://www.rogerebert.com/reviews/the-ref-1994*>

3. Marc Savlov, '*The Ref*', in *The Austin Chronicle*, 18 March 1994.
    <*https://www.austinchronicle.com/events/film/1994-03-18/the-ref/*>

4. Caryn James, 'Reviews/Film: *The Ref*: A Christmas That Upends Christmas', in *The New York Times*, 9 March 1994.
    <*https://www.nytimes.com/1994/03/09/movies/reviews-film-the-ref-a-christmas-that-upends-christmas.html*>

5. Claire Donner, '*The Ref* (1994): Lookback/Review', in *Den of Geek*, 18 December 2012.
    <*https://www.denofgeek.com/movies/the-ref-1994-lookbackreview/*>

6. Michael Wilmington, 'Dysfunctional *Ref* a Shouting Match', in *The Chicago Tribune*, 11 March 1994.
    <*https://www.chicagotribune.com/news/ct-xpm-1994-03-11-9403110097-story.html*>

7. David Nusair, '*The Ref*', in *Reel Film Reviews*, 4 March 2003.
    <*https://www.reelfilm.com/ref.htm*>

8.	Jeff Shannon, 'Family Feud A Fate Worse Than Jail For *The Ref*, in *The Seattle Times*, 11 March 1994. *<https://archive.seattletimes.com/archive/?date=19940311 &slug=1899594>*

9.	Kenneth Turan, 'Movie Reviews: *The Ref:* Razor-Sharp', in *The Los Angeles Times*, 9 March 1994. *<https://www.latimes.com/archives/la-xpm-1994-03-09-ca-31725-story.html>*

10.	James.

11.	Savlov.

12.	James Berardinelli, '*The Ref*, in *ReelViews*, 11 March 1994. *<https://www.reelviews.net/reelviews/ref-the>*

13.	Kelly Vance, 'Cutting Contest', in *The Chicago Reader*, 7 April 1994. *<https://chicagoreader.com/film/cutting-contest/>*

14.	Desson Howe, '*The Ref*, in *The Washington Post*, 11 March 1994. *<https://www.washingtonpost.com/wp-srv/style/ longterm/movies/videos/therefrhowe_a0b03a.htm>*

15.	Hal Hinson, '*The Ref*, in *The Washington Post*, 12 March 1994. *<https://www.washingtonpost.com/wp-srv/style/ longterm/movies/videos/therefrhinson_b009de.htm>*

16.	Ryan Cracknell, '*The Ref*, in *Movie Views*, 19 December 2003. *<https://movieviews.ca/the-ref>*

17.   George Rother, '*The Ref*', in *MovieGuy 24/7*, 9 December
        2012.
        <*https://movieguy247.com/iMovies/index.php/blog/holid
        ay-movies/689-the-ref*>

18.   Andy Webb, '*The Ref*', in *The Movie Scene*, 2009.
        <*https://www.themoviescene.co.uk/reviews/the-ref/the-
        ref.html*>

19.   Nusair.

12

The Preacher's Wife (1996)

Touchstone Pictures / The Samuel Goldwyn Company /
Mundy Lane Entertainment / Parkway Productions

Director: Penny Marshall
Producer: Samuel Goldwyn Jr.
Screenwriters: Nat Mauldin and Allan Scott, from an earlier
screenplay by Robert E. Sherwood and Leonardo Bercovici
and a novel by Robert Nathan

THE nineties not only witnessed a reaffirmation of many traditional Christmas conventions – it also saw numerous remakes and reimaginings of classic festive cinema which reasserted the relevance of the original films' themes while bringing their settings and characters right up to date. Les Mayfield's *Miracle on 34th Street* (q.v.) had brought a contemporary spin to George Seaton's much-loved 1947 original, whereas George Gallo's *Trapped in Paradise* (q.v.) had conjured up the spirit (if not explicitly the story) of Michael Curtiz's celebrated comedy *We're No Angels* (1955). Penny Marshall's *The Preacher's Wife* was to continue in this vein by breathing new life into Henry Koster's venerable Christmas tale *The Bishop's Wife* (1947), taking the central premise of that fondly-remembered post-war movie and giving it a thoroughly modern twist for 1990s audiences.

Koster's original film had involved a newly-minted Episcopal Bishop, Henry Brougham (David Niven), who had become so focused on the task of establishing a new cathedral in an affluent inner-city area that he had started to neglect his loving wife (Loretta Young) and their child. Thankfully a visiting angel named Dudley (Cary Grant) steps in to remind Henry of his priorities as a husband and father, and to help him establish a church community that puts fairness and mutual support ahead of the material concerns of the wealthier, more self-interested parishioners. *The Bishop's Wife* was adapted from Robert Nathan's 1928 novel of the same name, and won an Academy Award for Best Sound as well as being nominated for a further five Oscars (including Best Director for Henry Koster). With outstanding performances by the principal cast – especially Cary Grant as the dashing and refined Dudley, almost certainly the most debonair angel ever to be captured on film – the movie has gone on to become arguably one of the most critically well-regarded Christmas features of the genre's golden age.

The Preacher's Wife was to prove more than a simple retread of the 1947 original; the story was completely overhauled for modern audiences, the religious denomination of the eponymous protagonist changed, and the threat facing the pastor's church altered to make the story more relevant to contemporary viewers. The result was to be a film which was to resonate with the central themes of 1990s Christmas cinema – family and community, reaching mutual understanding and experiencing the transformative power of the festive season – while also reflecting motifs of personal faith that had become far less common since the more overtly religious Christmas films to appear in the late 1940s and early 50s. Andrew Horton explains that '*The Preacher's Wife* (1996) has

Denzel Washington as an angel sent down to help a troubled African American gospel church who falls in love with Whitney Houston, the preacher's wife. An anarchistic gospel screwball comedy, it is actually a remake of the 1947 comedy *The Bishop's Wife*. In [Penny] Marshall's update, the fantasy element – an African American angel – blends humorously and joyously with the festive gospel hand-clapping scenes for a true carnival of a Christmas-season film'.[1]

Helming this high-profile remake was director Penny Marshall, who by then was widely recognised as a highly successful creative talent in Hollywood. Having risen to public prominence in the role of Wisconsinite bottle-capper Laverne DeFazio in ABC's long-running series *Laverne & Shirley* (itself a spin-off from the same network's legendary situation comedy *Happy Days*), Marshall was nominated for three Golden Globe Awards for her performances in the show. In the 1980s, she moved into directing and soon generated a following amongst filmgoers for films such as early techno-thriller *Jumpin' Jack Flash* (1986), fantasy adventure *Big* (1988) and sporting comedy *A League of Their Own* (1992), and diversified into producing from the mid-nineties onwards. *The Preacher's Wife* was to be the penultimate film that she was to helm, and the only explicitly Christmas-themed movie that she would direct in her lifetime.

The Preacher's Wife was to be a production that was packed with performance talent, with many admired show-business personalities such as Denzel Washington, Whitney Houston, Courtney B. Vance, Gregory Hines and Jenifer Lewis appearing alongside four-time Grammy Award-winning singer Lionel Richie, formerly of The Commodores, in his feature film acting debut. Nat Mauldin and Allan Scott's screenplay for the film was based on the concepts and situations of the original 1947 movie, as scripted by Robert E. Sherwood and Leonardo Bercovici, and retained many of its key themes – a fact which appealed to some of the central cast. As *Jet* magazine clarified, '⟦Washington⟧ was attracted to the movie's positive theme of family closeness and church. "The story appealed to me because it's about the fundamental things we seem to have gotten away from in society – hope and faith in our fellow man, and in God, and the sense that family and church are the foundations of a community," he says. "I liked that about the story, as well as the idea of appearing in a film that would be saying positive, uplifting things"'.[2]

In a wintry city in the urban North-East of the United States, precocious preacher's son Jeremiah Biggs (Justin Pierre Edmund) explains that times are tough at his family's church. The weekly collection from the congregation is too meagre to pay the bills, and his father – the Reverend Henry Biggs (Courtney B. Vance) – is despairing at the challenges facing their faith community. He gives a heartfelt sermon about the need to have trust that God will help people through the hard times, while his wife Julia (Whitney Houston) tries to lighten the tone with some impromptu gospel singing as he speaks. Julia's wise and feisty mother, Margueritte Coleman (Jenifer Lewis), is staying with the family for the holidays and watches approvingly from the gathering of worshippers.

After the Sunday service is over, Henry's concerns are much more difficult to conceal. The area where the church is based is clearly suffering from underinvestment and various serious social issues, and Henry is worried that the church doesn't have the resources to offer enough practical support to the public. Julia offers him comforting words, knowing the depth of his anxiety, and notes approvingly that he has been revisiting some of the sermons written by her late father (the church's previous pastor). Even Margueritte notes that the teaching sounded almost as good the second time around. Further adding to the family's woes, Jeremiah's best friend Hakim (Darvel Davis Jr.) is set to go into the care of child welfare due to the advanced age of his grandmother, with whom he lives, and Henry notes with great regret that the local youth centre will be shutting down due to lack of funds. He intends to say goodbye to the children and young adults who attend it before the doors close for the final time.

Margueritte is troubled by Henry's deep dejection, and asks Julia if it is affecting their relationship. Julia shrugs off her mother's worries, but in truth Henry is questioning everything about his life – including the effectiveness of his ministry and way that he fears his value to the community may be diminishing. In desperation, he prays to God for some help in turning things around for the better. Little does he realise that the response to his prayer is much more immediate than expected, as a smartly-dressed gentleman named Dudley (Denzel Washington) suddenly appears outside his home as if arriving out of thin air. Jeremiah and Hakim are alarmed by the sudden presence of this benevolent stranger in their back yard, especially when he seems so oddly elated just to be there.

At the youth centre, Henry is saddened to see the many young individuals who used its facilities being forced out against their will. The building has been purchased for redevelopment by local real estate mogul Joe Hamilton (Gregory Hines), and while many of the young people rail against Henry for being unable to stop the closure, others thank him for having tried so hard to keep the building open. As he leaves, he is intercepted by Dudley, who introduces himself to the beleaguered pastor as having arrived in answer to his prayer. Henry is irritated, believing the encounter to be nothing more than a bad joke, and drives off – leaving the baffled newcomer in his wake.

Later, Dudley gets into a conversation with a pizza vendor (Jernard Burks) and asks if he knows Henry, casually pointing out that he has found him to be rather short-tempered and irritable. Infurated, the vendor informs him that the Reverend Biggs is a genuine pillar of the community, having baptised all five of his children and visited his wife in hospital every single day after she had surgery. Displeased that anyone would question the character of such a caring and hard-working pastor, he ejects Dudley and tells him never to return. Thus the newcomer is left in no doubt of the high regard in which Henry is held throughout the neighbourhood. Julia and Jeremiah pass by soon after, and the sharp-eyed boy immediately recognises Dudley as the man who had fallen from the sky earlier that day. However, the well-groomed stranger silently hushes him so as to keep his identity a secret. That night, Julia is saddened by Jeremiah's apprehension about the uncertain future of Hakim. He fears that he may never see his best friend again once he is taken into the care of the State. Henry watches the exchange from the doorway, feeling increasingly hopeless.

The next day, a robbery takes place at a liquor store near the church, and the owner (Jamie Tirelli) wrongly identifies the culprit as a local kid, Billy Eldridge (William James Stiggers Jr.), who happens to be standing on the opposite sidewalk next to a handgun discarded by the fleeing criminals. Billy just happens to have been in the wrong place at the wrong time, but is taken into custody when the police arrive. Henry is called down to the precinct where the young man is being held, but as the wrongly-accused Billy has a previous conviction from a few years previously it looks as though the innocent bystander may end up being sentenced in error. Returning to his car, the pastor is crestfallen when he discovers that the engine won't start, but a prayer for divine intervention leads to another encounter with Dudley.

Henry is dismayed to see the well-dressed gent again, believing him to be a harmless crank, but is taken aback when his hitherto-malfunctioning car suddenly starts up as soon as Dudley arrives. Suspiciously, he asks who Dudley really is, to which the stranger replies that he is an angel who has been sent to earth in order to assist Henry in getting through his troubles. The sceptical pastor clearly disbelieves this account, but Dudley emphatically retorts that angels are incapable of lying. The extraordinary guest confides that he had once been human many years ago, but had died while still a young man and has been waiting a long time for a return to the mortal world – even if it is only a temporary one. He also points out that Henry will only remember him until such time as Dudley's earthly mission is complete. As he drops the mysterious visitor off at a hotel, the pastor seems intrigued and suggests that Dudley make an appointment if he would like to talk further. They shake hands, and Henry looks stunned – as though affected by some higher power when they had temporarily made physical contact.

Back at the church, Julia leads a choir rehearsal while volunteers make repairs and redecorate the building's run-down interior. While the choir members' kids are treated to some Christmas stories, however, the church's ancient and ailing boiler is wheezing its way towards a total breakdown. Around the same time, a tired Henry is returning home ready to rest – only for Margueritte to tell him that Joe Hamilton had called for him earlier in the day and has invited the pastor to attend an important meeting the following morning.

A deafening explosion leads to the sudden evacuation of the church, and Henry is dismayed when he descends into the basement and discovers that the boiler has ruptured. Now more despairing than ever, the pastor tells Julia that he blames himself for all of it – the dwinding church membership, the building's crumbling condition, and the fact that no obvious answers are making themselves apparent. Neither of them realise that Dudley is outside their home, already working on solutions to improve their situation.

The next morning, Julia tells Henry that she is anxious that their marriage is suffering from the many stresses that are being placed on the pastor. No matter how well he shoulders the burdens of his responsibilities, he is ultimately only one human being. Before he can respond, however, he receives news that Billy's bail hearing has been moved forward, mean-ing that he has to race away from the breakfast table. While they talk, Dudley arrives and introduces himself to Beverly (Loretta Devine), Henry's industrious secretary. When he explains that he is there to assist the pastor, Beverly panics, believing that she is being replaced when she has three young children to support. But the smooth-talking angel assures her that his presence is strictly temporary.

At the court, Billy's attorney pleads his case, but the judge (Lizan Mitchell) is unwilling to accept that he was merely an innocent witness to the robbery. Henry agrees to post bail, but due to the seriousness of the crime the judge sets it at $25,000 – a cost that is far beyond the church's ability to pay. Meanwhile, Julia watches unhappily as Hakim is taken into the care of a foster family far from the town where he was brought up. Jeremiah is inconsolable at being separated from his best friend, even in spite of Julia's promises to help him write letters and keep in touch by telephone.

Beverly brings Dudley to the attention of Julia and Margueritte, still baffled at the arrival of a new assistant. However, Julia remembers Henry having written to the church council months beforehand in search of additional support and assumes that Dudley must be their appointee. The newcomer insists that he has been sent by 'the Top Man', and he is assured that he is welcome in the Biggs's home. Shortly afterwards, Dudley meets up with Jeremiah who remembers him from his unearthly arrival. The angel impresses him by magically repairing his toy ambulance – including the addition of sirens that were never previously there. Dudley explains that although Jeremiah is upset by the fact that he has been separated from Hakim, God always leaves the memory of a loved one with us even when they have had to part company.

Henry is dumbfounded when he returns home and finds Dudley hard at work in the church office. Offhandedly, the charming angel explains that he has given Beverly the day off to be with her children, and has been busy attending to her duties on her behalf. When the pastor discovers that Dudley has already ingratiated himself with his family, he is indignant and makes it clear that he doesn't appreciate a stranger inveigling their way into his life and work. But as Dudley patiently informs him, angels are never strangers.

Together with his new 'assistant', Henry heads for the meeting with Joe Hamilton. Still deeply distrustful of Dudley's motives, the pastor shuts him out of the meeting, but he soon discovers that many of his most prominent parishioners are already present in Hamilton's office. The fast-talking realtor explains that if Henry is willing to sign off on a brand new church for the community, a fresh era will dawn in the area.

He unveils a model of an ultra-modern glass and steel building with daycare facilities and a senior citizens' club. Hamilton even offers to provide a new boiler for the existing church to keep services going until the new complex is complete. Henry, however, is unconvinced. While the slick entrepreneur is presenting the new church as the answer to everyone's problems, the pastor can see that there will be issues in relocating the existing congregation to a totally new location. In other words, rather than solving the area's problems Hamilton intends to remove them permanently – by completely reshaping the neighbourhood out of all recognition.

Julia is directing rehearsals of the church's Nativity play, where Dudley is providing theatrical support to Jeremiah (who is portraying one of the manger's sheep). The angel watches, delighted, as the local kids run through their heartfelt musical numbers. Later, while Christmas shopping, Julia reveals to Dudley that she and Henry were childhood sweethearts, and that their marriage almost seemed preordained. The angel is touched to see that such an earnest love exists between the two. They take Jeremiah for lunch, but when Henry returns from the meeting – somewhat puzzled to see Dudley there – the angel offers to take the energetic youngster shopping at a toy store to let his parents talk in private.

Once they have departed, a conflicted Henry confesses to Julia that he has decided to take Joe Hamilton up on his offer. In exchange, a brand new boiler will be fitted into the existing church the following day. Julia is furious, perceiving that Hamilton is only really interested in building a monument to his own business acumen and seeing the replacement boiler as a blatant bribe in order to get his own way. Henry points out that the parishioners were strongly in favour of the new development, and that by making a move to the new building he may be able to do more good than he is currently able to. But Julia feels betrayed: not only had her late father entrusted the future of the church to Henry, but the well-meaning pastor has made an enormous decision – which affects both their lives – without even consulting her.

Back home, Margueritte entreats Julia to support Henry even in spite of her reservations about the new church. She points out that the main thing is that the parishioners will be better supported, which is more important than their personal attachment to the existing building. Julia later picks up a Christmas tree for the family with Dudley, who also implores her to forgive Henry for his decision to negotiate with Hamilton without talking the matter through with her first. Julia feels that her husband has increasingly been taking her for granted, which saddens Dudley. He hatches a plan to persuade her to share a romantic night on the town dancing with Henry. However, the long-suffering preacher has other ideas; he must pay hospital visits and take blankets to a home for senior citizens, and knows that no-one else will do it unless he does. Irritated at Dudley's well-intentioned attempts to support his marriage, Henry tells him that as he won't be available to take Julia out on a date night, the angel should go in his stead.

Dudley is frustrated that his efforts appear to be in vain, but when Julia is crestfallen that her husband has chosen pastoral duties over an evening with her, the kindly angel decides to take Henry up on his suggestion and invites Julia out instead. They enjoy the atmosphere of a local jazz club, which the Biggs' had frequently visited in their youth, and Dudley shares a dance with Julia – albeit that his dance moves, which are several decades out of date, bewilder the other patrons. Julia meets Britsloe (Lionel Richie), the club's owner, who speaks highly of Henry and recalls how the pastor has helped him out in years past. The pair reminisce about Henry proposing to Julia in the same club years previously, and chatting with Britsloe reminds her of the many times she sang there. At the urging of Dudley, she self-consciously agrees to a recital, and the angel is enraptured by her obviously-extensive performance talents.

While Julia sings, Henry is selflessly going about his duties, giving spiritual support to the ill member of his congregation in hospital and then serving food in a soup kitchen. This he does with a friendly smile on his face for all who encounter him, never betraying the true burden that he carries. Later that night, while making popcorn decorations for the family Christmas tree, Henry is discomfited when Jeremiah explains about Dudley window-shopping with Julia earlier in the day. He begins to wonder if the angel is really all that he seems to be. When Julia and Dudley return, Henry is aghast that they had spent the evening at a place that was so special to him and his wife – and that he had missed her singing there, which he had enjoyed so often in the early days of their relationship.

In spite of Henry's indignation, as soon as Julia has left the room Dudley tells the pastor that he is worried about his wellbeing. He knows that Henry has stopped believing in his ability to make a positive difference to the lives in his community – even as he continues to do exactly that. At the end of his tether, Henry angrily points out that he is already stretched to breaking point due to his increasingly taxing church duties. But Dudley begs him not to neglect his family's needs either: Julia is feeling increasingly overlooked, and Jeremiah is still lamenting the loss of his closest friend with all of the emotional pain that goes with a separation. The angel reminds the pastor not to take his loved ones for granted, even in spite of his many clerical responsibilities.

The next morning, Henry is present at the courthouse just as Billy is about to be sentenced. He meets with the troubled youth, and finds himself convinced that Billy was simply caught up in events beyond his control. The pastor suggests that Billy pray for a solution, but when the young man is unmoved by the prospect Henry tells him that even if the act of prayer is not appealing to him, he can look on it as simply being hope put into action. Newly energised, Henry walks into the courtroom – interrupting another trial – and pleads Billy's innocence to the judge. The pastor emphasises the young man's good character, and passionately states that no concrete evidence exists – beyond a faulty identification by a distressed victim – that Billy was involved in the crime. Henry's ardent defence impresses the judge, who relents and allows Billy to go free – much to the delight of his mother, Anna (Marcella Lowery).

While the courtroom drama is unfolding, Dudley has decided to take Julia and Jeremiah ice-skating. They are due to meet with Henry, little realising that the pastor is mysteriously being held up in traffic by a seemingly endless succession of traffic lights. Jeremiah soon tires, so he watches from the sidelines as Dudley treats Julia to a spirited display of skating. Eventually reasoning that Henry has been called off to other pastoral duties, they take a taxi home, but upon encountering Margueritte they find that she is becoming suspicious of Dudley's intentions towards her daughter. Julia assures her mother that her friendship with Henry's new assistant is purely platonic, but Margueritte – knowing the way that the pastor's responsibilities have been keeping him from his family – beseeches her to keep things that way.

Some time later, a supremely weary Henry finally arrives home, but his enthusiasm over getting Billy's charges dropped soon dissipates when he learns that Julia has been ice-skating with Dudley. The pastor marches into his office to confront him, demands that the angel no longer spend time with his wife, and then tells him that he is fired. Dudley tells him that he is unable to depart until he has completed his mission, leading Henry to angrily throw his Angel's Handbook into the office fireplace... leading to an unnatural flash of light. The pastor is baffled by the display, but Dudley feels certain this action will lead to no good. When Julia investigates the raised voices, Henry urges her to support his decision to terminate Dudley's employment, but she refuses to do so. On his way out of the office, the angel warns Henry that he would be facing the same problems with his marriage regardless of whether Dudley had arrived or not, but informs him that his ultimate duty is to ensure the survival of his church – the whole community will most assuredly suffer on account of its absence, not just Henry and Julia.

Margueritte intercepts Dudley as he leaves the house, and impresses on him the need to break off any romantic interest he may have in Julia. Dudley assures her that he is only present in order to help, and that the only relationship that concerns him is saving the one between Henry and his wife. Sternly, Margueritte informs him that she will gladly extend her stay at the Biggs's home until he leaves, so he should consider respecting Henry's wishes when it comes to departing. They shake hands, and in a moment of unspoken revelation Margueritte suddenly – and mysteriously – decides to give up her persistent smoking habit. Dudley's disconsolate mood is not improved when he spots Beverly striking up a new romance with Saul Jeffreys (Paul Bates), one of Henry's congregation, who runs a community transport service.

Dudley wanders alone from the jazz club to the church, but finds both deserted. Eventually he encounters Henry dropping off Christmas gifts at the homes of his parishioners, and uses a little angel magic to make him slip on an icy driveway and land harmlessly in the snow. Henry and Julia share a laugh as the angel watches glumly from the distance, knowing that he is helping them to remember the carefree larks they had shared in their youth. This simple action sparks off warm reminiscences which they impart during the rest of their festive deliveries.

On their arrival at home, Henry decides to check in on the volunteers who are preparing the church for the forthcoming Christmas celebrations. He soon discovers that, true to Joe Hamilton's word, a brand new boiler has been installed in the basement – just in time for the holidays. Seeing the pride that the volunteers are taking in their maintenance of the old church building, Henry seems contemplative.

The next day, which is Christmas Eve, he drives to Hamilton's palatial home and tells the property mogul that he has changed his mind about moving to the new church building. However, Hamilton will not be budged; as a trustee of the church (albeit a non-attending member), he owns the building's mortgage and intends to bulldoze the site at the heart of community in order to make way for luxury condominiums – complete with tennis courts. Henry is aghast, knowing that this will spell the end of the neighbourhood as he knows it. He begs Hamilton to come to the old church and see for himself the disastrous social impact that demolition will bring, but the realtor dismissively tells him that the local people will survive no matter what happens.

Later that night, Jeremiah is delighted to hear that he has been promoted from a sheep to a shepherd in the church's Nativity play. However, Henry and Julia have even more exciting news for him – they have arranged for Hakim to join the family for Christmas. Jeremiah's best friend will be with them until the new year, but Julia promises that they will do their best to arrange a longer stay if possible. With all of the many problems that are weighing down on him and his parish, Henry struggles to write his Christmas sermon, finding it difficult to pinpoint positive sentiment when there is so much to worry about. When he momentarily leaves to check the house's fuse box, Julia sneaks a peek at his notes and discovers that the text is very defeatist, suggesting that Henry has resigned himself to Hamilton's intention of demolishing the old church and thus scattering its existing congregation.

Unknown to Henry, Dudley makes his way to Hamilton's house and confronts the smooth-talking tycoon. Initially, Hamilton is indifferent and – believing that Henry has sent his assistant in his stead – simply demands that he leave. He starts to consider Dudley's claim of being an angel more seriously, however, when he notices his grand piano playing music of its own volition and hears a broken vintage radio set relaying one of his advertisements in spite of not even being plugged in. Hamilton tries to rationalise this as being simply the result of tricks and sleight-of-hand, but Dudley impresses on him the need to fully consider the negative effects that tearing down the church would have on the community.

Christmas Day arrives, and the church Nativity play goes down a storm with the parishioners. As Julia works behind the scenes to help the kids on and off the stage in the church, Dudley arrives and tells her that he will soon be taking his leave. Julia asks him to stay but, when he tells her that his work is done, she senses that their shared, unspoken attraction may be the reason for his departure. Before they can discuss the matter further, the girl playing the Virgin Mary drops out of the performance (due to a malfunction with the doll portraying the Baby Jesus), leading to Julia filling in for the closing musical number.

The time comes for Henry's sermon, but a teleprompter problem means that the text of his intended reading isn't available. Instead, he improvises an impassioned plea for greater involvement in the community so that the impoverished and the youth of the neighbourhood will all be supported. Reminding the congregation that God has gifted them all hope and love, he assures everyone present that the church can and will be saved. Little does he realise that Joe Hamilton is present among the members of the congregation, listening intently to the pastor's profound lesson.

Julia performs a rousing hymn to close the service, and she and Henry embrace knowing that the Christmas observance couldn't have gone better. As Britsloe takes over the church piano to accompany the choir's stirring rendition of 'Joy to the World', Hamilton finds himself full of the joy of the season and can barely contain his elation. Once the service is over, he tells Henry that he has come to the conclusion that the church really is of vital importance to the local community, and offers to discuss reworking the mortgage as soon as the holidays are over. The existential question mark hanging over the building has been removed at last.

As Henry and Julia leave the church, Dudley warmly wishes them both the compliments of the season... but it is clear that neither of them have the slightest recognition of him. Jeremiah, however, remembers his kind supernatural friend perfectly. The Biggs family return home, where they discover their Christmas tree has been lavishly decorated – and with an enigmatic, well-dressed angel perched on the top. Knowing now that his work is done at last, with Henry and Julia reasserting their shared love and the church safe in the heart of the neighbourhood, a wistful Dudley leaves the family to their happy future together.

Like Henry Koster's original 1947 film, *The Preacher's Wife* is fundamentally a movie which explores faith, and which makes a distinction between belief in oneself and trust in a higher power. This was naturally a challenge in a world which had become considerably more secular than the America of the immediate post-war period had been, but the primary theme of faith being challenged and then reaffirmed was essentially the same. Shayne Lee makes the point that 'Jeremiah's questions and the refrain of the opening song of St Matthew's choir, which introduces a God who "may not come when you want Him, but He'll be right there on time," foreshadow the film's salute to a supernatural God. But the distressed look on Reverend Biggs's face suggests that the pastor does not believe his own choir's exhortation, "Help is on the way." [...] As the plot unfolds, the struggling pastor overcomes doubt and grows in confidence through the angel's guidance and intervention'.[3] Henry's unstinting desire to support his parishioners and aid the community is, of course, directly tied into his own faith journey, and the screenplay makes this connection with subtlety and perceptiveness without ever allowing it to dominate the film's action.

The Preacher's Wife has, of course, become particularly well-known for the way in which it showcased the exceptional vocal talents of its female lead, Whitney Houston. One of the bestselling music artists in history, Houston was hugely influential in her lifetime and was the recipient of six Grammy

Awards, two Emmy Awards, 16 *Billboard* Music Awards and no less than 28 Guinness World Records in the course of her remarkable career. She remains the only artist to have seven number one singles charting consecutively in the *Billboard* Hot 100. Alongside her bestselling albums *Whitney Houston* (1985), *Whitney* (1987) and *I'm Your Baby Tonight* (1990), by the time of *The Preacher's Wife* she had also delivered prominent lead acting performances in *The Bodyguard* (Mick Jackson, 1992) and *Waiting to Exhale* (Forest Whitaker, 1995). Houston was reportedly initially reluctant to accept the role of Julia Biggs, but at the prompting of her eventual co-star Denzel Washington she ultimately changed her mind about the part. In an interview with *Jet* magazine, she later explained that the film's musical heritage held particular appeal to her: 'For Houston, performing as Julia also gave her a chance to return to her gospel roots. She grew up singing gospel in the New Hope Baptist Church in Newark, NJ. "This was the most exciting thing for me," the pop-soul superstar singer-actress allows. "It gave me the opportunity to sing gospel, the music I love most. I've been waiting a long time to do something like this. Also, like Denzel, I believe in the theme of the film, that the church is the glue that holds the community together'.[4] Her enthusiasm for the movie's musical content was certainly reflected in its commercial success; the original soundtrack for *The Preacher's Wife* went on to become the best-selling gospel album of all time, with a remarkable six million copies being sold globally.

As in *The Bishop's Wife*, much of the film's success revolves around the character interactions between the central love triangle of Henry, Julia and Dudley. The audience is left in no doubt of the love Reverend Biggs has for his wife and son, but are likewise aware of the balancing act he must achieve in also making himself available to his congregation and their often-pressing needs. Dudley, meanwhile, is every bit as mindful of his primary mission as he is to his growing feelings for Julia but – as in the original Koster film – this understated romance is cleverly restrained. Peter Stack makes the point that 'Director Marshall made a smart move in never letting passions ignite, instead trusting in the old-fashioned power of innuendo to create a romantic glow',[5] and the film is all the more powerful for the intricacy of the strong emotions and sentimental entanglements that are depicted within.

Dudley's presence may have been the answer to a prayer, but in his feelings for Julia it is clear that his earthly mission ultimately plays out in ways he had not anticipated. Unlike Cary Grant's original portrayal, where the inscrutable angel's backstory remains a mystery, the Denzel Washington incarnation of Dudley is fleshed out with a far more detailed character origin. As Roger Ebert has observed, 'Eagle-eyed theologians will have already asked themselves how an angel can fall in love. They have spotted a large hole in the story: Dudley is not, strictly speaking, an angel at all, but a human who died 30 years earlier and has now been sent from heaven on this aid mission. But he calls himself an angel, and one of the Three Laws of Angels is "Angels cannot lie," so either he (1) thinks he is an angel but is sincerely mistaken, or (2) is a human, and lying. Surely the makers of this film do not believe that humans go to heaven and become angels. As we all know, angels were created by God as his first companions, and he created humans much later, presumably after tiring of companions who never lied'.[6] Whatever Dudley's true genesis may be, Washington imbues the character with abundant compassion and charisma, and it is obvious why Julia would

reciprocate the attraction of the unconventional angel's captivating appeal.

While Washington effortlessly matches Cary Grant for
warmth, charm and sophistication as the angel Dudley,
Courtney B. Vance is arguably a far more sympathetic and
likeable pastor figure than the rather priggish and distant
Bishop Henry Brougham – the fussy, often-disagreeable character that the suave David Niven had been saddled with back
in the 1940s. This distinction is echoed in the predicament
faced by the two individuals; whereas Brougham was actively
overseeing the construction of a new cathedral and struggled
to keep his vision of a community of faith from being contam-
inated by the whims of materialistic, ostentatious and affluent
parishioners (all of whom were only interested in having their
monetary contributions recognised by all and sundry, rather
than donating solely for the sake of the church's mission),
Reverend Biggs instead faces the closure of his beloved church
and its replacement by an unabashedly commercial enterprise
antithetical to his altruistic beliefs – a dilemma much closer in
nature to that which confronted the characters in *The Bells of
St Mary's* (Leo McCarey, 1945).

The theme of Christmas altruism overcoming the ava-
rice of unfettered commercialism was hardly a new theme,
having been explored in one capacity or another since the genre's glory days in the 1940s, but *The Preacher's Wife* brought
a slightly new angle to the theme in that the ambitious self-
made millionaire Joe Hamilton really does intend to provide
new, modern worship facilities... but based far from the
community that really needs the support of the church. Many
of Henry's duties in the film emphasise the need for faith in
action, and that a church isn't a building – old or new – but
rather a group of like-minded people taking collective action in

the furtherance of their spiritual beliefs. While the notion of authentic, run-down inner-city neighbourhoods being redeveloped against the will of their inhabitants to make the way for luxury residences was the subject of other films around the same time, perhaps most notably *Life Stinks* (Mel Brooks, 1991), rarely was the issue of displaced lives and neglected social issues made with quite such panache – nor a supplication for Christian faith communities to put their convictions into practice made quite so frankly.

Marshall does an excellent job of updating Koster's original film for the modern world of the 1990s, and retains fidelity to the themes of the 1947 movie while also striking out in new directions – not least in the phenomenal gospel music provided by the Georgia Mass Choir. Some changes were simply reflective of advancements in technology over the course of the fifty years since *The Bishop's Wife*; for instance, whereas Cary Grant's Dudley magically operates a typewriter without so much as pressing a key, we now see Denzel Washington's variation of the character getting to grips with the complexities of Microsoft Windows via supernatural means instead. The film does possibly suffer from its lack of a substitute for Monty Woolley's Professor Wutheridge, however. The curmudgeonly scholar from Koster's original has no counterpart in Marshall's movie, which is all the more regrettable given the gruff charm of Woolley's portrayal and the fact that Wutheridge's character journey from the rationality of atheism to the optimism of faith complemented the film's core theme of turning bleak existential despondency into the constructive practicality of hope. That being said, the new screenplay by Nat Mauldin and Allan Scott introduces fresh challenges – most notably the trial of the wrongly-accused Billy Eldridge, and the difficult domestic problems that conspire to separate Jeremiah from his close friend Hakim – which illustrate by other means the same premise of faith re-shaping lives. Gladys Cooper's officious Mrs Agnes Hamilton is ably succeeded by Gregory Hines's charismatic realtor Joe Hamilton, and while his redemption is achieved by different means, the musical aspect to Dudley's encounter with them remains common to both variations of the character. However, as Barbara Shulgasser notes, the characters' shift in function from affluent funding donor to silver-tongued entre-preneur – and the shift in tone necessary to accommodate this alteration – did necessitate the elimination of one of the original film's most famous sequences: 'I would like to have seen more of the scenes from the original in which Dudley proves that he is, in fact, an angel by performing little tricks for the skeptical Henry. And Dudley was a mesmerizing presence in the earlier version, able to elicit a girlish giggle out of the rev-erend's no-nonsense secretary. [...] In general, Dudley seems a bit too mortal here, not quite otherworldly enough. I'm sorry to have to report that the director – Penny Marshall, who you'd think would know better – left out the funniest scene from the original – in which David Niven is embarrassingly glued to a chair by angel magic in the stately home of his con-gregation's wealthiest contributor. I'll bet Vance would have done it well'.[7]

Whereas the location filming of the original *The Bish-op's Wife* had taken place in Minneapolis, Minnesota (with interiors shot at Samuel Goldwyn Studios in West Holly-wood), *The Preacher's Wife* was instead filmed across a number of States including Maine, New Jersey and New York, as well as at Silver Screen Studios in New York City. The ice-skating sequence between Julia and Dudley, which had been one of the most iconic scenes in the original, was filmed at Deering Oaks Park in Portland, Maine, for *The Preacher's Wife*. The location had been chosen on account of its scenic ice pond, but – due to an unexpected rise in temperature at the time of the production – the ice and snow had largely gone when filming was due to begin. This meant that the production team were eventually reliant on the use of artificial ice and snow to shoot the scene, though even this proved to be a challenge as the frozen pond remained on the cusp of melting due to the unanticipated heatwave – something which naturally proved testing for the actors involved.

The interior shots of the fictional St Matthew's Baptist Church give an excellent portrayal of a vibrant faith community in action. Intriguingly, however, this was not a specially-constructed set but rather the elegant internal confines of the real-life Trinity United Methodist Church based in Newark, New Jersey. The production team reportedly made a number of temporary changes to the church interior during filming to be suggestive of a Baptist, rather than Methodist, layout when it came to pews, the pulpit and so on, and this meant that it also had to be reverted back to its original configuration once the production was at an end. In a surprising twist that makes reality seem stranger than fiction, whereas Reverend Biggs's church in the movie required a new boiler due to its existing, antiquated model constantly breaking down (and occasionally exploding), the actual Trinity United Methodist Church really *was* in need of a replacement boiler system, and as a result of its participation in the filming of *The Preacher's Wife* the church was able to purchase a refit for the benefit of its congregation. The exterior of the fictitious St Matthew's Church, on the other hand, was actually the Good Shepherd Presbyterian Church in Nodine Hill, Yonkers, in New York.

The soundtrack by Hans Zimmer brilliantly evokes a warm, festive ambience while allowing for emotive moments that never tip into mawkish sentiment. Zimmer was at the time best-known for his original scores for films such as *Rain Man* (Barry Levinson, 1988), *Driving Miss Daisy* (Bruce Beresford, 1989), *Thelma & Louise* (Ridley Scott, 1991) and *The Lion King* (Roger Allers and Rob Minkoff, 1994), amongst many others, and he has since gone on to major international success which has seen him win two Academy Awards, four Grammy Awards, and nominations for two Emmy Awards and a Tony Award. With its skilfully underplayed emotional evocation, the orchestral score for *The Preacher's Wife* is arguably one of the most underrated soundtracks of any 1990s Christmas movie – largely on account of the fact that the main commercially-released soundtrack album, which contained vocal performances rather than instrumental tracks, was so monumentally successful, remaining for a total of 38 weeks in the *Billboard* 200 chart and an even more incredible 49 weeks in the *Billboard* Top R&B Albums chart.

Aside from the skill of its production, *The Preacher's Wife* makes a powerful statement about personal responsibility to the community as much as to the individual, and – as Henry makes plain in the film – this is not exclusively a religious duty, but one that helps to make life better for everyone irrespective of their spiritual beliefs. The central tenets of love and hope are values which are universally relevant, regardless of whether one has a religious faith or otherwise, and – as James Berardinelli suggests – in this sense the movie fits perfectly into the wider canon of festive cinema: 'The uplifting moral here is that miracles can happen for those who believe. *The Preacher's Wife* is about reclaiming lost faith and spreading the message of love. These are themes common to almost every beloved holiday classic. So, as a Christmas film, *The Preacher's Wife* has all the right sentiments, and presses the expected buttons. On the other hand (call me a Scrooge if you will), I'm not sure I'd want to see this movie at any other time of the year. If not for the pervasive spirit of the season, something like this could easily send me into sugar shock. It's a little too nice and happy'.[8]

There is no doubting that, just as *The Bishop's Wife* had been a film that had exuded star power, this characteristic was amply matched by its successor. Star Denzel Washington was already one of the most instantly-recognisable actors in Hollywood, having been active on stage and television before making his cinematic debut in comedy-drama *Carbon Copy* (Michael Schultz, 1981). He made a huge critical breakthrough in the role of anti-apartheid activist Steve Biko in Richard Attenborough's *Cry Freedom* (1987), for which he received his first Academy Award nomination, and then made appearances in such high-profile features as *Glory* (Edward Zwick, 1989), *Malcolm X* (Spike Lee, 1992), *The Pelican Brief* (Alan J. Pakula, 1993), *Philadelphia* (Jonathan Demme, 1993) and *Crimson Tide* (Tony Scott, 1995). He has since become one of the most decorated actors of the modern age, with ten Academy Award nominations (winning twice, for performances in *Glory* and Antoine Fuqua's 2001 crime drama *Training Day*), nine Golden Globe Award nominations (winning three times, including the much-coveted Cecil B. DeMille Award in 2016), two nominations for Primetime Emmy Awards, a Grammy Award nomination, and two Tony Award nominations (winning in 2010 for his lead performance in August Wilson's stage drama *Fences*). Amongst his many other accolades, Washington received the

Presidential Medal of Freedom in 2022, awarded by President Joe Biden.

Courtney B. Vance has also been the recipient of a Tony Award and two Primetime Emmy Awards, alongside many other industry awards and nominations for his work in film, television and on stage. First active in stage acting, he made an immediate impact with his film debut in John Irvin's *Hamburger Hill* (1987), with many well-received later roles in movies including *The Hunt for Red October* (John McTiernan, 1990), *Dangerous Minds* (John N. Smith, 1995) and *The Last Supper* (Stacy Title, 1995). Gregory Hines was a multiple nominee for Emmy Awards and Tony Awards, amongst many other industry prizes, and made an impression on the cinema of the time due to his performances in films such as *Wolfen* (Michael Wadleigh, 1981), *The Cotton Club* (Francis Ford Coppola, 1984), and *Running Scared* (Peter Hyams, 1986). Jenifer Lewis initially began her career on the stage and specifically in Broadway musicals. Her many memorable film performances throughout the 1980s and 90s included parts in *Beaches* (Garry Marshall, 1988), *Sister Act* (Emile Ardolino, 1992) and *What's Love Got to Do with It* (Brian Gibson, 1993). While Lewis received critical praise for playing Julia Biggs's mother in *The Preacher's Wife* (not least because, in reality, she was only six years older than the superstar performer), a less well-known fact was that Whitney Houston's real mother – Cissy Houston – makes a cameo appearance in the film as the strong-willed Mrs Havergal, who sings with the church choir.

When *The Preacher's Wife* opened in cinemas, it did so to the general approval of critics – with the caveat that, with such high regard for Henry Koster's 1947 original, comparisons to the silver screen classic were not always favourable.

Russell Smith, for instance, noted that, 'There's a sense that everyone is being just a bit too respectful of precedent to transform this film according to their own vision. So even though *The Preacher's Wife* is far from a waste of time, it begs the question of whether anyone would have felt compelled to do a remake if this had been the original. As with other passable but uninspired remakes such as *Sabrina* and *Love Affair*, I'm guessing the answer is no'.[9] That being said, the wide-ranging endorsement of the film's creative intentions did shine through, even with reservations; as Ebert put it, '*The Preacher's Wife* is a sweet and good-hearted comedy about the holiday season, and I suppose that is enough, although I would have liked it with more punch and bite. [...] I found myself enjoying *The Preacher's Wife*, for its simple but real pleasures: For the way Houston sings, for the glimpses of the people in the church congregation, and for the way preacher tries his hardest to do the right thing. And also for Denzel Washington, who is able to project love without lust, and goodness without corniness. This movie could have done more, but what it does, it makes you feel good about'.[10]

The Preacher's Wife did elicit praise for its understated but powerful evocation of social issues and the wide-ranging impact these concerns had on individuals and communities. Some critics – Esther Iverem among them – commended the film's excellent achievement in world-building, even when decrying a perceived lack of depth in its characterisation: 'In Biggs's church, there are cracks in the walls and the boiler is about to blow. Young men in the neighborhood are being carted off to jail and foster homes. With this milieu established so well, the story still founders. It's not that it tries to tell too many stories at once but that the stories seem predictable and disjointed. The script and directing fail to draw us close enough to the main characters so that they appear more than cutouts. 〚...〛 There are many good reasons for going to see *The Preacher's Wife*. Just don't go looking for a blessing'.[11] The strength of the film's performances was appreciated by reviewers, albeit that some did reflect that the cast's talents may have proven even more impressive had they been presented with more robust material. Desson Howe remarked, for instance: 'Besides Washington's likable presence, Vance has amusing moments as the put-upon straight man, as does Lewis as Julia's tell-it-like-it-is mother, Margueritte. When Julia protests that – as far as Dudley goes – she's only window-shopping, Margueritte has a no-nonsense response. "You'd better not go window-shopping with money in your pocket," she says sternly. "And you'd better not put money in the layaway plan." Where you stand on sitcom-standard jokes like this is probably where you'll stand on enjoying the movie'.[12]

Ultimately, however, while commentators seemed satisfied with most elements of *The Preacher's Wife*, there was still a sense that in comparison with its illustrious forebear it had been found wanting. While the two movies had shared many of the same concepts and character archetypes, the transition from the golden age of Christmas cinema to the complex nuances of the contemporary world was not without its accusations of a resulting loss of charm in the new interpretation. Typical of this line of criticism was Berardinelli, who observed that:

Those looking for something truly uplifting will find more than they could possibly want in this movie. Creatively, however, it's on shaky ground. Beneath the warm sentiments and likable personalities, *The Preacher's Wife* is rather trite. I think I

369

would probably react the same way if someone produced a passable remake of *It's a Wonderful Life*. I enjoy that film immensely, but my affinity for it results largely from a nostalgia for the period during which it was made and in which it transpires. A modernized version of Capra's movie would lack that crucial quality, and, consequently, the viewing experience would suffer. Much the same can be said about *The Preacher's Wife*. It has better production values than its predecessor, but the intangibles aren't the same. An element of the magic is missing.[13]

More recent analysis of *The Preacher's Wife* has retained the diversity of opinion which was in evidence during the original screenings of the movie. Some, such as J.P. Roscoe, have reflected on the way in which the film's key principles have broadly corresponded to wider trends in popular culture, while lamenting the comparative temerity of its artistic objectives: '*The Bishop's Wife* is an odd story and the movie adaptation is an odd movie. The idea of an angel visiting and helping isn't that odd. *It's a Wonderful Life*, *Highway to Heaven* and *Touched by an Angel* were series based on this concept, and angel and the holidays go hand-in-hand… in that case *The Preacher's Wife* makes sense. [...] *The Preacher's Wife* is tolerable. It isn't great, it isn't awful. It feels a bit like a better holiday TV movie than a major motion picture, and Penny Marshall directs it that way… nothing will surprise you'.[14] Others, including Keith Phipps, instead made clear their view that the remake – and its principal cast – had struggled to reignite the celebrated creative spark of the initial movie: 'While the original was sappy – any movie about an angel returning to earth to help a struggling clergyman is going to be – it worked because of its fine performances. Denzel Washington occasionally gets to show that he can play comedic scenes, but he has two big things working against him: a treacly, simplistic script and Whitney Houston, whose acting ranges from delighted surprise (eyebrows raised) to sulking anger (brow furrowed)'.[15]

Overall, however, most modern critics have reached a fairly broad consensus that *The Preacher's Wife* was a competent, well-intentioned remake with solid imaginative aims. In the analysis of some, such as Andy Webb, this almost seemed like damning the movie with faint praise: 'Like with many movies that focus on the Christmas period it delivers a blend of warmth, a little romance and some comedy. It's a pleasant enough blend with plenty of scenes which will make you smile although rarely reaching the point of laughing, something it strives to do. [...] What this all boils down to is that *The Preacher's Wife* is a nice enough movie. It keeps you entertained with some comedy, a little emotion, probably more musical moments that were necessary and a performance from Denzel Washington which brings it all together. But it lacks that little bit of magic which makes you believe that if you Hope things will happen'.[16] Conversely, a few commentators have instead come to regard *The Preacher's Wife* as a neglected jewel of 1990s festive cinema, with some among them – including George Rother – advocating greater attention for the film than it has hitherto received: 'A pleasant little movie that didn't attract much attention at the box office over the Christmas movie season in '96, *The Preacher's Wife* combines elements of several different genres (comedy, drama, romance, musical and fantasy) and makes one of the nicest Christmas-themed movies of the 90s. [...] Is *The Preacher's Wife* a religious movie? Not necessarily, but it should appeal to the same

crowd that shows up to see the Tyler Perry movies on opening weekend. Even though it runs a bit longer than it should,
The Preacher's Wife works on a few different levels and it's
worth checking out around the holiday season'.[17]

The Preacher's Wife was nominated in the category of
Best Music, Original Musical or Comedy Score for composer
Hans Zimmer at the Academy Awards, and was also nominated for many other industry plaudits including at the
NAACP Image Awards (winning in two categories, for Outstanding Lead Actress and Outstanding Supporting Actress)
and the MovieGuide Awards, while the soundtrack was nominated for an American Music Award and a Blockbuster
Entertainment Award.

Given its explicit celebration of faith, love and church
communities, *The Preacher's Wife* was arguably the most
explicitly faith-based mainstream Christmas movie in many
years, and would remain so until the release of Biblical adaptation *The Nativity Story* (Catherine Hardwicke, 2006) a
decade later. In its full-throated defence of family, friendship
and reaching out to the wider neighbourhood for the recipro-
cal support of all, the film chimed in perfectly with the
traditional conventions of Christmas cinema which were being reiterated throughout the course of the 1990s. Perhaps
most crucially of all, it acknowledged – albeit in the most indi-
rect of ways – that while secularism was very much on the
increase amongst the general population since the time of the
original Koster film's production, people still related to the
sentiment of that 1947 classic: namely the importance of encouraging and caring for our loved ones, of maintaining
friendships and celebrating close acquaintances, and of never
taking the benefits of community spirit for granted. With an
approach that unifies rather than divides, these universal aims

transcended religious denomination or spiritual belief and aimed to bring people together rather than encourage dissent and discord. And, at its core, what aim could be more in the spirit of the best Christmas movies than that?

REFERENCES

1. Andrew Horton, *Laughing Out Loud: Writing the Comedy-Centred Screenplay* (Berkeley: University of California Press), p.161.

2. Anon., 'Whitney Houston, Denzel Washington, Courtney B. Vance and Jenifer Lewis Star in *The Preacher's Wife*', in *Jet*, Vol.91, No.5, 16 December 1996, 58-62, pp.59-60.

3. Shayne Lee, *Cinema, Black Suffering, and Theodicy: Modern God* (Lanham: Lexington Books, 2022), p.164.

4. Anon., in *Jet*, pp.60-61.

5. Peter Stack, '*The Preacher's Wife*', in *The San Francisco Chronicle*, 2 May 1997.
    <*https://www.sfgate.com/movies/article/FILM-REVIEW-Preacher-s-Divine-Comedy-2843077.php*>

6. Roger Ebert, '*The Preacher's Wife*', in *The Chicago Sun-Times*, 13 December 1996.
    <*https://www.rogerebert.com/reviews/the-preachers-wife-1996*>

7. Barbara Shulgasser, '*Preacher's Wife* is Touched by an Angel', in *The San Francisco Examiner*, 13 December 1996.
    <*https://www.sfgate.com/news/article/Preacher-s-Wife-is-touched-by-an-angel-3110063.php*>

8. James Berardinelli, '*The Preacher's Wife*', in *ReelViews*, 13 December 1996.
    <*https://www.reelviews.net/reelviews/preacher-s-wife-the*>

9.   Russell Smith, '*The Preacher's Wife*', in *The Austin Chronicle*, 13 December 1996.
       <*https://www.austinchronicle.com/events/film/1996-12-13/the-preachers-wife/*>

10.   Ebert.

11.   Esther Iverem, '*The Preacher's Wife*: A Wan Sermon', in *The Washington Post*, 12 December 1996.
       <*https://www.washingtonpost.com/wp-srv/style/longterm/review96/preacherswifeiver.htm*>

12.   Desson Howe, '*The Preacher's Wife*: One Foot in Heaven', in *The Washington Post*, 13 December 1996.
       <*https://www.washingtonpost.com/wp-srv/style/longterm/review96/preacherswifehowe.htm*>

13.   Berardinelli.

14.   J.P. Roscoe, '*The Preacher's Wife* (1996)', in *Basement Rejects*, 16 December 2011.
       <*http://basementrejects.com/review/the-preachers-wife-1996/*>

15.   Keith Phipps, '*The Preacher's Wife*', in *AV Club*, 29 March 2002.
       <*https://www.avclub.com/the-preachers-wife-1798195900*>

16.   Andy Webb, '*The Preacher's Wife*', in *The Movie Scene*, 2011.
       <*https://www.themoviescene.co.uk/reviews/the-preachers-wife/the-preachers-wife.html*>

17.   George Rother, '*The Preacher's Wife*', in *MovieGuy 24/7*, 16 March 2012.

<https://movieguy247.com/iMovies/index.php/blog/holida
y-movies/472-the-preachers-wife>

13

Jingle All the Way (1996)

1492 Pictures / Twentieth Century Fox

Director: Brian Levant
Producers: Michael Barnathan, Chris Columbus and
Mark Radcliffe
Screenwriter: Randy Kornfield

WITHOUT question, one of the predominant themes to emerge from Christmas cinema has been the conflict which has emerged between the un-selfishness of the season of giving and the unfettered material-ism of the increasingly commercial aspect of the modern holiday period. Reaching all the way back to the genre's gold-en age in the immediate post-war period of the 1940s, many Christmas movies have wrestled with the divergence which exists between the joy of gifting and the unabashed acquisi-tiveness encouraged by the growing commoditification of the festive season. Few, however, have come out in favour of all-out yuletide mercantilism quite so enthusiastically as *Jingle All the Way*.

The basic premise of the film centres around the phe-nomenon – familiar since at least the 1980s – of the annual in-demand toy that inevitably sells out in the lead up to Christ-mas, usually creating scenes of commercial pandemonium as parents battle it out in stores across the land to ensure that their child won't be the only one to wake up on Christmas morning without the must-have gift of the year. As James Berardinelli sagely remarks, 'Almost everyone has memories of a birthday, Christmas, or other holiday when they either got or didn't get a gift they had been coveting. From a parent's perspective, trying to purchase such a present, especially if it's the "hot" toy of the year (remember Cabbage Patch Dolls and Transformers?), can be an agonizing experience, especially if they wait until the last minute'.[1] Working on the assumption that most people in the audience would be well aware of this depressingly familiar commercial phenomenon, and may well have fallen foul of it themselves, the story progresses from the nightmare scenario of a parent who has only the tiny window of Christmas Eve's trading hours to track down and acquire the most-wanted toy of the season – even in spite of widespread incredulity that anyone could achieve such a feat.

Jingle All the Way enjoyed a conspicuous publicity campaign which featured action star Arnold Schwarzenegger cast against type as a hapless family man. Though he had become a household name thanks to his performances in high octane action movies throughout the 1980s and 90s – among them *Conan the Barbarian* (John Milius, 1982), *The Terminator* (James Cameron, 1984), *Commando* (Mark L. Lester, 1985) and *Predator* (John McTiernan, 1987) – by the late nineties the former international body-builder had begun to diversify his career. This included a move into directing and producing, and perhaps most notably appearances in mainstream comedies including Ivan Reitman's *Twins* (1988), *Kindergarten Cop* (1990) and *Junior* (1994), all of which allowed him to show his lighter side and impressive sense of comic timing. Thus *Jingle All the Way* allowed him to fill the shoes of an ill-fated everyman with much aplomb, far from the extreme violence of his earlier films such as *Red Heat* (Walter Hill, 1988) and *Total Recall* (Paul Verhoeven, 1990), though in actual fact Schwarzenegger was no stranger to Christmas movies, having directed (and made an uncredited cameo in) a Turner Pictures TV movie remake of *Christmas in Connecticut* (1992), a modern day updating of the celebrated Peter Godfrey film from 1945 which had succeeded original star Barbara Stanwyck with Dyan Cannon in the lead role.

Directing *Jingle All the Way* was Brian Levant, who had been active in television (initially as a writer) since the mid-1970s before making a move into cinema with features including family comedy *Beethoven* (1992) and live-action cartoon adaptation *The Flintstones* (1994). Randy Kornfield was responsible for the screenplay, having established experience in the industry thanks to the scripts he had developed for movies such as *Sweet Revenge* (Mark Sobel, 1987) and *The Secretary* (Andrew Lane, 1995).

In order to conjure the frantic spirit of Christmas Eve shopping in a wintry urban environment, the decision was made to film the movie on location around the beautiful State of Minnesota, including Minneapolis, St Paul and Bloomington. Terry Rowan notes that, 'Inspired by real-life Christmas toy sell-outs for products such as the Cabbage Patch Kids [...] and the Mighty Morphin [Power] Rangers, the film [...] was shot in the Twin Cities of Minnesota at a variety of locations, including Bloomington's Mall of America'.[2] Some impressive production design was involved in making these inner-city scenes appear suitably frosty (the movie was actually filmed between the April and August of 1996, with the Minnesota sections being recorded for five weeks from April onwards before the production moved to Universal Studios Hollywood in California), and scores of extras were required to create the ambience of busy Christmas shoppers cramming the streets and malls in their search for last-minute festive gifts.

Life has become complicated for high-powered sales executive Howard Langston (Arnold Schwarzenegger). Not only do his workaholic tendencies mean that he willingly allows his professional duties to exclude him from office social events, but he is constantly missing out on landmark family occasions – much to the frustration of his long-suffering wife, Liz (Rita Wilson). Though he tries his best to be in two places at once, random factors such as heavy traffic mean that he is almost always late or unable to attend.

As Christmas approaches, Howard proves to be a no-show at a karate demonstration which features his son, Jamie (Jake Lloyd). Liz is exasperated by her husband's lack of reliability, and almost as annoyed by the unsubtle efforts of slimy local lothario Ted Maltin (Phil Hartman) to ingratiate himself with her. Recently divorced, Ted is on the lookout for a new partner, but Liz clearly has no interest in his rather transparent advances. Jamie is downcast that his father does not appear in time to see him perform; Howard arrives so late, due in part to an unexpected confrontation with a traffic cop (Robert Conrad) on account of dangerous driving, that everyone has already left the building by the time he gets there.

Howard is less than impressed when, on finally returning home, he discovers Ted on the Langstons' roof fitting Christmas lights – pointedly, he explains, because the harried businessman hasn't had time to do it himself. Ted also tells Howard that he has recorded the karate display on video so he can watch it later, even though he was unable to attend in person... a revelation which irks Howard, knowing that he is being deliberately needled. He finds a considerably frostier reception inside the house, where Liz laments his constant unreliability and Jamie – due to his profound disappointment – gives him the silent treatment.

Jamie is obsessed with the action-oriented, merchandise-driven *Turbo Man* TV series, watching intently as the eponymous superhero (Daniel Riordan) battles the evil Dementor (Richard Moll) to free the US President (Harvey Korman) and First Lady (Laraine Newman). His life seems to revolve around watching *Turbo Man* commercials and reading comics starring the aforementioned character. So when Howard asks if there is anything special that his son wants for Christmas – desperately hoping to get back into his good books – Jamie has no hesitation in telling him that would like most of all is the *Turbo Man* action figure. It is, he claims, that year's must-have toy, and all of his friends have asked Santa Claus to deliver one.

Howard congratulates himself on having devised a plan to win his son's forgiveness for his constant non-appearance at his school events, but his contentment proves to be short-lived when Liz tells him that not only does she know that this is Jamie's dream Christmas gift, but that she had asked Howard to buy one several weeks earlier... only for him to have immediately forgotten about it at the time. Liz is horrified by the prospect that Howard hadn't got hold of the hard-to-find action figure as promised, so to reassure her he casually lies that he'd picked one up as requested and hidden it away. Just as well, his wife explains, as the toy is so popular it would surely be next to impossible to find one this close to Christmas.

The next morning is Christmas Eve, and Jamie is in his *Turbo Man* pyjamas tucking into *Turbo Man* breakfast cereal as Howard tries to sneak out. Liz is puzzled at his claim that he needs to complete a few tasks at the office, but he conspiratorially tells her that he needs to pick up the action figure which (he claims) he has accidentally left at his workplace. Jamie is disappointed that his father appears to be heading back to work yet again, as he wants the whole family to be together for the annual Christmas parade, not least as there is set to be a special appearance by (who else?) *Turbo Man*.

As soon as Howard sets foot out of his front door, he is accosted by an unusually hostile reindeer. Ted is on the other end of the reins, and explains that its presence is a little festive treat for his son – he will happily go to any length to create Christmas magic for his loved ones, which rankles Howard even more. When Howard tells him that he's heading to pick up a *Turbo Man* action figure, Ted is the very picture of *schadenfreude* – the toy has been such a runaway success, he had to buy one for his son months ago, and it is now safely nestled beneath his family Christmas tree. This news goes down like a lead balloon with Howard, who is increasingly starting to realise that the odds are stacked against him.

With bustling crowds everywhere, Howard arrives in the city and elbows his way to the front of a queue for a huge toy store. However, the staff don't intend to let customers in until nine o'clock precisely, so Howard is angrily shoved back in line. A good-natured bystander, Myron Larabee (Sinbad), defends Howard as being just a hard-working dad trying to do the best for his children. The two strangers introduce themselves to each other, and Myron explains that as a postal worker, he hasn't had any opportunity to buy gifts for his family until now – hence his belated presence in the city on Christmas Eve. It transpires that he too is searching for a *Turbo Man* toy, albeit grudgingly; he is bitter about the fact that the action figure has been so continuously hyped by TV commercials that everyone has essentially been manipulated into buying one for their kids, lest they feel bad about their own child feeling left out.

When the toy store finally opens, the massed customers storm into the building and promptly tear the place apart in their desperate search for last-minute gift ideas. Howard and Myron are both aghast to discover that the *Turbo Man* displays are completely bereft of stock, having sold out weeks beforehand, and the staff react with uncontrolled hilarity when Howard asks if they have any new supplies which haven't yet reached the shelves. They gleefully inform him that the action figure isn't just the hottest gift that year, but the most commercially successful toy in history.

Under duress, one of the employees eventually reveals that another customer has just picked up the final *Turbo Man* action figure in the store – solely because she'd had it reserved some time earlier. Overhearing this, Myron goes dashing after the person in question, and Howard realises that it's now a case of every parent for themselves. Using a remote-controlled car to trip up the racing mailman, Howard rushes into the street and identifies the departing customer... just as they drive away in their car. He desperately tries to flag her down in the hope of making her an offer to buy the *Turbo Man* toy, but she believes him to be a crank and accelerates away.

Howard calls into every toy store he can find in the city, including a toy museum, but is singularly unable to track down the much-sought-after action figure. After hours and hours of unsuccessful searching through jam-packed crowds of people, his temper is seriously starting to fray. Little does he realise that back home, the sleazy Ted has arrived and offers Liz some time off from her busy cooking schedule; he suggests that she go and relax while he looks after things for her. Liz, who knows only too well what her obsequious neighbour's intentions are, eventually realises that he won't take no for an answer.

Howard calls home from a payphone to tell Liz that he will likely be late, only to be confused when Ted answers the phone instead. Unable to offer any explanation for his presence in the Langston family kitchen beyond the fact that he is watching over a batch of cookies in the oven, Ted promises to pass on the message once Liz gets out of the shower, then abruptly hangs up. Howard is growing concerned by his neighbour's predatory behaviour, but his thoughts are interrupted when he encounters Myron again. The mailman apologises for their earlier brawl, and Howard admits that they are both willing to do whatever it takes to track down the in-demand toy. Myron suggests joining forces, but Howard – finding that the motor-mouthed delivery man is grating on his nerves – politely refuses. Before they can argue further, a passing shopper excitedly alerts them to the fact that a toy store in the Mall of America is expecting a late delivery of *Turbo Man* figures, prompting a mad scramble. Unfortunately for Howard, in his haste to drive away he accidentally collides with a motorcycle... which, as luck would have it, belongs to the same traffic cop he had encountered the previous day. Elated to see his rival being held up, and thus losing precious time, Myron hurries away into the distance.

Some time later, the pair are reunited at the toy store in the mall, where the beleaguered manager (Lewis Dauber) wearily informs the obstreperous crowd gathering in his shop that as only a small quantity of *Turbo Man* toys are scheduled to be delivered, they will be drawing lottery numbers to determine who will be able to purchase one. Worse still, due to the frantic demand for the action figures, the manager has decided to double the retail price – knowing full well that people will pay almost anything for the boxed figures at this stage. The assistants handing out numbered rubber balls for the draw are soon overwhelmed, leading to a near-riot as everyone scrambles to grab one.

There is a furious struggle between Howard and Myron over one of the rubber balls, and the errant sphere ends up bouncing through the vast mall – with Howard in hot pursuit – until it eventually comes to rest in a children's play area. Now bereft of all common sense, the burly businessman ends up squeezing his way through the activity centre in pursuit of the child who has accidentally caught the ball, but is soon set upon by angry parents. As he rapidly departs, he meets a shady mall Santa Claus (James Belushi) who claims to have a spare *Turbo Man* action figure that he is willing to part with – for the right price. Howard immediately detects a scam, but is now desperate enough to try just about anything.

The mall Santa instructs Howard to drive him to an inner-city cemetery, where he enters a password-protected warehouse. Inside, Howard is astonished to discover a complex operation being overseen by many costumed Santa Clauses and elves boxing up obvious knock-off goods. He is asked to pay the vastly-inflated price of $300 for the promised toy, but upon opening the package (against the protestations of 'Santa') he discovers a cheap imitation with foreign language voice recordings which is already falling apart. Realising that he has been hoodwinked, Howard demands his money back, but he is curtly told that all transactions are considered final. A fight breaks out between him and the festively-attired crooks, which initially goes well until he confronts a gigantic, musclebound Santa (Paul 'The Giant' Wight) and is then tasered. Only a sudden police raid saves Howard at the last minute; impersonating a detective, he bluffs his way out of the ensuing mass arrests and gets back on the road again.

Ted has arranged a street party for the kids of the neighbourhood, but Jamie is upset that once again Howard has let him down by being absent all day. He hears the house's phone ring, and discovers his dad on the other end of the line. His car having run out of fuel, Howard tries to inform Liz of his whereabouts, but Jamie believes that he is calling to say that he won't be home in time for the parade and gets upset. Liz overhears the last few moments of the conversation and disappointedly draws the same conclusion.

Howard meets Myron at a diner, and both bemoan the fact that they have been unable to find the coveted *Turbo Man* toy in spite of their best efforts. Myron confides that he has always blamed the fact that he didn't get his own dream toy in youth for his personal disappointments in later life, which spurs Howard on to one final burst of effort. A local radio DJ (Martin Mull) proudly proclaims over the airwaves that their station has a single *Turbo Man* action figure to give away as a prize to the first caller who can correctly identify all eight of Santa's reindeer. Another mad jostle takes place as both Myron and Howard battle for control of the diner's payphone, but they end up wrecking it in the process. The diner owner suggests that as the radio station is based only a couple of blocks away, the squabbling pair should head there to enter the competition in person.

After sprinting to the station, Howard makes it to the DJ's recording studio and frantically blurts out the answer to the competition question. Thinking that he is being accosted by a madman (which at this stage isn't too far from the truth), the DJ calls the police, but – just when he thinks things can't get any worse – Myron arrives with a suspicious package that he claims contains an improvised explosive device. According to Myron, he intercepted it in the mail and decided to hold on to it in case it was ever needed to get out of a tight spot. A struggle breaks out and the package goes flying through the air... only to reveal (to the relief of the others) that it contains a harmless music box rather than a bomb. The DJ admits that there is no *Turbo Man* toy on the premises, but rather that the station is giving away a gift certificate that can be exchanged for an action figure (assuming that anyone can actually find one).

Upon leaving the DJ's studio, Howard and Myron are intercepted by a team of police officers responding to the 911 call. Myron pulls the same stunt with another package which he claims contains an explosive device, allowing him and Howard to leave. One of the officers claims to be a bomb squad veteran and opens the package, believing it to be nothing more than a harmless parcel... only for it to blow up (much to the surprise of the retreating Myron, who had considered it to be another fake). Thankfully the resulting detonation is limited, and none of the police officers are injured.

Returning to the diner, Howard discovers that his car has been badly vandalised and is now undriveable – even if it had any fuel in the tank. He arranges for it to be towed for (extensive) repairs, and is dropped off at home. Howard is livid when he spots Ted putting the finishing touches to the decorations on the lavishly-bedecked Langston Christmas tree, knowing that he has been currying favour with Liz while Howard has had the worst Christmas Eve imaginable. Seeing red, Howard dreams up a heartless revenge strategy. Knowing that Ted has a *Turbo Man* toy safely wrapped up underneath his Christmas tree, the indignant Howard decides to break into his neighbour's house to claim it for himself.

Quickly spotting the parcel in question (swathed, to no great surprise, in *Turbo Man* wrapping paper), Howard grabs it... but then discovers the arrival of carol singers at the front of Ted's house, making his departure impossible. Sneaking out of the back door, however, he has a sudden attack of conscience and realises that he can't deprive Ted's son of his much-desired Christmas gift. But before he can return it, he is attacked by the obstinate visiting reindeer, which chases him back into Ted's house, causes untold damage to the interior, and accidentally starts a fire when scattered festive decorations stray into the living room's open fireplace. Howard desperately tries to extinguish the flames, but only succeeds in drawing attention to himself by inadvertently breaking a window. When a horrified Ted arrives on the scene, with Liz close behind him, Howard tries to explain the carnage. However, with him being caught red-handed with Ted's *Turbo Man* gift, Liz immediately pieces together what has happened – and, being tired of her husband's constant lies, excuses and broken promises – leaves in disgust to take Jamie to the Christmas street parade... with Ted.

His family heading off to the city, Howard makes peace with the errant reindeer and drowns his sorrows with a beer. Spotting one of Jamie's drawings of his happy family inside a garden playhouse Howard had built for him during a previous Christmas, however, he is galvanised to make things right once and for all. At the Holiday Wintertainment Parade, Jamie watches in awe as wave after wave of characters from popular culture marches along the street – though given the current TV sensation, he knows that the organisers will be saving *Turbo Man* until last. Howard, trying to get there by taxi, is snarled up in traffic and decides to run to the parade on foot.

As Liz firmly rebuffs Ted's unwanted advances for the umpteenth time, Howard arrives and sees the two of them in an apparent embrace. Losing his temper, he dashes to confront them but ends up colliding with his old nemesis the traffic cop again. He is thus oblivious to the fact that Liz, appalled by Ted's increasingly inappropriate overtures, has walloped him with a flask of his own alcohol-free eggnog. A game of cat and mouse plays out between Howard and the outraged policeman, and – to evade detection – he ducks into one of the buildings being used by the parade organisers. However, before he can get his bearings he is mistaken for an actor and rapidly put into costume so that he can appear in the parade. Baffled by this turn of events, Howard is unable to get a word in edgeways before he is put onto a parade float – not even aware of what character he is supposed to be playing.

Once the float gets underway, everything suddenly becomes clear: Howard has been dressed in a *Turbo Man* costume, and thanks to some timely guidance from his faithful sidekick Booster (Curtis Armstrong) – is informed that he must do battle with his arch-enemy Dementor while also choosing a child from the audience in order to gift them a rare customised *Turbo Man* toy. Howard is elated to finally get his hands on the much-prized action figure after all this time, cheered on by the spectators. Spotting Jamie in the crowd, he invites his son onto the float to gift him the *Turbo Man* he so fervently wants. Just as he does so, however, Dementor ziplines his way onto the float... and reveals himself to be none other than Myron, who has tied up the actor who was supposed to be playing the arch-villain. The now-unhinged mailman has become so obsessed with getting hold of a *Turbo*

Man toy, he has decided to challenge Howard for it in a furious confrontation that plays out in front of the public.

Howard stashes the toy in Jamie's backpack before he and Myron battle out their differences with their suit-aided superpowers. As Howard is pinned down by Dementor's minions, Myron attempts to intercept Jamie but is thwarted. The plucky youth races through the parade, his pursuer hot on his tail. Eventually Jamie climbs onto the roof of a building, his shocked mother watching in distress from the street. The crowd cheers, believing this all to be part of the show. Eventually Howard breaks free of his antagonists and, seeing Myron pinning Jamie down on a rooftop Christmas display, ignites his jetpack… only to immediately lose control and go rocketing through the skies above the city.

After several near-misses, Howard eventually gets back to ground level, but Myron and Jamie end up in grave peril when the Christmas decorations on the roof give way. Myron snatches the *Turbo Man* toy from Jamie, but ends up losing his grip and falling to the parade below – where he lands harmlessly on the police float and is immediately arrested. Howard reignites his jetpack and saves Jamie from falling in the nick of time, then returns his son to Liz. While exhilarated by his unexpected adventure, the young boy still voices disappointment that Howard couldn't be there to witness the escapade for himself. But he is overjoyed when his dad removes *Turbo Man*'s helmet and reveals his true identity, promising to no longer neglect time with his family. The traffic cop returns the stolen toy to Jamie while Myron is taken into custody. However, Jamie decides that he wants to voluntarily give the action figure to Myron so that his own son isn't disappointed on Christmas morning, reasoning that he is lucky enough to have *Turbo Man* as his own dad and thus has no real need of the once-cherished toy.

In a post-credits sequence, Howard places the star atop his family's Christmas tree, and he and Liz embrace after a long and impossibly arduous Christmas Eve. Wistfully, Liz points out that he is such a good father to have gone to such effort just to avoid letting down his son, and this leads her to wonder... if Howard risked everything – including his own safety – just to get hold of an action figure for his son, what could he have possibly bought for her to match all that effort? In response, Howard can only gape in silent horror.

Jingle All the Way is, as Christmas films go, strictly high concept entertainment. With its frantic pace and non-stop action, its hectic energy perfectly mirrors the chaos involved in trying to find an in-demand gift during last-minute Christmas shopping. Arnold Schwarzenegger seems to revel in the role of a put-upon suburban father who is simply doing his best to ensure that his son is not let down at the holidays, though there is a definite postmodern edge to Howard accidentally being turned into an action hero – the exact type of part that had made Schwarzenegger's career throughout the eighties – and quietly admitting to himself that he could get used to this kind of thing.

It is true, of course, that the film contains certain elements which would be considered far from acceptable in the present day. These include Howard punching a bad-tempered reindeer unconscious (and, perhaps just as bad, giving it bottles of beer to drink as they reconcile afterwards); the hapless father ending up in an anarchic scrap with countless costumed Santas; and – most infamously – Jamie escaping from Myron's clutches by kicking him in a rather sensitive area that is, quite literally, below the belt. There are also a number of strange illogicalities throughout which are never explained. Why does Myron insist on bringing along his mail bag from work to a shopping expedition – especially when it constantly seems to be spilling out letters and packages in all directions? Would the comparatively weedy Ted really be stupid enough to make a move on his neighbour's wife when the man in question is built like the musclebound former Mr Universe, Arnold Schwarzenegger? When the constantly-harassed traffic cop, Officer Hummell, is drenched in boiling hot coffee when Howard collides with him at the parade, why is he mysteriously bone dry when he then gives chase? Why does Ted voluntarily choose to leave his home to attend the Christmas parade when it has suffered fire damage, has a fire still burning in the grate, and his living room window is smashed? Fortunately the film's pace is so frenzied, few of these inconsistencies are likely to give viewers much pause for thought.

There was a considerably metafictional aspect to *Jingle All the Way*, in that the film – which was aggressively marketed at the time of its release – cheerfully pokes fun at the excessive merchandising of popular franchises. The visual style and action of the in-movie *Turbo Man* TV series is a very obvious pastiche of Saban Entertainment's hugely popular *Mighty Morphin Power Rangers*, which originally ran from 1993 to 1995 and produced endless spin-off merchandise. We then see endless *Turbo Man* spin-offs peppered throughout the various scenes, including breakfast cereal, comics, and even a *Turbo Man* movie playing at a local theatre. Among the endless fictional merchandise on display, in a rather tongue-in-cheek twist, we constantly see boxed action figures of the anthropomorphic lion Booster, *Turbo Man*'s sidekick – the archetypal toy which nobody ever seems to want, which is always in abundant supply while the main *Turbo Man* toy is nowhere to be found. In the ultimate breaking of the fourth wall, a real-life *Turbo Man* action figure was produced as a tie-in to the film, though its emergence did not create anything close to the shopping frenzy amongst the public that was depicted throughout the film.

In spite of these ingenious variations and subversions of expectation, the film's depiction of commercial hysteria at the festive season did not play well with many commentators. Karal Ann Marling, for instance, noted that:

> *Jingle All the Way* (1996) with Arnold Schwarzenegger [was] filmed in part at the Mall of America, where the frenzy of Christmas Eve shopping was simulated for the cameras on a blistering midsummer weekend. [...] *Jingle All the Way* is a thoroughly unpleasant film in which the desperate father bullies and attacks the retail world relentlessly for eighty-five minutes in the effort to get the last 'Turbo Man' action figure. In a way, Schwarzenegger's role is a parody of the wham-bang brutes he has always played in the movies: he *is* 'Turbo Man', a Hollywood action figure. But the real target of the satire, if the movie can be described as satire, seems to be the terrible, empty materialism of Christmas, which the film ultimately endorses.[3]

The enormous Mall of America in Bloomington was an inspired location for the film, which spotlighted perfectly the vast multiplicity of choice when it came to Christmas gift-buying. With a total of 520 stores at time of writing, and no less than 12,300 car parking spaces, the huge mall has featured as a filming location in numerous productions, but seemed

393

perfectly suited to the frantic hustle and bustle of *Jingle All the Way*'s Christmas Eve shopping expedition. (The film's world premiere was held at the mall on 16 November 1996.) However, Howard's search for the elusive *Turbo Man* toy seems to take him around most of Minnesota, with more than a few reflections on the profit-making mercantilism of the festive season being thrown into the mix along the way. As Rowan alludes, 'Producer Chris Columbus rewrote the script, adding in some interesting elements of satire about the commercialization of Christmas',[4] and this aspect of the film is perhaps its most noteworthy.

The unabashed wallowing in material acquisition at the heart of *Jingle All the Way* marked it out as somewhat controversial amongst reviewers, some of whom felt that – irrespective of whether the film lampooned the materialism of the intense hysterics surrounding Christmas gift-buying or celebrates the relief of pinpointing that ideal yuletide present – that there was a degree of danger in allowing audiences to draw the conclusion that this is what the festive season should really be about. Ryan Cracknell spoke for many when he highlighted that the film's uneven approach to this issue ultimately led to the risk of it communicating mixed messages: 'Who would want their children to see something that so openly embraces the idea that Christmas is all about the special gift? And I'm not talking ambiguously or symbolic here either. I'm talking commercialism. ⟦...⟧ *Jingle All the Way* makes an argument for consumerism. Although it finishes with the expected sentimental reunion of sorts and an act of goodwill, it's not genuine. ⟦...⟧ In its Christmas setting, *Jingle All the Way* backs up the notion that the season is all about presents and the insanity that goes into the build-up. Regardless of whether you view Christmas as a religious celebration

of birth or a day to spend with family, this is frightening ideology with dire implications'.[5]

The film does, in a wider sense, raise interesting questions about the ability of companies to manipulate consumers
through the creation of hype and social buzz about particular
products, and then the corresponding ability of children to
pressure their parents into purchasing these items – largely
because the kids themselves are suffering extreme peer pressure to make sure that they appear the same as their
contemporaries. George Rother makes the point that:

> In general, *Jingle All the Way* is a pleasing little
> comedy, but I must take issue with the underlying
> message about buying somebody's love with mate-
> rial goods. It's like Jamie is saying that he'll love
> his father if he gives him a specific object, is this
> the lesson people would like to impart to their
> children? These days, children already have a pret
> ty good grasp of materialism and manipulating
> their parents into buying them something to com-
> pensate for any perceived shortcomings they might
> have. While I don't agree with the idea of any par-
> ent ignoring their children in favor of their career,
> it seems rather harsh for the children to use emo-
> tional blackmail to guilt their parents into buying
> them things.[6]

There was a general critical consensus that Levant's
film presented a rather erratic and disordered approach to the
issue of commercialism, never quite confident enough in its
message to be a satire and yet lacking enough bite to act as an
attack on unfettered consumer excess. While the thematic un-
derpinnings were certainly established to make some

withering observations about this phenomenon, not least in the surreal underworld warehouse operation being run by the illicit Santas and elves, Randy Kornfield's screenplay pulls its punches at exactly the wrong moments, making the film's eventual climax – where Jamie finally realises that having a good relationship with his father is worth immeasurably more than a faddish toy that will almost certainly be forgotten by the following year – seem somewhat overly expedient and thus unconvincing. Andy Webb makes the point that: 'It's sad really that a movie which shows a sort of glimpse at the commercialism of Christmas with children demanding a certain gift for Christmas, the insane marketing of the toy as well as acknowledging the state of modern family life where the father is too busy working that it ends up ignoring the depth for slapstick farce. This could have turned into a clever and witty look at modern Christmas rather than the one joke wonder it ended up being'.[7]

While the movie is clearly a star vehicle which is dominated by Schwarzenegger's vast celebrity status, the supporting actors were as effective as they were eclectic. Sinbad (real name David Adkins) is a well-known stand-up comedian and actor who by that point had made numerous appearances on television and was active in film since the mid-1980s thanks to appearances in features such as *That's Adequate* (Harry Hurwitz, 1989), *Coneheads* (Steve Barron, 1993) and *Houseguest* (Randall Miller, 1995). He brings great personality to the role of Myron – reportedly, many of his lines were improvised, which fit the character of the fast-talking mailman perfectly. He faced an uphill struggle, however, in the sense that it is often difficult to know exactly how to regard the character: as a sympathetic friend, an opportunistic enemy, a 'frenemy' whose allegiances constantly shift, or something else entirely. Phil Hartman was well-known for his many appearances on NBC's *Saturday Night Live* between 1986 and 1994, where he became especially renowned for his impersonations of US Presidents Ronald Reagan and Bill Clinton. He made numerous appearances in film throughout the 1980s and 90s, mostly in comedies, with roles in movies as varied as *Pee-Wee's Big Adventure* (Tim Burton, 1985), *Three Amigos* (John Landis, 1986), *Fletch Lives* (Michael Ritchie, 1989) and *Quick Change* (Bill Murray and Howard Franklin, 1990). And of course Jake Lloyd was only a few years away from achieving worldwide recognition as the young Anakin Skywalker in George Lucas's *Star Wars: The Phantom Menace* (1999), though he was not the only actor to hit the big time soon afterwards – watch out too for a pre-*Austin Powers* Verne Troyer as one of the pugilistic elves in the counterfeit goods warehouse.

Jingle All the Way was comprehensively blasted by critics at the time of its release, though critics were divided when it came to identifying the alleged failings of the film. Marc Savlov, for instance, blamed the movie's underlying cynicism for blunting the impact of its core theme: '*Jingle All the Way* is yet another scary, mean-spirited, holiday "comedy" that's about as much fun as a stocking full of dead spiders. [...] Try as it might, the film's practical message about the perils of Yuletide consumerism is lost in the shuffle, ground under the sooty, hobnailed boots of evil Santas and line readings so wooden you could heat your house with them for weeks at a time. Unfunny and worse, unpleasant, *Jingle All the Way* is holiday cheer from the warped psyche of a Scrooge. Even the Grinch wouldn't like this one'.[8] Roger Ebert, on the other hand, took issue with the choice of emphasising relentless, frenetic on-screen anarchy at the cost of characterisation: 'I liked a lot of the movie, which is genial and has a lot of energy, but I was sort of depressed by its relentlessly materialistic view of Christmas, and by the choice to go with action and (mild) violence over dialogue and plot. Audiences will like it, I am sure, but I have to raise my hand in reluctant dissent and ask, please, sir, may we have some more goodwill among men? Even Turbo Men?'[9]

Others, such as Berardinelli, instead identified the film's unmemorable approach as seeming somewhat by-the-numbers, meaning that it failed to convincingly make its mark in the highly competitive field of Christmas movie-making: 'The real problem with *Jingle All the Way* has nothing to do with its suitability for certain age groups, but its suitability in general. Being good-natured and family-friendly has little to do with being consistently entertaining. *Jingle All the Way* is forgettable, and that, more than anything else, is why I recommend passing up this holiday offering'.[10] More common was a wider disdain for the way in which *Jingle All the Way* raises concerns over the dangers of the over-commercialisation of Christmas, only to then ultimately embrace this commoditisation. Barbara Shulgasser is representative of this line of opinion when she wrote, 'No one should sell his birthright to see this icky movie, a slick, overblown, special effects extravaganza that, in its attempt to mock the marketing fest Christmas has become, only congratulates us all for our materialism. [...] Perhaps other people will have greater tolerance for seeing this one-joke movie through to its inevitable end'.[11] This view was shared by Edward Guthmann, who approved of the apprehensions raised by the film but was unconvinced by Levant's execution of these premises: 'When *Jingle All the Way* isn't pitting Arnold and Sinbad against each other like cartoon nemeses, or spoofing American consumerism and

Christmas-shopping hysteria, it tries to say something important about the quality of family relationships and the need to make time for the kids. That's a valuable message, but the movie makes it too late and without conviction. *Jingle* wants to warm our hearts and establish Schwarzenegger as a family man – but devotes so much time to goony violence and broad physical comedy that the last-reel schmaltz feels hollow and tacked-on'.[12]

While more recent appraisals of *Jingle All the Way* have shown slightly greater polarisation in comparison to the wholesale drubbing it received from critics back in 1996, even the more positive appraisals have been somewhat qualified in their response. On one hand, reviewers such as Jeremiah Chin have sounded a cautious note of appreciation while being all too aware of the movie's limits: 'Overall *Jingle All the Way* is a great example of Schwarzenegger's comedic genius that you can interpret as awesomely bad or intentional, but either way it's still funny. Sure you could go into some of the finer points of the films plot and writing that try to be a critique on consumerism only to reaffirm the need for materialism, but I don't feel particularly pretentious so I'll just leave it at a Schwarzenegger "family" style comedy that hits some great comedic notes and pulls out some funny performances from nearly everyone'.[13] But on the opposing end of the spectrum, commentators like Keith Phipps have held unreceptive views much closer to that of the critical reaction to the film's original release, lamenting that: 'As mirthful as an icicle straight up your ass, the long-awaited pairing of Arnold Schwarzenegger and Sinbad finally hits the silver screen. [...] If there is a bottom of the Hollywood barrel, *Jingle All The Way* has been gleaned from the filth upon which that bottom rests'.[14]

The professional quality of the performances, and the way that they tend to transcend the material offered by the screenplay, was the focus of some critics. Representative of this view, Kevin Matthews identified the cast's spirited enactment of the chaotic action to be the film's most successful aspect: '*Jingle All The Way* is quite a horrid movie, there's no doubt about it. Whereas many other Christmas movies have celebrated the good feeling and traditional cheer that can come along with it (as well as, let's not forget, the darker aspects that can accompany the holiday), *Jingle All The Way* celebrates the materialism that has come to dominate the proceedings. [...] If it wasn't for those game performances by Schwarzenegger, Conrad and Hartman, this movie would be unwatchable. As it stands, it's barely tolerable but only watch it around the holiday season if you really, really can't avoid it'.[15] Others have lamented the fact that, with only a few improvements in key areas of the movie's productions, it may have been a considerably more successful creative endeavour – reflecting that the film's confused tone works against it, perhaps necessitating a more explicitly adult approach to the subject matter than was possible in a family feature. J.P. Roscoe, for example, observes that: '*Jingle All the Way* with a stronger script and a more appropriate cast could have worked. As it stands now, it is a mess. There are moments that are almost laughable (that are supposed to be), like Schwarzenegger breaking into his neighbor's house to steal presents, that were kind of funny... but then the characters have remorse and "do the right thing". If only they had no remorse and just went all out evil for the holidays. Cold-hearted and cruel parents bent on making the perfect Christmas and no drunk reindeer... that is a Christmas movie I'd watch'.[16] Finally, there are commentators who have reflected on the fact that nostalgia for the cinema of the time may aid in viewing *Jingle All the Way* through more forgiving eyes, harking back to an era where Internet shopping and home delivery had not yet become all-pervasive. As Chris Olson explains:

> Christmas is a time for forgiveness, and if you can forgive the achingly poor script and bizarre characterisation, there is still a lot wrong with *Jingle All the Way*. That being said, there is also a nostalgic charm to the movie, not least in seeing Schwarzenegger throwing down calamity everywhere he goes; tackling toddlers for bingo balls or five-knuckle-sandwiching a Santa are just some of his Yuletide antics. There is also an enjoyable pace which is laid down early on by the Christmas Eve deadline, and kept steady throughout the duration. Scenes of comic capering are done with gleeful childishness, never taking themselves too seriously, and delivering plenty of spectacle.[17]

Jingle All the Way was to win Sinbad a Blockbuster Entertainment Award – in the category of Favorite Supporting Actor: Family – the following year. Many years later, the film received a sequel (albeit in name only) in the form of Alex Zamm's *Jingle All the Way 2*. A direct-to-video production starring Larry the Cable Guy, Brian Stepanek and Santino Marella, the movie was a co-production between 20th Century Fox and WWE Studios which featured none of the actors or characters from the original film. The central premise was, however, immediately recognisable: a truck driver is determined to get hold of that year's must-have Christmas toy ('Harrison the Talking Bear') for his young daughter, but is thwarted at every turn by the new husband of his former wife who seeks to cast the hard-working father in a bad light. The critical response to the film was generally not favourable.

Jingle All the Way had reinforced the recurring theme of 1990s Christmas film-making, which was to commemorate and advocate the family unit as well as celebrating friendship and community as a means of mutually overcoming adversity. While we see in Howard's reconciliation with Jamie and Liz the traditional affirmation of the nuclear family, there is also a sense with Ted – a divorced father who is determined to give his son the perfect holiday season experience single-handedly – that the depiction of the family unit was continuing to broaden in response to changing social mores. While its (largely inconsistent) note of caution surrounding the over-commercialisation of Christmas had its origins in much earlier festive cinema, Levant's film never leans to hard on this aspect of the narrative – indeed, it is arguably even contradicted at times – and the emphasis continuously returns to madcap action rather than contemplative social reflection. *Jingle All the Way* may not have been the most critically lauded Christmas movie of the 1990s by some measure, but thanks to the enormous popularity of its star it certainly made a decent mark on the box-office of the time.

REFERENCES

1. James Berardinelli, '*Jingle All the Way*', in *ReelViews*, 22 November 1996.
    <*https://www.reelviews.net/reelviews/jingle-all-the-way*>

2. Terry Rowan, *Having a Wonderful Christmas Time Film Guide* (Morrisville: Lulu Press, 2014), p.110.

3. Karal Ann Marling, *Merry Christmas!: Celebrating America's Greatest Holiday* (Cambridge: Harvard University Press, 2001) [2000], p.347.

4. Rowan, p.110.

5. Ryan Cracknell, '*Jingle All the Way*', in *Movie Views*, 5 December 2003.
    <*https://movieviews.ca/jingle-all-the-way*>

6. George Rother, '*Jingle All the Way*', in *MovieGuy 24/7*, 15 December 2011.
    <*https://movieguy247.com/iMovies/index.php/blog/holiday-movies/677-jingle-all-the-way*>

7. Andy Webb, '*Jingle All the Way*', in *The Movie Scene*, 2007.
    <*https://www.themoviescene.co.uk/reviews/jingle-all-the-way/jingle-all-the-way.html*>

8. Marc Savlov, '*Jingle All the Way*', in *The Austin Chronicle*, 29 November 1996.
    <*https://www.austinchronicle.com/events/film/1996-11-29/jingle-all-the-way/*>

9.   Roger Ebert, '*Jingle All the Way*', in *The Chicago Sun-Times*, 22 November 1996.
     <*https://www.rogerebert.com/reviews/jingle-all-the-way-1996*>

10. Berardinelli.

11. Barbara Shulgasser, 'Arnold: Don't toy with us', in *The San Francisco Examiner*, 22 November 1996.
     <*https://www.sfgate.com/news/article/Arnold-Don-t-toy-with-us-3112507.php*>

12. Edward Guthmann, 'Film Review: Arnie Doesn't Ring Any Comedy Bells', in *The San Francisco Chronicle*, 22 November 1996.
     <*https://www.sfgate.com/movies/article/FILM-REVIEW-Arnie-Doesn-t-Ring-Any-Comedy-2958581.php*>

13. Jeremiah Chin, '*Jingle All The Way: Family Fun Edition*', in *DVD Compare*, 2 March 2009.
     <*https://dvdcompare.net/review.php?rid=975*>

14. Keith Phipps, '*Jingle All the Way*', in *AV Club*, 29 March 2002.
     <*https://www.avclub.com/jingle-all-the-way-1798194998*>

15. Kevin Matthews, '*Jingle All the Way* (1996)', in *FlickFeast*, 13 December 2011.
     <*https://www.flickfeast.co.uk/reviews/film-reviews/jingle-1996/*>

16. J.P. Roscoe, '*Jingle All the Way* (1996)', in *Basement Rejects*, 18 December 2011.
     <*http://basementrejects.com/review/jingle-all-the-way-1996/*>

17.   Chris Olson, '*Jingle All the Way*', in *UK Film Review*, 14
      December 2015.
      *<https://www.ukfilmreview.co.uk/post/jingle-all-the-way-
      1996>*

14

I'll Be Home For Christmas (1998)

Walt Disney Pictures / Mandeville Films / Kyra Productions

Director: Arlene Sanford
Producers: David Hoberman and Tracey Trench
Screenwriters: Tom Nursall and Harris Goldberg,
from a story by Michael Allin

ARRIVING at the end of the 1990s, *I'll Be Home for Christmas* would prove to be an oddly apposite bookend for the decade's festive cinema. Given that the earliest and most commercially successful Christmas movie of the nineties, *Home Alone* (q.v.), had been concerned with the defence of the home as both sanctuary and site of family unity, *I'll Be Home for Christmas* would instead centre around another familiar trope of festive cinema – the long, difficult but ultimately rewarding return home – albeit with something of a twist in that the protagonist has little enthusiasm for the journey, and the family unit is both fractured and distinctly post-nuclear in its composition.

Rather than offering nostalgia for the family Christmas celebrations of years past, *I'll Be Home for Christmas* instead presented a family that had been separated by death and re-marriage, setting up the opportunity for reconciliation between an estranged father and his somewhat emotionally disaffected son. Crucially, however, the youthful protagonist has no desire to embrace home and hearth, and his self-interested motivation is anything but altruistic. Thus while so many Christmas films of the 1990s had focused upon the nuclear family as a kind of ideal, and had often concentrated on a need for belonging at the festive season, this film was to subvert the traditional homecoming as an embrace of Christmas past and instead established the foundation for a gradual transformation of individual character at the festive season: a theme with even greater resonance to the established themes of past Christmas cinema.

In its unorthodox melange of festive tradition and nineties cynicism, *I'll Be Home for Christmas* skewers the literal (and metaphorical) return home familiar to many previous yuletide features, instead presenting audiences with a charming but largely unsympathetic character who is forced to overcome adversity in order to fulfil a familial obligation to rejoin his widowed father (and his new partner) over the holidays. Contrary to all convention in festive film-making, returning home for Christmas is depicted not as an ideal but rather as something of a chore. Initially the central character has to be bribed in order to make the journey back to his father, though over time he begins to change and develop as the festive season transforms his attitudes. He begins to realise the importance not just of family and home, but also a need to embrace a common humanity that benefits not just the people around him, but also himself. As Mick LaSalle has remarked, 'There are three kinds of holiday movies: those that instill a holiday feeling; those that kindle an already present holiday feeling; and those that threaten to wreck a holiday. *I'll Be Home for Christmas* is in that middle category. For someone like me, who starts looking forward to Christmas not long after the Fourth of July, the picture is a modest diversion with an extra dose of coziness because it's getting near the holidays. And a movie like this needs all the coziness it can get'.[1]

The director of the movie was Arlene Sanford, a highly experienced television director who in later years would go on to be nominated for two Primetime Emmy Awards for helming episodes of the Fox Network's legal comedy-drama *Ally McBeal* in 1999 as well as ABC's Massachussetts-set *Boston Legal* in 2008. While she had directed episodes of many high-profile TV series including *The Wonder Years* (1988), *Dream On* (1990), *Friends* (1994) and *Dawson's Creek* (1998), Sanford had also helmed a theatrical feature, *A Very Brady Sequel* (1996), which was a comedic continuation to the previous year's *The Brady Bunch Movie* (Betty Thomas, 1995). She would return to festive film-making later in her career with the Lifetime Television Network's *12 Men of Christmas* (2009), starring Kristin Chenoweth, and the Disney Channel's TV movie *Good Luck Charlie, It's Christmas!* (2011), featuring Bridgit Mendler and Leigh-Allyn Baker.

Featuring prominently in the promotional materials for *I'll Be Home for Christmas* was its youthful star, Jonathan Taylor Thomas (better known in the pop culture of the time by his initials, JTT). Though an experienced voice actor, particularly well-recognised as the voice of the young Simba in Disney's animated musical *The Lion King* (Roger Allers and Rob Minkoff, 1994), Thomas had made live-action appearances in films as wide-ranging as *Tom and Huck* (Peter Hewitt, 1995) and *Wild America* (William Dear, 1997), but was almost certainly best-known for his long-running role as series regular Randy Taylor in ABC's situation comedy *Home Improvement* between 1991 and 1999. Already a multiple award-winner and nominee at the time of *I'll Be Home for*

Christmas, which was released when he was only seventeen years of age, Thomas's career had earned him a legion of fans, and the hope was that he would follow in the footsteps of his *Home Improvement* co-star Tim Allen who had achieved success in Christmas cinema with *The Santa Clause* (q.v.) four years earlier.

At Palisades College in sunny Los Angeles, too-cool-for-school student Jake Wilkinson (Jonathan Taylor Thomas) is the life and soul of the party on campus. Slick, opportunistic and always ready with a wisecrack, he glides through life on a wave of self-serving charm. The only blot on his horizon is the devious and conniving Eddie Taffet (Adam LaVorgna), who bullies and coerces his fellow students in order to ensure he always gets his own way.

While popular amongst the student body there in California, Jake is originally from Larchmont in New York. Christmas is approaching, and Jake hasn't been home for the holidays since the death of his mother, resenting his father (Gary Cole) for having remarried ten months later. His father has sent him two plane tickets to return to New York, but Eddie asks his roommate and habitual fixer Ian (Blair Slater) to go on the Internet and have the destination changed to Cabo San Lucas instead. He intends to ask his girlfriend, Allie Henderson (Jessica Biel) to accompany him for a sunny Christmas on the beach, but – already harassed due to a final exam taking place just before the holidays – she tells him that she intends on going home to see her family, and admonishes him for not doing the same. Knowing that her parents would be deflated if she didn't spend the festive season with them (also in Larchmont), she suggests that Jake should finally bury the hatchet with his father. The odious Eddie arrives and tries to flirt with Allie, but only succeeds in reversing his new car into a nearby BMW – much to Jake's amusement.

Later, Jake's dad calls him to once again ask if he will be joining the family for Christmas. Knowing too well his son's smooth-talking fabrications, he makes it clear that he knows that Jake has tried to transfer the plane tickets to another destination, and beseeches him to come back to join him, his new wife Carolyn (Eve Gordon) and Jake's younger sister Tracey (Lauren Maltby) for the holidays. When his wayward son continues to protest, the older man pulls out the final ace from his sleeve – if Jake gets back home by 6pm on Christmas Eve, he will gift him his beloved vintage 1957 Porsche 356 that they had restored together years earlier. While Jake still has no enthusiasm to return home to see his family, he considers the bribe to be one that he can't refuse. Carolyn is astounded that her husband would make such a generous offer when his son has been so deceitful and cavalier with other people's feelings, but as far as Jake's dad is concerned he will do anything to have his elusive offspring back for Christmas for the first time in years.

Jake catches up with Allie after her exam and spins her a yarn about having had a change of heart. He conveniently avoids telling her about the offer of his father's Porsche, and she agrees to accompany him home for the holidays. Before he can depart, however, Jake has made arrangements with three dim-witted jocks (P.J. Prinslow, Kevin Hansen and James Sherry) to help them pass their own exams – for a nominal fee. He hatches an elaborate plan with Ian to look up the paper's answers on the Internet and then send them into exam room via pager before the deadline is called. All goes until a vengeful Eddie picks up on the scheme and stops Ian from transmitting the answers, ensuring that the jocks end up failing the exam paper.

Later on, Jake is boasting of his soon-to-be-acquired Porsche when Eddie and the jocks arrive and pin him down. They accuse him of deliberately sabotaging their chances in the exam, but – as Ian has been trapped inside his locker by Eddie – Jake has nobody to back up his side of the story. As always, he tries to talk himself out of trouble, but Eddie and his crew are resistant to his silver-tongued charm and decide to enact their revenge.

The next morning, Allie is ready to depart with Jake, little realising that Eddie and his trio of assailants have dressed him in a Santa Claus suit and abandoned him in the middle of a desert. Worse yet, the hat and beard have been glued in place, making them impossible to remove. Allie assumes that the almost-always-unreliable Jake has simply stood her up, but Eddie arrives (knowing too well that her boyfriend will be out of circulation for the foreseeable future) and offers to transport her across the country to her family in New York. Knowing Eddie of old, she is reluctant to accept his deceptively benevolent offer, but in Jake's absence she can see no other choice and thus grudgingly gets into his (miraculously already repaired) new car.

After staggering through the wilderness for hours, Jake eventually finds a remote garage and calls Allie, only to reach her answering machine (which isn't working properly). He then calls his dad and asks him to wire him money to get home. However, having lied constantly to his father over the years, the older man assumes that it is yet another of his son's ploys to avoid returning to Larchmont and abruptly hangs up. Fortunately for Jake, four elderly Tom Jones fans (Amzie Strickland, Natalie Barish, Kathleen Freeman and Celia Kushner) are heading through the area on the way to an event in Las Vegas and offer to give him a lift. However, still worse for the wear from the night before, the jarring car ride leads him to vomit copiously into one of the women's handbags, ensuring that he is soon ejected from the vehicle and forced to hitch-hike. But when thrown out of the car somewhere in Nevada, his glued beard detaches (painfully), which he considers to be at least a minor benefit.

Allie calls her answering machine remotely from a public call box and is confused when she hears Jake's garbled message. Eddie, who has stopped the car temporarily to buy some supplies, assures her that it is probably nothing to worry about, but panics when he discovers that – by a million to one chance – Jake is hitch-hiking from a position across the street. Being none too pleased to see his assailant, Jake heads in his direction, but Eddie panics and races off at high speed, confusing Allie in the process. Jake, for his part, is baffled at why his girlfriend appears to be travelling in a car with his nemesis.

Jake's continued attempts to hitch-hike are unsuccessful, forcing him to spend the night sleeping in a decorative Santa's sleigh (until he is later turfed out by a civic employee). His luck changes the following day when he is picked up by eccentric van driver Nolan (Andrew Lauer), who only narrowly avoids knocking him down. Allie and Eddie pass them on the road, the former still relentlessly fending off the advances of the latter. Nolan accelerates to intercept them at Jake's urging, but attracts the attention of a traffic cop who flags down the van for speeding. This alarms Nolan, who reveals that the back of the vehicle is crammed full of stolen goods. Thinking quickly, Jake persuades him to put on a Christmas hat and pretends that the unconventional driver is actually his elf, who goes by the name of 'Snow Puff'. He explains to the sceptical policeman (Sean O'Bryan) that they are headed for the next town and that the contents of the van are intended as gifts for a children's hospital. To the dismay of Jake and Nolan, the cop is so moved by the story that he offers to escort them all the way to the nearby settlement, Red Cliff.

Jake hopes against hope to give the kind-hearted policeman the slip when they reach the hospital, but – when he insists on helping to distribute the presents – Jake and Nolan are forced to spread Christmas cheer to ill and injured children as they hand out obviously-purloined goods such as toasters and hairdryers. Much to Jake's relief, the traffic cop never suspects the reality behind the situation. The final child to speak with Santa, Esteban (Mark De La Cruz), emotionally admits that he doesn't want the offered gift of a cordless vacuum cleaner – all he desires for the holidays is to be reunited with his family who are missing him back home. This causes even the cynical Jake to reflect on his own situation.

Nolan reveals to Jake that he has realised the error of his ways, and rather than fencing stolen goods he intends to return to his family back west for Christmas. This infuriates Jake, who still needs to travel east to get back to his own family's home, but the traffic cop unwittingly saves the day when he pleads with Jake to speak to his estranged wife at the restaurant where she works in Nebraska and plead with her to reconcile with him for the holidays. While the prospect of acting as a *de facto* marriage guidance counselor doesn't much appeal to Jake, he agrees when he realises that it will bring him several hours closer to his final destination.

Now off-duty, the policeman – who reveals that his name is Max – agrees with Jake that if the would-be Santa can persuade his separated wife to return home for the holidays, he will pay for a bus ticket so that Jake can travel direct-ly from Nebraska to New York. They arrive at a restaurant named Turf and Turf, where Max's wife Marjorie (Lesley Boone) is a waitress, but she proves impervious to Jake's charm as he tries to persuade her to give the hapless cop a second chance. She is livid that Max was caught kissing an old flame, in spite of his protestations that it was a purely platonic gesture, but the fast-talking teen tries to convince her that most relationship misunderstandings can be overcome. Is it really worth throwing away their marriage over a quarrel that may simply have its basis in a painful false impression?

Now desperate to encourage any kind of reconcilation, Jake hijacks a passing bluegrass band and urges them to help out. Max serenades his wife to the sound of banjo music and makes a heartfelt apology (Jake feeding him lyrics literally as soon as he has jotted them down). Surprised by her husband's sincerity and desire to heal the rift between them, Marjorie changes her mind and the pair resolve their differences. Max then makes good on his promise to buy Jake a bus ticket to New York.

Meanwhile, Allie and Eddie are passing through Iowa when they spot a Bavarian-themed village in Iowa named Edelbrück. Tired of Eddie's inane conversation, Allie suggests that they stay there overnight before resuming their journey in the morning. They find the village surprisingly charming, and discover more chemistry than either of them had bar-gained for when they kiss under the mistletoe. As it happens, the kiss is televised, and Jake ends up watching the live broad-cast from the waiting area at the bus station. Incensed at Eddie making a move on his girlfriend, Jake hatches a plan to divert the bus from its direct course to New York so that he can intercept Allie and Eddie in Iowa. Mocking up an organ transplant transport container, he claims that it holds a live liver and that there is only limited time to get it to the recipient – whom, he claims, is in Edelbrück.

As the village is almost completely booked up for the holidays, Eddie and Allie are told that only one room is left – the honeymoon suite – and that they will have to share. However, any hope Eddie has of developing a romance in such dreamy surroundings is rapidly put on ice as Allie makes clear her continued resistance to his overtures. The next morning, the New York-bound bus arrives, and the put-upon driver (Peter Kelamis) warns Jake that he has a maximum of ten minutes before he must get back on the road. Promptly ditching the fake liver, he steals a cleaner's room rota to track down Allie. Reunited, he explains the ordeal he has been through. His girlfriend seems reluctant to believe him given his usual track record of deceit, but Jake insists that he has been unable to contact her due to having been left abandoned in the desert prior to their intended departure. Eddie gloats at the success of his plan, and Jake's furious reaction convinces her that his story is genuine. Allie and Jake appear to reconcile their differences, but when he accidentally gives away the fact that he is only returning home for Christmas in order to claim his father's luxury automobile, Allie fumes that he had blatantly lied to her about having a change of heart.

Finally pushed to the limit by Jake's dishonesty and manipulation, Allie tells him that they are finished – she has reached a point where she literally can't believe a thing that he tells her. This fact is compounded when she boards the New York bus, taking Jake's place, and discovers to her indignation that he had told everyone on board that she was the recipient of the fake liver transplant. As she heads off east, leaving Jake in the dust, Eddie takes pity on his rival and of-

416

fers to give him a ride in his car. Driving north from Iowa to Wisconsin, however, Eddie eventually pieces together the fact that if he helps Jake get back to his family before 6pm, his old foe will get access to his father's Porsche, grow in popularity and presumably have a greater chance of winning Allie back. To this end, he comes to his senses and unceremoniously drops Jake off on the sidewalk before speeding away into the distance.

Jake despairs at this latest turn of bad luck until he realises that he has accidentally landed at the starting line for a fun run – with all of the participants dressed in Santa Claus suits. Realising that there is a $1,000 prize for the winner, Jake registers in the hope of securing another way back to New York. Fortunately for him, many of the other Santas are out of shape, and the early favourite (Ernie Jackson) ends up sabotaging his own chances due to an accidental collision with some Christmas decorations. The race looks like a dead heat, but when Jake loses his Santa hat – one of the prerequisites of winning at the finish line – his closest competitor (Ian Robison) displays great sportsmanship and holds back until the younger man can retrieve it, allowing Jake to win the competition.

Collecting his winnings, Jake is amused when he spots Eddie being driven away by the local police, having harassed them while trying to leave the town while the race was taking place and subsequently being taken into custody. Jake hails a cab for a ride to the airport, but finds himself conflicted when the taxi driver (Kurt Max Runte) reveals that the Santa who was beaten by Jake in the run is actually Mayor Wilson, who wins every year and always donates his winnings to good local causes. Wrestling with his conscience, Jake asks the driver to take him to the mayor's house, where he passes on the prize cash so that it can be used to help others. Mayor Wilson thanks him for his unexpected generosity and asks if he will join his family for a Christmas meal, but Jake gently refuses the kind offer as there is somewhere else he needs to be.

Now penniless again, Jake phones home and speaks with Tracey. She assumes that he is ringing to make yet another excuse to avoid returning home, but when she realises that he now seems unconcerned even about claiming the Porsche it finally dawns on her that he is genuinely facing difficulties. She offers to use her savings to wire him a plane ticket to the nearest airport in Madison, Wisconsin. However, when he goes to collect it he is told that he can't board the plane without proper identification – to which, of course, he doesn't have access. Just when all seems lost, Jake notices a passing animal transport container and manages to secrete himself inside with a friendly (if flatulent) canine named Ringo. He thus manages to stow himself away on a cargo flight to John F. Kennedy Airport in New York, creating a diversion on his arrival to sneak away undetected.

Back at Larchmont, Jake's dad is melancholic as the hours count down to his six o'clock deadline. Little does he realise that Jake is jumping from train to train – without the cash for his fare – as he gets ever closer to his destination. Unable to hitch a car ride, he eventually becomes desperate enough to jump on top of an automobile heading in the right direction (unbeknownst to the driver), then upon reaching Larchmont he commandeers a horse-drawn carriage from the local Christmas parade. However, his haste is not due to the agreement to take ownership with his father's Porsche at 6pm – instead, he heads for Allie's home and assures her of his good intentions. He swears that his cross-country tribulation has revealed his character flaws and helped him to become a better, more selfless individual as a result. Allie senses his honesty and realises that he really has changed due to his recent ordeal.

The pair get into the sleigh and speed off to Jake's home. However, he surprises her when they arrive with one minute to spare and he refuses to enter until after six o'clock has come and gone. Inside, his father gloomily reflects that even the prospect of a classic Porsche wasn't enough to bring his son home for the holidays. His despondency soon turns to jubilation when Jake storms through the front door and joyfully reunites with his loved ones. Jake's dad offers him the keys to the luxury car – even though he is a few seconds late – but his son refuses, telling him that he would rather continue to work with him on restoring it for years yet to come. He also makes clear not just his acceptance of his father's marriage to the genial Carolyn, but also his heartfelt approval of it. As the family celebrate Jake's arrival, the street parade passes the house and recognise the stolen sleigh. Thankfully as Jake is still attired in the (now somewhat haggard) Santa suit, he looks the part when it comes to driving the sleigh in the parade, and his family and Allie hop aboard as he gleefully swaps any prospect of owning the Porsche for a mode of transport more befitting jolly old Saint Nick.

I'll Be Home for Christmas was rather unconventional fare for a family-oriented festive movie, with many critics noting that as its approach seemed too unsophisticated for an adult audience and yet too urbane for children, it appeared to be made for no specific viewership in particular. Playing out like a Christmas-oriented fusion of *National Lampoon's Vacation* (Harold Ramis, 1983) and the Thanksgiving-set *Planes, Trains and Automobiles* (John Hughes, 1987), albeit with more family-friendly humour, the film's tone seemed wildly patchy for a Walt Disney Picture, leading some commentators – such as John R. McEwen – to remark on its perplexing sense of moral confusion: 'There are some cute moments, and some funny characters, but one cannot help but notice that there is not a respectable "role model" in the film. I don't mean to preach, but I'm not at all sure of what message is being sent here. Jake is supposed to be the protagonist, but he is invariably selfish, inconsiderate, and deceitful to everyone he meets, including those he's supposed to care about. Is this a kids' film?'[2]

The realism of Jake's character journey from self-serving charmer to altruistic do-gooder is admittedly hard to swallow due to his general tendency towards tall tales and con artistry – it is difficult to know when he is being sincere and when he is double-dealing, even after his supposed epiphany near the end of the movie. While Allie's conversations with the narcissistic Eddie reveal her experience of a more cultured, sensitive side to Jake than we ever see the character demonstrate on-screen, the fact is that he is a figure so defined by his balance between blatant untrustworthiness and smooth persuasiveness (a fact aided by the considerable charisma of Jonathan Taylor Thomas's peformance) that we can sympathise with Allie's complaint that Jake and Eddie are essentially two sides of the same coin. Yet whereas Jake has the benefit of a poetic soul and a gift for loquacity, Eddie seems more blunt and uncompromising by comparison, and it is his refusal to change – even when an evolution and redemption of his character finally seems probable – that ultimately condemns him to a cell in a police station over Christmas while Jake is celebrating the holidays with his family and girlfriend.

Jake's moral transformation may have been in the best tradition of Christmas movies past, but the speed and directness of that development was difficult to accept and has led to accusations of convenient ethical fruition simply for the sake of it rather than a heartfelt progression in his worldview. As Andy Webb observes, 'We are meant to have some depth as the self-centred Jake discovers the true meaning of Christmas on his travels through the various people he meets. As such he meets a sick child who is going to spend Christmas in hospital but would love to be home with his family and also a Mayor who donates money to the needy all of which leads to Jake discovering the joy of family and giving. But to be frank this isn't some road to Damascus conversion because basically Jake goes from being shallow to understanding in the blink of an eye'.[3] It is, of course, a matter of some subjectivity as to whether Jake always had this capacity for self-sacrifice and common humanity but was simply seeking the means to release it; his estrangement from his family and reluctance to return home in the first place, it is hinted, derives from his inability to accept that life has moved on, suggesting that his nostalgia for Christmas is tied to memories of his late mother and father still being together, thus meaning that accepting her loss is too painful a burden for him to bear. Because so little of his character is revealed in detail, however, it has led to sharp criticism from reviewers such as Hollis Chacona, who have derided the efficacy of Jake's conversion to selflessness: 'The story is supposedly about a boy who learns the meaning of Christmas on his cross-country odyssey, but a Norman Rockwell ending can't fill the shallow emptiness of this picture. *I'll Be Home for Christmas* is like the tableau in a snow globe – after all the whirling (and blatantly artificial) snow has settled, not a single figure has actually moved or changed'.[4]

Quite aside from how convincingly – or not – Jake's change in character is depicted, the film contains a number of enjoyable performances ranging from the long-running sibling rivalry between Lauren Maltby's Tracey and Jake through to the growing disappointment of Jake's dad at his son's non-appearance and his loving relationship with his supportive new wife Carolyn. Sadly none of these interactions are given enough screen time to allow the characters to fully develop, meaning that the movie is left to pivot almost entirely on Jake's choice of whether to save his romance with Allie or go for broke to take ownership of his father's car – and slowly realising that for once in his life, he can't have both. Fortunately Jessica Biel delivers a savvy and likeable performance as Allie, whose disillusionment with Jake's falsehoods and manipulation are balanced by the character's genuine affection for the charming prevaricator. While the chemistry between the couple is strained, both Biel and Thomas do their best to breathe life into the slight material they are given.

There is also a number of strange plot illogicalities which are never addressed, not least why Jake – when he discovers that he has been deliberately stranded in the desert – doesn't simply decide to get back to his room at the college campus, which is significantly closer than his father's home in New York. (When he is able to access a phone, he could easily have made arrangements to return to the college – perhaps by taxi – and then pick up his plane ticket from there, shortening his journey considerably.) On that same note, if he is travelling via the most direct route possible from California to New York, why does he end up in a northern-situated State like Wisconsin when it is many hundreds of miles out of his path? Would any exam invigilator really be so naïve as to allow pagers into an exam room during a paper, even in the 1990s?

What would make Allie trust the shady Eddie enough to travel across the country with him by road when Jake has her plane ticket – and how did Eddie get his car repaired so quickly when he had damaged it in a crash only the previous day? Similarly, with cellphones (and indeed pagers) much more readily accessible in 1998 than at the beginning of the decade, can Jake really not conceive of any way of getting a message to Allie while he is on the road? While pondering these details too closely would undoubtedly have bogged down the film's frenetic pace, the fact that their reasoning isn't even vaguely considered seems strange – and overly convenient when it comes to the smooth running of the central plotline.

Arlene Sanford's direction always proves capable, and she maintains a sense of intense pace and urgency throughout. The cinematography of Hiro Narita brings considerable charm to the film, moving from the sunny climes of southern California through to frostier environments depicted in Iowa, Wisconsin and New York. In reality, the film was shot on location in Canadian settings throughout Alberta and British Columbia, as well as in Californian sites such as Red Rock Canyon State Park and San Bernardino National Forest. The campus of Jake's college was, in reality, filmed at Mount Saint Mary's University in Los Angeles. The film also benefits from a dynamic but controlled original score by John Debney, which hit all of the relevant emotional beats while still containing the requisite touches of festive whimsy where required.

Thomas was aided in no small part by a reliable line-up of supporting performers, foremost among them Jessica Biel as Jake's girlfriend Allie. Still at the beginning of her career at this stage, Biel had made her cinematic debut the previous year in the drama *Ulee's Gold* (Victor Nunez, 1997), for which she received a Young Artist Award in the category of Best Performance in a Feature Film: Supporting Young Actress. However, she was more readily recognised as series regular Mary Camden in The WB's family drama 7th *Heaven*, which ran between 1996 and 2003. She has since gone on to develop a very successful acting career which has seen her nominated for a Golden Globe Award, a Primetime Emmy Award and two MTV Movie Awards, amongst many others. Gary Cole was already a veteran of the acting world at the time of *I'll Be Home for Christmas*, having been active on stage and television since the mid-1980s. Equally capable in comedic and dramatic roles, his performances on film had included features such as romantic comedy *Lucas* (David Seltzer, 1986), political thriller *In the Line of Fire* (Wolfgang Petersen, 1993), tongue-in-cheek sitcom spoof *The Brady Bunch Movie* (Betty Thomas, 1995) and crime drama *A Simple Plan* (Scott B. Smith, 1998). He had, however, arguably been even more well-known for his many guest appearances in popular TV series of the time, with roles in high profile shows including *American Playhouse* (1984), *The Twilight Zone* (1985), *Miami Vice* (1986), *Moonlighting* (1987) and *The Outer Limits* (1998), along with starring roles in series such as NBC's talk radio drama *Midnight Caller* (1988-91) and CBS's cult classic *American Gothic* (1995-96).

I'll Be Home for Christmas tanked at the box-office, bringing in takings of $12.2 million[5] against a budget of approximately $30 million.[6] This may, in part, have been a result of its decidedly unenthusiastic reception from the critics of the time, who were deeply unconvinced of the film's perceived merits. Many at the time of release considered its tone to be too cynical and uneven to achieve success amongst other family fare of the same period. Lawrence Van Gelder, for example, remarked: 'Here's the good part about *I'll Be Home for Christmas*: It's short. Here's the dangerous part: If you've never had the urge to kick Santa Claus, this might be just the irksome misadventure into comedy that will drive you over the edge. [...] Although the spirits behind *I'll Be Home for Christmas* treat the audience to vomit in the back of the old ladies' car and a flatulent dog, they make nothing of the comic possibilities of the lederhosen crowd. Mel Brooks, where are you when we need you?'[7] Others instead took issue with the movie's contrivance with the passing of time, allowing for strange temporal plot convolutions which bore little resemblance to reality during Jake's long-haul trip from California to New York. As Michael O'Sullivan noted, 'Chronology seems to expand and contract like a sci-fi time warp as it takes the spoiled brat only two days to get as far as Wisconsin, and then barely an afternoon to complete the journey (with a spare hour or so to run a 5K race in between). Continuity is not as big a problem, however, as the film's terminal lack of humor. [...] *I'll Be Home for Christmas* is too sophisticated for thumb-suckers, but far too stupid for anyone else'.[8]

The film's awkwardly-pitched methodology was of concern to several commentators, who took issue with the way that the action and characterisation were being presented in what was offered as family entertainment while the film simultaneously contained significant cynicism and moral ambiguity. This line of criticism was picked up on by reviewers such as Chacona, who observed:

> Beware of seasonal comedies whose titles echo Christmas carol refrains. Remember *Jingle All the Way?* Heed the omen. Oh, *I'll Be Home for Christmas* doesn't have the aggravating decibel level or nearly the mindless mayhem of *Jingle*'s

massive affront to the senses, nor does it fill the void with warmth or mirth or much of anything else. [...] With a funny script or some genuine tenderness, I might have been able to overlook the sloppy direction and shoddy production values. But the film, despite a constant stream of pranks and mishaps, is mired in comic inertia and poorly pieced together. It's the sort of effort you'd get from a tired and tipsy parent late on Christmas Eve, trying to put together a complicated, assembly-required toy for Christmas morning. The intent was good-hearted, but the result leaves much to be desired.[9]

While the critical reception was not entirely negative, even the more favourable reviews contained caveats in their approval. Roger Ebert was not alone in noting that while the film conformed to the general conventions of festive filmmaking, it would prove too insipid to make a convincing mark on the genre: 'The star is Jonathan Taylor Thomas, from TV's *Home Improvement*, who is an immensely likable actor. But even his easy grin seems to weary a little by the later stretches of the film, which is unrelentingly corny. [...] *I'll Be Home for Christmas* will appeal to people who fail to care if nothing good happens in a movie, just as long as nothing bad happens in it'.[10] This moderated praise was largely representative of critical opinion as a whole at the time of the movie's release, in that the feature had proven disappointing largely on account of squandered opportunities and the curiously amorphous demographic of its target audience.

More recent analysis of *I'll Be Home for Christmas* has done little to improve its standing amongst other festive films of the nineties, with modern appraisals continuing to regard the movie as lacklustre and unremarkable. Critics such as Jason Rugaard have echoed earlier reviewers in considering the film's ill-judged intended viewership range to be at the core of its issues: '1990s television heartthrob, Jonathan Taylor Thomas attempts to make the leap to big-screen romantic leading man in Disney's *I'll Be Home for Christmas*. It's an unsuccessful transition as the young actor isn't able to captivate our attention for the duration of a feature-length film. Who is the intended audience for this picture? It's too childish for the teen crowd, and it will bore smaller children. [...] *I'll Be Home for Christmas* is a tamer version of *Planes, Trains, and Automobiles* for family viewing. It's innocuous and inoffensive, but it's also dull and charmless. JTT, who comes off so well on TV, is too bland to register in a longer format'.[11] Thomas's star quality was observed favourably by some, though only in the context that the film is overly dependent on the charm of his on-screen personality to keep audiences interested. Webb, for instance, declared: 'Remove Jonathan Taylor Thomas from the equation and what *I'll Be Home for Christmas* ends up is a mediocre at best comedy about an eventful journey home for Christmas. [...] *I'll Be Home for Christmas* is a mediocre mishap journey home for Christmas movie with nothing about it which is really stand out. And in truth it is a movie which predominantly relies on Jonathan Taylor Thomas's boyish charms and popularity and unfortunately it over relies on them'.[12]

While some reviewers, such as Keith Phipps, have tended more towards the negative end of the critical spectrum when it came to *I'll Be Home for Christmas*, he focuses on the success of Thomas's inclusion as being largely subjective in the sense that the viewer's enjoyment of the movie is likely to rest almost entirely on their appreciation of his easygoing charisma

– and for those immune to his appeal, there was less to recommend: 'The only pleasure in watching *I'll Be Home For Christmas*, aside from a few cool Christmas novelty songs on the soundtrack, comes from the fact that the teen idol formerly known as JTT is forced to wear a Santa costume through pretty much the entire movie, including an extended sequence in the desert and a scene that places Thomas in a pet carrier with a large, overly friendly-looking dog. It looks extremely uncomfortable'.[13] In the final analysis, however, *I'll Be Home for Christmas*'s underwhelming commercial performance has generally been considered to be less a direct result of any singular fault on the part of the movie, and more a case that it simply lacked enough in the way of memorable qualities to stand out amongst an increasingly well-populated field of festive entertainment at the time. As David Nusair reflected:

> It's a decidedly sitcom-like premise that is, at the outset, employed to less-than-enthralling effect by director Arlene Sanford, as the filmmaker, working from a script by Tom Nursall and Harris Goldberg, initially gears the proceedings towards younger viewers to an extent that's nothing short of oppressive. It's only as the story unfolds and Jake embarks on his road trip that *I'll Be Home For Christmas* starts to become a more than just a misbegotten holiday comedy, with the inclusion of several sappy yet heartwarming episodes near the film's conclusion cementing its place as a perfectly watchable (yet admittedly forgettable) piece of work.[14]

With its late-in-the-day affirmation of the family unit at Christmas, as well as its note of warning over prizing material gain over the mutual support of friendship and kinship, *I'll Be Home for Christmas* had engaged with themes which had been repeatedly addressed throughout the 1990s. Gradually, Jake begins to realise that the ephemeral popularity of his college peers is essentially surface and transient when compared with the enduring love of his father and wider family, and discovers a renewed sense of belonging which coincides with his awareness that commercial goods alone are not enough to ensure a happy and fulfilled life – especially at the festive season. As in so many Christmas movies, not least in the nineties, we see the tendency of the holiday spirit to correct a dysfunctional situation even in spite of insurmountable odds, the character transformation of a self-serving cynic into a reformed humanitarian, and two people finding that shared commonality develops into a lasting bond of romance. While the defence of the family unit had been a recurrent theme of Christmas film-making during the nineties, *I'll Be Home for Christmas* would again make the point that family no longer necessarily referred to the traditional nuclear model; given changing social conventions, increasingly family had become a more inclusive concept which meant that the term essentially now encompassed any group of people that any individual chose to include. This was a journey in attitudes which had gradually evolved throughout the decade, from *All I Want for Christmas* (q.v.) through to *The Santa Clause* (q.v.), and demonstrated a much more wide-ranging tendency to bring people together – the kind of inclusive development that was very much at the heart of the Christmas message as it was so often presented on film.

    I'll Be Home for Christmas was one of the last festively-themed movies to be released in the 1990s, and it arrived at a time when the commercial approach to Christmas film-making was undergoing a considerable change in direction. Whereas the cinematic output of the eighties and nineties had been heavily influenced by particular key themes, whether in relation to attitudes towards materialism or the importance of the domestic environment in engendering contentment and mutual cooperation, the coming decade would see a major and crucial difference in the production of Christmas cinema. Although the immediate post-millennial period was to bear witness to a considerable expansion in the number of features being produced with intrinsic Christmas topicality or distinctively festive settings, this new proliferation of films would not share any one common thematic thread. While they would continue to draw upon the accepted tropes of filmmaking in the genre which had by now become instantly recognisable, they would also capitalise upon this audience familiarity to deconstruct and re-examine elements of the Christmas movie and question if, and why, they remained relevant to contemporary society.

The nineties had demonstrated a multifaceted clash between tradition and modernity, taking into account the complex ways that family relations were changing and the manner in which increasingly sophisticated modes of technology were having an impact on how we worked, lived and communicated, while simultaneously reinforcing the need to honour long-standing Christmas conventions. In this sense, the decade was to lay the groundwork for further explorations of these topics in the years ahead, with cultural topicality, social mores and changing technology all playing a part in the films of the dawning new century. Audiences were about to enter the era of the thoroughly postmodern Christmas, and festive cinema was never to be quite the same again.

REFERENCES

1. Mick LaSalle, '*I'll Be Home* Travels Far on Holiday Spirit', in *The San Francisco Chronicle*, 13 November 1998. <https://www.sfgate.com/movies/article/I-ll-Be-Home-Travels-Far-on-Holiday-Spirit-2979100.php>

2. John R. McEwen, '*I'll Be Home for Christmas*' in *Film Quips Online*, 13 November 1998. <http://www.filmquipsonline.com/illbehomeforchristmas.html>

3. Andy Webb, '*I'll Be Home for Christmas*', in *The Movie Scene*, 2004. <https://www.themoviescene.co.uk/reviews/ill-be-home-for-christmas/ill-be-home-for-christmas.html>

4. Hollis Chacona, '*I'll Be Home for Christmas*', in *The Austin Chronicle*, 20 November 1998. <https://www.austinchronicle.com/events/film/1998-11-20/142259/>

5. Box-office data from *The-Numbers.com*. <http://www.the-numbers.com/movie/Ill-Be-Home-For-Christmas>

6. Budgetary data from *BoxOfficeMojo.com*. <https://www.boxofficemojo.com/title/tt0155753/>

7. Lawrence Van Gelder, 'Film Review: *All I Want for Christmas* is a Porsche and a Purpose', in *The New York Times*, 13 November 1998. <https://www.nytimes.com/1998/11/13/movies/film-review-all-i-want-for-christmas-is-a-porsche-and-a-purpose.html>

8.   Michael O'Sullivan, '*I'll Be Home for Christmas*', in *The Washington Post*, 13 November 1998. <*https://www.washingtonpost.com/wp-srv/style/movies/reviews/illbehomeforchristmasosullivan.htm*>

9.   Chacona.

10.   Roger Ebert, '*I'll Be Home for Christmas*', in *The Chicago Sun-Times*, 13 November 1998. <*https://www.rogerebert.com/reviews/ill-be-home-for-christmas-1998*>

11.   Jason Rugaard, '*I'll Be Home for Christmas*', in *Movie Mavericks*, 24 December 2021. <*https://moviemavericks.com/2021/12/ill-be-home-for-christmas-1998-review/*>

12.   Webb.

13.   Keith Phipps, '*I'll Be Home for Christmas*', in *AV Club*, 29 March 2002. <*https://www.avclub.com/ill-be-home-for-christmas-1798196024*>

14.   David Nusair, 'Two Christmas Movies from Disney', in *Reel Film Reviews*, 23 December 2010. <*https://reelfilm.com/dischr1.htm#ill*>

15

Other Christmas Films of the 1990s

C HRISTMAS settings were popular in 1990s film-making, with numerous films dealing with themes or scenarios related to the festive season being produced throughout the decade. However, many of them were far from traditional yuletide fare. In this section, I have listed a number of movies which, though not often seasonal in and of themselves, nonetheless feature Christmas in one capacity or another – sometimes as merely a backdrop to the action, while in many cases the festive season appears as an integral aspect of the plot:

1. *Alice* (Woody Allen, 1990)
2. *Anywhere But Here* (Wayne Wang, 1999)
3. *Babe* (Chris Noonan, 1995)
4. *Batman Returns* (Tim Burton, 1992)
5. *Bed of Roses* (Michael Goldenberg, 1996)

6. *Beyond Silence* (a.k.a. *Jenseits der Stille*) (Caroline Link, 1996)
7. *Boogie Nights* (Paul Thomas Anderson, 1997)
8. *City of Lost Children* (Marc Caro and Jean-Pierre Jeunet, 1995)
9. *Come See the Paradise* (Alan Parker, 1990)
10. *Convicts* (Peter Masterson, 1991)
11. *Croupier* (Mike Hodges, 1998)
12. *Dark Angel* (a.k.a. *I Come in Peace*) (Craig R. Baxley, 1990)
13. *Dear God* (Garry Marshall, 1996)
14. *Digging to China* (Timothy Hutton, 1998)
15. *Donnie Brasco* (Mike Newell, 1997)
16. *End of Days* (Peter Hyams, 1999)
17. *Enemy of the State* (Tony Scott, 1998)
18. *English Patient, The* (Anthony Minghella, 1996)
19. *Entrapment* (Jon Amiel, 1999)
20. *Europa* (a.k.a. *Zentropa*) (Lars von Trier, 1991)
21. *Everyone Says I Love You* (Woody Allen, 1996)
22. *Eyes Wide Shut* (Stanley Kubrick, 1999)
23. *Go* (Doug Liman, 1999)
24. *Goodfellas* (Martin Scorsese, 1990)
25. *Grumpy Old Men* (Donald Petrie, 1993)
26. *Hard Eight* (a.k.a. *Sydney*) (Paul Thomas Anderson, 1996)
27. *Heavenly Creatures* (Peter Jackson, 1994)
28. *Hook* (Steven Spielberg, 1991)
29. *House of the Spirits* (Bille August, 1993)
30. *Howards End* (James Ivory, 1992)
31. *Hush* (Jonathan Darby, 1998)
32. *In the Bleak Midwinter* (a.k.a. *A Midwinter's Tale*) (Kenneth Branagh, 1995)

33. *Inventing the Abbotts* (Pat O'Connor, 1997)
34. *Jack Frost* (Troy Miller, 1998)
35. *Johns* (Scott Silver, 1996)
36. *Land Girls, The* (David Leland, 1998)
37. *Last Night* (Don McKellar, 1998)
38. *Life with Mikey* (James Lapine, 1993)
39. *Little Women* (Gillian Armstrong, 1994)
40. *Log, The* (a.k.a. *La bûche*) (Danièle Thompson, 1999)
41. *Long Kiss Goodnight, The* (Renny Harlin, 1996)
42. *Long Walk Home, The* (Richard Pearce, 1990)
43. *Look Who's Talking Now* (Tom Ropelewski, 1993)
44. *Lovers on the Bridge, The* (a.k.a. *Les Amants du Pont-Neuf*) (Leos Carax, 1991)
45. *Man Bites Dog* (a.k.a. *C'est arrivé près de chez vous*) (Rémy Belvaux, André Bonzel and Benoît Poelvoorde, 1992)
46. *Man on the Moon* (Milos Forman, 1999)
47. *Metropolitan* (Whit Stillman, 1990)
48. *Michael* (Nora Ephron, 1996)
49. *Midnight in the Garden of Good and Evil* (Clint Eastwood, 1997)
50. *Money Train* (Joseph Ruben, 1995)
51. *Mortal Thoughts* (Alan Rudolph, 1991)
52. *Mouth to Mouth* (a.k.a. *Boca a boca*) (Manuel Gómez Pereira, 1995)
53. *Mr and Mrs Bridge* (James Ivory, 1990)
54. *My Father's Glory* (a.k.a. *La gloire de mon père*) (Yves Robert, 1990)
55. *My Favourite Season* (a.k.a. *Ma saison préférée*) (André Téchiné, 1993)

56. *My Mother's Castle* (a.k.a. *Le château de ma mère*) (Yves Robert, 1990)
57. *Night Sun* (a.k.a. *Il sole anche di notte*) (Paolo Taviani and Vittorio Taviani, 1990)
58. *Once Around* (Lasse Hallström, 1991)
59. *One True Thing* (Carl Franklin, 1998)
60. *Oscar and Lucinda* (Gillian Armstrong, 1997)
61. *Outside Providence* (Michael Corrente, 1999)
62. *Peter's Friends* (Kenneth Branagh, 1992)
63. *Postcards from America* (Steve McLean, 1994)
64. *Reckless* (Norman René, 1995)
65. *RoboCop 3* (Fred Dekker, 1993)
66. *Rogue Trader* (James Dearden, 1999)
67. *Ronin* (John Frankenheimer, 1998)
68. *Rover Dangerfield* (James L. George and Bob Seeley, 1991)
69. *Rudolph the Red-Nosed Reindeer: The Movie* (William R. Kowalchuk Jr., 1998)
70. *Santa Claws* (John A. Russo, 1996)
71. *Santa with Muscles* (John Murlowski, 1996)
72. *Scenes from a Mall* (Paul Mazursky, 1991)
73. *Shadowlands* (Richard Attenborough, 1993)
74. *Simon Birch* (Mark Steven Johnson, 1998)
75. *Slipping-Down Life, A* (Toni Kalem, 1999)
76. *Smoke* (Wayne Wang, 1995)
77. *Soldier* (Paul W.S. Anderson, 1998)
78. *Some Mother's Son* (Terry George, 1996)
79. *Stepmom* (Chris Columbus, 1998)
80. *Strange Days* (Kathryn Bigelow, 1995)
81. *Sunshine* (István Szabó, 1999)

82. *Those Who Love Me Can Take the Train* (a.k.a. *Ceux qui m'aiment prendront le train*) (Patrice Chéreau, 1998)
83. *Toy Story* (John Lasseter, 1995)
84. *Truman Show, The* (Peter Weir, 1998)
85. *Turbulence* (Robert Butler, 1997)
86. *Twelve Monkeys* (Terry Gilliam, 1995)
87. *Untamed Heart* (Tony Bill, 1993)
88. *While You Were Sleeping* (Jon Turteltaub, 1995)
89. *Whole Wide World, The* (Dan Ireland, 1996)
90. *Will It Snow for Christmas?* (a.k.a. *Y'aura t'il de la neige à Noël?*) (Sandrine Veysset, 1996)
91. *Winter Sleepers* (a.k.a. *Winterschläfer*) (Tom Tykwer, 1997)

Filmography

HOME ALONE (1990)

Production Company: Hughes Entertainment/Twentieth Century Fox Film Corporation.

Distributor: Twentieth Century Fox Film Corporation.

Director: Chris Columbus.

Producer: John Hughes.

Associate Producer: Mark Radcliffe.

Executive Producers: Tarquin Gotch, Mark Levinson and Scott M. Rosenfelt.

Screenplay: John Hughes.

Cinematography: Julio Macat.

Film Editing: Raja Gosnell.

Original Score: John Williams.

Production Design: John Muto.

Casting: Janet Hirshenson and Jane Jenkins.

Art Direction: Dan Webster.

Set Decoration: Eve Cauley and Dan Clancy.

Costume Design: Jay Hurley.

Running Time: 103 minutes.

Main Cast: Macaulay Culkin (Kevin McCallister), Joe Pesci (Harry Lyme), Daniel Stern (Marv Merchants), John Heard (Peter McCallister), Roberts Blossom (Marley), Catherine O'Hara (Kate McCallister), Angela Goethals (Linnie), Devin Ratray (Buzz), Gerry Bamman (Uncle Frank), Hillary Wolf (Megan), John Candy (Gus Polinski), Larry Hankin (Officer Balzak), Michael C. Maronna (Jeff), Kristin Minter (Heather), Daiana Campeanu (Sondra), Jedidiah Cohen (Rod), Kieran Culkin (Fuller), Senta Moses (Tracy), Anna Slotky (Brooke), Terrie Snell (Aunt Leslie), Jeffrey Wiseman (Mitch Murphy), Virginia Smith (Georgette), Matt Doherty (Steffan), Ralph Foody (Johnny/Gangster #1), Michael Guido (Snakes/Gangster #2), Ray Toler (Uncle Rob), Billie Bird (Woman in Airport), Bill Erwin (Man in Airport), Gerry Becker (Officer #1), Victor Cole (Officer #2), Porscha Radcliffe

(Cousin), Brittany Radcliffe (Cousin), Clarke Devereux (Officer Devereux), Dan Charles Zukoski (Pizza Boy), Lynn Mansbach (French Woman), Peter Siragusa (Lineman), Alan Wilder (Scranton Ticket Agent), Hope Davis (French Ticket Agent), Dianne B. Shaw (Airline Counter Person), Tracy J. Connor (Check Out Girl), Jim Ryan (Stock Boy), Ken Hudson Campbell (Santa), Sandra Macat (Santa's Elf).

ALL I WANT FOR CHRISTMAS (1991)

Production Company: Paramount Pictures.
Distributor: Paramount Pictures.
Director: Robert Lieberman.
Producer: Marykay Powell.
Co-Producer: Vicky Herman.
Associate Producer: Robert P. Cohen.
Executive Producer: Stan Rogow.
Screenplay: Thom Eberhardt and Richard Kramer.
Original Music: Bruce Broughton.
Director of Photography: Robbie Greenberg.
Film Editing: Peter E. Berger and Dean Goodhill.
Production Design: Herman F.Zimmerman.
Art Direction: Randall McIlvain.
Set Decoration: John M. Dwyer.
Costume Design: Nolan Miller.
Running Time: 97 minutes.
Main Cast: Harley Jane Kozak (Catherine O'Fallon), Jamey Sheridan (Michael O'Fallon), Ethan Randall (Ethan O'Fallon), Kevin Nealon (Tony Boer), Thora Birch (Hallie O'Fallon), Andrea Martin (Olivia), Lauren Bacall (Lillian Brooks), Amy Oberer (Stephanie), Renée Taylor (Sylvia), Leslie Nielsen (Santa), Felicity LaFortune (Susan), Camille Saviola (Sonya), Michael Alaimo (Frankie), Joanne Baron (Salesdervish #2), Alan Brooks (Mr Chase), Elizabeth Cherney (Paige), Otto Coelho (Bruiser), Joe Costanza (Burly #2), J. Teddy Davis (Santa's Helper), Tracy Diane (Girl in Line), Joey Gaynor (Shep), Frank Girardeau (Burly #1), Darrell Kunitomi (Salesdervish #3), Patrick LaBrecque (Marshall), Phil Leeds (Mr Feld), Neal Lerner (Caterer), Harriet Medin (Mrs Graff), Devin Oatway (Kevin Mars), Kavi Raz (Cabbie #2), Bernardo Rosa Jr. (Paramedic #1), J.D. Stone (Lollipop Kid), Edith Varon (Stella), Joshua Wiener (Brad).

29TH STREET (1991)

Production Company: Twentieth Century Fox/JVC Entertainment Net-
works/Largo Entertainment/Permut Presentations.
Distributor: Twentieth Century Fox.
Director: George Gallo.
Producer: David Permut.
Co-Producer: Ellen Erwin.
Executive Producer: Jerry A. Baerwitz.
Screenplay: George Gallo, from a story by Frank Pesce and James Francis-
cus.
Original Music: William Olvis.
Cinematography: Steven Fierberg.
Film Editing: Kaja Fehr.
Production Design: Robert Ziembicki.
Art Direction: Dayna Lee.
Set Decoration: Hugh Scaife.
Costume Design: Peggy Farrell.
Running Time: 101 minutes.
Main Cast: Danny Aiello (Frank Pesce, Sr.), Anthony LaPaglia (Frank
Pesce, Jr.), Lainie Kazan (Mrs Pesce), Frank Pesce (Vito Pesce), Robert
Forster (Sgt. Tartaglia), Ron Karabatsos (Philly the Nap), Rick Aiello
(Jimmy Vitello), Vic Manni (Louie Tucci), Paul Lazar (Needle Nose
Nipton), Pete Antico (Tony), Donna Magnani (Madeline Pesce), Dar-
ren Bates (Sal Las Benas), Tony Sirico (Chink Fortunado), Richard K.
Olsen (Father Lowery), Richard Cerenzio (Dom the Bomb), Philip Cic-
cone (Rocky Sav), Joey Gironda (Carmine Tucci), Vic Noto (Auggie
Falcone), Sal Ruffino (Angelo), Sam Shamshak (Irv the Pawnbroker),
Adam LaVorgna (Frankie, age 8), Frank Acciarto (Jimmy, age 8), Don
Blakely (Sgt. Jones), Hope Alexander-Willis (Lucy Sills), Leonard Ter-
mo (Dr Puccini), Lou Criscuolo (Ticket Buyer), Karen Duffy (Maria
Rios), Julie Lott (Julie the Usherette), David Ferraro (Cousin Leo), Ted
Cleanthes (Pit Boss), Vincent Chase (Army Eye Doctor), Shirley
Swanger (Nun), Tom Ellis (Newscaster), Tony Lipp (Nicky Bad
Lungs), Vinnie Curto (Zippers Bad Lungs), Mario Todisco (Zippers'
Bodyguard), Richard Tacchino (Social Club Waiter), Rocco Savastano
(Social Club Bartender), Jerry Guarino (Chickens), Bill Ricci (Mickey
the Dwarf), Nicky 'Pops' Anest (Tommy the Geep), George 'Aggie'
Anest (Joe Numbers), Vito 'Baldie' Boccanfuso (Johnny Cake), Anne
Sterling (Maternity Nurse), William Phillips (Lottery Finalist), Joe

441

Roberto (Patrolman Tollen), Jim Ondatje (Patrolman #2), Tony Monte (Jesus Rios), Jessen Noviello (Needle Nose, age 8), Charles Haugk (Tucci's Driver), Alexander Fehr Blue (Baby on Train), Ingrid Van Dorn (Nurse).

THE MUPPET CHRISTMAS CAROL (1992)

Production Company: Jim Henson Productions/The Jim Henson Company/ Walt Disney Pictures.

Distributor: Buena Vista Pictures.

Director: Brian Henson.

Producers: Brian Henson and Martin G. Baker.

Co-Producer: Jerry Juhl.

Line Producer: David Barron.

Executive Producer: Frank Oz.

Screenplay: Jerry Juhl, from the novella by Charles Dickens.

Director of Photography: John Fenner.

Film Editing: Michael Jablow.

Original Score: Miles Goodman.

Music and Lyrics: Paul Williams.

Production Design: Val Strazovec.

Casting: Mike Fenton, Gilly Poole and Suzanne Crowley.

Art Direction: Dennis Bosher.

Supervising Art Director: Alan Cassie.

Set Decoration: Michael Ford.

Costume Design: Ann Hollowood and Polly Smith.

Running Time: 85 minutes.

Main Cast: Michael Caine (Ebenezer Scrooge), Dave Goelz (The Great Gonzo as Charles Dickens/Waldorf as Robert Marley/Dr Bunsen Honeydew as Charity Collector #1/Bettina Cratchit/Rat/Voice of Zoot), Steve Whitmire (Kermit the Frog as Bob Cratchit/Rizzo the Rat/Beaker as Charity Collector #2/Bean Bunny/Belinda Cratchit/Beetle/Sprocket the Dog), Frank Oz (Miss Piggy as Emily Cratchit/Fozzie Bear as Fozziwig/Sam the Eagle as Headmaster of Junior High School Graduates/Animal/George the Janitor), Louise Gold (Mrs Dilber/Spider), Jerry Nelson (Statler as Jacob Marley/Ma Bear/Lew Zealand/Mouse/Penguin/Mr Applegate/Pig Gentleman/Pops/Robin the Frog), David Rudman (Peter Cratchit/Swedish Chef), Steven Mackintosh (Fred, Scrooge's

Nephew), Robin Weaver (Clara), Meredith Braun (Belle), Kristopher Milnes (Young Scrooge), Russell Martin (Young Scrooge), Raymond Coulthard (Young Scrooge), Edward Sanders (Young Scrooge), Theo Sanders (Young Scrooge), Anthony Hamblin (Boy #1), Fergus Brazier (Boy #2), Jessica Fox (Voice of Ghost of Christmas Past), Karen Prell (Ghost of Christmas Past (Muppet Performer)/Voice of Additional Muppets), Robert Tygner (Ghost of Christmas Yet to Come (Muppet Performer)/Ghost of Christmas Past (Muppet Performer)/Turkey), William Todd Jones (Ghost of Christmas Past/Additional Muppets), Donald Austen (Ghost of Christmas Present (Muppet Performer)/Ghost of Christmas Yet to Come (Muppet Performer)), Mike Quinn (Pig Gentleman/Voice of Undertaker), David Shaw Parker (Voice of Old Joe), Marcus Clarke (Voice of Puppeteer), David Barclay (Additional Muppet Performer), Robbie Barnett (Additional Muppet Performer), Sue Dacre (Additional Muppet Performer), Geoff Felix (Additional Muppet Performer), Nigel Plaskitt (Additional Muppet Performer), Simon Williamson (Additional Muppet Performer), Tim Rose (Additional Muppet Performer).

A MIDNIGHT CLEAR (1992)

Production Company: A&M Films/Beacon Pictures/Beacon Communications.
Distributor: InterStar Releasing/Rank Film Distributors.
Director: Keith Gordon.
Producers: Bill Borden and Dale Pollock.
Associate Producer: Margaret Hillard.
Executive Producers: Marc Abraham, Armyan Bernstein, Margaret Hilliard and Tom Rosenberg.
Screenplay: Keith Gordon, from a novel by William Wharton.
Original Score: Mark Isham.
Cinematography: Tom Richmond.
Film Editing: Doin Brochu.
Art Direction: David Lubin.
Set Decoration: Janis Lubin.
Costume Design: Barbara Tfank.
Running Time: 108 minutes.

Main Cast: Peter Berg (Bud Miller), Kevin Dillon (Cpl. Mel Avakian), Arye Gross (Stan Shutzer), Ethan Hawke (Sergeant Will Knott), Gary Sinise (Vance 'Mother' Wilkins), Frank Whaley (Paul 'Father' Mundy), John C. McGinley (Major Griffin), Larry Joshua (Lieutenant Ware), David Jensen (Sergeant Hunt), Curt Lowens (Older German Soldier), Rachel Griffin (Janice), Tim Shoemaker (Eddie), Kelly Gately (Young German Soldier), Bill Osborn (American Sentry), Andre Lamal (German Soldier).

THE NIGHTMARE BEFORE CHRISTMAS (1993)

Production Company: Touchstone Pictures/Skellington Productions Inc.
Distributor: Buena Vista Pictures.
Director: Henry Selick.
Producers: Tim Burton and Denise Di Novi.
Co-Producer: Kathleen Gavin.
Associate Producers: Danny Elfman, Jill Jacobs, Diane Minter and Philip Lofaro.
Screenplay: Caroline Thompson, based on a story and characters by Tim Burton.
Director of Photography: Pete Kozachik.
Film Editing: Stan Webb.
Original Score: Danny Elfman.
Production Manager: Philip Lofaro.
Casting: Mary Gail Artz and Barbara Cohen.
Art Direction: Deane Taylor.
Running Time: 76 minutes.
Main Cast: Chris Sarandon (Voice of Jack Skellington), Danny Elfman (Singing Voice of Jack Skellington/Voice of Barrel/Voice of Clown with the Tear Away Face), Catherine O'Hara (Voice of Sally/Voice of Shock), William Hickey (Voice of Dr Finklestein), Glenn Shadix (Voice of Mayor), Paul Reubens (Voice of Lock), Ken Page (Voice of Oogie Boogie), Ed Ivory (Voice of Santa), Susan McBride (Voice of Big Witch/Voice of WWD), Debi Durst (Voice of Corpse Kid/Voice of Corpse Mom/Voice of Small Witch), Gregory Proops (Voice of Harlequin Demon/Voice of Devil/Voice of Sax Player), Kerry Katz (Voice of Man Under Stairs/Voice of Vampire/Voice of Corpse Dad), Randy Crenshaw (Voice of Mr Hyde/Voice of Behemoth/Voice of Vampire), Sherwood Ball (Voice of Mummy/Voice of Vampire), Carmen Twillie

(Voice of Undersea Gal/Voice of Man Under the Stairs), Glenn Walters (Voice of Wolfman), Mia Brown (Additional Voice), L. Peter Callender (Additional Voice), Ann Fraser (Additional Voice), Jennifer Levey (Additional Voice), Jesse McClurg (Additional Voice), John Morris (Additional Voice), Robert Olague (Additional Voice), Bobbi Page (Additional Voice), Elena Praskin (Additional Voice), Trampas Warman (Additional Voice), Judi Durand (Additional Voice), Doris Hess (Additional Voice), Daamen Krall (Additional Voice), Christina MacGregor (Additional Voice), David McCharen (Additional Voice), Gary Raff (Additional Voice), David J. Randolph (Additional Voice), Gary Schwartz (Additional Voice).

MIRACLE ON 34TH STREET (1994)

Production Company: Twentieth Century Fox / Hughes Entertainment.
Distributor: Twentieth Century Fox.
Director: Les Mayfield.
Producer: John Hughes.
Executive Producers: William S. Beasley and William Ryan.
Screenplay: John Hughes, from a screenplay by George Seaton and a story by Valentine Davies.
Original Score: Bruce Broughton.
Cinematography: Julio Macat.
Film Editing: Raja Gosnell.
Production Design: Doug Kraner.
Art Direction: Steve Arnold.
Set Decoration: Leslie E. Rollins.
Costume Design: Kathy O'Rear.
Running Time: 114 minutes.
Main Cast: Richard Attenborough (Kriss Kringle), Elizabeth Perkins (Dorey Walker), Dylan McDermott (Bryan Bedford), J.T. Walsh (Ed Collins), James Remar (Jack Duff), Jane Leeves (Alberta Leonard), Simon Jones (Mr Shellhammer), William Windom (C.F. Cole), Mara Wilson (Susan Walker), Robert Prosky (Judge Harper), Kathrine Narducci (Mother), Mary McCormack (Myrna Foy), Alvin Greenman (The Doorman), Allison Janney (The Woman), Greg Noonan (Commander Coulson), Byrne Piven (Dr Hunter), Peter Gerety (Cop), Jack McGee (Tony Falacchi), Joe Pentangelo (Bailiff), Mark Damiano II (Daniel), Casey Moses Wurzbach (Grandson), Jennifer Morrison (Den-

ice), Peter Siragusa (Cabbie), Samantha Krieger (Sami), Horatio Sanz (Orderly), Lisa Sparrman (Mrs Collins), Kimberly Smith (Court Clerk), Mike Bacarella (Santa), Harve Kolzow (Businessman), Bianca Rose Pucci (Little Girl), Jimmy Joseph Meglio (Little Boy), Hank Johnston (Boy), Margo Buchanan (Another Mother), Bill Buell (Band Director), Ron Beattie (Priest), Alexandra Michelle Stewart (Child), Paige Walker Leavell (Tricia), Rosanna Scotto (News Anchor), Michele Marsh (News Anchor), Joe Moskowitz (News Anchor), Lester Holt (Newscaster), Susie Park (Newscaster), Janet Kauss (Newscaster).

THE SANTA CLAUSE (1994)

Production Company: Walt Disney Pictures/Outlaw Productions/Hollywood Pictures.
Distributor: Buena Vista Pictures.
Director: John Pasquin.
Producers: Brian Reilly, Robert Newmyer and Jeffrey Silver.
Co-Producers: Caroline Baron and William W. Wilson III.
Associate Producers: Jennifer Billings and Susan E. Novick.
Executive Producers: Richard Baker, Rick Messina and James Miller.
Screenplay: Leo Benvenuti and Steve Rudnick.
Cinematography: Walt Lloyd.
Film Editing: Larry Bock.
Original Score: Michael Convertino.
Production Design: Carol Spier.
Casting: Renée Rousselot.
Art Direction: James McAteer.
Set Decoration: Elinor Rose Galbraith.
Costume Design: Carol Ramsey.
Running Time: 97 minutes.
Main Cast: Tim Allen (Scott Calvin/Santa Claus), Judge Reinhold (Dr Neil Miller), Wendy Crewson (Laura Calvin Miller), Eric Lloyd (Charlie Calvin), David Krumholtz (Bernard the Elf), Larry Brandenburg (Detective Nunzio), Mary Gross (Miss Daniels), Paige Tamada (Judy the Elf), Peter Boyle (Mr Whittle), Judith Scott (Susan Perry), Jayne Eastwood (Judy the Waitress), Melissa King (Sarah the Little Girl), Bradley Wentworth (Elf at North Pole), Azura Bates (Elf in Hangar), Joshua Satok (Larry the Elf), Joyce Guy (Principal Compton),

Jesse Collins (Ad Executive), Steve Vinovich (Dr Pete Novos), Aimee McIntyre (Ruth), Tabitha Lupie (Future Ballet Girl), Dennis O'Connor (Mailman), David Sparrow (Bobby's Dad), Ron Hartmann (Judge G. Whelan), Nic Knight (Quintin), Scott Wickware (Officer Malone), Gene Mack (Officer Newman).

TRAPPED IN PARADISE (1994)

Production Company: Twentieth Century Fox/Permut Presentations.
Distributor: Twentieth Century Fox.
Director: George Gallo.
Producers: Jon Davison and George Gallo.
Co-Producers: David Coatsworth and Ellen Erwin.
Executive Producer: David Permut.
Screenplay: George Gallo.
Original Music: Robert Folk.
Director of Photography: Jack N. Green.
Film Editing: Terry Rawlings.
Art Direction: Gregory P. Keen.
Set Decoration: Gordon Sim.
Production Design: Bob Ziembicki.
Costume Design: Mary E. McLeod.
Running Time: 111 minutes.
Main Cast: Nicolas Cage (Bill Firpo), Richard B. Shull (Father Ritter), Jon Lovitz (Dave Firpo), Dana Carvey (Alvin Firpo), Jack Heller (Chief Parole Officer), Mike Steiner (Monty Dealer), Greg Ellwand (Cop #1), Kirk Dunn (Cop #2), Blanca Jansuzian (Shopkeeper), Florence Stanley (Ma Firpo), Cherie Ewing (Woman in Restaurant), Jeff Levine (Man in Restaurant), Sandra Myers (Diner #1), Frank Berardino (Diner #4), Mabel (Merlin), Sarge (Merlin), Paul Lazar (Deputy Timmy Burnell), Andrew Miller (Deputy Myers), Sean McCann (Chief Burnell), Gerard Parkes (Father Gorenzel), Madchen Amick (Sarah Collins), Donald Moffat (Clifford Anderson), Frank Blanch (Rutag Guard), John Ashton (Ed Dawson), John Bergantine (Clovis Minor), Angela Paton (Hattie Anderson), Vivian Reis (Lila), Bernard Behrens (Doc Milgrom), Bunty Webb (Hertha Wayerhauser), Kay Hawtrey (Rose Weyerhauser), Vic Manni (Vic Mazzucci), Frank Pesce (Caesar Spinoza), Vic Noto (Inmate #1), Nicky 'Pops' Anest (Inmate #2), Rocco Savastano (Inmate #3), George 'Aggie' Anest (Inmate #4), George Gal-

lo Sr. (Don Vito), Al Cerullo (Helicopter Pilot), James W. Evangelatos (Agent #2), Richard Jenkins (Agent Peyser), Jonathan Allore (Agent Boyle), Mark Melymick (Agent Cooper), Scott Wickware (Agent Giardello), Sean O'Bryan (Dick Anderson), Zoe Erwin (Marla Anderson), Tripod (Tripod), John Dawe (Newscaster), Marcia Bennett (Bus Station Clerk), Brett Miller (State Trooper), Richard McMillan (Agent #1), Robert Thomas (Agent #3), Pierre Larocque (Trucker #1), Tom McCleary (Trucker #2), Bill Currie (Bus Driver).

MIXED NUTS (1994)

Production Company: TriStar Pictures.
Distributor: TriStar Pictures.
Director: Nora Ephron.
Producers: Joseph Hartwick, Paul Junger Witt and Tony Thomas.
Co-Producer: John L. Solomon.
Executive Producers: Delia Ephron and James W. Skotchdopole.
Screenplay: Nora Ephron and Delia Ephron.
Original Music: George Fenton.
Director of Photography: Sven Nykvist.
Film Editing: Robert Reitano.
Art Direction: Dennis Bradford.
Set Decoration: George DeTitta Jr.
Production Design: Bill Groom.
Costume Design: Jeffrey Kurland.
Running Time: 97 minutes.
Main Cast: Steve Martin (Philip), Madeline Kahn (Mrs Munchnik), Robert Klein (Mr Lobel), Anthony LaPaglia (Felix), Juliette Lewis (Gracie), Rob Reiner (Dr Kinsky), Adam Sandler (Louie), Liev Schreiber (Chris), Rita Wilson (Catherine), Parker Posey (Rollerblader), Jon Stewart (Rollerblader), Joely Fisher (Susan), Steven Randazzo (Detective), Christine Cavanaugh (Police Officer), Henry Brown (Police Officer), Garry Shandling (Stanley), Steven Wright (Man at Pay Phone), Brian Markinson (Policeman/Voice of Obscene Caller), Caroline Aaron (Voice of Hotline Caller), Mary Gross (Voice of Hotline Caller), Mary Kelly (Voice of Hotline Caller), Donald L. Lee Jr. (Voice of Hotline Caller), Victor Garber (Voice of Irate Neighbor), Sidney Armus (Chris' Father), Michele Singer (Vanessa), Haley Joel Osment (Little Boy), Diane Sokolow (Chris' Mother), Michael

Badalucco (AAA Driver), Joann Lamneck (Woman Doctor), France Iann (Nurse), Jacqueline Murphy (Nurse).

THE REF (1994)

Production Company: Touchstone Pictures/Don Simpson/Jerry Bruckheimer Films.
Distributor: Buena Vista Pictures.
Director: Ted Demme.
Producers: Ron Bozman, Richard LaGravenese and Jeff Weiss.
Executive Producers: Jerry Bruckheimer and Don Simpson.
Screenplay: Richard LaGravenese and Marie Weiss, from a story by Marie Weiss.
Original Music: David A. Stewart.
Director of Photography: Adam Kimmel.
Production Design: Dan Davis
Film Editing: Jeffrey Wolf.
Art Direction: Dennis Davenport.
Set Decoration: Jaro Dick.
Costume Design: Judianna Makovcky.
Running Time: 97 minutes.
Main Cast: Denis Leary (Gus), Judy Davis (Caroline), Kevin Spacey (Lloyd), Robert J. Steinmiller Jr. (Jesse), Glynis Johns (Rose), Raymond J. Barry (Huff), Richard Bright (Murray), Christine Baranski (Connie), Adam LeFevre (Gary), Phillip Nicoll (John), Ellie Raab (Mary), Bill Raymond (George), John Scurti (Steve), Jim Turner (Phil), Herbie Ade (Bartender), Ron Gabriel (Limo Driver), Scott Walker (Prosecutor), Edward Saxon (Reporter), Donna Holgate (Newscaster), Kenneth Utt (Jeremiah Willard), Marilyn Stonehouse (Store Cashier), Victoria Mitchell (Store Customer), Cort Day (Salvation Army Volunteer), Robert Ridgely (Bob Burley), Charles Kerr (Town Citizen), Derek Keurvorst (Town Citizen), Caroline Yeager (Town Citizen), J.K. Simmons (Siskel), Max Piersig (Cadet), Victor Erdos (Cadet), John Benjamin Hickey (Old Baybrook Policeman), James Burke (Old Baybrook Policeman), Chris Phillips (Old Baybrook Policeman), Stephen Hunter (Old Baybrook Policeman).

THE PREACHER'S WIFE (1996)

Production Company: Touchstone Pictures/The Samuel Goldwyn Company/Mundy Lane Entertainment/Parkway Productions.

Distributor: Buena Vista Pictures.

Director: Penny Marshall.

Producer: Samuel Goldwyn Jr.

Co-Producers: Timothy M. Bourne, Debra Martin Chase and Amy Lemisch.

Associate Producer: Bonnie Hlinomaz.

Executive Producers: Elliot Abbott and Robert Greenhut.

Screenplay: Nat Mauldin and Allan Scott, from an earlier screenplay by Robert E. Sherwood and Leonardo Bercovici and a novel by Robert Nathan.

Original Music: Hans Zimmer.

Director of Photography: Miroslav Ondricek.

Film Editing: George Bowers and Stephen A. Rotter.

Production Design: Bill Groom.

Art Direction: Dennis Bradford.

Set Decoration: George DeTitta.

Costume Design: Cynthia Flynt.

Running Time: 124 minute.

Main Cast: Denzel Washington (Dudley), Whitney Houston (Julia Biggs), Courtney B. Vance (Reverend Henry Biggs), Gregory Hines (Joe Hamilton), Jenifer Lewis (Margueritte Coleman), Loretta Devine (Beverly), Justin Pierre Edmund (Jeremiah Biggs), Lionel Richie (Britsloe), Paul Bates (Saul Jeffreys), Lex Monson (Osbert), Darvel Davis Jr. (Hakim), William James Stiggers Jr. (Billy Eldridge), Marcella Lowery (Anna Eldridge), Cissy Houston (Mrs Havergal), Aaron A. McConnaughey (Teen), Shyheim Franklin (Teen), Taral Hicks (Teen), Kennan Scott (Teen), Jernard Burks (Pizza Man), Michael Alexander Jackson (Robber), Jamie Tirelli (Liquor Store Owner), Shari Headley (Arlene Chattan), Lizan Mitchell (Judge), Robert Colston (Bailiff), Victor Williams (Robbie), Juliehera Destefano (Receptionist), Charlotte d'Amboise (Debbie Paige), Delores Mitchell (Mary Halford), David Langston Smyrl (Hanley's Waiter), Harsh Nayyar (Christmas Tree Man), Mervyn Warren (Pianist), Roy Haynes (Drummer), George Coleman (Sax Player), Ted Dunbar (Guitar Player), Jamil Nasser (Bass Player), Helmar Augustus Cooper (Johnson Keeley), Mary Bond Davis (Bernita), Toukie Smith (Teleprompter Operator).

JINGLE ALL THE WAY (1996)

Production Company: 1492 Pictures/Twentieth Century Fox.
Distributor: Twentieth Century Fox.
Director: Brian Levant.
Producers: Michael Barnathan, Chris Columbus and Mark Radcliffe.
Associate Producers: Paula DuPré Pesmen and Warren Zide.
Co-Producer: James Mulay.
Executive Producer: Richard Vane.
Screenplay: Randy Kornfield.
Original Score: David Newman.
Cinematography: Victor J. Kemper.
Film Editing: Kent Beyda, Wilton Henderson and Adam Weiss.
Art Direction: Thomas Fichter.
Supervising Art Director: Tony Fanning.
Production Design: Leslie McDonald.
Set Decoration: John Anderson and Ronald R. Reiss.
Costume Design: Jay Hurley.
Casting: Judy Taylor.
Running Time: 89 minutes.
Main Cast: Arnold Schwarzenegger (Howard Langston), Sinbad (Myron
    Larabee), Phil Hartman (Ted Maltin), Rita Wilson (Liz Langston),
    Robert Conrad (Officer Hummell), Martin Mull (D.J.), Jake Lloyd
    (Jamie Langston), James Belushi (Mall Santa), E.J. de la Pena (Johnny),
    Laraine Newman (First Lady), Justin Chapman (Billy), Harvey Korman
    (President), Richard Moll (Dementor), Daniel Riordan (Turbo Man),
    Jeff Deist (T.V. Booster/Puppeteer), Nada Despotovich (Margaret),
    Ruth Afton Hjelmgren (Single Mother Judy), Caroline Kaiser (Single
    Mother Mary), Samuel B. Morris (Sensei), Shawn Hamilton (Sensei
    Assistant), Lewis Dauber (Toy Store Manager), Bill Schoppert (Father
    at Toy Store), Courtney Goodell (Little Girl at Toy Store), George
    Fisher (Daring Shopper), Chris Parnell (Toy Store Sales Clerk), Patrick
    Richwood (Toy Store Co-Worker), Kate McGregor-Stewart (Toy
    Store Customer), Marcus Toji (Little Boy with Car Remote), Steve
    Hendrickson (Father on Phone #1), Mo Collins (Mother on Phone),
    Peter Syvertsen (Father on Phone #2), John Rothman (Mall Toy Store
    Manager), Christopher Slater (Mall Toy Store Employee #1), Robert
    Southgate (Mall Toy Store Employee #2), Allison Benner (Toddler),
    Hayley Benner (Toddler), Sandra K. Horner (Toddler's Angry Mom),
    Phyllis Wright (Angry Mom #2), Marvette Knight (Angry Mom #3),

Danny Woodburn (Tony the Elf), Bruce Bohne (Santa at Warehouse Door), Paul 'The Giant' Wight (Huge Santa), Ron Gene Browne (Santa in Warehouse), Robert Tee Clark (Santa in Warehouse), James Riddle (Santa in Warehouse), Bill Wilson (Santa in Warehouse), Alan Blumenfeld (Cop at Santa's Warehouse), Traci Christofore (Little Girl Petting Reindeer), Sandy Thomas (Mother in Neighborhood), Martin Ruben (Father in Neighborhood), Nick La Tour (Counterman), Peter Breitmayer (Sparky), Marianne Muellerleile (Tow Truck Driver), Phil Morris (Gale Force), Amy Pietz (Liza Tisch), Judy Sladky (Snoopy), Walter von Huene (Taxi Driver), Steve Van Wormer (Turbo Man Float Parade Worker), Curtis Armstrong (Chain Smoking Booster), Jim Meskimen (Police Officer at Parade), Martin Valinsky (Police Officer Escorting Myron), Rochelle Vallese (Girl at Parade), Deena Driskill (Barbie), Spencer Klein (Kid in Turbo Man Commercial), Danny Pritchett (Kid in Turbo Man Commercial).

I'LL BE HOME FOR CHRISTMAS (1998)

Production Company: Walt Disney Pictures/Mandeville Films/Kyra Productions.
Director: Arlene Sanford.
Producers: David Hoberman and Tracey Trench.
Co-Producer: Justis Greene.
Executive Producer: Robin French.
Screenplay: Tom Nursall and Harris Goldberg, from a story by Michael Allin.
Original Music: John Debney.
Director of Photography: Hiro Narita.
Film Editing: Anita Brandt-Burgoyne.
Production Design: Cynthia Charette.
Costume Design: Maya Mani.
Art Decoration: Alexander Cochrane.
Set Decoration: Lin MacDonald.
Running Time: 86 minutes.
Main Cast: Jonathan Taylor Thomas (Jake), Jessica Biel (Allie), Adam LaVorgna (Eddie), Gary Cole (Jake's Dad), Eve Gordon (Carolyn), Lauren Maltby (Tracey), Andrew Lauer (Nolan), Sean O'Bryan (Max), Lesley Boone (Marjorie), Amzie Strickland (Tom Tom Girl Mary), Natalie Barish (Tom Tom Girl Darlene), Mark De La Cruz

(Esteban), Kathleen Freeman (Tom Tom Girl Gloria), Jack Kenny (Gabby), Celia Kushner (Tom Tom Girl Mama), Blair Slater (Ian), P.J. Prinslow (The Brandt-Man), Kevin Hansen (The Murph-Man), James Sherry (The Ken-Man), Alexandra Mitchell (Little Girl in Hospital), Eric Pospisil (Little Boy at Bus Station), Cathy Weseluk (Wendy Richards), Peter Kelamis (Conway The Bus Driver), Betty Linde (Older Lady On The Bus), Awaovieyi Agie (Service Man), Brendan Beiser (Bellhop), Graeme Kingston (Pizza Eating Santa), Ian Robison (Mayor Wilson), Ernie Jackson (Kenyan Santa), Kurt Max Runte (Taxi Driver), Nicole Oliver (Ticket Agent), Tasha Simms (Parade Manager), Dmitry Chepovetsky (Angel), Delores Drake (Fraulein Maid), Chris Willis (Race Official), Nick Misura (Groundskeeper), Mark Acheson (Sandwich Passenger), Bart Anderson (Turf 'n' Turf Customer #1), J.B. Biven (Port-a-Potty Santa), Annette Dreeshen (Nose Strip Girl), Manami Hari (Edelbruck Clerk), Tom Heaton (Turf 'n' Turf Customer #2), Sarah May (Sierra), Alexander Milani (Wet Lap Boy), Ron Timms (Party Guy), David Neale (Running Santa), Paul Norman (Hick on Bus), Michael P. Northey (Freight Handler), Eileen Pedde (Turf 'n' Turf Customer #3), Melissa Barker Sauer (Teenage Mom on Bus), Mike Battie (Santa on Stilts).

Bibliography

Agajanian, Rowana, '"Peace on Earth, Goodwill to All Men": The Depiction of Christmas in Modern Hollywood Films', in *Christmas at the Movies: Images of Christmas in American, British and European Cinema*, ed. by Mark Connelly (London: I.B. Tauris, 2000), pp.143-164.

Aiello, Danny, with Gil Reavill, *I Only Know Who I Am When I Am Somebody Else: My Life on the Street, on the Stage and in the Movies* (New York: Gallery Books, 2014).

Aldgate, Anthony, and Jeffrey Richards, *Best of British: Cinema and Society from 1930 to the Present* (London: I.B. Tauris, 2002).

Allon, Yoram, Del Cullen and Hannah Patterson, eds, *Contemporary British and Irish Film Directors: A Wallflower Critical Guide* (London: Wallflower Press, 2001).

—, eds, *Contemporary North American Film Directors: A Wallflower Critical Guide* (London: Wallflower Press, 2000).

Ames, Caroline, '*All I Want for Christmas* (1991) Review', in *Let's Go to the Movies*, 17 December 2013.
<*https://letsgotothemovies.co.uk/2013/12/17/all-i-want-for-christmas-1991-review/*>

Anon., 'Whitney Houston, Denzel Washington, Courtney B. Vance and Jenifer Lewis Star in *The Preacher's Wife*', in *Jet*, Vol.91, No.5, 16 December 1996, pp.58-62.

Ansen, David, 'Movies: Tim Burton Looks at Holiday Hell', in *Newsweek*, 31 October 1993.
<*https://www.newsweek.com/movies-tim-burton-looks-holiday-hell-194070*>

Arnold, Jeremy, *Christmas in the Movies: 30 Classics to Celebrate the Season* (New York: Hachette Book Group, 2018).

Ashby, Justine, and Andrew Higson, eds., *British Cinema, Past and Present* (London: Routledge, 2000).

Attebery, Brian, *Stories About Stories: Fantasy and the Remaking of Myth* (Oxford: Oxford University Press, 2014).

Austin, Joe, and Michael Nevin Willard, eds, *Generations of Youth: Youth Cultures and History in Twentieth-Century America* (New York: New York University Press, 1998).

Avins, Mimi, 'Ghoul World', in *Tim Burton: Interviews*, ed. by Kristian Fraga (Jackson: University Press of Mississippi, 2005), pp.95-101.

Babington, Bruce, and Peter William Evans, *Biblical Epics: Sacred Narrative in the Hollywood Cinema* (Manchester: Manchester University Press, 1993).

Baker, Neil, 'Seven Underrated Christmas Movies', in *Cinerama Film*, 12 December 2020.
<*https://cineramafilm.com/2020/12/12/eight-underrated-christmas-movies/#h-all-i-want-for-christmas-1991*>

Barnes, Harper, '*The Nightmare Before Christmas*', in *The St Louis Post-Dispatch*, 22 October 1993, p.3.

Baumgarten, Marjorie, '*All I Want for Christmas*', in *The Austin Chronicle*, 8 November 1991.
<*https://www.austinchronicle.com/events/film/1991-11-08/139224/*>

—, '*The Nightmare Before Christmas*', in *The Austin Chronicle*, 29 October 1993.
<*https://www.austinchronicle.com/events/film/1993-10-29/140073/*>

Berardinelli, James, '*A Midnight Clear*', in *ReelViews*, 20 December 2018.
<*https://www.reelviews.net/reelviews/midnight-clear-a*>

—, '*Jingle All the Way*', in *ReelViews*, 22 November 1996.

<https://www.reelviews.net/reelviews/jingle-all-the-way>

—, '*Mixed Nuts*', in *ReelViews*, 21 December 1994.
<https://www.reelviews.net/reelviews/mixed-nuts>

—, '*The Preacher's Wife*', in *ReelViews*, 13 December 1996.
<https://www.reelviews.net/reelviews/preacher-s-wife-the>

—, '*The Ref*', in *ReelViews*, 11 March 1994.
<https://www.reelviews.net/reelviews/ref-the>

—, '*The Santa Clause*', in *ReelViews*, 11 November 1994.
<https://www.reelviews.net/reelviews/santa-clause-the>

Bishop, John, '*A Midnight Clear + Inside Monkey Zetterland*', in *Mind of Frames*, 25 March 2015.
<https://mind-of-frames.blogspot.com/2015/03/a-midnight-clear-inside-monkey.html>

Bohm-Duchen, Monica, *The Private Life of a Masterpiece* (Berkeley: University of California Press, 2001).

Booker, M. Keith, *Disney, Pixar, and the Hidden Messages of Children's Films* (Santa Barbara: Praeger, 2010).

Bradshaw, Peter, '*Home Alone* review: 1990 Christmas cracker resurfaces', in *The Guardian*, 30 November 2018.
<https://www.theguardian.com/film/2018/nov/30/home-alone-review-yuletide-rerelease>

—, '*The Muppet Christmas Carol* Review: Michael Caine shows spirit in magical extravaganza', in *The Guardian*, 29 November 2017.
<https://www.theguardian.com/film/2017/nov/29/the-muppet-christmas-carol-review-michael-caine-kermit-miss-piggy>

Browne, Ray B., and Glenn J. Browne, *Laws of Our Fathers: Popular Culture and the U.S. Constitution* (Bowling Green: Bowling Green State University Popular Press, 1986).

—, and Pat Browne, *The Guide to United States Popular Culture* (Madison: University of Wisconsin Press, 2001).

Bruce, Pamela, '*The Muppet Christmas Carol*', in *The Austin Chronicle*, 11 December 1992.
<*https://www.austinchronicle.com/events/film/1992-12-11/the-muppet-christmas-carol/*>

Brunson, Matt, 'Ho-Ho-No: The Worst Christmas Movies of All Time', in *Film Frenzy*, 22 December 2018.
<*https://thefilmfrenzy.com/2018/12/22/ho-ho-no-the-worst-christmas-movies-of-all-time/*>

Canby, Vincent, 'Review/Film: *A Midnight Clear*, War Recalled as Surreal Muddle', in *The New York Times*, 24 April 1992.
<*https://www.nytimes.com/1992/04/24/movies/review-film-a-midnight-clear-war-recalled-as-a-surreal-muddle.html*>

Catcher, Jessica, '12 Awesome Facts You Didn't Know About the Original *Miracle on 34th Street*', in *ViralNova*, 12 December 2014.
<*http://www.viralnova.com/miracle-34-trivia/*>

Chacona, Hollis, '*I'll Be Home for Christmas*', in *The Austin Chronicle*, 20 November 1998.
<*https://www.austinchronicle.com/events/film/1998-11-20/142259/*>

—, '*Miracle on Thirty-Fourth Street*', in *The Austin Chronicle*, 18 November 1994.
<*https://www.austinchronicle.com/events/film/1994-11-18/138400/*>

—, '*Mixed Nuts*', in *The Austin Chronicle*, 6 January 1995.
<*https://www.austinchronicle.com/events/film/1995-01-06/mixed-nuts/*>

—, '*The Santa Clause*', in *The Austin Chronicle*, 18 November 1994.
<*https://www.austinchronicle.com/events/film/1994-11-18/the-santa-clause/*>

Chapman, James, 'God Bless Us, Every One: Movie Adaptations of *A Christmas Carol*', in *Christmas at the Movies*, ed. by Mark Connelly (London: I.B. Tauris, 2000), pp.9-37.

Chard, Holly, *Mainstream Maverick: John Hughes and New Hollywood Cinema* (Austin: University of Texas Press, 2020).

Chin, Jeremiah, '*Jingle All The Way: Family Fun Edition*', in *DVD Compare*, 2 March 2009.
<*https://dvdcompare.net/review.php?rid=975*>

Coffel, Chris, 'The Tao of Nicolas Cage: *Trapped in Paradise*', in *Film School Rejects*, 23 December 2016.
<*https://filmschoolrejects.com/the-tao-of-nicolas-cage-trapped-in-paradise-206546a5c80c/*>

Collins, Ace, *Stories Behind the Great Traditions of Christmas* (Grand Rapids: Zondervan, 2003).

Connelly, Mark, ed., *Christmas at the Movies* (London: I.B. Tauris, 2000).

—, 'Santa Claus: The Movie', in *Christmas at the Movies*, ed. by Mark Connelly (London: I.B. Tauris, 2000), pp.115-134.

Cook, David C., *The Inspirational Christmas Almanac: Heartwarming Traditions, Trivia, Stories, and Recipes for the Holidays* (Colorado Springs: Honor Books, 2006).

Cooper, Jeanne, '*Home Alone*', in *The Washington Post*, 16 November 1990.
<*https://www.washingtonpost.com/wp-srv/style/longterm/movies/videos/homealonepgcooper_a09ecc.htm*>

Corliss, Richard, 'A Sweet and Scary Treat: *The Nightmare Before Christmas* spins a fun-house fantasy for two holidays', in *Time*, 11 October 1993.
<*https://content.time.com/time/subscriber/article/0,33009,979351-2,00.html*>

Cracknell, Ryan, '*All I Want for Christmas*', in *Movie Views*, 10 December 2003.
<*http://movieviews.ca/all-i-want-for-christmas*>

—, '*Jingle All the Way*', in *Movie Views*, 5 December 2003.

<*https://movieviews.ca/jingle-all-the-way*>

—, '*Miracle on 34th Street* (1994)', in *Movie Views*, 13 December 2003.
<*https://movieviews.ca/miracle-on-34th-street-1994*>

—, '*The Ref*', in *Movie Views*, 19 December 2003.
<*https://movieviews.ca/the-ref*>

Crouse, Richard, *The 100 Best Movies You've Never Seen* (Toronto: ECW Press, 2003).

Crump, William D., *The Christmas Encyclopedia*, 3rd edn (Jefferson: McFarland and Company, 2013).

Cruz-Tan, Zachary, '*The Santa Clause* (1994)', in *The Critical Reel*, 26 November 2014.
<*http://thecriticalreel.com/the-santa-clause-1994/*>

D'Angelo, Mike, '*A Midnight Clear*', in *AV Club*, 27 December 2010.
<*https://www.avclub.com/a-midnight-clear-1798223380*>

D'Ecca, Artemisia, *Keeping Christmas Well* (Dublin: Phaeton Publishing, 2012).

Dance, Liz, *Nora Ephron: Everything is Copy* (Jefferson: McFarland, 2015).

Davis, Hugh H., 'A Weirdo, a Rat and a Humbug: The Literary Qualities of *The Muppet Christmas Carol*', in *Studies in Popular Culture*, Vol. 2, No. 3, April 1999, 95-105.

Davis, Steve, '*Trapped in Paradise*', in *The Austin Chronicle*, 9 December 1994.
<*https://www.austinchronicle.com/events/film/1994-12-09/trapped-in-paradise/*>

Deacy, Christopher, *Faith in Film: Religious Themes in Contemporary Cinema* (Aldershot: Ashgate Publishing, 2005).

Denby, David, 'Getting Serious', in *New York Magazine*, 18 May 1992, p.55.

Detora, Lisa M., ed., *Heroes of Film, Comics and American Culture: Essays on Real and Fictional Defenders of Home* (Jefferson: McFarland, 2009).

Deutsch, James, '*A Midnight Clear*', in *War and American Popular Culture: A Historical Encyclopedia*, ed. by M. Paul Holsinger (Westport: Greenwood, 1999), pp.284-85.

deVillalvilla, Carlos, '*The Santa Clause*', in *Cinema365*, 24 December 2011. <*https://carlosdev.wordpress.com/2011/12/24/the-santa-clause/*>

DeVito, Carlo, *Inventing Scrooge: The Incredible True Story Behind Dickens' Legendary* A Christmas Carol (Kennebunkport: Cider Mill Press, 2017).

Dickens, Charles, *The Christmas Books* (Ware: Wordsworth Editions, 1995) [1852].

Docker, John, *Postmodernism and Popular Culture: A Cultural History* (Cambridge: Cambridge University Press, 1994).

Doidge, Kristin Marguerite, *Nora Ephron: A Biography* (Chicago: Chicago Review Press, 2022).

Donner, Claire, '*The Ref* (1994): Lookback/Review', in *Den of Geek*, 18 December 2012.
<*https://www.denofgeek.com/movies/the-ref-1994-lookbackreview/*>

Duralde, Alonso, *Have Yourself a Movie Little Christmas* (New York: Limelight Editions, 2010).

Ebert, Roger, '*29th Street*', in *The Chicago Sun-Times*, 1 November 1991.
<*https://www.rogerebert.com/reviews/29th-street-1991*>

—, '*A Midnight Clear*', in *The Chicago Sun-Times*, 1 May 1992.
<*https://www.rogerebert.com/reviews/a-midnight-clear-1992*>

—, '*All I Want for Christmas*', in *The Chicago Sun-Times*, 8 November 1991.
<*https://www.rogerebert.com/reviews/all-i-want-for-christmas-1991*>

—, '*Home Alone*', in *The Chicago Sun-Times*, 16 November 1990.
<*https://www.rogerebert.com/reviews/home-alone-1990*>

—, '*I'll Be Home for Christmas*', in *The Chicago Sun-Times*, 13 November 1998.
<*https://www.rogerebert.com/reviews/ill-be-home-for-christmas-1998*>

—, '*Jingle All the Way*', in *The Chicago Sun-Times*, 22 November 1996.
<*https://www.rogerebert.com/reviews/jingle-all-the-way-1996*>

—, '*Miracle on 34th Street*', in *The Chicago Sun-Times*, 18 November 1994.
<https://www.rogerebert.com/reviews/miracle-on-34th-street-1994>

—, '*Mixed Nuts*', in *The Chicago Sun-Times*, 21 December 1994.
<*https://www.rogerebert.com/reviews/mixed-nuts-1994*>

—, '*The Muppet Christmas Carol*', in *The Chicago Sun-Times*, 11 December 1992.
<*https://www.rogerebert.com/reviews/the-muppet-christmas-carol-1992*>

—, '*The Nightmare Before Christmas*', in *The Chicago Sun-Times*, 22 October 1993.
<*https://www.rogerebert.com/reviews/tim-burtons-the-nightmare-before-christmas-1993*>

—, '*The Preacher's Wife*', in *The Chicago Sun-Times*, 13 December 1996.
<*https://www.rogerebert.com/reviews/the-preachers-wife-1996*>

—, '*The Ref*', in *The Chicago Sun-Times*, 11 March 1994.
<*https://www.rogerebert.com/reviews/the-ref-1994*>

—, '*The Santa Clause*', in *The Chicago Sun-Times*, 11 November 1994.
<*https://www.rogerebert.com/reviews/the-santa-clause-1994*>

—, '*Trapped in Paradise*', in *The Chicago Sun-Times*, 2 December 1994.
<*https://www.rogerebert.com/reviews/trapped-in-paradise-1994*>

Ellis, John, *Visible Fictions: Cinema, Television, Video* (London: Routledge, 1989) [1982].

Errigo, Angie, '*Miracle on 34th Street* Review', in *Empire*, January 1995. <*https://www.empireonline.com/movies/reviews/miracle-34th-street-review/*>

Fairclough, Norman, *Critical Discourse Analysis: The Critical Study of Language* (Harlow, Longman: 1995).

Felton, Bruce, *What Were They Thinking?: Really Bad Ideas Throughout History*, rev. edn (Guilford: Lyons Press, 2007).

Fisher, Doug, '*29th Street*', in *Bohica*, 14 September 2015. <*https://movieguy1970.blogspot.com/2015/09/29th-street-1991-12.html*>

Fishwick, Marshall W., *Popular Culture in a New Age* (Binghampton: Haworth Press, 2002).

Forbes, Bruce David, *Christmas: A Candid History* (Berkeley: University of California Press, 2007).

Fraga, Kristian, ed., *Tim Burton: Interviews* (Jackson: University Press of Mississippi, 2005).

Francis, R.D., 'Exploring: Gangster Films Inspired by *GoodFellas*', in *B&S About Movies*, 20 November 2021. <*https://bandsaboutmovies.com/2021/11/20/exploring-gangster-films-inspired-by-goodfellas/*>

Frow, John, *Genre* (London: Routledge, 2006).

Gabbard, Glen O., and Krin Gabbard, *Psychiatry and the Cinema*, 2nd edn (Washington D.C.: American Psychiatric Press, 1999).

Garlen, Jennifer C., and Anissa M. Graham, eds, *Kermit Culture: Critical Perspectives on Jim Henson's Muppets* (Jefferson: McFarland and Company, 2009).

Garrett, Greg, *The Gospel According to Hollywood* (Louisville: Westminster John Knox Press, 2007).

Giddings, Robert, and Erica Sheen, eds, *The Classic Novel: From Page to Screen* (Manchester: Manchester University Press, 2000).

Glavin, John, ed., *Dickens on Screen* (Cambridge: Cambridge University Press, 2003).

Gleiberman, Owen, '*Home Alone*', in *Entertainment Weekly*, 25 July 2007.
<*https://ew.com/article/2007/07/25/home-alone-2/*>

—, 'Tim Burton's *The Nightmare Before Christmas*', in *Entertainment Weekly*, 7 August 2012.
<*https://ew.com/article/2012/08/07/tim-burtons-nightmare-christmas-2/*>

Green, Stanley, *Hollywood Musicals Year by Year*, 2nd edn, rev. by Elaine Schmidt (Milwaukee: Hal Leonard, 1999).

Guida, Fred, A Christmas Carol *and Its Adaptations: A Critical Examination of Dickens' Story and Its Productions on Stage, Screen and Television* (Jefferson: McFarland, 2000).

Guthmann, Edward, 'Film Review: Arnie Doesn't Ring Any Comedy Bells', in *The San Francisco Chronicle*, 22 November 1996.
<*https://www.sfgate.com/movies/article/FILM-REVIEW-Arnie-Doesn-t-Ring-Any-Comedy-2958581.php*>

Hales, Stephen D., 'Putting Claus Back into Christmas', in *Christmas: Philosophy for Everyone*, ed. by Scott C. Lowe (Chichester: Blackwell, 2010), pp.161-71.

Hallenbeck, Bruce G., *Comedy-Horror Films: A Chronological History, 1914-2008* (Jefferson: McFarland and Company, 2009).

Hardy, Phil, ed., *The Aurum Film Encyclopedia: Science Fiction* (London: Aurum Press, 1995).

Harrington, Richard, '*The Nightmare Before Christmas*', in *The Washington Post*, 22 October 1993.
<*https://www.washingtonpost.com/wp-srv/style/longterm/movies/videos/thenightmarebeforechristmaspgharrington_a0ab93.htm*>

Hartl, John, 'An Animation Dream – *Nightmare Before Christmas* is Visual Treat, But it Lacks Vision', in *The Seattle Times*, 22 October 1993. <*https://archive.seattletimes.com/archive/?date=19931022&slug=1727371*>

Hicks, Chris, 'Film review: *Home Alone*', in *Deseret News*, 21 November 2000. <*https://www.deseret.com/2000/11/21/20087760/film-review-home-alone*>

Hildebrand, Douglas, 'Les Mayfield', in *Contemporary North American Film Directors: A Wallflower Critical Guide*, ed. by Yoram Allon, Del Cullen, and Hannah Patterson (London: Wallflower Press, 2001) [2000].

Hill, John, and Pamela Church Gibson, eds, *The Oxford Guide to Film Studies* (Oxford: Oxford University Press, 1998).

Hinson, Hal, '*A Midnight Clear*', in *The Washington Post*, 1 May 1992. <*https://www.washingtonpost.com/wp-srv/style/longterm/movies/videos/amidnightclearrhinson_a0a76a.htm*>

—, '*Home Alone*', in *The Washington Post*, 16 November 1990. <*https://www.washingtonpost.com/wp-srv/style/longterm/movies/videos/homealonepghinson_a0a9b9.htm*>

—, '*Miracle on 34th Street*', in *The Washington Post*, 18 November 1994. <*https://www.washingtonpost.com/wp-srv/style/longterm/movies/videos/miracleon34thstreetpghinson_a0a86e.htm*>

—, '*Mixed Nuts*', in *The Washington Post*, 21 December 1994. <*https://www.washingtonpost.com/wp-srv/style/longterm/movies/videos/mixednutspg13hinson_a0a884.htm*>

—, 'The Ref', in *The Washington Post*, 12 March 1994. <*https://www.washingtonpost.com/wp-srv/style/longterm/movies/videos/therefrhinson_b009de.htm*>

—, '*Trapped in Paradise*', in *The Washington Post*, 2 December 1994. <*https://www.washingtonpost.com/wp-srv/style/longterm/movies/videos/trappedinparadisepg13hinson_c01357.htm*>

Hischak, Thomas S., *American Literature on Stage and Screen: 525 Works and Their Adaptations* (Jefferson: McFarland, 2012).

Hjort, Mette, and Scott MacKenzie, *Cinema and Nation* (London: Routledge, 2000).

Hoffman, Robert C., *Postcards from Santa Claus: Sights and Sentiments from the Last Century* (New York: Square One Publishers, 2002).

Hollows, Joanne, and Mark Jancovich, eds, *Approaches to Popular Film* (Manchester: Manchester University Press, 1995).

Holsinger, M. Paul, ed., *War and American Popular Culture: A Historical Encyclopedia* (Westport: Greenwood, 1999).

Honeycutt, Kirk, *John Hughes: A Life in Film* (New York: Race Point Publishing, 2015).

Horton, Andrew, *Laughing Out Loud: Writing the Comedy-Centred Screenplay* (Berkeley: University of California Press).

Howe, Desson, '*29th Street*', in *The Washington Post*, 1 November 1991. <https://www.washingtonpost.com/wp-srv/style/longterm/movies/videos/29thstreetrhowe_a0b356.htm>

—, '*All I Want for Christmas*', in *The Washington Post*, 8 November 1991. <https://www.washingtonpost.com/wp-srv/style/longterm/movies/videos/alliwantforchristmasghowe_a0ae7f.htm>

—, '*Miracle on 34th Street*', in *The Washington Post*, 18 November 1994. <https://www.washingtonpost.com/wp-srv/style/longterm/movies/videos/miracleon34thstreetpghowe_a0b090.htm>

—, '*The Muppet Christmas Carol*', in *The Washington Post*, 11 December 1992.
<https://www.washingtonpost.com/wp-srv/style/longterm/movies/videos/themuppetchristmascarolghowe_a0af54.htm>

—, '*The Preacher's Wife*: One Foot in Heaven', in *The Washington Post*, 13 December 1996.

<https://www.washingtonpost.com/wp-srv/style/longterm/review96/
preacherswifehowe.htm>

—, '*The Ref*', in *The Washington Post*, 11 March 1994.
<https://www.washingtonpost.com/wp-srv/style/longterm/movies/
videos/therefrhowe_a0b03a.htm>

—, '*The Santa Clause*', in *The Washington Post*, 11 November 1994.
<https://www.washingtonpost.com/wp-srv/style/longterm/movies/
videos/thesantaclausepghowe_a0b08e.htm>

—, '*Trapped in Paradise*', in *The Washington Post*, 2 December 1994.
<https://www.washingtonpost.com/wp-srv/style/longterm/movies/
videos/trappedinparadisepg13howe_a0b093.htm>

Hunter, Allan, ed., *The Wordsworth Book of Movie Classics* (Ware:
Wordsworth, 1996) [1992].

Iverem, Esther, '*The Preacher's Wife*: A Wan Sermon', in *The Washington
Post*, 12 December 1996.
<https://www.washingtonpost.com/wp-srv/style/longterm/review96/
preacherswifeiver.htm>

James, Caryn, 'Film Review: What Do You Say, Virginia?', in *The New
York Times*, 18 November 1994.
<https://www.nytimes.com/1994/11/18/movies/film-review-what-do-you-
say-virginia.html>

—, 'Review/Film: Holiday Black Comedy for Modern Children', in *The
New York Times*, 16 November 1990.
<https://www.nytimes.com/1990/11/16/movies/review-film-holiday-black-
comedy-for-modern-children.html>

—, 'Reviews/Film: *The Ref*: A Christmas That Upends Christmas', in *The
New York Times*, 9 March 1994.
<https://www.nytimes.com/1994/03/09/movies/reviews-film-the-ref-a-
christmas-that-upends-christmas.html>

Jeffers, H. Paul, *Legends of Santa Claus* (Minneapolis: Lerner Publishing
Group, 2001).

Johnston, Hank, and John A. Noakes, eds, *Frames of Protest: Social Movements and the Framing Perspective* (Oxford: Rowman and Littlefield, 2005).

Jones, Ken D., Arthur F. McClure and Alfred E. Twomey, *Character People* (New York: A.S. Barnes, 1977).

Jordan, Chris, *Movies and the Reagan Presidency: Success and Ethics* (Westport: Praeger, 2003).

Kalaga, Wojciech H., and Marzena Kubisz, eds, *Multicultural Dilemmas: Identity, Difference, Otherness* (Frankfurt am Main: Peter Lang, 2008).

Kehr, Dave, '*Home Alone*', in *The Chicago Tribune*, 16 November 1990. <*https://www.chicagotribune.com/ct-home-alone-review-1990-20150929-story.html*>

Kemp, Philip, '*The Muppet Christmas Carol*', in *Sight and Sound*, February 1993.
<*https://www2.bfi.org.uk/news-opinion/sight-sound-magazine/reviews-recommendations/muppet-christmas-carol-deconstructed-dickins*>

Kempley, Rita, '*All I Want for Christmas*', in *The Washington Post*, 8 November 1991.
<*https://www.washingtonpost.com/wp-srv/style/longterm/movies/videos/alliwantforchristmasgkempley_a0a27d.htm*>

Klady, Leonard, '*Miracle on 34th Street*', in *Variety*, 6 November 1994. <*https://variety.com/1994/film/reviews/miracle-on-34th-street-2-1200439489/*>

—, '*The Santa Clause*', in *Variety*, 10 November 1994. <*https://variety.com/1994/film/reviews/the-santa-clause-1200439443/*>

Knapp, Raymond, *The American Musical and the Performance of Personal Identity* (Princeton & Oxford: Princeton University Press, 2006).

Langford, Barry, *Post-Classical Hollywood: Film Industry, Style and Ideology Since 1945* (Edinburgh: Edinburgh University Press, 2010).

LaSalle, Mick, '*I'll Be Home* Travels Far on Holiday Spirit', in *The San Francisco Chronicle*, 13 November 1998.
<*https://www.sfgate.com/movies/article/I-ll-Be-Home-Travels-Far-on-Holiday-Spirit-2979100.php*>

Lee, Shayne, *Cinema, Black Suffering, and Theodicy: Modern God* (Lanham: Lexington Books, 2022).

Leitch, Thomas M., *Film Adaptation and Its Discontents: From* Gone with the Wind *to* The Passion of the Christ (Baltimore: Johns Hopkins University Press, 2007).

Lester, Meera, *Why Does Santa Wear Red?... and 100 Other Christmas Curiosities Unwrapped* (Avon: Adams Media, 2007).

Levi, Ross D., *The Celluloid Courtroom: A History of Legal Cinema* (Westport: Greenwood Publishing Group, 2005).

Lewis, Morgan R., '*Trapped in Paradise*', in *Morgan on Media*, 8 December 2013.
<*https://morganrlewis.wordpress.com/2013/12/08/trapped-in-paradise/*>

Liebman, Lisa, 'Film: The Gentle Art of Creating a Family Film', *The New York Times*, 27 November 1994.
<*https://www.nytimes.com/1994/11/27/movies/film-the-gentle-art-of-creating-a-family-film.html*>

Linville, Susan E., *History Films, Women, and Freud's Uncanny* (Austin: University of Texas Press, 2004).

Long, Mike, '*The Muppet Christmas Carol*', in *DVD Sleuth*, 8 November 2012.
<*https://www.dvdsleuth.com/MuppetChristmasCarolReview/*>

—, '*The Nightmare Before Christmas*', in *DVD Sleuth*, 26 August 2008.
<*https://www.dvdsleuth.com/NightmareBeforeChristmasReview/*>

—, '*The Santa Clause Trilogy* (1994-2006)', in *DVD Sleuth*, 16 October 2012.
<*https://www.dvdsleuth.com/TheSantaClauseTrilogyReview/*>

Loukides, Paul, and Linda K. Fuller, eds, *Beyond the Stars: Plot Conventions in American Popular Film* (Bowling Green: Bowling Green State University Popular Press, 1991).

—, eds, *Beyond the Stars: Studies in American Popular Film Volume 5: Themes and Ideologies in American Popular Film* (Madison: Popular Press, 1996).

Lowe, Scott C., ed., *Christmas: Philosophy for Everyone* (Chichester: Blackwell, 2010).

Mackenzie, Michael, '*Home Alone: Family Fun Edition* Review', in *DVD Times*, 1 December 2006.
<*https://www.thedigitalfix.com/film/dvd_review/home-alone-family-fun-edition/*>

Magala, Slawomir, *Cross-Cultural Competence* (Abingdon: Routledge, 2005).

Mansour, David J., *From Abba to Zoom: A Pop Culture Encyclopedia of the Late 20th Century* (Kansas City: Andrews McMeel Publishing, 2005).

Marling, Karal Ann, *Merry Christmas!: Celebrating America's Greatest Holiday* (Cambridge: Harvard University Press, 2001) [2000].

Maslin, Janet, 'Film Review: 3 Mismatched Brothers in a Small-Town Caper', in *The New York Times*, 2 December 1994.
<*https://www.nytimes.com/1994/12/02/movies/film-review-3-mismatched-brothers-in-a-small-town-caper.html*>

—, 'Film Review: Hysterics All Dressed Up for the Holidays', in *The New York Times*, 21 December 1994.
<*https://www.nytimes.com/1994/12/21/movies/film-review-hysterics-all-dressed-up-for-the-holidays.html*>

—, 'Review/Film: Kermit, Etc. Do Dickens Up Green', in *The New York Times*, 11 December 1992.
<*https://www.nytimes.com/1992/12/11/movies/review-film-kermit-etc-do-dickens-up-green.html*>

Matthews, Kevin, '*Jingle All the Way* (1996)', in *FlickFeast*, 13 December 2011.
<*https://www.flickfeast.co.uk/reviews/film-reviews/jingle-1996/*>

—, '*Miracle on 34th Street* (1994)', in *FlickFeast*, 23 December 2011.
<*https://www.flickfeast.co.uk/reviews/film-reviews/miracle-34th-street-1994/*>

McCarthy, Todd, '*Trapped in Paradise*', in *Variety*, 4 December 1994.
<*https://variety.com/1994/film/reviews/trapped-in-paradise-1200439821/*>

McEwen, John R., '*I'll Be Home for Christmas*' in *Film Quips Online*, 13 November 1998.
<*http://www.filmquipsonline.com/illbehomeforchristmas.html*>

McGee, Patrick, *Cinema, Theory, and Political Responsibility in Contemporary Culture* (Cambridge: Cambridge University Press, 1997).

Mechling, Jay, 'Rethinking (and Reteaching) the Civil Religion in Post-Nationalist American Studies', in *Post-Nationalist American Studies*, ed. by John Carlos Rowe (Berkeley: University of California Press, 2000), pp.63-80.

Miller, Toby, and Robert Stam, eds., *A Companion to Film Theory* (Oxford: Blackwell, 2004) [1999].

Mitchell, Jeremy, and Richard Maidment, eds., *The United States in the Twentieth Century: Culture* (London: Hodder and Stoughton, 1994).

Moore, Kenneth, *The Magic of 'Santa Claus': More Than Just a Red Suit!* (Martinez: Ken Moore Productions, 2006).

Munby, Jonathan, 'A Hollywood Carol's Wonderful Life', in *Christmas at the Movies: Images of Christmas in American, British and European Cinema*, ed. by Mark Connelly (London: I.B. Tauris, 2000), pp.39-57.

Murphy, Robert, ed., *The British Cinema Book*, 2nd edn (London: British Film Institute, 2001).

Murray, Noel, '*Home Alone*', in *A V Club*, 13 December 2006.

<https://www.avclub.com/home-alone-1798202206>

Nash, Jay, *The Encyclopedia of Best Films: A Century of all the Finest Movies: Volume 4* (New York & London: Rowman and Littlefield, 2019).

Neale, Steve, *Genre and Hollywood* (London: Routledge, 2000).

Neff, Alan, *Movies, Movie Stars, and Me* (Bloomington: AuthorHouse, 2008).

Norwitz, Leonard, '*Home Alone* (Blu-ray)', in *Lens Views*, 8 December 2008.
<http://www.dvdbeaver.com/film2/DVDReviews43/home_alone_blu-ray.htm>

—, '*Miracle on 34th Street* (Blu-Ray)', in *Lens Views*, 22 October 2009.
<http://www.dvdbeaver.com/film2/DVDReviews47/miracle_on_34th_street_1994_blu-ray.htm>

Nusair, David, '*29th Street*', in *Reel Film Reviews*, 20 April 2005.
<https://www.reelfilm.com/anchbay2.htm#29th>

—, '*Jingle All the Way*', in *UK Film Review*, 14 December 2015.
<https://www.ukfilmreview.co.uk/post/jingle-all-the-way-1996>

—, '*The Ref*', in *Reel Film Reviews*, 4 March 2003.
<https://www.reelfilm.com/ref.htm>

—, 'Two Christmas Movies from Disney', in *Reel Film Reviews*, 23 December 2010.
<https://reelfilm.com/dischr1.htm#ill>

O'Sullivan, Michael, '*I'll Be Home for Christmas*', in *The Washington Post*, 13 November 1998.
<https://www.washingtonpost.com/wp-srv/style/movies/reviews/illbehomeforchristmasosullivan.htm>

Olson, Chris, '*Miracle on 34th Street* (1994) film review', in *UK Film Review*, 23 December 2015.

<https://www.ukfilmreview.co.uk/post/miracle-on-34th-street-1994-film-review>

—, '*The Muppet Christmas Carol*', in *UK Film Review*, 24 December 2015. <https://www.ukfilmreview.co.uk/post/the-muppet-christmas-carol-1992-film-review>

—, '*The Nightmare Before Christmas* Film Review', in *UK Film Review*, 22 December 2015. <https://www.ukfilmreview.co.uk/post/the-nightmare-before-christmas-1993-film-review>

Patel, Sonja, *The Christmas Companion* (London: Think Books, 2008).

Paulding, Barbara, Suzanne Schwalb and Mara Conlon, *A Century of Christmas Memories 1900-1999* (New York: Peter Pauper Press, 2009).

Phipps, Keith, '*I'll Be Home for Christmas*', in *AV Club*, 29 March 2002. <https://www.avclub.com/ill-be-home-for-christmas-1798196024>

—, '*Jingle All the Way*', in *AV Club*, 29 March 2002. <https://www.avclub.com/jingle-all-the-way-1798194998>

, '*The Nightmare Before Christmas*', in *AV Club*, 29 March 2002. <https://www.avclub.com/the-nightmare-before-christmas-1798195605>

—, '*The Preacher's Wife*', in *AV Club*, 29 March 2002. <https://www.avclub.com/the-preachers-wife-1798195900>

Pitts, Leonard, Jr., '*Christmas* is Beguiling: A Predictable Plot is Wonderfully Executed', in *The Miami Herald*, 8 November 1991, p.61.

Purves, Barry J.C., *Stop Motion: Passion, Process and Performance* (Oxford: Focal Press, 2008).

Quart, Leonard, and Albert Auster, *American Film and Society Since 1945*, 3rd edn (Westport: Greenwood Publishing Group, 2002).

Rainer, Peter, 'Movie Review: Muppets Take on Dickens' *Carol*', in *The Los Angeles Times*, 11 December 1992.

<*https://www.latimes.com/archives/la-xpm-1992-12-11-ca-1527-story.html*>

Reid, John Howard, *Hollywood Movie Musicals: Great, Good and Glamorous* (Morrisville: Lulu.com, 2006).

—, *Movies Magnificent: 150 Must-See Cinema Classics* (Morrisville: Lulu.com, 2005).

Romney, Jonathan, '*The Muppet Christmas Carol*', in *The New Statesman*, December 1992-January 1993, p.60.

Roscoe, J.P., '*Jingle All the Way* (1996)', in *Basement Rejects*, 18 December 2011.
<*http://basementrejects.com/review/jingle-all-the-way-1996/*>

—, '*The Preacher's Wife* (1996)', in *Basement Rejects*, 16 December 2011.
<*http://basementrejects.com/review/the-preachers-wife-1996/*>

—, '*The Santa Clause* (1994)', in *Basement Rejects*, 13 December 2011.
<*http://basementrejects.com/review/the-santa-clause-1994/*>

Rosenbaum, Jonathan, '*All I Want for Christmas*', in *The Chicago Reader*, 3 December 2012.
<*https://chicagoreader.com/film/all-i-want-for-christmas/*>

—, '*Home Alone*', in *The Chicago Reader*, 26 October 1990.
<*https://chicagoreader.com/film/home-alone-2/*>

—, '*Trapped in Paradise*', in *The Chicago Reader*, 29 November 1994.
<*https://chicagoreader.com/film/trapped-in-paradise/*>

Rother, George, '*Jingle All the Way*', in *MovieGuy 24/7*, 15 December 2011.
<*https://movieguy247.com/iMovies/index.php/blog/holiday-movies/677-jingle-all-the-way*>

—, '*Mixed Nuts*', in *MovieGuy 24/7*, 1 December 2011.
<*https://movieguy247.com/iMovies/index.php/blog/holiday-movies/772-mixed-nuts*>

—, '*The Preacher's Wife*', in *MovieGuy 24/7*, 16 March 2012.

<https://movieguy247.com/iMovies/index.php/blog/holiday-movies/472-the-preachers-wife>

—, 'The Ref', in MovieGuy 24/7, 9 December 2012.
<https://movieguy247.com/iMovies/index.php/blog/holiday-movies/689-the-ref>

—, 'Trapped in Paradise', in MovieGuy 24/7, 9 December 2012.
<https://movieguy247.com/iMovies/index.php/blog/holiday-movies/672-trapped-in-paradise>

Rowan, Terry, Having a Wonderful Christmas Time Film Guide (Morris-ville: Lulu Press, 2014).

Rowe, John Carlos, ed., Post-Nationalist American Studies (Berkeley: University of California Press, 2000).

Rugaard, Jason, 'I'll Be Home for Christmas', in Movie Mavericks, 24 December 2021.
<https://moviemavericks.com/2021/12/ill-be-home-for-christmas-1998-review/>

Rutter, Troy, 'Film Review: All I Want For Christmas', in Heartland Film Review, 4 December 2020.
<https://heartlandfilmreview.com/2020/12/04/film-review-all-i-want-for-christmas/>

Ryan, Michael, and Douglas Kellner, Camera Politica: The Politics and Ideology of Contemporary Hollywood (Indianapolis: Indiana University Press, 1988).

Samuel, Raphael, Theatres of Memory: Volume 1: Past and Present in Contemporary Culture (London: Verso, 1994).

Santino, Jack, All Around the Year: Holidays and Celebrations in American Life (Champaign: University of Illinois Press, 1994) [1985].

—, New Old-Fashioned Ways: Holidays and Popular Culture (Knoxville: University of Tennessee Press, 1996).

Savlov, Marc, '*A Midnight Clear*', in *The Austin Chronicle*, 5 June 1992.
<*https://www.austinchronicle.com/events/film/1992-06-05/a-midnight-clear/*>

—, '*Home Alone*', in *The Austin Chronicle*, 11 January 1991.
<*https://www.austinchronicle.com/events/film/1991-01-11/home-alone/*>

—, '*Jingle All the Way*', in *The Austin Chronicle*, 29 November 1996.
<*https://www.austinchronicle.com/events/film/1996-11-29/jingle-all-the-way/*>

—, '*The Ref*', in *The Austin Chronicle*, 18 March 1994.
<*https://www.austinchronicle.com/events/film/1994-03-18/the-ref/*>

Scheib, Richard, '*Miracle on 34ᵗʰ Street*', in *Moria: Science Fiction, Horror and Fantasy Review*, 2009.
<*https://www.moriareviews.com/fantasy/miracle-on-34th-street-1994.htm*>

Schochet, Stephen, *Hollywood Stories: Short, Entertaining Anecdotes about the Stars and Legends*, 2nd edn (Los Angeles: Hollywood Stories Publishing, 2013).

Schrodt, Paul, 'Why *Mixed Nuts* is the Best Holiday Movie You've Never Seen', in *Esquire*, 24 December 2014.
<*https://www.esquire.com/entertainment/movies/reviews/a31592/mixed-nuts-holiday-movie/*>

Schwartz, Dennis, '*29ᵗʰ Street*', in *Dennis Schwartz Movie Reviews*, 24 June 2004.
<*https://dennisschwartzreviews.com/29thstreet/*>

Seravia, Jerry, 'The Thieving Magpies of *Paradise*', in *Jerry Saravia on Cinema*, 28 November 2011.
<*https://jerrysaravia.blogspot.com/2011/11/thieving-magpies-of-paradise.html*>

Shail, Robert, *British Film Directors: A Critical Guide* (Edinburgh: Edinburgh University Press, 2007).

Shannon, Jeff, 'Allen Delivers Belly Laughs In Amusing *Santa Clause*', in *The Seattle Times*, 11 November 1994.
<*https://archive.seattletimes.com/archive/?date=19941111&slug=1941324*>

—, 'Family Feud A Fate Worse Than Jail For *The Ref*', in *The Seattle Times*, 11 March 1994.
<*https://archive.seattletimes.com/archive/?date=19940311&slug=1899594*>

Shulgasser, Barbara, 'Arnold: Don't toy with us', in *The San Francisco Examiner*, 22 November 1996.
<*https://www.sfgate.com/news/article/Arnold-Don-t-toy-with-us-3112507.php*>

—, '*Preacher's Wife* is Touched by an Angel', in *The San Francisco Examiner*, 13 December 1996.
<*https://www.sfgate.com/news/article/Preacher-s-Wife-is-touched-by-an-angel-3110063.php*>

Simpson, Paul, ed., *The Rough Guide to Cult Movies* (London: Haymarket Customer Publishing, 2001).

Smith, Edison, 'Keep the Change, You Filthy Animal: How *Home Alone* Became a Festive Record Breaker', in *VHS Revival*, 17 December 2020.
<*https://vhsrevival.com/2020/12/17/keep-the-change-you-filthy-animal-how-home-alone-became-a-festive-record-breaker/*>

Smith, Russell, '*The Preacher's Wife*', in *The Austin Chronicle*, 13 December 1996.
<*https://www.austinchronicle.com/events/film/1996-12-13/the-preachers-wife/*>

Stack, Peter, '*The Preacher's Wife*', in *The San Francisco Chronicle*, 2 May 1997.
<*https://www.sfgate.com/movies/article/FILM-REVIEW-Preacher-s-Divine-Comedy-2843077.php*>

Staiger, Janet, *Perverse Spectators: The Practices of Film Reception* (New York: New York University Press, 2000).

Stead, Ezra, '*Trapped in Paradise*', in *Ruthless Reviews*, 7 December 2020.

<https://www.ruthlessreviews.com/47463/trapped-in-paradise-1994/>

Stelle, Ginger, '"Starring Kermit the Frog as Bob Cratchit": Muppets as Actors', in *Kermit Culture: Critical Perspectives on Jim Henson's Muppets*, ed. by Jennifer C. Garlen and Anissa M. Graham (Jefferson: McFarland and Company, 2009), pp.94-102.

Strupp, Phyllis, *The Richest of Fare: Seeking Spiritual Security in the Sonoran Desert* (Scottsdale: Sonoran Cross Press, 2004).

Svehla, Gary J., '*The Muppet Christmas Carol*', in Gary J. Svehla and Susan Svehla, *It's Christmas Time at the Movies* (Baltimore: Midnight Marquee Press, 1998), 197-99, p.199.

—, and Susan Svehla, *It's Christmas Time at the Movies* (Baltimore: Midnight Marquee Press, 1998).

Svitil, Torene, '*All I Want for Christmas* Review', in *Empire*, 3 December 2012.
<https://www.empireonline.com/movies/reviews/want-christmas-review/>

Tatum, Charles T., Jr., '*Trapped in Paradise*', in *500 Terrible Films*, 2 September 2022.
<https://500filmstowatch.blogspot.com/2022/09/82-trapped-in-paradise-1994.html>

Thomas, Tony, *A Smidgeon of Religion* (Bloomington: AuthorHouse, 2007).

Thompson, Frank, *American Movie Classics' Great Christmas Movies* (Dallas: Taylor Publishing Company, 1998).

Turan, Kenneth, 'Movie Reviews: Burton Dreams Up a Delightful *Nightmare*', in *The Los Angeles Times*, 15 October 1993.
<https://www.latimes.com/archives/la-xpm-1993-10-15-ca-45836-story.html>

—, 'Movie Review: The *Miracle* of 1947, 47 Years Later', in *The Los Angeles Times*, 18 November 1994.

<https://www.latimes.com/archives/la-xpm-1994-11-18-ca-64068-
story.html>

—, 'Movie Reviews: *The Ref*. Razor-Sharp', in *The Los Angeles Times*, 9
March 1994.
<https://www.latimes.com/archives/la-xpm-1994-03-09-ca-31725-
story.html>

Turner, Graeme, *Film as Social Practice* (London: Routledge, 1999).

Turner, Sam, '*A Midnight Clear*. Blu-ray Review', in *Film Intel*, 10 April
2012.
<http://www.film-intel.com/2012/04/midnight-clear-blu-ray-review.html>

Tyler, Don, *Music of the Postwar Era* (Westport: Greenwood Publishing
Group, 2008).

Upchurch, Michael, '*Clear* and Present Danger', in *The Seattle Times*, 1
May 1992.
<https://archive.seattletimes.com/archive/?date=19920501&slug=1489485>

Van Gelder, Lawrence, 'Film Review: *All I Want for Christmas* is a Porsche and a Purpose', in *The New York Times*, 13 November 1998.
<https://www.nytimes.com/1998/11/13/movies/film-review-all-i-want-for-
christmas-is-a-porsche-and-a-purpose.html>

Vance, Kelly, 'Cutting Contest', in *The Chicago Reader*, 7 April 1994.
<https://chicagoreader.com/film/cutting-contest/>

Watt, Kate Carnell, and Kathleen C. Lonsdale, 'Dickens Composed: Film
and Television Adaptations 1897-2001', in *Dickens on Screen*, ed. by John
Glavin (Cambridge: Cambridge University Press, 2003), pp.201-16.

Webb, Andy, '*29th Street*', in *The Movie Scene*, 2005.
<https://www.themoviescene.co.uk/reviews/29th-street-1991/29th-street-
1991.html>

—, '*I'll Be Home for Christmas*', in *The Movie Scene*, 2004.
<https://www.themoviescene.co.uk/reviews/ill-be-home-for-christmas/ill-
be-home-for-christmas.html>

—, 'Jingle All the Way', in The Movie Scene, 2007.
<https://www.themoviescene.co.uk/reviews/jingle-all-the-way/jingle-all-the-way.html>

—, 'Miracle on 34th Street', in The Movie Scene, 2009.
<https://www.themoviescene.co.uk/reviews/miracle-on-34th-street/miracle-on-34th-street.html>

—, 'Mixed Nuts', in The Movie Scene, 2008.
<https://www.themoviescene.co.uk/reviews/mixed-nuts/mixed-nuts.html>

—, 'The Ref', in The Movie Scene, 2009.
<https://www.themoviescene.co.uk/reviews/the-ref/the-ref.html>

Werts, Diane, Christmas on Television (Westport: Greenwood Press, 2006).

Westbrook, Caroline, 'The Muppet Christmas Carol', in Empire, January 1993.
<https://www.empireonline.com/movies/reviews/muppet-christmas-carol-review/>

Wilmington, Michael, 'Dysfunctional Ref a Shouting Match', in The Chicago Tribune, 11 March 1994.
<https://www.chicagotribune.com/news/ct-xpm-1994-03-11-9403110097-story.html>

—, 'Movie Review: Midnight a Clear-Eyed Anti-War Film', in The Los Angeles Times, 1 May 1992.
<https://www.latimes.com/archives/la-xpm-1992-05-01-ca-1382-story.html>

—, 'The Santa Clause', in The Chicago Tribune, 11 November 1994.
<https://www.chicagotribune.com/news/ct-xpm-1994-11-11-9411110127-story.html>

Wilson, Richard, Scrooge's Guide to Christmas: A Survival Manual for the Festively Challenged (London: Hodder and Stoughton, 1997).

Young, Jordan R., Roman Polanski: Behind the Scenes of His Classic Early Films (Lanham: Applause Books, 2022).

Zyber, Joshua, 'The Nightmare Before Christmas', in High-Def Digest, 25 August 2008.
<https://bluray.highdefdigest.com/1207/nightmarebeforechristmas.html>

Index

484

486

F

492

I

J

M

498

Acknowledgements

I am most grateful to my family, Julie Christie and Mary Melville, and to my friends Amy Leitch, Professor Roderick Watson, Eddy and Dorothy Bryan, Alex Tucker and Kelley Nave, Ian and Anne McNeish, Dr Colin M. Barron and Vivien Barron, Vincent and Elizabeth Connell, and Robert Murray and Eleanor Jewson for their fellowship and encouragement throughout the course of this project.

Best wishes also to my pals Scott and Caroline Boulton and Joy Furmage – Christmas movie enthusiasts one and all!

With special thanks, as ever, to my dear friends Joe and Mary Moore of the North Pole Press, who always keep the Christmas spirit alive all the year round!

About the Author

Dr Thomas Christie has many years of experience as a literary and publishing professional, working in collaboration with several companies including Cambridge Scholars Publishing, Crescent Moon Publishing and Applause Books. A passionate advocate of the written word and literary arts, over the years he has worked to develop original writing for respected organisations such as the Stirling Smith Art Gallery and Museum and a leading independent higher education research unit based at the University of Stirling. Additionally, he is regularly involved in public speaking events and has delivered guest lectures and presentations about his work at many locations around the United Kingdom.

Tom is a Fellow of the Royal Society of Arts and a member of the Royal Society of Literature, the Society of Authors, the Federation of Writers Scotland and the Authors' Licensing and Collecting Society. He holds a first-class Honours degree in English Literature and a Masters degree in Humanities with British Cinema History from the Open University in Milton

Keynes, and a Doctorate in Scottish Literature awarded by the University of Stirling.

He is the author of a number of books on the subject of modern film which include *Liv Tyler: Star in Ascendance* (2007), *The Cinema of Richard Linklater* (2008), *John Hughes and Eighties Cinema: Teenage Hopes and American Dreams* (2009), *Ferris Bueller's Day Off: Pocket Movie Guide* (2010), *The Christmas Movie Book* (2011), *The James Bond Movies of the 1980s* (2013), *Mel Brooks: Genius and Loving It!: Freedom and Liberation in the Cinema of Mel Brooks* (2015), *A Righteously Awesome Eighties Christmas: Festive Cinema of the 1980s* (2016), *The Golden Age of Christmas Movies: Festive Cinema of the 1940s and 50s* (2019) and *John Hughes FAQ* (2019).

His other works include *Notional Identities: Ideology, Genre and National Identity in Popular Scottish Fiction Since the Seventies* (2013), *The Spectrum of Adventure: A Brief History of Interactive Fiction on the Sinclair ZX Spectrum* (2016), *Contested Mindscapes: Exploring Approaches to Dementia in Modern Popular Culture* (2018) and *A Very Spectrum Christmas: Celebrating Seasonal Software on the Sinclair ZX Spectrum* (2021). He has also written a crowdfunded murder-mystery novel, *The Shadow in the Gallery* (2013), which is set during the nineteenth century in Stirling's historic Smith Art Gallery and Museum.

Additionally, Tom has written two Scottish travel guides in collaboration with his sister, Julie Christie, which are entitled *The Heart 200 Book: A Companion Guide to Scotland's Most Exciting Road Trip* (2020) and *Secrets and Mysteries of the Heart 200 Route* (2021).

For more details about Tom and his work, please visit his website at:
www.tomchristiebooks.co.uk

Also Available from Extremis Publishing

The Spectrum of Adventure
A Brief History of Interactive Fiction on the Sinclair ZX Spectrum

By Thomas A. Christie

The Sinclair ZX Spectrum was one of the most popular home computers in British history, selling over five million units in its 1980s heyday. Amongst the thousands of games released for the Spectrum during its lifetime, the text adventure game was to emerge as one of the most significant genres on the system.

The Spectrum of Adventure chronicles the evolution of the text adventure on the ZX Spectrum, exploring the work of landmark software houses such as Melbourne House Software, Level 9 Computing, Delta 4 Software, the CRL Group, Magnetic Scrolls, and many others besides.

Covering one hundred individual games in all, this book celebrates the Spectrum's thriving interactive fiction scene of the eighties, chronicling the achievements of major publishers as well as independent developers from the machine's launch in 1982 until the end of the decade in 1989.

A Righteously Awesome Eighties Christmas
Festive Cinema of the 1980s

By Thomas A. Christie

The cinema of the festive season has blazed a trail through the world of film-making for more than a century, ranging from silent movies to the latest CGI features. From the author of *The Christmas Movie Book*, this new text explores the different narrative themes which emerged in the genre over the course of the 1980s, considering the developments which have helped to make the Christmas films of that decade amongst the most fascinating and engaging motion pictures in the history of festive movie production.

Released against the backdrop of a turbulent and rapidly-changing world, the Christmas films of the 1980s celebrated traditions and challenged assumptions in equal measure. With warm nostalgia colliding with aggressive modernity as never before, the eighties saw the movies of the holiday season being deconstructed and reconfigured to remain relevant in an age of cynicism and innovation.

Whether exploring comedy, drama, horror or fantasy, Christmas cinema has an unparalleled capacity to attract and inspire audiences. With a discussion ranging from the best-known titles to some of the most obscure, *A Righteously Awesome Eighties Christmas* examines the ways in which the Christmas motion pictures of the 1980s fit into the wider context of this captivating and ever-evolving genre.

Also Available from Extremis Publishing

The Golden Age of Christmas Movies
Festive Cinema of the 1940s and 50s

By Thomas A. Christie

Today the Christmas movie is considered one of the best-loved genres in modern cinema, entertaining audiences across the globe with depictions of festive celebrations, personal reinvention and the enduring value of friendship and family. But how did the themes and conventions of this category of film come to take form, and why have they proven to be so durable that they continue to persist and be reinvented even in the present day?

This book takes a nostalgic look back at the Christmas cinema of the 1940s and 50s, including a discussion of classic films which came to define the genre. Considering the unforgettable storylines and distinctive characters that brought these early festive movies to life, it discusses the conventions which were established and the qualities which would define Christmas titles for decades to come.

Examining landmark features of the period, *The Golden Age of Christmas Movies* delves into some of the most successful festive films ever produced, and also reflects upon other movies of the time that—for one reason or another—have all but disappeared into the mists of cinema history. Considering films which range from the life-affirming to the warmly sentimental, *The Golden Age of Christmas Movies* investigates the many reasons why these memorable motion pictures have continued to entertain generations of moviegoers.

Also Available from Extremis Publishing

A Very Spectrum Christmas
Celebrating Seasonal Software on the Sinclair ZX Spectrum

By Thomas A. Christie

Throughout the 1980s, thousands of British children were lucky enough to discover a Sinclair ZX Spectrum under their Christmas trees and soon found their eyes opened to a virtual world of wonder. But Santa Claus did more than deliver computers – sometimes he appeared on them, too.

From the author of *The Spectrum of Adventure* and *A Righteously Awesome Eighties Christmas*, this book delves into the Spectrum's extraordinary pantheon of seasonal games: the good, the bad, the surprising, the unabashedly surreal and the occasionally rather tenuous.

From the machine's formative days in the early eighties right through to the latest independent releases, *A Very Spectrum Christmas* takes a look at what makes a truly memorable festive title for the vintage home micro-computer... as well as unearthing a few games that may have become lost in the mists of Christmas past for good reason.

Fully illustrated with colour screenshots of all the games under discussion, *A Very Spectrum Christmas* is a treasure trove of yuletide software experiences – where eighties nostalgia collides with modern day homebrew innovation with frequently unexpected results!

Contested Mindscapes
Exploring Approaches to Dementia in Modern Popular Culture

By Thomas A. Christie

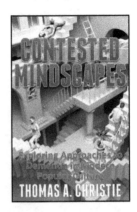

Dementia is a mental health condition which affects an estimated 50 million people worldwide. Yet it has, until recently, been an unfairly neglected subject in popular culture.

Contested Mindscapes considers the ways in which the arts have engaged with dementia over the past twenty years, looking at particular examples drawn from the disciplines of film and television, popular music, performance art, and interactive entertainment.

Examining a variety of creative approaches ranging from the thought-provoking to the controversial, *Contested Mindscapes* carefully contemplates the many ways in which the humanities and entertainment industries have engaged with dementia, exploring how the wide-ranging implications of this complex condition have been communicated through a variety of artistic nodes.

Love Christmas? Then don't miss the *Traditionally Speaking* podcast!

Available from streaming audio providers worldwide, a brand new episode of *Traditionally Speaking* is released monthly. Join authors and lifelong Christmas enthusiasts Tom Christie and Joe Moore as they explore the differences in festive traditions on both sides of the Atlantic.

Find out more on the official *Traditionally Speaking* website at: **www.traditionally-speaking.com**

For details of new and forthcoming books
from Extremis Publishing, including our
monthly podcast, please visit our official
website at:

www.extremispublishing.com

or follow us on social media at:

www.facebook.com/extremispublishing

www.linkedin.com/company/extremis-publishing-ltd-/

Lightning Source UK Ltd.
Milton Keynes UK
UKHW021948021222
413123UK00017B/638